STARTING STRONG

365 Days to Spark Personal Revival

CHANCE WALTERS

ISBN: 1983505048
ISBN 13: 9781983505041

Dedication.

To my amazing family,
you know who you are.
A part from your prayers, I would
not be here.
Thank you for never giving up on me.

One day, someone asked me, who is your target audience for the book, "Starting Strong." And the reality is; I penned every word for you. Over the course of two years, my heart waited patiently before the Lord to listen like one being taught. The words you are about to read came from the secret place of my souls delight. From here forward, may you feast on the fairest of ten thousand and be drawn closer to the Saviors side by Starting everyday Strong!

Acknowledgments

Books may be written by one person but they are influenced by many waters. My deepest appreciation goes to:

My beautiful wife Kacie, you are the inspiration that moves me, the safe harbor that shelters me and the anchor that holds everything together. You are my beloved, my best friend and the greatest example of Christ in my life. You are God's gift to me, our family and countless others. I adore you more and more everyday! May we continue to write the greatest love story ever told...

To my three individually remarkable children, Victory Ann, Glory Rae and Hyatt Chance. When I look into your eyes, my heart is suddenly swept away to the greatness of God's grace and majesty. The truth is; He sent you here to change the world. May this book be a constant reminder that you can do anything you put your mind to. May you go farther, accomplish more and see God move in unprecedented ways in your generation. Always know, Daddy loves you dearly and I'm so proud of you!

To my parents, Cecil and Shelia. Your prayers, personal sacrifice and godly influence has paved the way for me. Our family, ministry and future impact will always find its roots in your faith. Thank you for your impeccable example of integrity, sincerity and steadfastness. May the fire that you fanned forever burn in the hearts of man.

To my sister Kelly and my brother-in-law Len; I couldn't imagine a life without you. You're a constant stream of support, a city set on a hill and a faithful friend to so many. It's my honor to call you family. May the spirit of excellence that you carry be multiplied to the nations. You challenge me, mold me and make me a better follower of Christ. May we forever walk hand in hand.

To all of our ministry partners, this book is for you. Without your continued love, prayers and support none of this would be possible. God has used you to literally change the landscape of thousands of lives all over the world. It's true. Together, we are *"Sparking Revival Worldwide!"* May we finish stronger than we started.

And lastly, to my Lord and Savior Jesus Christ; No words could ever articulate the love that is bound up in my heart for you. If it were a novel, all the books in the world could not contain the thoughts of my gratitude toward you. Indeed, I am in debt to your mercy and grace. Take my life and use me as you will. Until the whole world hears, Thank you Jesus.

JANUARY 1

Happy New Year!

"He has made everything beautiful in its time."

Ecclesiastes 3:11

I believe with my whole heart that this year is going to be your best year yet! However, before you get well into the New Year, you have to get something new into you. God's word says, *"He makes all things new including His mercies for you everyday."* This is Good News, but it also poses these questions for you? What do you want to do this year? What do you want to accomplish? What changes do you want to make? Where do you want to go? Who do you want to see? On the other side, maybe you should stop doing something. I can't answer these questions for you because I don't know the desires of your heart but I do know the *"Art of the Start"* is the most important part. How you transition into a new season will determine the outcome of your days. As far as this goes, let's be sure to not miss anything God has in store for us this year! *When God speaks to your heart you have to start! You have to go! You have to put our hand to the plow and never look back. Are you ready?*

If so, here's my challenge: Listen to what God told the Prophet Jeremiah in scripture. God told him, *"Write in a book all the words I have spoken to you." What better way to start strong for the New Year!* Get a notepad or a notebook and write down what you hear the Lord saying this year. More importantly, write down what He wants you to do. Habakkuk 2:2 says, *"Write the vision down and make it plain on tablets so that those who see it may run with it."*

If your desire never leaves your mouth but remains in your mind, your dream will never manifest and you will always wonder what would have happened if you had trusted the Lord. So, share your aspirations with your spouse, pastor and accountability partner. But first and foremost, you have to write your dreams and visions down & believe the word of the Lord for yourself.

<u>Step to Start Strong:</u>

Re-Examine your Day

JANUARY 2

Fast Forward

"However, this kind does not go out except by prayer and fasting."

Matthew 17:21

Fasting & prayer is like sowing seed. The words you speak by faith are planted in the ground of your soul and watered by the word of God everyday as you fast & pray. Most likely, what you plant today in prayer will not bring you a harvest over-night. You have to wait for the seed of the word of God to germinate below the surface in your soul. Any disturbance with the seed can abort the purpose for which it was planted. The seed has to have a season of isolation before it can endure the pressure from above to produce the long-lasting fruit of the spirit. This is our ultimate goal; *"to produce fruit."* Fruit falls to the ground to do what? To provide food for others to eat! The fruit of the spirit is produced in you for others to consume & be changed into the image of Christ. However, this process begins with a single seed; a time of submission and surrender to God.

This is a perfect picture of fasting. Other than a select few, nobody knows you are fasting. You are partaking of a private discipline that will eventually bring you public reward. You are committing the whole year to God by giving Him a First-fruit Offering of Fasting & Prayer. What you are doing today will reap a Harvest of Righteousness the rest of the year if you do not give up. You are sacrificing for a season but you will inherit the enduring blessing of lifetime. Don't let the world of instant gratification discourage & deter you from fulfilling the call God has upon your life. If one thing is for sure; There is more is store! Keep doing good because God is always good! The proper time is coming because He is an on-time God...

Step to Start Strong:

Set aside a Season of Prayer and Fasting.

JANUARY 3

Bible 101.

"If you abide in Me, and My words abide in you, ask whatever you wish, and it will be done for you."

John 15:7

In order for you to be sustained during a season of fasting and prayer, you are going to need a healthy, well-balanced diet. At the top of every menu should be a smorgasbord of the Word of God. I invite you to imitate the Prophet Ezekiel and do whatever it takes to get the word of God on the inside of you. God commanded him in Exodus 3, *"Son of man, Eat this scroll I am giving you and fill your stomach with it."* So He did and it tasted as sweet as honey in my mouth. Ezekiel literally had the word for breakfast & surprisingly, it tasted like honey to his soul. *What does this mean?* Reading to you may sound like a chore or a daily duty. However, I have found out there is another type of devotion. Many people think they have to read, fast and pray but they miss out on a better way. It's called the secret place! A place where you long to be with the Lord. The first is religion and the second is relationship. It's not about if you do, but do you want to! There's a big difference!

Pray this prayer today: God, *"Put a burning desire inside of my soul to seek you with my whole heart this year."* Deliverance is losing the desire to do what you don't want to do but dependence upon God is set-up the same way. It all starts with this word: Desire. What we need is a deep, deep desire to do what God has called us to do!

Reading God's Word on a daily basis during fasting & prayer is like throwing desire on the fire. Proverbs 28:1 says, *"Where there is no wood, the fire goes out."* The wood refers to the Word of God. I have to ask: Does your spiritual desire seem dim? All you need is a few more logs on the fire. If you will commit yourself to reading the Word of God on a consistent basis this month you will regain your flame. Let's make it a holy habit to read, pray & meditate upon God's Precepts this Year!

Steps to Start Strong:

Find a Bible Reading Plan

JANUARY 4

21 Seconds to Change your World

"In this manner, therefore, pray: Our Father in heaven, Hallowed be Your name. Your kingdom come. Your will be done, On earth as it is in heaven. Give us this day our daily bread. And forgive us our debts, As we forgive our debtors. And do not lead us into temptation, But deliver us from the evil one. For Yours is the kingdom and the power and the glory forever, amen."

Matthew 6:9-13

Evangelist Billy Graham once said, *"The 3 most important things you could do today is pray, pray & pray some more!"* That's what we are doing today; We, as the body of Christ, are bombarding Heaven with the desires of our heart. I love what Joel 2:14 says, *"Who knows? He may turn and relent and leave behind a blessing."* One of the greatest blessings, God has given us as His children, is the opportunity to approach Him in prayer. Prayer connects us to our Heavenly Father. To be more specific, our words prepare the way. Matthew 6:11 says, *"When you pray say!"* God wants you to talk to Him with child-like faith. Be open. Be brutally honest. Be transparent. Just be yourself. If you have trouble praying like many people. Here are the next step to jump-start your year: Pray the Lord's Prayer everyday.

Dr. Mark Rutland released a book entitled, *"21 Seconds to Change your World."* In the book, he discusses the average time to say the Lord's Prayer is only 21 seconds. You heard it right. *Just 21 seconds?* Can you give God 21 seconds of our schedule? Of course, you can! Romans 10:17 says, *"Faith cometh by hearing & hearing the word of God."* When you pray the word out loud, you hear the word and the word produces faith inside of your soul especially when you're the one doing the praying!

Here's my challenge to you today: Pray the Lord's Prayer everyday when you wake up. You can pray it in the shower, on the sofa or walking down the street. Find a place & pray! This prayer will activate your spirit & get you ready for whatever God has in store for you that day. Jesus said when you pray, pray this way. Give it try. His word works! Remember, principles don't have to be profound to be powerful. It's the simple steps that we take on a daily basis that give us the strength to stay the course. Just pray, pray, pray and pray some more!

Step 2 Start Strong:

Pray the Lord's Prayer Everyday.

JANUARY 5

It is Written

"But He answered and said, 'It is written, 'Man shall not live by bread alone, but by every word that proceeds from the mouth of God.'"

Matthew 4:4

Do you deal with discouragement? Have you ever felt like giving up? Do you feel weak & worthless. If you do; Relax. This is completely normal. I have found out in life but especially when you fast & pray that your flesh begins to cry out. Your emotions can be tossed around like a wave in the sea. Your body is screaming to your soul, *"What are you doing to me?"* So, take heart Mighty Warrior! Though outwardly you are wasting away, inwardly you are being renewed each day. At least this is what the Word says.

For example, when Jesus fasted for 40 days in the wilderness, He experienced a time of isolation & temptation. He was all alone and the enemy used this opportunity to tempt Him and tell Him what He should do. I wonder what thoughts and temptations have been presented to you this week? If you haven't experienced opposition yet, be on guard. The enemy will do anything possible to keep you out of your Promised Land.

You may ask: When I am down, *"How do I overcome Satan's devices?"*

Well, *"How did Jesus do it?"* He spoke the word. The word cannot work unless you speak it. Jesus combated His enemy by quoting scripture in the midst of temptation. (Matthew 4)

In this particular passage, Jesus was tempted in the 3 major categories of temptation: Provision, Protection & Power. However, according to scripture God has promised to provide, protect & to give us the power to accomplish everything He has set before us. The crutch of every temptation is the tendency to depend upon our strength instead of depending on the spirit. Human dependency always produces pride but on the contrary humility will produce the fruit of the spirit. Therefore, what should you do if you are discouraged? Speak the Word and Worship!

Step to Start Strong:

Speak the Word!

JANUARY 6

THE VALLEY OF GEHENNA

"These will go away into eternal punishment, but the righteous into eternal life."

Matthew 26:46

The Valley of Gehenna was a real place in ancient Israel. It was the city's garbage dump. This area was known to be dirty, dusty & disgusting. Anywhere there is garbage, there will be flies, worms & maggots. To make matters worse, there was a perpetual fire burning there, 24 hours a day, every day of the year. It was literally a *"Hell Hole."*

Jesus used the Valley of Gehenna as an illustrated sermon in scripture. In the Bible, the word Gehenna refers to *"a lake of fire"* located in Hell. Literally, a place of weeping and gnashing of teeth. Jesus came to save us from ever experiencing this place. Despite, unpopular belief, Hell is a real place. However, Hell was not created for you, it was created for the devil and His demons. God desperately desires for everyone to choose the free gift us grace through His Son Jesus Christ. God doesn't send anyone to Hell. He gives us the choice; Hell or Him.

As you pray, don't forget your lost family and friends in prayer. Stand in the gap on their behalf. Believe for their deliverance this year. Call their name out to God. May God free your family and friends from the fire of Hell and grant you *"Household Salvation"* this year! What greater gift could we receive? Think about it: eternal life with Him.

<u>Step to Start Strong:</u>

Make a Prayer List

JANUARY 7

Isaiah 58

The 58th Chapter of Isaiah gives us the most exhaustive description about Fasting in scripture. While meditating upon this passage a few years ago, I discovered a great deal of insight about this spiritual discipline. I began to underline the action verbs in my Bible & here's what I came up with. There are 10 things that I should not do while fasting, 10 things I should do while fasting and 20 things God would do if I will fast and pray His way today! Remember this: God can do exceedingly and abundantly more than we could ever ask or think during our sacrifice! If we do our part, God has promised to do His part. What's your part? What's His part?

"Cry aloud, spare not; Lift up your voice like a trumpet;

Tell My people their transgression, And the house of Jacob their sins. Yet they seek Me daily, And delight to know My ways, As a nation that did righteousness, And did not forsake the ordinance of their God. They ask of Me the ordinances of justice; They take delight in approaching God. 'Why have we fasted,' they say, 'and You have not seen? Why have we afflicted our souls, and You take no notice?' "In fact, in the day of your fast you find pleasure, And exploit all your laborers. Indeed you fast for strife and debate,

And to strike with the fist of wickedness. You will not fast as you do this day, To make your voice heard on high. Is it a fast that I have chosen, A day for a man to afflict his soul? Is it to bow down his head like a bulrush, And to spread out sackcloth and ashes? Would you call this a fast, And an acceptable day to the Lord? "Is this not the fast that I have chosen: To loose the bonds of wickedness, To undo the heavy burdens, To let the oppressed go free, And that you break every yoke? Is it not to share your bread with the hungry, And that you bring to your house the poor who are cast out; When you see the naked, that you cover him, And not hide yourself from your own flesh? Then your light shall break forth like the morning, Your healing shall spring forth speedily, And your righteousness shall go before you; The glory of the Lord shall be your rear guard. Then you shall call, and the Lord will answer; You shall cry, and He will say, 'Here I am.' "If you take away the yoke from your midst, The pointing of the finger, and speaking wickedness, If you extend your soul to the hungry And satisfy the afflicted soul, Then your light shall dawn in the darkness, And your darkness shall be as the noonday. The Lord will guide you continually, And satisfy your soul in drought, And strengthen your bones; You shall be like a watered garden, And like a spring of water, whose waters do not fail. Those from among you Shall build the old waste places; You shall raise up the foundations of many generations; And you shall be called the Repairer of the Breach, The Restorer of Streets to Dwell In. "If you turn away your foot from the Sabbath, From doing your pleasure on My holy day, And call the Sabbath a delight, The holy day of the Lord honorable, And shall honor Him, not doing your own ways, Nor finding your own pleasure, Nor speaking your own words, Then you shall delight yourself in the Lord; And I will cause you to ride on the high hills of the earth, And feed you with the heritage of Jacob your father. The mouth of the Lord has spoken."

Step to Start Strong:

Meditate upon Isaiah 58

JANUARY 8

Complete Victory!

"But thanks be to God, who gives us the victory through our Lord Jesus Christ."

1st Corinthians 15:57

Victory is when you completely overcome your enemy. Victory is cutting off the head of your Goliath and dancing on the grave of your adversary. Victory is the picture of someone still standing at the end of the storm.

The Greek word for Victory in the New Testament is *"Nike."* We all know the tagline for The Nike Company. You said it! Just do it! When God gives you a word, you can rest assure, the word is reliable. Trust Him and do whatever He says to do this year. Indeed, one word can change your life forever.

The 1st miracle Jesus ever performed was at a Wedding in Cana. (John 2) In fact, His mother pushed him into his purpose. In the story Jesus said, *"woman, my time has not yet come,"* but she made a statement there that day that paved the way for all miracles to manifest in the future. Mary told the servants, *"whatever He says, just do it!"* She laid the foundation for all faith forward. When God speaks, Jump! When you do, He will confirm His word with signs, miracles & wonders. Go ahead. Give it a try!

Are you in need of a miracle? What has God ask you to do? If you haven't heard an answer, keep praying for a clear direction and directive. When He gives you an ear to hear what His Spirit is saying, just do exactly what He says, nothing more, nothing less. Remember, sometimes you have to look ridiculous before you can be victorious! Just do it! "Victory is mine, says the Lord!" Your promise will come to pass at last!

Step to Start Strong:

Trust and Obey.

JANUARY 9

Divine Direction

"Trust in the Lord with all your heart, And lean not on your own understanding; In all your ways acknowledge Him, And He shall direct your paths."

Proverbs 3:5-6

In 2013, like every other year, we were fasting & praying to start off strong. This particular year, I was praying for God to speak to me concerning my relationship with Kacie. I loved her & desired for her to be my wife but I wanted the nod of God or the approval of God, if you will. She was fasting with me so we plowed through and finally made it to the day of completion. Over the years, we have created the 21st day of fasting to be a segway to a celebration. We always like to break-fast in a special way. That year we decided to drive to Wilmington for a weekend spent with my sister at the beach. We arrived late that morning and we were desperate to go eat lunch at one of our favorite places downtown by the river. All of us pitched in to unpack the car but before we gorged ourselves with seafood we paused to pray. We wanted to thank God for giving us strength to endure yet another 21 days of sacrifice. So the three of us joined hands and made a prayer circle. As we began to call out to God, suddenly a sweet presence of the Lord moved upon us. It was a very special moment I will never forget. I can remember it like yesterday. God was with us in a very tangible way. It was almost like He way saying, *"Thank you for drawing near to me, I am here & I love you so much."*

After the prayer, Kacie stepped outside & I heard a ding! The noise was an incoming text message from who? Turbo Tax of course! Nobody knew but my plan was to use my tax refund check that year to go buy Kacie a ring & ask her to marry me! My federal refund was processed early and the notice came to me as soon as we said, *"Amen!"* God's timing couldn't have been more perfect! This was my confirmation. In this moment, I knew God was releasing me to marry Kacie. This may sound simple to you but it was God showing Himself strong to me. In this moment, Kacie walked back into the house that day & ask me, *"Is everything all right?"* With tears flowing down my face, I said, "Everything is going to be just fine." God said Yes & she did too! The rest is His-Story still being written.

Do you need divine direction? Do you need the nod of God? Are you seeking God for clarity? Keep fasting, keep praying and keep believing! Your answer is on the way. Your ding will be a little different but the spiritual sound will echo the same. Something on the inside of you will know it's the Lord giving you confirmation to move forward.

Step to Start Strong:

Be Specific when you Pray.

JANUARY 10

SHHH...IT'S A SECRET.

"He who dwells in the secret place of the Most High
Shall abide under the shadow of the Almighty."

Psalm 91:1

In Matthew Chapter 6, Jesus teaches us about the three private disciplines that bring public reward. These are giving, praying & fasting. When you implement these three instructions into your life, you are a chord with three strands that is not easily broken. You will start strong but most importantly, you will stand strong through the storms of life. We are challenged to give, pray & fast but we must do it the right way.

In order to stand, you have to take a step. However, before you start successful, you must be able to keep a secret. What do I mean? Jesus said in this passage of scripture, *"Your Heavenly Father sees what you do in secret."* God has His eye on you. He has a plan & a purpose for you this year. He sees & hears everything you do on a daily basis. Hopefully, your actions are creating an atmosphere that attracts the presence of God. Remember, your motive is a magnet. Why you do, what you do is equally important to what you do. If your desire is to be seen by men, the attention you get from men will be the only reward you will ever see. However, if you humble your heart and seek God in the secret place, your private acts of righteousness will reap a public reward.

Here is the Good News: God wants to bless you! For real! Not only does He want to bless you but He wants to take it public. He wants to bring His blessing out of the closet. In this moment, people will begin to notice the favor that follows you and eventually, you'll be approached with this question: *What is it about you? Where does you joy ad peace come from? How have you received such favor?* This will be the time for you to share your secret. My friend, until then, Shhh!Keep giving, keep praying and keep fasting! God is orchestrating His promise of prosperity & promotion! Can you keep a secret?

Step to Start Strong:

Set Giving, Praying and Fasting Goals.

JANUARY 11

The Bread of Life

"And Jesus said to them, 'I am the bread of life. He who comes to Me shall never hunger, and he who believes in Me shall never thirst."

John 6:35

In New Testament Times, Bread was the main course at meal time. When you pulled up a chair at the dinner table, one thing was for sure, there may not be any meat, sweets or side dishes but the bread was hot and ready. This reminds me of what Jesus said in John 6:35. He said, *"I am the Bread of Life."* In this culture, they fully understood what He meant by this statement. He was illustrating to His disciples that He was the source and sustainer of life, the centerpiece of all creation. The focal point for all people groups.This tells me, Jesus desires to be on your time table. He doesn't want to be a side dish or condiment. Something you add on after you indulge. That's nonsense! Jesus wants to be on the forefront of our minds. This is why He calls Himself, Our Daily Bread. Someone once said, *"The main thing is to keep the main thing the main thing!"* What's the main thing? The main thing is your relationship with Jesus. Don't allow *"weapons of mass distraction"* to destroy your appetite for what matters most in life. Do what Jesus did and clear the tables in your temple by un-cluttering your life. Take time to sit down with your Savior. Involve Him in every activity of your life. Ask Him what He thinks.It may save you from more than your sins? Bread anyone?

Step to Start Strong:

Take Personal Communion

JANUARY 12

THE UPPER ROOM

"When the Day of Pentecost had fully come, they were all with one accord in one place."

Acts 2:1

The Upper Room was a popular place for the early church. It was here that they celebrated the Passover Meal the night Jesus was betrayed. Soon after the crucifixion, where did they retreat? The Upper Room. They also ran to this room after Jesus gave them The Great Commission. This was obviously a safe haven for the disciples in that day. Indeed, a place of protection and prayer.

Consequently, the Bible records another event that took place in the Upper Room in Acts Chapter Two. Listen to what happened this time:

"When the Day of Pentecost had fully come, they were all in one place, (in the Upper Room) & in one accord. Suddenly, there came a sound from heaven, as of a mighty rushing wind, and it filled the whole house where they were sitting. Then there appeared to them

as divided tongues of fire, and one sat upon each of them. And they were all filled with the Holy Spirit and began to speak with other tongues, as the Spirit gave them utterance."

What you just read was the Birth-day of the Church. On the day of Pentecost, one-hundred twenty people were present to experience the infilling of God's presence, the Holy Spirit. When you unify your hearts with corporate prayer and fasting, your faith releases a greater measure of the presence & power of God! And one thing is for sure, *"We need the presence & power of God!"* This is true: We all need an Upper Room Revelation and a Personal Pentecost Experience.

In Acts 13:2-3, God gives us another key. *"As they ministered to the Lord & fasted, the Holy Spirit said, 'Now separate to Me Barnabas and Saul for the work to which I have called them." Then, having fasted and prayed, they laid their hands on them & they sent them on their way."*

Fasting & prayer not only releases God's presence & power but the Holy Spirit will speak to you and prepare you for your purpose. After fasting, the Holy Spirit spoke in this story & said, *"Separate these two apostles so I can fulfill their purpose."* I wonder what the Holy Spirit is going to ask you to do this year? What kind of separation needs to take place for you to focus on your purpose? All I know is, you're going to need the presence & power of God to accomplish your purpose. We need the Upper Room to get from Passover to Pentecost & from Pentecost to our Purpose. Amen.

Step to Start Strong:

Find a Prayer Partner

JANUARY 13

The Warrior's Creed

"You therefore, my son, be strong in the grace that is in Christ Jesus. And the things that you have heard from me among many witnesses, commit these to faithful men who will be able to teach others also. You therefore must endure hardship as a good soldier of Jesus Christ."

2 Timothy 2:1-3

I am a soldier in the Army of my God. The Lord Jesus Christ is my Commanding Officer. The Holy Scripture is my code of conduct. Faith, prayer and the Word are my weapons of warfare. I have been taught by the Holy Spirit, trained by experience, tried by adversity and tested by fire. I am a volunteer in this army, and I am enlisted for eternity.

I will not get out, sell out, be talked out or pushed out. I am faithful, reliable, capable and dependable. If my God needs me, I am there.I am a soldier.

I am not a baby. I do not need to be pampered, petted, primed up, pumped up, picked up, or pepped up.

I am a soldier.

No one has to call me, remind me, write me, visit me, entice me or lure me. I am a soldier. I am not a wimp. I am in place, saluting my King, obeying His orders & praising His Holy name! No one has to send me flowers, gifts, food, cards or candy, or give me handouts. I do not need to be cuddled, cradled, cared for or catered to. I am committed. I cannot have my feelings hurt bad enough to turn me around. I cannot be discouraged enough to turn me aside. I cannot lose enough to cause me to quit. When Jesus called me into this army, I had nothing. If I end up with nothing, I will still come out ahead. I will win. My God has supplied all of my needs & I am more than a conqueror. I will always triumph. I can do all things through Christ who gives me the strength that I need. Devils cannot defeat me. People cannot disillusion me. Weather cannot weary me. Sickness cannot stop me. Battles cannot beat me. Money cannot buy me. Governments cannot silence me, and hell cannot handle me.

I am a soldier. Even death cannot destroy me!

I am a soldier in the army of the Lord! I will not give up, back down or turn around! I am a soldier in the Army of the Lord and I am marching Heaven-bound! Can I get a witness?

Step to Start Strong:

Re-Read this Creed with your Whole Heart

JANUARY 14

The Year of 1863

In 1863, President Abraham Lincoln declared a National Day of Fasting & Repentance. It's easy to see. America needs to repent and turn back to God. Please take time to Read this Proclamation: By the President of the United States,

Whereas, the Senate of the United States, devoutly recognizing the Supreme Authority and just Government of Almighty God, in all the affairs of men and of nations, has, by a resolution, requested the President to designate and set apart a day for National prayer and humiliation.

And whereas it is the duty of nations as well as of men, to own their dependence upon the overruling power of God, to confess their sins and transgressions, in humble sorrow, yet with assured hope that genuine repentance will lead to mercy and pardon; and to recognize the sublime truth, announced in the Holy Scriptures and proven by all history, that those nations only are blessed whose God is the Lord.

And, insomuch as we know that, by His divine law, nations like individuals are subjected to punishments and chastisements in this world, may we not justly fear that the awful calamity of civil war, which now desolates the land, may be but a punishment, inflicted upon us, for our presumptuous sins, to the needful end of our national reformation as a whole People? We have been the recipients of the choicest bounties of Heaven. We have been preserved, these many years, in peace and prosperity. We have grown in numbers, wealth and power, as no other nation has ever grown. But we have forgotten God. We have forgotten the gracious hand which preserved us in peace, and multiplied and enriched and strengthened us; and we have vainly imagined, in the deceitfulness of our hearts, that all these blessings were produced by some superior wisdom and virtue of our own. Intoxicated with unbroken success, we have become too self-sufficient to feel the necessity of redeeming and preserving grace, too proud to pray to the God that made us! It behooves us, then, to humble ourselves before the offended Power, to confess our national sins, and to pray for clemency and forgiveness.

Now, therefore, in compliance with the request, and fully concurring in the views of the Senate, I do, by this my proclamation, designate and set apart Thursday, the 30th. Day of April, 1863, as a day of national humiliation, fasting and prayer. And I do hereby request all the People to abstain, on that day, from their ordinary secular pursuits, and to unite, at their several places of public worship and their respective homes, in keeping the day holy to the Lord, and devoted to the humble discharge of the religious duties proper to that solemn occasion.

All this being done, in sincerity and truth, let us then rest humbly in the hope authorized by the Divine teachings, that the united cry of the Nation will be heard on high, and answered with blessings, no less than the pardon of our national sins, and the restoration of our now divided and suffering Country, to its former happy condition of unity and peace. In witness whereof, I have hereunto set my hand and caused the seal of the United States to be affixed. *By the President: Abraham Lincoln*

What would Abraham Lincoln say today?

Step to Start Strong:

Pray for America.

JANUARY 15

Declaration of Dependence

"Therefore we do not lose heart. Even though our outward man is perishing, yet the inward man is being renewed day by day."

2 Corinthians 4:16

Your life is made up of three parts. Your body, soul and spirit. You are a spiritual being with a body that just so happens to have a mind & will with emotions which together is called your soul. God is a spirit so this is the part in you that was created in His image. When you receive Him as your Savior, His Holy Spirit is birthed on the inside of your spirit man which makes you alive *"in Christ."* Your body is the part that is wasting away, however, your soul is the part that needs to be regenerated and renewed each day. Your spirit was made perfect but your soul struggles. Does anybody bear witness?

Now, watch this: This is where prayer and fasting comes into play. Prayer connects you to God and fasting disconnects you from the flesh. What does the flesh represent? The Bible refers to the flesh as your body & soul. Fasting doesn't allow you to feed your soul and selfish desires. If you feed your flesh, its inevitable; your body will follow. However, if you feed your spirit your flesh will follow too! Jesus said, *"Follow me."* The Academy Award Winning Question is: *"Who has control of you?" Your flesh or your spirit?*

If you're struggling, keep fasting & praying. Fasting is like signing a personal Declaration of Dependence. You are saying to yourself, *"God is the source of my strength and my hope is in Him alone." You can depend upon Him for anything.* Go to God first this year. This is the basis of starting the year off strong. We want to cut off all dependencies other than Christ alone. By doing so, you not only strengthen the fruit of self-control but you strengthen your will to depend upon Him. So be strong today! Be Spirit-filled and be Spirit-led!

Step to Start Strong:

Feed your Spirit Man all you Can.

JANUARY 16

PREACHING PENNIES

"He who wins souls is wise."

Proverbs 11:20

Think about a penny? Really insignificant and overlooked to say the least. For you math majors, you know it takes hundreds of pennies to purchase anything these days. Most people wouldn't take the time to pick up a penny by the gas pump. Its safe to say, pennies are depreciating in value like many other things. However, for me, I like to picture people as pennies. Think about this: Planet earth is home for over 7 billion souls and they all need a Savior. Some are dirty, others are forgotten, many are overlooked and under appreciated but all of them are loved by God. A matter of fact, I believe each of them deserves to hear the Gospel at least one time in their life. "Don't you think so?" This is the Great Commission. Our only mission! *"To seek & save that which was lost."* Pennies may not have significance is the eyes of our society but they certainly do in the eyes our Savior. There are pennies put in your path everyday but do you see them through the eyes of Christ? I'll never forget, the year I was celebrating my 12th Spiritual Birthday, I picked up a young man on the side of the street. He was peddling for money as He held up a sign that said, *"My mom just died. I'm homeless & I really need help."* I normally don't do this but I felt so compelled to help this young man with more than money. In ministry, we've heard it all. All the same scams and lies just to get another high. However, this guy was different. I sensed a I a dire need for divine intervention. I later found out his mom really did die & he had nowhere to go. Heroin took her life and if he didn't get some help soon drugs would destroy his destiny too. To make a long story short, we brought him to the house for food & a hot shower. We packed his bags and checked him into a 90 day program by midnight that very day. Indeed, God prepared the way for this guy! A 21 year old Jewish boy who had never heard the Gospel, not only heard the Gospel that day but more importantly, experienced it. Remember, Simple obedience brings radical results.

Why am I telling you this? Because that night when I got home, Kacie was already asleep, so I slipped into the washroom to clean up. As I sat down to kick off my shoes, I looked down & guess what I found? Surprisingly, *"One shiny penny,"* and I said, *"you've got to be kidding me?"* The Spirit of the Lord said, *"Happy Birthday!"* I knew exactly what this meant. I teared up & said, *"God, you couldn't have given me a greater gift."* This was the greatest present for me. *"Another Soul Saved & I still have the penny."* I have to wonder what God is gonna give us this year? Many more saved souls would definitely be ok.

Step to Start Strong:

Pick up a Penny. Lead Someone to the Lord.

JANUARY 17

My Promise

"When the Lord restored the fortunes of Zion, we were like those who dreamed. Our mouths were filled with laughter, our tongues with songs of joy. Then it was said among the nations, "The Lord has done great things for them." The Lord has done great things for us, and we are filled with joy. Restore our fortunes, Lord, like streams in the Negev. Those who sow with tears will reap with songs of joy. Those who go out weeping, carrying seed to sow will return with songs of joy, carrying their harvest with them."

Psalm 126

God gave me this promise in Psalm 126 years ago as I was studying the scripture. It actually cross references to Jeremiah 29:10-14 which says: "When seventy years are completed for Babylon, I will come to you and fulfill my good promise to bring you back to this place. For I know the plans I have for you," declares the Lord, "plans to prosper you and not to harm you, plans to give you hope and a future. Then you will call on me and come and pray to me, and I will listen to you. You will seek me and find me when you seek me with all your heart. I will be found by you," declares the Lord, "and I will bring you back from captivity. I will gather you from all the nations and places where I have banished you," declares the Lord, "and will bring you back to the place from which I carried you into exile."

The interesting part of this passage is the 70 year revelation that Daniel received when was when He was in the mist of prayer and fasting. (Daniel 9 and 10) Yes, He was fasting while was reading Jeremiah's prophetic word concerning this powerful promise. It was actually in this moment that God gave Him the revelation that He was in the right place at the right time to take this prophetic word to a place of fulfillment. He thought, *"It has been 70 years!"* Now is the time for God's people to be free so why are they still in captivity?

Here is the principle: *"Fasting was the key that released the revelation for Daniel to understand the signs of the times in which He was living."* Ultimately, He was the end of the spear that brought about Israel's deliverance. However, we have to remember that fasting sharpened His blade of sensitivity to fulfill what the Spirit of the Lord had intended. What was God's intention? Psalm 126; It all started with a dream but it ended with a Harvest! Circle the Promise of Jeremiah 29:11 & Psalm 126 in your Bible. Remember, *"Those who sow in tears, shall come forth with shouts of Joy carrying their harvest with them."* This is your Promise.

Step 2 Start Strong:

Stand of the Promises of God.

JANUARY 18

Soul-Food

"My food is to do the will of God for the one who sent me."

John 4:34

For those of us who were raised in the South, dinner doesn't get any better than fried chicken, mashed potatoes & gravy and home-made biscuits. Oh, how could I forget the cornbread & chow-chow! You can call this "Soul-Food" or as some may say, "Comfort-Food." In fact, you can call it whatever you wanna call it but I know what I call it, I call it Good!

Here's my point: Food is to our belly as fasting & prayer is to our soul. Our soul needs food too folks! Jesus put it this way, *"The food I eat nobody knows about."* (John 4:32) What was He saying? He was saying that there is more to life than eating & drinking! There is another type of substance that satisfies our deepest desires and I believe He was speaking of spiritual disciplines such as fasting and praying right here.

This month we are setting aside a First-Fruit Offering, not unto ourselves but unto the King who holds everything in His hands. His is worthy and I want to say today, *"What we are doing is worth it!"* May the hunger pains in your soul outweigh the one inside of your stomach. As one preacher put it, *"Now is the time to De-throne King Stomach!"* Take time to feed yourself spiritually. You wouldn't skip a free meal at your favorite restaurant would you? Absolutely not, so don't miss out of the opportunity set a smorgasbord of soul-food before your spirit-man on a daily basis.

Jesus goes on to say, *"My food is to do the will of God for the one who sent me."* (John 4:34) I don't know about you but I am hungry after the one who saved me and sent me into the world to be a witness. May your soul be satisfied in Him today. He is worth it all.

Step to Start Strong:

Keep a Well-Balanced Diet.

JANUARY 19

All Things are Possible!

"Jesus said to him, 'If you can believe, all things *are* possible to him who believes."

Mark 9:23

Listen to this provoking thought from the late Pastor and Preacher, A. W. Tozer:

> *"God is looking for people through whom He can do the impossible. What a pity that we plan only things we can do by ourselves."*

Do we spend most of our time and energy doing what we could do all by ourselves? Think about it this way: If the Holy Spirit hid himself for a day, would we even know He was missing? I don't know about you but I am in the place in my life where if my dream doesn't drive me to a deeper dependance upon God, I just keep dreaming bigger! I don't want to look back into the rearview mirror of my life and see mediocracy. I want to leave behind a life of legacy! How about you?

Mark 9:23 says, *"All things are possible!"* But most people aren't experiencing the impossible. Why? Because we don't understand the second half of that verse. It says, *"All things are possible to those who believe."* Most people don't experience the impossible because they don't believe in the God of the Impossible. Therefore, they never attempt to do anything outside of themselves. *Do you really believe?* Test yourself because your actions determine what you *"really"* believe. Are you stuck in a religious rut? If so, remember, prayer and fasting will push you into God's plan & purpose for your life.

Evangelist Reinhart Bonnke says, *"Don't plan with what's in your pocket. Plan with what's in God's pocket!"* Don't let what you don't have dictate what you do. Where there is vision, there is always provision and If it is God's will, it is God's bill. Your Heavenly Father will supply all your needs according to His riches in glory! God's got His eye on you but the question is: Do you have your eyes on Him?

Step to Start Strong:

Dream Big Dreams.

JANUARY 20.

True Story

"The Lord is not slow in keeping his promise."

2 Peter 3:9

One of my favorite characteristics about the Lord and His ways is His divine timing. Yes, not just what He does but when He does it! God can do anything He wants to do but He chooses to do it at *"just the right time."* By operating this way, He leaves us in a place where we have these *"Gotta Be God moments!"*

Have you ever experienced this before? It's during seasons of deep prayer and fasting that I feel the most in sync with the Holy Spirit. For instance, one day I was in a meeting with one of our Board of Directors discussing the need to develop a more user friendly website. After 30 minutes of writing down changes to be made online and looking at other websites to model after, I receive a Facebook message from a friend of a friend. Really random but what I read almost caused me to almost fall out of my seat! Here's the message, Check it out:

> *"Hey Chance! I am looking to fill ten spots for my company over the next two months. We do christian marketing and story telling. We are funded by a board of trustees, so the tab will be completely covered by them. We do websites, design, and social campaigns for people with a mission for Christ. Are you interested in any of these services?*

Am I interested? You bet! Within 2 minutes, this guy was on speaker phone sharing the vision of their ministry and how they want to help ministries who have a low budget to get set-up with a successful on-line presence. What I was hearing was almost too good to be true. However, I am proud to announce, we launched a completely new website and the best thing about it? It was completely free! Now, do you think this was a coincidence? No sir, I believe it was a God Incident! His timing is so divine!

How can you apply this to your life? Well, what God did for me, he can do for you. As a matter of fact, "Your life could change in 24 hours." Just ask Joseph, as He went from the pit to the palace in a 24 hour period. Maybe ask Ruth, she woke up one day begging for food and she went to sleep that very night at the feet of Boaz! One phone call, one meeting, one encounter could literally change your life and your circumstances forever. May this true story leave you in a place of true expectancy as you seek God wholeheartedly.

Step to Start Strong:

Let Him who Boast, Boast in the Lord.

JANUARY 21

Great for God

"The Lord gave the word; Great was the company of those who proclaimed it."

Psalm 68:11

One day, a pastor friend of mine gave me a book entitled, *"Great for God."* The author, Davis Shibley, tells the story of 25 missionaries that have changed the world. One of these missionaries was Hudson Taylor who truly led *"The Exchanged Life,"* as He laid down His life for the nation of China. Some Historians say, He was the most fruitful missionary since the Apostle Paul. Only Heaven will tell but what we do know is Galatians 2:20 was his life verse. Listen to what it says:

"I am crucified with Christ & I no longer live but the life that I now live in the body, I live by faith in the Son of God who loved me & gave Himself for me."

Hudson heard a call from God at 5 years old to be a missionary. Many people would laugh at Him and say, *"Well, young man just where will that be?* He would immediately say with confidence, *"China."*

Indeed, God did whisper these words into His spirit at a very young age and years later in 1832, Hudson Taylor sailed the ocean blues all the way to Shanghai. He was ready to preach the Gospel and win souls but to his surprise, he faced great opposition and persecution. Much like the life of the Apostle Paul, His autobiography tells of all the tragedies and heartache he experienced there. His plea to His partners back in England was over 1 million souls are dying here each day and we must do something to save them!

One of His famous quotes is, *"There are three stages in every great work of God: first, it is impossible, then it is difficult, then it is done."* His work was eventually finished in 1907 but the impact of His legacy is still living. Remember, If God's work is done in God's way, your time is never wasted.

What is God whispering in your spirit? Where is your mission field? When will you start? Are you ready to go? May you Be Great for God this year.

<u>Step to Start Strong:</u>

Live your Life on Mission.

JANUARY 22

I CAN ONLY IMAGINE

"You understand my thought from afar."

Psalm 139:2

One of the greatest gifts God has given you is your imagination. He created you with the ability to see outside yourself into a realm of the unknown. Anyone who has spent anytime with children understands this concept completely. Its like they can flip a switch and automatically be transported to the movie set of Frozen or their favorite Fairy-Tale scene. It absolutely amazes me! However, we have to remember, we were the same way when we were small. The sad thing is most people stop using their imagination as they grow more mature along the way.

This reminds me of a scripture found in Matthew 18:3, *"Truly I tell you, unless you change and become like little children, you will never enter the kingdom of heaven.*

It's almost like God knows as we grow older we tend to lose the child-like characteristics that He wants us to keep in our relationship with Him. Like trust, tenderness & truth just to name a few. The truth is, w*e must change & become like little children when we approach Him as our Heavenly Father.* There are many facets of faith in the life of a child but my all-time favorite is their ability to use their imagination.

My pastor in Bible School once told me that He had a thinking chair. After a long day, He would sit in His recliner at home and clear His mind as He meditated upon the word of God. He told me God had given Him answers to problems, words of wisdom and creative counsel in that chair. This thought never left me and till this day I try to do the same thing. I do my best to take time everyday to get away from the noise and let my imagination run wild. It's in this chair, if you will, that I find strength through my struggles and power in my weaknesses. I can only imagine what God will do for you if you will withdraw to a solitary place today. Find a place. Find a chair. Use your imagination! God gave it to you for a reason. Don't relinquish it! Use it to your advantage! Its time to dream again!

Step to Start Strong:

Find a Thinking Chair.

JANUARY 23

STAR WARS

"Finally, my brethren, be strong in the Lord and in the power of His might."

Ephesians 6:10

If you know me, you know one of my favorite ministries to follow is Free Chapel with Pastor Jentezen Franklin. The devotion written today was entitled,"Starting Strong," so I wanted to share a piece of it with you.

"*The Force Awakens* recently blew the doors off the box office with record earnings of $249 million dollars opening weekend. Known for epic battle scenes of good versus evil, right versus wrong and light versus darkness, it has packed theaters for decades. No matter how knowledgeable you may be on the series, the bad guy is easily pinpointed. With his outfit, his voice and his demeanor, he basically screams, "Hey! Over here! I am the villain!"Our real life enemy is not so easily distinguishable. His destructive plan for your life doesn't come in a box clearly marked *TNT*, nor will he parade around dressed in black with obvious respiratory issues. On the contrary, he masks himself as an appealing angel of light, and fights with subtle mistruths, discouragements and defeats. He is strategic, strong and sinister. If you don't know much about him, you probably wouldn't even realize he is at work. But he certainly is.

"*For we do not wrestle against flesh and blood, but against the rulers, against the authorities, against the cosmic powers over this present darkness, against the spiritual forces of evil in the heavenly places* (Ephesians 6:12 ESV)."

Lucky for us, he is also DEFEATED!

What comfort there is in knowing the resolve before entering the conflict. As you go about your week, be intentional about clothing yourself in the armor Jesus has provided. Pull tight that belt of integrity. Shoulders back in your breastplate of purity. Double knot your boots of peace. Hold fast to that shield of certainty. Strap tight your helmet of sanity and sharpen up with His word.

You were never created to be a paying spectator in someone else's battle. So suit up, there is a war to win.

Oh, and let His force be with you!

Step to Start Strong:

Keep Fighting the Good Fight of Faith.

JANUARY 24

The Desert of Judea

"It was good for me to be afflicted so that I might learn your decrees."

Psalm 119:71

You read a lot about the desert in scripture. The children of Israel were in the desert wandering for 40 years. Jesus was tempted by the devil in the desert for 40 days. Many other people have experienced desert seasons in their life and ministry including you and I. The desert is a destination of loneliness and lifelessness. The desert is a tough place. A place of testing and trouble.

Maybe you're in a tough place today? Maybe you are being tested with trouble? Maybe you feel lonely or lifeless.

If so, the Bible speaks very clearly that the desert experience can lead you to a place of victory. Think about it? The Israelites left the desert by crossing through the Red Sea representing the Blood of Jesus. Once they made it the other side, they began to step into the promises of God found in Canaan. What promises have you heard from God? They will ultimately be fulfilled by the blood of the lamb if you believe His word and keep following the leading of the Holy Spirit.

Take time to consider Jesus; He was led into the desert by the Holy Spirit to be tempted by the devil right? We read that He resisted the enemy and came out of the desert full of the Spirit's power to begin His earthly ministry. It seems the desert experience is a prerequisite to God's promises?

Many times your misery becomes your ministry. At other times, your test becomes your testimony. King David would say so as He said in Psalm 119, *"I thank the Lord for my affliction because it has made me a man of God's word."* Think about it? We typically don't thank the Lord for our trial but after we triumph over it, we look back & think, *"My struggle has made me stronger."* So embrace the desert and resist the dessert and believe that Isaiah 35 will be a reality for you:

> *"The desert and the parched land will be glad; the wilderness will rejoice and blossom. Like the crocus, it will burst into bloom; it will rejoice greatly and shout for joy. The glory of Lebanon will be given to it, the splendor of Carmel and Sharon for they will see the glory of the Lord, the splendor of our God. So, strengthen your feeble hands & steady your knees that give way; because God's promises are on the way."* And All God's people said, *"Amen!"*

<u>Step to Start Strong:</u>

Resist Temptation.

JANUARY 25

Somebody is Watching You

"The eyes of the LORD are in every place, Watching the evil and the good."

Proverbs 15:3

In the world that we live in, somebody is always watching. Between smart phones, satellites & drones you almost feel like it is impossible to be completely alone. It's equally amazing to me what you can see on Cable TV. People can catch the most catastrophic events on camera? What used to be told on tv can now be tweeted and seen around the world in a matter of minutes. There is an eye in the sky if you will.

However, the same is true in the spiritual world. 2 Chronicles 16:9 says, "*The eyes of the LORD range throughout the earth to strengthen those whose hearts are fully committed to him.*" This means that God has got His eye on you. He sees your faithfulness and He sees your faults. He sees your struggle and He sees your successes. The writer of Hebrews wrote in chapter 4 verse 13, "*Nothing in all creation is hidden from God's sight."* Indeed, the Lord is watching every aspect of your life very closely.

This could be good or not so good for you. It all depends upon your day to day activities and personal integrity. The definition of true character is who you are when no one else is looking. This is who you really are! Think about it? The best part: God knows you better than yourself. Why is this good? This reality should set you free to be yourself. It's ok to be brutally honest with God.

In fact, you are the apple of His eye. Other people see some things but God sees all things. Make your Heavenly Father proud today and be all He created you to be.

Step to Start Strong:

Be Yourself

JANUARY 26

The Prayer Globe

"Ask of me, I will give you the nations as your inheritance. The ends of the earth as your possession."

Psalm 2:8

When I gave my life to the Lord on April 29th 2003, God birthed a dream inside of me to go to the nations. He later quickened a verse in my spirit found in Psalm 2:8. This scripture has become one of our foundational verses for the vision of our ministry.

Again it says, *"Ask of me, I will give you the nations as your inheritance. The ends of the earth as your possession."*

So, what does this verse say to do? Just ask and God will do what? He will give me the nations. So what did I do? I simply started asking God to send me to the nations and now look what God has done. He has sent us to 6 of the 7 continents on the earth and what a ride it has been. However, it all started with a

Prayer Globe. When I was in Teen Challenge, my mom gave me a small globe of the earth and I would pace around my room in prayer asking God to send me to the nations.

I would pray this prayer repetitiously, *"If you can use anything Lord you can use me. Touch my hands Lord and my feet. Touch my heart Lord and speak through me. If you can use anything Lord you can use me."* This prayer still moves me in my spirit today.

This was the beginning of a deep, deep desire for me to see people saved and saved free in every nation across the sea. We can't forget that Jesus gave us the "Great Co-mmission." He said, "Go therefore and make disciples of all the nations and behold I am with you always. This is the Great Commission and it's our only mission. It's not a Great Suggestion. There is no other option. It is a mandate from Heaven from our Commander-in-chief, the Lord Jesus Christ. God is still saying Go & now is the time. The Greek word for go means *"as you are going."* So as you go about your day today, be a mission. Look for ways to be used by God. Someone said, "availability is always better than ability when it come to witnessing."

Step to Start Strong:

Make yourself Available to Be used by the Lord.

JANUARY 27

The Gate Beautiful

"Now Peter and John went up together to the temple at the hour of prayer, the ninth hour. And a certain man lame from his mother's womb was carried, whom they laid daily at the gate of the temple which is called Beautiful, to ask alms from those who entered the temple; who, seeing Peter and John about to go into the temple, asked for alms. And fixing his eyes on him, with John, Peter said, "Look at us." So he gave them his attention, expecting to receive something from them. Then Peter said, "Silver and gold I do not have, but what I do have I give you: In the name of Jesus Christ of Nazareth, rise up and walk." And he took him by the right hand and lifted him up, and immediately his feet and ankle bones received strength."

Acts 3:1-7

There are three people we can focus on in this passage. We can turn our attention to Peter and John or we could turn our attention to the beggar by the gate beautiful. The two disciples just so happened to be up and the other guy like many of us at times was down. This is a perfect picture of everyday life. One day you're up

& the other day you're down. One day I'm the guy helping others and the next day I'm the one who needs help. This is the purpose of the church. The Apostle Paul put it this, *"When you have the opportunity, do good to all people, but especially to the household of believer's.*

Peter & John were in a beautiful place but they encountered an ugly situation. They could had turned an eye or just rushed by this guy. However, they took notice of his situation and this was the first notable miracle recorded in the book of Acts after the ascension of Jesus. For these two, it was now or never.

I wonder if the potential for your next miracle is in the form of something that you are stepping over? Let me put it this way: What are you overlooking that God wants you to see? This man was looking for money but He got a miracle! All He wanted was some spare change but on the contrary, God changed His life forever!

Here's a good life principle: *"If you will give God your attention, He will always exceed your expectation."* In Acts 1, God gave us the promise of the Holy Spirit. In Acts 2, He fulfilled the promise with the power of the Holy Spirit and In Acts 3, Peter and John knew it was time to put the promise into practice. Give God your attention today and expect Him to do His part; The Supernatural.

Step to Start Strong:

Be an Answered to Someone Else's Prayer

JANUARY 28

TODAY MATTERS

"Your life is but a vapor, it appears for a little while & then vanishes away."

James 4:14,

If one thing is for sure, life has a way of passing us by. With this in mind, may we make everyday count in light of eternity.

Mahatma Gandhi, a civil rights activist in South Africa coined the popular phrase, *"Live like you would die tomorrow but learn like you would live forever."* I say let's live this year like it was our last year! Not a bad idea huh? Try asking yourself this question: *"If you only had 12 months to live, what would you do?"* What would you focus on? Who would you help? How would you spend your time? Whatever your answer is; this is what you should really be doing. Within reason of course but what I mean is; Don't waste your life! It's way too precious and way too short.

In conclusion, I love how the Message Translation of the Bible articulates Ephesians 5:11-21 and with this we will close:

> *"Don't waste your time on useless work on the barren pursuits of darkness. Expose these things for the sham that they are. It's a scandal when people waste their lives on things they must do in the darkness where no one will see. Rip the cover off those frauds and see how attractive they look in the light of Christ. Wake up from your sleep, Climb out of your coffins; Christ will show you the light! So watch your step. Use your head. Make the most of every chance you get. These are desperate times! Don't live carelessly, unthinkingly. Make sure you understand what the Master wants. Don't drink too much wine. That cheapens your life. Drink the Spirit of God, huge draughts of him. Sing hymns instead of drinking songs! Sing songs from your heart to Christ. Sing praises over everything in the name of our Lord & Savior, Jesus Christ."*

Remember, *Today Matters.*
Do your best and let God do the rest!

Step to Start Strong:

Live Before you Die.

JANUARY 29.

LISTEN TO HIM!

"A cloud appeared and overshadowed Peter, James and John on the Mount of Transfiguration and a voice came out of the cloud saying, "This is my beloved Son, Listen to Him!"

Mark 9:7

In this story, the Father affirms His son with love but also, confirms our need to Listen to Him! One of the essential elements of loving someone is listening to them. You cannot live strong in relationships if you do not take time to listen to your love ones. God gave us two ears so we would listen twice as much as we are talking. This is a struggle for some people. It reminds me of a joke:

"Three friends decided to go deer hunting together. One was a lawyer, one a doctor, and the other a preacher. As they were walking, along came a big buck. The three of them shot simultaneously. Immediately the buck dropped to the ground and all three of them rushed up to see how big it actually was. Upon reaching the deer, they found out that it was not only dead but it had only one bullet hole. Thus a debate followed concerning whose big buck it was. A few minutes later a game officer came by and asked what all the fuss was about. The doctor told him their reason for the debate. The officer told them he would take a look and tell them who shot it. Within a few seconds the game officer said with much confidence, *"The pastor shot the buck!"* They all wondered how he knew that so quickly. The officer said, *"The diagnosis was easy.The bullet went in one ear and out the other."*

Sad to say, many times when the Lord speaks to us, it goes in one ear and out the other. Let us not live our lives in such a way. If God speaks, let us be obedient and do what He says to do. I feel like many people don't hear from God because He knows if He speaks their not going to do what He said anyway. God doesn't speak to be heard, He speaks to be obeyed. Let's listen to Him this year! He might give you further instructions if you go back and do what He asked you to due in a recent season. It's just a thought. May we keep walking by faith and not by sight.

<u>Step to Start Strong:</u>

Be a Doer of the Word and Not a Hearer Only.

JANUARY 30

True Confession

"If we confess our sins, He is faithful and just to forgive us our sins and to cleanse us from all unrighteousness."

1 John 1:9

One of my favorite study techniques for the Bible is defining certain words in their original language. The Old Testament was written in Hebrew because this was the common dialect of its day. When the New Testament Times was canonized, the universal language was Greek. Somebody told me once, *"I know a little greek, He owns the delicatessen down the street."* This is a little different but you know what I mean. The Greek word for *"confession"* in the Bible literally means, *"to say the same thing."* When you confess your sins, He is faithful and just to forgive you of your sins and cleanse you from ALL unrighteousness. Amen. (1st John 1:9)

So, how do you truly confess your sins? You say the same thing about your sin that God says about your sin. When you mess up; You say, *"I was wrong."* Will you please forgive me and help me to never do this again! When you lie, you say, God I lied! When you gossip, you say God I gossiped! When you doubt, you say, God, I let fear creep in. You have to call it as He sees it. Don't sugar coat it!

A story in the Bible that illustrates this point is the account of Jacob in Genesis 32. There was no one who hated Jacob more than himself. He lied to his father, stole from his brother and ran away from home to hide from his sin. Indeed, misery was his best friend, until one day he decided to face His failure. He repented from his rebellion, changed his direction and found himself headed back home again after 20 years of seclusion. The night before he met his brother, he decided to wrestle with God in prayer. Something we all need to do from time to time.

It was during this encounter that God asked Jacob a question. Now, let me remind you, God never asks a question because He needs the information. Why is this so? Because He already knows the answer! Whenever God asks you a question, *He is creating an awareness inside of you for something that needs to change.* What was the question He asked Jacob that day? God said, *"Son, what's your name?"* Jacob's name literally meant deceiver. This was the most significant moment in this man's life. Instead of making excuses and saying what he wanted to say about his sin, he said what God said about his sin. He said, *"My name is Jacob."* Simply meaning, He was confessing His sin of deception. In fact, this True Confession caused a True Conversion. Now, we serve the God of Abraham, Isaac & Jacob.

<u>Step to Start Strong</u>:

Confess you Sins to God.

JANUARY 31.

GROUND ZERO

"Remember me, O LORD, in Your favor toward Your people; Visit me with Your salvation."

Psalm 106:4

What's your first thought when you hear the words, *"Ground Zero?"* If I were a betting man, I would say 100% of you reading this devotion thought of the 9/11 terrorist attack against our country. This was my thought as well. September 11, 2001, will have a lasting impact on every person that lived during that day. In fact, if I asked you where you were when you first heard of this catastrophe, almost all of you would remember this as well. The popular theme says, we will never forget and indeed we will not.

We serve a *"Ground Zero God."* The Webster definition of ground zero means a starting point. The Apostle Paul put it this way, *"You can be confident of this very thing, He who started a good work in you will bring it to completion in the day of Christ Jesus (Phil 1:6)."* Our God is the author and the perfecter of our faith! When God came into your life, you were at *"ground zero."* When you got saved this was your spiritual starting point! The scripture says, Adam and Eve were the first humans in history. Noah started civilization over again after the flood. Abraham lived a life of faith by leaving his homeland. Moses started when He left Pharaoh's palace and dwelt on the backside of the desert and the list goes on and on and on.

God loves ground zero. Don't you ever forget where He found you. What did your life look like? Better yet, what did you look like? What situation were you in? Maybe it was a pile of rubble. Maybe it was in the mist of pain? Whatever day this was for you, write it down.

For me, Ground Zero was April 29, 2003. Fast forward almost 8 years & you will find the day I was ordained into the Gospel Ministry of Jesus Christ. This just so happened to be 9/11, 2011. A Day I will never forget. He who called you is faithful and He will do it! Do not despise the day of small beginning because the Lord rejoices when a work is begun! Lay a strong salvation and let the Holy Spirit build your structure. He is the God who turns Zero's into Hero's! Hallelujah!

<u>Step to Start Strong:</u>

Write your Spiritual Birthday in your Bible

FEBRUARY 1

The Year of ?

"For the vision is yet for the appointed time; It hastens toward the goal and it will not fail Though it tarries, wait for it; For it will certainly come, it will not delay."

Habakkuk 2:3

Finish this sentence: This Year is The Year of _________?

What are you believing God for this year? What word would you use to describe this year? Think of it this way: What does this year represent for you in the spirit?

Every year, I seek the Lord to see what His theme is for me. I even dig a little deeper to discover a theme verse for the year. Pastors do this for their congregations, businesses do this for their employees but what about you. Cooperate campaigns are great to grow bottom line but these are only temporal ideas. What about you & your personal relationship with Jesus? Jesus has a theme for your timeline. He has a victory verse for you to stand on during the upcoming days. Think about it? What's your word?

One of the covenantal names of Christ is Jehovah Nissi. This Hebrew word means, *"The Lord is my Banner."* Moses used this term in the battle with the Amalekites in Exodus 17. As long as Moses held his staff up to the Heavens, Joshua and the Israelites would succeed in the valley. On the contrary, when he lowered his staff, the enemy would gain ground against them. This simple act of obedience was their key to victory. I want you to see that the staff represents the truth of the word of God. An actual staff supports a person naturally but God's word will support and sustain you supernaturally. The word of God has supernatural power!

So, fly your banner high this year. Ask God to give you a word to stand on. Believe God for this staff to support and sustain you! Hold your hands high and declare that God is going to do exceeding and abundantly more than you could ever ask or think. I've got my word. What's your's?

This Year is The Year of __________?

Step to Start Strong:

Write down a Verse that Describes this Year for You

FEBRUARY 2

The Super Bowl

"The twenty-four elders fell down before the Lamb, each having a harp, and golden bowls full of incense, which are the prayers of the saints."

Revelation 5:8

The imagery of the scriptures are amazing to me. Picture this: Here you are on earth, with a finite mind, praying the best you can for whatever situation you're in. While you pray, angels in Heaven capture your petitions and store them in bowls as incense around the throne of God. You may forget what you prayed from one day to the next but God can't. The prayer you prayed when you were 8 in the altar of your church is still stored. The prayers you uttered in the darkest season in your life. Your first prayer and your last prayer will never be wasted. All the questions, all the promises and all the tears have been stored up in Heavenly places. Prayer is the greatest retirement plan! The return is out of this world! Picture this: The prayers you prayer each day reach the ear of God and they're being poured out like incense before the one who can save you and set you free.

Let your faith be built up right now. You are walking on the pavement that has been laid by the prayers of past generations. Take action today and pray. Just like young Samuel in the scripture, *"No word will be wasted."*

In fact, Prayer is not asking. It is a longing of the soul. It is a daily admission of one's weakness. It is better in prayer to have a heart without words than words without a heart.

This is the Original Super Bowl which stores the prayers of the saints.

Step to Start Strong:

Participate in the Super Bowl: Prayer Today.

FEBRUARY 3

EARS TO HEAR

"The sovereign Lord has given me an instructed tongue, to know the word that sustains the weary. He awakens me morning by morning, He awakens my ear to listen like one being taught. The sovereign Lord has opened my ears and I have not been rebellious and I have not drawn back. I will set my face like flint because I know I will not be put to shame."

Isaiah 50:4

What a prayer to pray everyday! Many years ago, I found this verse and I pray the principle found here very often. Let's lean in and glean this morning:

Did you know that you can know the word that sustains the weary of heart? Many times, we know not because we ask not. As a Christian, you can know what to do in any situation. I can't count the times people have approached me and said, *"What you said was exactly what*

I needed to hear." Now, I didn't know what they were facing. I wasn't stalking them on Facebook fishing for information. I just spoke what God spoke to me very simply. We don't know all things but the Spirit of God who lives on the inside of you knows everything. If you will ask, God will answer. He will give you an ear to hear. Let me be plain, this is not only for those behind the pulpit. The Holy Spirit can speak to you concerning anyone you meet. The passing thought that pops in your mind, at just the right time, just might be God. Be obedient and speak what He says with confidence.

Revelation 2:7 says, "*Now, to him who has ears, let him hear what the spirit is saying.*" (The Lord is not speaking of natural ears here.) Everybody has ears but not everybody can hear! He is speaking specifically about your spiritual ears of understanding. What He whispers in your ear, shout from the rooftops! (Matthew 10:27) Take what you hear God say privately and make it public. (Only if He released you to do so:) Yes, God speaks to me concerning many things but He only releases me to share some things. Why does He do this? One reason is so we can know how to pray. Ask God to give you an ear to hear. There are many sounds of distraction but only one Holy Spirit. Do you have an ear to hear his voice?

Here's my prayer for you today: *"Just as God awakens you every morning, may He awaken your spiritual ears. Whatever you do, Don't draw back! Do what God says to do and say what God says to say. By doing so, you will walk in a greater measure of grace, in Jesus name! Amen!"*

Step to Start Strong:

Train your Spiritual Ears to Hear

FEBRUARY 4

But God?

"Zechariah and Elizabeth were upright in the sight of God, observing all the Lord's commandments and regulations blamelessly but they had no children."

Luke 1:6

Now you and I both know when someone uses the conjunction "but" in a sentence, what the person is really trying to convey is a sharp contrast between two subjects. For instance, The panthers played terrible Sunday night in the Super Bowl but hopefully, they will win next year! See, the contrast and see the truth! This is exactly what God is wanting you to see in this scripture. Zechariah and Elizabeth loved God with all their heart and they were blameless by the law which means they kept all the man-made traditions of the day. But there was a problem; They had no children. So what's the big deal? The contrast occurs because in this culture, to be barren meant you were cursed by God. So how can they be blameless and blessed but cursed by sin in the same sentence. God was trying to prove a point in this passage.

Even though the people looked upon this couple with great misfortune, God was about to look upon them with favor because of their faithfulness. The laity held one view of the Law but the Lord ultimately held their victory!

My question for you today is: *"Have you connected your faith to a negative connotation?"* Zechariah and Elizabeth was upright in the sight of God but they had not children. What does your conjunction represent? God has called me to do this but I'm too old or I don't have enough money or I'll never be smart enough or nobody cares about me or my church doesn't support me or my spouse and I are in disunity. And the contrast continues…

The people in this passage placed a label upon this couple. What labels have you allowed in your life? Notice that despite popular belief God had other plans. God was about to shake the nation of Israel through their soon coming son John the Baptist and they didn't even know it. This revelation tells the story:

The Hebrew name Zechariah means God remembers. Sarah's name means His promises. Read the rest of the story and you'll see how they bore a son named John the Baptist. His name means Grace. Put them all together and what do you say: *"God remembers His promises of Grace."*

Remove your negative connotation today. Instead of saying, the Word says But? Try saying, I know what the world says, But God makes a difference.

Step to Start Strong:

Don't ever forget His promises of Grace.

FEBRUARY 5

A Move of God

Miracles are the easiest part of my job. Do you know why? Because I don't perform them! We serve a God who is omnipotent, omniscient and omni-present who is the same yesterday, today and forevermore! What God did way back when, He can do right now and He still does. We dwell in the dispensation of grace and grace is what I want to focus on today.

I love miracles more than anybody. We've seen many miracles in the life of our ministry and I believe even more miracles are on the way. However, many times our perception of a mighty move of God is skewed. The Greatest Miracle is you. *Can I ask, what happened when you got saved?* It was a divine exchange. You repented of your sins and asked God to forgive you and what did God do? He forgave you and cast your sins as far as the East is from the West! Wow! Now, this was a mighty move of God by the Grace of God. Would you agree?

My point is: *"One of the greatest miracles you will ever see is one person going to another person to ask for forgiveness."* Matthew 5:23-24 says,

"Therefore, if you are offering your gift at the altar and remember that your brother or sister has something against you, leave your gift in front of the altar. Go first and be reconciled to them and then come back and offer your gift to God." So we see, in order to be in right standing with God, God places utmost importance upon our relationships.

One of the best ways to show your love for God is to show His love to people. However, its inevitable. Relationships lead to offense and offense leads to deep hurt and division. Should this cause you to give up on people? Certainly not! Has God given up on you? So, let the love of God move you today to a place of repentance and reconciliation with your relationships. Remember this: One person calling another person for the purpose of forgiveness is an undeniable mighty move of God. A modern day miracle I call it. However, we live in a day where most people are envious, jealous and quick to bring vengeance. This is not the character of Christ. He is quick to forgive, slow to anger and full of mercy.

So I ask you, What relationship do you need to mend? Has someone offended you? When I said this, the Holy Spirit spoke to you. This is the relationship that God wants to restore. Let God move you. He still performs miracles.

Step to Start Strong:

Freely Forgive as Christ Forgave You

FEBRUARY 6

All 4 One

"A great crowd of people followed him because they saw the signs he had performed by healing the sick."

John 6:2

When you read through the Gospels, you'll notice how the crowds followed Jesus by the masses just to hear His message. Nobody preached like Jesus. Everybody wanted to be by His side. However, it amazes me to see how Jesus stepped away from the stage, if you will, just to witness to one lost soul. Some scholars say, 80% of His ministry was fulfilled on a one-on-one basis. One of these instances is found in Luke Chapter 8. The scripture says, *"A large crowd had gathered and began to follow Jesus as He traveled."* One day Jesus said to His disciples, *"Let's go to the other side of the lake."* Now, in this moment, I believe He heard a word from the Holy Spirit to go. So what does He do? He left the crowd to cross the lake. *But watch what happens next?* Jesus tired from the tour decides to take a nap. The disciples settle in and begin to row the boat. Now, in the course of this transition, a violent storm arises on the horizon. If you've ever been on a boat when this happens, you know how quickly the weather can change. One minute the sun is out and the next minute a storm hits with high winds & waves. Many times, it's the same way, when you transition in life. Someone said, *"You're either going into a storm, coming out of a storm or right in the middle of a storm."* Have you ever felt this way before? Furthermore, you have to remember, the disciples willingly agreed to go with Jesus to the other side. But now they find themselves shaking Him profusely in the boat thinking their about to die! What does Jesus do? He rises up, rebukes the storm and goes back to His resting place. *Wow!* Even the winds and waves obey Him! Now, I want give the disciples some grace. The greek word for storm is only used in one other place in scripture; When Jesus died on the cross. So what happened here? All Hell broke loose. Literally! The sun turned black and darkness covered the earth. Dead men were raised from the grave and the ground began to shake. You could only imagine the fear that gripped everyones heart. So, the best way to relate is to say that the disciples were in a category 5 hurricane on the lake. This illuminates the Psalm that says, *"Many are the afflictions of the righteous but God delivers him out of them all."* We've all found out that living a life of obedience in not easy but it's worth it. Why is this so? Because of what happens when you get to the other side. When they weathered the storm and finally made it to the other side, they immediately encountered a man who was bound by Satan. He was a demoniac living in the graveyard. Jesus said one sentence and set Him free. After this ministry moment, He said, *"Ok, our work here is finished. Let's set sail and go back to where we were."* This event proves a powerful point; Jesus will leave the flock and endure anything to go find the one lost sheep. At one point in our life, this was you and me. Are you grateful? If so, How you can show it? By leaving the crowd. By leaving your comfort zone. By enduring the storm! Now you know what the storms is for? The storm is trying to keep you from going to the other side. May your faith be awakened today in Jesus name! Remember, Perfect Peace is His will. The wind & the waves have to be still. It's not All 4 Nothing, It's All 4 One!

Step to Start Strong.

Find the One and Share your Faith.

FEBRUARY 7

The Last Days

"But understand this, in the last days there will be times of difficulty. People will be lovers of self, lovers of money, proud, arrogant, abusive, disobedient to their parents, ungrateful, unholy, heartless, unappeasable, slanderous, without self-control, brutal, not loving good, treacherous, reckless, swollen with conceit, lovers of pleasure rather than lovers of God, having the appearance of godliness, but denying its power. Avoid such people."

2 Timothy 3: 1-5

This list describes the 21st Century. God's word is relevant and right concerning the signs of the times. Many people believe we are living in the last seconds of the last days and I would strongly agree. As Children of God, we have to stay strong because the love of many will wax cold. God's word says, *"That those who endure till the end shall be saved."* (Matthew 24) The scripture is clear, there will be a great falling away in the last days. We see it everyday. There is a falling away of absolute truth built on

Biblical principles, a falling away of morality and constitutional guidelines, a falling way of faith and family. We are living in a generation where the core values of America are disintegrating like the sand on the sea shore. So, what should we do? God gives us a key in 2nd Timothy Chapter 3 verse 5. As Christians, we should avoid such people who live like the list above. Now, this doesn't mean, we shouldn't associate, befriend and love other people who have different beliefs. But this does mean we should be careful who we let in our inner circle. God knows how subtle Satan can slip into our souls and lead us down paths of unrighteousness so He gives us a strong warning here. *Beware of such people! If the blind leads the blind, want both fall in the ditch?* (Luke 6:39) The church has to lead even when it hurts. We have to stand even when we're the only one standing.

Psalm 1 Paints a Picture of a Downward Spiritual Progression: *"Blessed is the man who walks not in the counsel of the wicked, nor stands in the way of sinners, nor sits in the seat of scoffers; but his delight is in the law of the Lord, and on his law he meditates day and night."*

This verse describes a man who was walking with God but somewhere along the way, He started listening to the counsel of the wicked. The ungodly influence caused Him to stop walking with God, so he started standing with sinner's. Before long, he got tired of standing in his sin so he finally sat down with scoffers. This man went from walking, to standing to sitting. This represents the downward spiritual progression of our nation and many believers today. Some were raised in church but never experienced true salvation. Others backslid because of ungodly influence. Many sat in complacency but now there sitting in the pews of our churches scoffing about everybody else's condition. How did we ever get here? Because we didn't avoid subtle sin. The steps of a righteous man are ordered by the Lord but the steps of an unrighteous man or ordered by Satan. Who are you walking with? Who's in your inner circle? What are you standing up for? Or better yet, who are you standing up for May the Bride of Christ go from sitting, to standing, to soaring with our Soon Coming King! Let's live out loud in the last days!

<u>Step to Start Strong:</u>

Stand your Ground

FEBRUARY 8

Born Again

Jesus answered him, *"Truly, truly, I say to you, unless one is born again he cannot see the kingdom of God."* Nicodemus, a Pharisee and member of the Sanhedrin, said to him, *"How can a man be born when he is old? Can he enter a second time into his mother's womb and be born?"* Jesus answered, *"Unless one is born of water and the Spirit, he cannot enter the kingdom of God. That which is born of the flesh is flesh, and that which is born of the Spirit is spirit. Do not marvel that I said to you, 'You must be born again.'*
8 The wind blows where it wishes, and you hear its sound, but you do not know where it comes from or where it goes. So it is with everyone who is born of the Spirit."

John 3:3-8

Do you remember the day you were born? Well, you probably don't really remember it or at least I hope not. That would be traumatizing! What I mean is, *"Do you know the date?"* Of course you do!

For me, it was January 19th, 1980. The Greatest Day in History! But what about you? You remember your Birth-day but what about your New-Birth-Day? Can you remember the Day you were saved?

Scripture is clear. No one will see the Kingdom of God unless they are Born Again. Children are born into the world by water but we are born into the Family of God by the Spirit. It's two different experiences. For me, I was born again on April 29th, 2003. This was the night Jesus changed everything for me. I not only know the day but I know the exact spot. The Holy Spirit convicted me, I knelt down on my knees and I began to cry out to God to forgive me and set me free. To my surprise, He answered me and gave me another chance at life. The next day, I entered the Teen Challenge program and made my decision public by going to the altar. This decision altered the course of my destiny and ultimately my family. There have been many times over the past 12 years, where I have asked myself this question, *"Where would I be without the Lord in my life?"* As I sit here typing this devotional, the thought brings tears to my eyes and chills down my spine. The question leaves me with this thought: *"We all need the Lord." Where would you be without Him?*

Do you remember your Salvation Birthday? If you do, write down the Day in the cover of your Bible. If you don't know the day, do your best to remember the season & write down a day that is close. It's important to celebrate the stages of your spiritual success. You have come such a long way and here's the Good News, *"He's not through with you yet!"*

I think God would say, *"Finish Well thy Faithful Worker."*

<u>Step to Start Strong:</u>

Re-member your Salvation Story

FEBRUARY 9

THE PURPOSE OF PLOWING

"Judah must plow, and Jacob must break up the ground. Sow righteousness for yourselves, reap the fruit of unfailing love, and break up your unplowed ground: for it is time to seek the Lord, until he comes and showers his righteousness on you."

Hosea 10:11-12

For all of you farmers out there, you know how important it is to prepare your soil before you plant your seed. Every seed has great potential but the secret to the seed is in the soil. A seed will always be a seed until you decide to sow it in soil.

The seed in scripture represents the Word of God but the soil speaks of the condition your heart. So, what do you do when the soil of your heart is hard? The Book of Hosea says that, *"Judah must plow."* Judah means praise. So its safe to say that Judah represents praise. Think of tithes way: Praise must plow! If your heart has grown hard, praise & worship will break up the ground and prepare it for the seed of the Word of God.

Now remember, worship is what you give to God but the word is what God gives you. So, don't walk into worship late. Always prepare yourself. Don't go a day without praise and worship! You praise God for what He has done for you but you worship God for who He is!

So, do you feel down today? Sing! Do you feel discouraged? Make a melody in your mind! Is your heart hard? Plow the ground with praise! May His name be continually on your lips today! It's something about singing that makes you more receptive to the things of the spirit. So, prepare your soul by singing and making melody in your heart on a daily basis. By doing so, you will plant the seed of the word of God in soft seasoned soil. Your harvest will be 30, 60 or 100 fold this year! I can almost hear the Lord saying, *"Judah keep plowing, keep praising, your breakthrough is on the way!"*

Step to Start Strong:

Plow the Soil of your Heart with Praise

FEBRUARY 10.

House of Prayer

"Jesus said, It is written, My house will be called a House of Prayer."

Matthew 21:13

Do we sing? *Yes,! Do we give? You bet! Do we preach? Most definitely! Do we give God the leftovers in prayer? What would be your answer...*

If we all answered honestly, most of us would say we struggle in the area of personal prayer. You may pray before you eat with your family, pray over the offering at church and you may pray when tragedy strikes. And don't get me wrong, all these things are vitally important for victory but I believe there's more. God so desires to walk and talk with you every moment of everyday. He wants to celebrate with you, cry with you and commune with you on a very personal level.

1st Thessalonians 5:6 says, "Let us not sleep as others do, but let us keep watch & pray."

Now, I understand that some people have the gift of intercessory prayer. They can pray for an hour and it feel like a few mins but when I pray for an hour, it feels like an hour! *Can I get an amen?*

But this truth doesn't exclude me from daily conversation with Jesus Christ. His Spirit abides in me and He is a whisper away. Can I ask you, *"Have you heard from Him lately?"*

The Common Denominator in many of our meetings the past few years is a call to bring God's people back to the Secret Place of Prayer. Prayer is where we find our power. Prayer is better than our man-made programs. Prayer is the key to complete victory! Lets pray! Let's start today!

What does your daily routine look like:

- When do you pray?
- Where do you pray?
- How do you pray?

Remember, Prayer is the #1 Priority of the Believer.

John Bunyan said, *"You can do more than pray after you have prayed but you cannot do more than pray until you have prayed."*

Step to Start Strong:

Pray, Pray, Pray.

FEBRUARY 11

Is that you God?

The most important factor for the success of your future is the ability to discern God's voice. Nothing is more important than knowing and obeying the voice of the Lord. Do you hear God clear? Do you know God's voice? Do you struggle with what to do and where to go? If so, God's got a word for you today and He spoke it through the Prophet Habakkuk. Habakkuk was a Watchmen on the Walls of Israel and he shares the 5 steps every believer should take to hear the voice of God in Chapter 2:1-3. There are major truths in the minor prophets so listen up...

#1 <u>He withdrew to His Watchtower</u>: Habakkuk knew he had to get away from the noise if he was going to hear God's voice. He withdrew from the world if you will. The Bible also says, in 5 different occasions that, *"Jesus withdrew to a solitary place to pray."* The #5 represents Grace. There is grace in the solitary place. Find a place to pray today.

#2 <u>He Waited</u>: He calmed his thoughts and settled his emotions. He stationed Himself meaning He stayed still. Remember, *"Hurry is the dagger that puts prayer to death."* If haven't heard from

God lately, you might be too busy. God will speak to those who take the time to listen. This is the most important part of your day. Your inner calm will create a channel for God to speak to you. Just take a deep breathe & relax. Focus on your Heavenly Father.

#3 Read the Word of God: The first verse goes on to say, *"I will look to see what God has to say."* This doesn't even sound right. It doesn't say, listen to what God has to say, but look at what God has to say. What does this mean? It's speaking about the scriptures. We need to know what the word of God says for every situation and we do this by meditation. God will never contradict His word because His will is His word. If you are seeking direction, stop waiting on a voice and start looking for a verse. Stop looking for some sign in a sky. If you open God's mouth, He will speak to you. Read the Bible everyday and the Bible will begin to read you.

#4 Write down what God says to you: Habakkuk 2:2 says, *"Write down the revelation and make it plain on tablets."* In the first chapter of this book, the prophet begins to ask God a bunch of questions. In the second chapter, he waits for the answer and when God gives him the word, he writes it down. We need to be more disciplined in our diary. Journaling is not a weakness but more like a weapon. Jesus kept a journal! Why? Because He knew He was going to die, so he wrote down His word so that His word would live forever! So, make it priority to keep a personal memoir. *"Write down every word God speaks to you in a book!"* (Jeremiah 30:2)

#5: Lastly, Review Regularly: This speaks of Remembrance. If one word can change your life forever. Why would you take a chance and overlook it? Whatever you do, don't forget what God whispers in your spirit. Rehearse the word. Re-member the revelation. Think about it. Build your life upon it! It will give you strength when you are struggling to stay true to your call. If God has branded you with a vision, *"Though it linger, I will wait for it; because it will certainly come and it will not delay."* Psalm 62:5 says, *"My soul sits in silence before God."* Until you are comfortable will silence you will always struggle to hear the voice of God. Try taking these 5 strategic steps to hear clear from Christ: *Withdraw, wait, read the word, write down the revelation that God gives you & review it often.*

Step to Start Strong:

Sit in Silence before your Savior.

FEBRUARY 12

Stepping Stones

"When the whole nation had finished crossing the Jordan, the Lord said to Joshua, 'Choose twelve men from among the people, one from each tribe, and tell them to take up twelve stones from the middle of the Jordan, from right where the priests are standing, and carry them over with you and put them down at the place where you stay tonight. These stones are to be a memorial to the people of Israel forever."

Joshua 4:1-7

Joshua is a type of Christ in the Old Testament. His name is translated, *"The one who saves."* To fulfill the prophecy attached to His name, God raised up this young man at the age of 17 to be the predecessor of Moses. What Moses started to do, Joshua would ultimately finish. You know the story, the Israelites wandered in the desert for 40 years until all the people who did not believe the promises of God had past away. (Except Joshua & Caleb of course.) These two men believed the report of the Lord so they lived long enough to go with the next generation to conquer the land of Canaan.

Joshua & Caleb were ready to fight! They were full of faith as they stood on the riverbank that day. At this time of the year, the Jordan River was at flood stage but they had come too far to back down or turn around. The priest picked up the Ark of the Covenant, which was the presence of the Lord, and they stepped into deep that day. Simultaneously, the water was cut off upstream and an estimated 4 million people passed through into the promised land. How could this be? All because of two men who took a step of obedience.

It's interesting to see, once they made it to the other side, God told Joshua to send 12 men back. To do what? To pick up 12 stones from the bottom of the riverbed to set up a memorial for future generations to see. These were what I lie to call, *"Stepping Stones."* God knew the stones would give His people a firm place to stand that day. If it were not for the stones, the Israelites would have never made it to the other side. They were on the bottom. I've been at the bottom a time or two. How about you?

So, what does this mean? We can't forget where we came from and who has helped us to get to where you are today? Who have you stepped on? Who held you up? Sir Isaac Newton said, *"If we have seen further, it is because we are standing on the shoulders of the giants in past generations."* The stones will be a memorial forever. For God hasn't forgotten the people who helped you or the people you have helped. We're all on a journey. We all need one another and we all need Jesus (All day-Everyday) Indeed, Life is a stepping stone.

Step to Start Strong:

Lay Some Stepping Stones

FEBRUARY 13

7 Supernatural Blessings

"Blessed is he who considers the poor; The Lord will deliver him in time of trouble. The Lord will preserve him and keep him alive, And he will be blessed on the earth; You will not deliver him to the will of his enemies. The Lord will strengthen him on his bed of illness; You will sustain him on his sickbed."

Psalm 41:1-3

One of my heroes in the faith is the late David Wilkerson. He was a powerful preacher of the gospel and pioneer of multiple ministries that are still impacting the world. He made a statement one day that lodged in my spirit and reminded me of Psalm 41 and I quote, *"If you want God to bless your ministry, find the poor & do whatever it takes to help them."*

In the Life of Jesus, we see him helping the people who could not help themselves. God did not send His Son to those who were healthy but to those who needed a doctor. (Luke 5:31) Giving with the motive to get is not godly giving at all. As Christians, we give to give and we help to help.

Psalm 41 says, "*Blessed are those who have regard for the poor.*" After this, God describes a list of "7 Supernatural Blessings" that will fall on you if you give to the least of these. In other words, if you will, He will.

#1 He will Deliver you in time of Trouble!
#2 He will Preserve your Life, Body & Belongings!
#3 He will Satisfy you will a Long Life!
#4 He will give you Supernatural Favor!
#5 He will give you Divine Protection!
#6 He will give you Supernatural strength!
#7 He will give you Divine Healing!

Remember, *"What you do for others, God will do for you!"*
Ephesians 6:8

<u>Step to Start Strong:</u>

Help the Poor

FEBRUARY 14

Phantom Pains

"If one part suffers, every part suffers with it; if one part is honored, every part rejoices with it. Now you are the body of Christ, and each one of you is a part."

1st Corinthians 12:26

The Church is the Body of Jesus Christ. I can't do what you can do and you can't do what I do. We all look different, act different and think differently. God has given us different types of gifts and talents because it takes all of us to get The Word Out! When we look around the world & see the need, it may seem overwhelming. But one thing is for sure, we can't be all things to all people. Mother Teresa said, *"You can't help everybody but you can help somebody."* All we can do is be faithful to the one who called us and do what He has ask us to do. Growing up, I remember working with my uncles during the summer to pick up some extra money since I was out of school. They owned a siding company and most construction sites can always use a gopher to help here and go there. The first week on the job, I remember standing on the walk-board in the hot summer sun trying to act like I knew what I was doing. I've never been a Tim the Tool-Man Taylor type so that day I swung my hammer, missed the nail & smashed my thumb. Not a good way to start my career. To my demise, I bit my tongue and acted like nothing happened. No need to say anything right? Nobody needed to know. So I tried to hide it and work my way through. For the rest of day, I had a lot of thoughts but not one time, did I say to myself, *"I don't really need my thumb."* Should I just go ahead and cut it off? Certainly not! Even though, my thumb bled & turned blue, I knew it would heal and be ok in a day or two. Have you ever been there before? I think you have in one way or another. When you hurt one part of your body, you whole body feels the effect. It's the same way within the Church. *"If one part suffers, we all suffer."* Many times, when people suffer, they try to hide it in because they feel like no one would understand. But we all need someone we can talk to. We should always be there for the ones suffering within the sphere of our influence. No one should be permanently *"cut off."*

This reminds me of the medical condition called, *"Phantom Pains."* These particular pains strike a person who's had a limb cut off or amputated from their body. This sensation effects their nervous system as the body tries to get use to living without the missing body part. We've all experienced Phantom Pains in a spiritual sense. When the body of Christ loses someone to a death or even over a division, we all pay the price. It's hard to move on when you lose a close friend or family member especially when you know you're better together. So, whatever you do, remember to *"rejoice with those who rejoice, suffer with those who suffer and above all things stick together."*

Step to Start Strong:

Love one another.

FEBRUARY 15

Be a Tree

"Jesus entered Jericho and was passing through. A man was there by the name of Zacchaeus; he was a chief tax collector and was wealthy. He wanted to see who Jesus was, but because he was short he could not see over the crowd. So he ran ahead and climbed a sycamore-fig tree to see him, since Jesus was coming that way. When Jesus reached the spot, he looked up and said to him, "Zacchaeus, come down immediately. I must stay at your house today." So he came down at once and welcomed him gladly. All the people saw this and began to mutter, "He has gone to be the guest of a sinner." But Zacchaeus stood up and said to the Lord, "Look, Lord! Here and now I give half of my possessions to the poor, and if I have cheated anybody out of anything, I will pay back four times the amount." Jesus said to him, "Today salvation has come to this house, because this man, too, is a son of Abraham. For the Son of Man came to seek and to save the lost."

Luke 19: 1-10

Zacchaeus was a wee little man and a wee little man was he! He climbed up in the sycamore tree for the Lord He wanted to see. You know the ole Sunday school song. This was an actual story! So think with me for a minute: The tree was the support system for this sinful man to see Jesus. If it were not for the tree, where would Zacchaeus be? The tree gave this man a different perspective so he could receive His salvation. God is calling you to *"Be a Tree."*

If people know you are a christian, they will watch you to see how you react in certain situations. If you pass their impression test one day they will test you personally. They will pull on your thought processes, climb on your character and step on your salvation experience to see if they really want to trust this Jesus with their life as well. Don't bend your branches or give into their temptations. Let your roots grow deep into the soil of God's word so your family & friends want fall by the wayside. Be a Tree!

This reminds me of the parable of the mustard seed. Jesus said, *"The Kingdom of God is like a mustard seed, which a man took and planted in his garden. It grew and became a tree, and the birds perched in its branches."* If you take on the characteristics of a tree, God will send people to perch in your branches. It's not about you, it's all about them seeing the Savior. My prayer for you today is that you would *"Be a Tree: An Oak of Righteousness in Jesus Name!"* (Isaiah 61)

Step to Start Strong.

Be a Tree!

FEBRUARY 16

First Impressions

You never have a second chance to make a first impression. True or False? The Apostle Paul put it this way, *"Make the most out of every opportunity."* God gives you gifts of opportunity and what you do with those opportunities are your gift back to God. What opportunities have been given to you lately? Are they from God or are they a distraction?

How do you know the difference? I'm glad you asked. In today's devotion, I want to give you *"5 ways to Test an Impression."* An impression is something you feel when you have a decision to make in your life. Should I do this or should I not? How do you know what to do? This fool-proof filter will help you live your life by facts rather than feelings.

"5 Ways to Test an Impression"

#1 Is the thought consistent with the Word of God? Does it line up with the Lord. *"The grass withers & the flowers fade but the word of God will stand forever."* (Isaiah 40:8) We should always anchor every major decision in our lives to God's word. I have found the more

I meditate upon God's word, the more opportunity I give God to speak to me.

#2 Will it make me more Christlike: Our ultimate goal is to be like Jesus. It may sound cliche, but what would Jesus do if He were in your shoes. Study the Character of Christ. It is God's will that you would have the attitude of Christ Jesus. (Philippians 2)

#3 Does my "church family" agree. Is your decision encouraged by your leaders, mentors and family. You don't need everybody's input and support but you do need somebody's. Some people will tell you what you want to hear but others will tell you what you need to hear. Ephesians 3:10 says, *"God's intent was through the church the manifold wisdom of God would be made known." Christianity is not just believing, but its also belonging. Seek Godly counsel.*

#4 Is it consistent with how God shaped me: Ephesians 2:10 says, *"We are God's workmanship created in Christ Jesus to do good works which He planned beforehand for us to do."* God has a pattern for your life and whatever He calls you to do should be straight forward. You shouldn't be tossed to and fro by every new thing. If it's new, it's not true. God's not a schizophrenic; He doesn't make you one way and use you another way. He knit you in your mothers womb for a specific purpose to impact the world around you. So, stay true to your calling.

#5 Do I sense God's peace: Here is the sure way to discern if God is leading you to a certain decision. Do you have the piece of peace. Colossians 3:15 says, *"Let the peace of God rule in your heart."* Jesus was never in a hurry. This means the Holy Spirit will always guide you gently. If you don't have peace, I advise you to stay put until you do. You can do the right thing at he wrong time. Always take your time when making major decisions. God isn't trying to hide His will from you. He will speak to you, if you will wait. I picture an airplane landing on the runway in the night. You're descending toward your decision in the dark but the closer you get to your destination the runway lights appear. The lights secure a safe landing for you & your family. God's word is a lamp unto your feet and the runway lights to your path. These 5 Impressions will prevent you from experiencing a crash landing. Look for these lights.

Step to Start Strong:

Let Peace be your Guide

FEBRUARY 17

DRY SEASONS

"And all Israel crossed over on dry ground."

Exodus 14:22

Have you ever felt dry spiritually? Like you weren't making a difference or moving forward in your faith. You may have prayed, *"Where are you Lord?"* and the ceiling seemed like brass. Can you relate to the seasons where your circumstances didn't line-up with the promises of God? I think we all can. Especially those who have walked with God for quite sometime. *There is a time and a season for every activity under the sun.* (Eccles. 3:1) We all have to endure dry seasons in our spiritual life from time to time. These seasons may not come from a direct result of sin or struggle. Sometimes the Holy Spirit will send us into the desert just to prove His love and faithfulness to us.

Case & Point: When the children of Israel finally escaped 400 years of captivity in Egypt. The Lord directed their course with a cloud by day and a fire by night to a place where they were surrounded on every side. The land literally ran out! The Red Sea was in front of them, Egyptians Soldiers were behind them and they were thinking that God had given up on them. However, I have found out that God loves to put his people in predicaments where they have to depend upon His power. If there is a deep demand in your life today, the supply of God's grace is deeper! So, what did the children of Israel do? They began to cry out to God. What did God do? He parted the Red Sea with a sneeze. Achoo!

The Sea splits and the children of God walked safety through. But don't miss this thought! Exodus 14:22 says, *"The Israelites walked through the sea on dry ground."* Dry ground? Yes, you read that right. Dry ground! The dry season that you are experiencing in your life could be the pathway to victory! This phrase is mentioned 3 different times in 3 different situations in scripture. In each story, the children of Israel is in transition. However, in order to get to the other side, they had to endure the dry season. Why? Because the enemy will always attack you in a place where you are most vulnerable. When we feel dry spiritually, we feel weak but remember God is proving His power to you. When the enemy comes in like a flood the Lord will raise up a standard against thee! I want to speak to those who feel surrounded on every side today. You feel like God has forgotten you but as you go through this dry season, your enemy will be silenced. Keep praying and preserving. You will make it to the other side. If you feel dry spiritually. Know this is your pathway to victory! You're closer to your breakthrough than ever before. Don't give up now. You've come way too far! Indeed, you're surrounded by the Red Sea which speaks of the precious blood of Jesus Christ. What better place to be? Stand still and see the salvation of the Lord. You may dry but you'll never be defeated!

Step to Start Strong:

Listen to the leading of the Holy Spirit

FEBRUARY 18

YOUR RHEMA WORD

Have you ever read the Bible and the words just jump off the page? Or maybe you were sitting in church and the pastor was preaching a message that should have been entitled, *"I know what happened to you this week?"* We've all encountered experiences like this before. I call them, *"Gotta be God moments."* But Biblically they're called *"Rhema words."* There are two greek words in the Bible that describe the Word of God. One is Logos and the other is Rhema. The logos word is the written word. When you read the Bible, you are reading the logos word. The written word. However, there is another word mentioned in scripture called, Rhema. This word is a word spoken in due season that is illuminated and anointed by the Holy Spirt. This word speaks right into your circumstance and normally creates faith inside of your soul.

A great verse that supports this point is Matthew 4:4 which says, *"Man shall not live by bread alone but by every 'rhema word" that proceeds from the mouth of God."* It's a now word! A faith-filled word that will encourage you to take the next step.

These words come to you when you least expect it. You're reading your Bible one day and boom! The Holy Spirit drops a bomb on you. You've read that passage before but you never understood it quite like you had this time. What happened? God opened your eyes. This is Logos vs. Rhema. Now you know why we don't read the Bible one time like a history book. We read it consistently because our circumstances change but the scriptures are constant. Before you do your daily Bible reading, take time to pause and pray. Simply ask God to give you a rhema word for the day. In fact, Holy Spirit speak to us today in Jesus name!

Step to Start Strong:

Open your eyes to the wondrous works of His word

FEBRUARY 19

How to Pray

"But you, when you pray, go into your room, and when you have shut your door, pray to your Father who is in the secret place; and your Father who sees in secret will reward you openly."

Matthew 6:6

We know that prayer was a priority for Jesus because what it practiced by the teacher is always imitated by the student. We see the evidence of this thought posed in a question asked by one of the disciples. Luke 11:1 says, *"Lord, would you teach us how to pray?"* Now at this point, the playing field was wide open. They could have asked Jesus for anything. Like Lord, teach us to walk on water or turn water into wine or maybe, Lord, teach us how to cleanse the lepers or to cast out devils. We never see those requests in the scripture. Only Lord, *"Teach us how to pray!"* They knew the secret to Jesus' public success was found in His intimate relationship with His Father which was developed and nurtured in His private prayer closet. This is why the disciples desired to pray the way Jesus prayed because when Jesus prayed the power of God was present. He wasn't wasting His time when He went away to pray. In fact, He was multiplying it. This reminds me of a quote from the great reformer Martin Luther; He said, *"Lord, I have so much to do today, I shall spend the first 3 hours of it in prayer."* This was a man who took prayer seriously and God used Him to change history.

My provoking thought for you today is, *"Pray the answer, not the problem."* Many of us go to God with our problems and that's certainly a step in the right direction. However, sometimes in the process, we magnify our problem rather than magnifying God. Do you have big problems or do you have a big God? In the process of talking about your problem, you can forget about God's promises. Let's try shifting our focus today. Stop asking God to deliver you from depression and start thanking God for giving you joy. Stop asking God to heal your body and start thanking Him for making you whole. See the difference? When you place your faith in the finished work of Christ, you see your situation differently. You see yourself as an over-comer rather than an under-achiever. This is how Jesus prayed. He called things that were not as if they were. How did He do this? By seeing with eyes of faith. How do you see yourself today? It will not only change the way you pray but it will change your outlook in life.

Step to Start Strong:

Pray the answer & not the problem

FEBRUARY 20

The Heart of Worship

"God is Spirit, and those who worship Him must worship in spirit and truth."

John 4:24

Recently, the Lord reminded me of Matt Redman's popular song, *"The Heart of Worship."* If you take time to look at the credits of many top christian hits, you will notice the name Matt Redman. Matt is a stunning songwriter and a world renown worship leader in the UK. Back in the early 1990s, the pastor of Soul Survivor Church in England, stood before his congregation one Sunday morning & said, *"We have lost our heart for worship."* The next few weeks, we will gather in the sanctuary of this church in absolute silence. No more musicians, no more music, no more noise. At first, he encountered resistance as you could only imagine. What did you say? Break our routine. Change the tradition? Yes,! He said, with a question, *"Do you even know why we worship?" It's quite amusing.* The believers didn't know what to do without the drums, lights & loud mics. Worship had become more like a concert rather than a time to connect with the Holy Spirit. So, here's what happened:

The people found their way back to the heart of worship. Yes, it took some time but eventually they got to the point where their heart was pointing toward God instead of pointing toward the pulpit and worship pastor. They became producers of worship rather than consumers of music. I had the thought, in some circles, people worship the music and the bands rather than worshipping God, the creator of man.

What do you do when you worship on Sunday morning? Worship is what you give to God and the Word is what God gives you. Do you show up late for worship? Worship prepares you for the word. Take this time seriously. This is the time to bring an offering of praise to your God. If you need to, close your eyes and calm your soul. Create an expectation to hear from the Holy Spirit. Worship Him. He is worthy of all of your praise.

Out of this experience, Matt Redman wrote the song, *"The Heart of Worship"* in his bedroom when his church was going through this season of consecration. Ultimately, they returned to their first love and discovered, *"It's always been about Jesus & it always will."* Read the lyrics to the song & you'll understand.

<u>Step to Start Strong:</u>

Develop a Heart for Worship.

FEBRUARY 21

Divine Appointments

"The steps of a righteous man are ordered by the Lord."

Psalm 37:23

The longer I walk by faith with the my Heavenly Father, the more I see this verse fulfilled in my life. God is a master weaver and every thread represents a person he is intertwining into your life for a greater purpose. Pay attention to those who cross your path. Remember, your steps are ordered by the Lord. God sits high and looks low. He knows how to give good gifts to this who love Him. The answer to your next miracle could come through someone who you meet today?

All day long, God works behind the scenes, to set you up for success and many times, we are so stuck in our normal routine that we miss his blessing. When you bump into someone on the sidewalk or in the parking lot of the supermarket that you haven't seen in a while, is this a coincidence? No, this is a God-Incident! God is directing your steps! May we arise every morning with great expectation that God is going to use you us and bless us every step of every day. God has google synced His calendar with yours in the name of Jesus. When is your next divine appointment? It could be today!

Isaiah 43:16-19 *"Thus says the Lord, who makes a way in the sea, a path in the mighty waters, who brings forth chariot and horse, army and warrior; they lie down, they cannot rise, they are extinguished, quenched like a wick: 'Remember not the former things, nor consider the things of old. Behold, I am doing a new thing; now it springs forth, do you not perceive it? I will make a way in the wilderness and rivers in the desert."*

Step to Start Strong.

Pay Attention to those Around you

FEBRUARY 22

Fresh Oil

"David said, I have been anointed with fresh oil."

Psalm 92:10

Oil in the scripture represents the anointing of the Holy Spirit. The word anointing means, *"to smear with."* So in context of this passage, we see David being anointed or smeared with the Holy Spirit in a fresh way. God has a fresh anointing for you everyday. This is Good News!

In Ephesians 4:18-21, God gives us 4 steps to receive a fresh anointing. Do you need a fresh touch of God today? If so, here's your Holy Inspired Instruction:

> *"Do not get drunk with wine, which leads to debauchery. Instead, be filled with the Spirit, speaking to one another with psalms, hymns, and songs from the Spirit. Sing and make music from your heart to the Lord, always giving thanks to God the Father for everything, in the name of our Lord Jesus Christ. Submit to one another out of reverence for Christ, for this is God's will for you."*

The phrase *"Filled with the Spirit"* is a continual participle. This is not a one time experience like salvation. It's an infilling of the Holy Spirit whom we drink from everyday. So, how do I drink from this fountain you say? It's simple. The Apostle Paul wrote the points in the passage above.

In order to be filled with the Spirit, we must speak the word to one another, sing in the spirit, sacrifice the offering of thanksgiving and submit to one another out of reverence to Christ. By doing these things, you will release the Spirit of God on the inside of you to move in a mighty way.

No matter how I feel, when I talk about Jesus, I always walk away feeling better. When I wake up in the morning and sing in the shower, no matter how bad I sound, I step out better than I stepped in. When I give thanks and portray an attitude of gratitude, I feel content within my situation even though I still have needs. These are the steps that lead to a fresh anointing? Indeed, God will fill you, if you follow this pattern.

The world is like a vacuum cleaner. It will suck the life right out of you. You need a fresh anointing of God's Spirit when you step out the door in order to conquer the circumstances that are set before you. Sadly, the anointing you receive on Sunday was never meant to carry you for 7 days. You will be weak by the end of the week. So, go ahead and practice this pattern. Start speaking the word, singing the scripture, sacrificing a thanks offering and submitting to those in your life. By doing these things, you will see a difference. It's His promise. The Holy Spirit will anoint you with fresh oil.

Step to Start Strong:

Speak, Sing, Sacrifice and Submit.

FEBRUARY 23

JEHOVA JIREH

"And the same God, who takes care of me, will supply all your needs from his glorious riches, which have been given to us in Christ Jesus."

Philippians 4:19

Provision is important. Without it, you can't do what God has called you to do. You need provision for yourself, your family, your finances and your health. When you really think about it, there's a lot we need on a daily basis. We depend upon God for everything but this is the way it was originated. God is the source of all things and everything else is the re-source.

Over the years, God has built my faith to a place where I know if its God's will, its God's bill. My part is to pray and His part is to provide. Someone said, *"Where God guides, He always provides,"* and I totally agree. Reinhart Bonnke says, *"You should never plan with what's in your pocket but plan with what's in God's pocket!*

Philippians 4:19 says, *"And my God shall supply all of my needs according to His riches that is in Christ Jesus."* There's not a shortage of finances in the world but there is a shortage of faith. If God has called you do something, outside yourself, you can literally take it to the bank. Where there no vision, people perish but where there is vision, there will always be pro-vision. Go ahead. Test the Lord and see if He will not open up the windows of Heaven and pour out a blessing on you! You will never know unless you take the first step. If you come into agreement with God, you will go places you have not known and God will use you in ways you would have never dreamed. Your Heavenly Father is the supplier of all your needs. His name is Jehovah Jireh!

Step to Start Strong:

Sow a Seed in your Time of Need

FEBRUARY 24

Follow the Star.

"Now after Jesus was born in Bethlehem of Judea in the days of Herod the king, behold, wise men from the East came to Jerusalem, saying, 'Where is He who has been born King of the Jews? For we have seen His star in the East and have come to worship Him."

Matthew 2:2

When the wise men saw the star in the sky, they changed their direction and followed this star by the Saviors side. Think about it? Where would these men be without the star? The North Star stood out from the other stars because of its close proximity to the sun. All these men were starstruck! This begs the question: Who has stood out in your life? Who has God used to guide you to the Savior's side? Your parents? Your grandparents? A Pastor or Sunday School teacher? Maybe even a friend? Whoever they were, I'm sure they stood out in your life. There was something different about them. They were close to Jesus and this drew your attention which led to your salvation.

Let's celebrate the Stars that God has placed in our lives today. We wouldn't be here without them. Let's pause and pray for them right now. God thank you for My Star. Thank you for my salvation and thank for leading me & guiding me. In Jesus Name. Amen.

Along the same lines, may we be a star for someone today. Many people need guidance in our day. Stay close to Jesus and you will shine like a star in the sky. People will follow you because you are following Jesus. Where is The Star of Heaven leading you? Keep Following Him. He is forever faithful even unto the end.

As The Old Song says,

O Star of wonder, Star of night
Star with royal beauty bright
Westward leading, still proceeding
Guide us to thy Perfect Light!

<u>Step to Start Strong:</u>

Follow the Star

FEBRUARY 25

The Shema

"Hear, O Israel: The Lord our God, the Lord is one!
You shall love the Lord your God with all your heart,
with all your soul, and with all your strength."

Deuteronomy 6: 4-5

Deuteronomy 6 is the passage of scripture referred to as *"The Shemah."* One of the most read and most memorized passages of scripture in Judaism. Jesus quoted from this chapter when He communicated the greatest commandment to His disciples which implied *"Loving God and Loving Others."* Let us meditate upon these precepts today and I pray God would reveal more of His heart to you, in Jesus name.

Deuteronomy 6 *"Now this is the commandment, and these are the statutes and judgments which the Lord your God has commanded to teach you, that you may observe them in the land which you are crossing over to possess, that you may fear the Lord your God, to keep all His statutes and His commandments which I command you, you and your son and your grandson, all the days of your life, and that your days may be prolonged. Therefore*

*hear, O Israel, and be careful to observe it, that it may be well with you, and
that you may multiply greatly as the Lord God of your fathers has promised
you—'a land flowing with milk and honey.' "Hear, O Israel: The Lord our
God, the Lord is one! You shall love the Lord your God with all your heart,
with all your soul, and with all your strength. "And these words which I command you today shall be in your heart. You shall teach them diligently to your
children, and shall talk of them when you sit in your house, when you walk
by the way, when you lie down, and when you rise up. You shall bind them as
a sign on your hand, and they shall be as frontlets between your eyes. 9 You
shall write them on the doorposts of your house and on your gates. Then it will
be righteousness for us, if we are careful to observe all these commandments
before the Lord our God, as He has commanded us."*

Step to Start Strong:

Love God and Love Others

FEBRUARY 26

Ingredients for Increase

"They devoted themselves to the apostles' teaching and to fellowship, to the breaking of bread and to prayer. Everyone was filled with awe at the many wonders and signs performed by the apostles. All the believers were together and had everything in common. They sold property and possessions to give to anyone who had need. Every day they continued to meet together in the temple courts. They broke bread in their homes and ate together with glad and sincere hearts, praising God and enjoying the favor of all the people. And the Lord added to their number daily those who were being saved."

Acts 2:42-47

The proper ingredients to make your favorite food is vital and important. This reminds me of the year my mom made her famous pecan pie for the family on Thanksgiving. The spread for the main course was absolutely scrumptious. Every was full but we're never too stuffed for dessert right? We passed the pie around the room and as I took a bite, I realized something was not quite right? I waited and looked at my wife as she took a bite and her face said the same thing. What was wrong? The pie looked better than ever. How could this be? To our surprise, Mom forgot to add the most important ingredient! *The sugar!* Thankfully, we had a back-up, the infamous chocolate cake and a few weeks later, a pecan pie for Christmas. *Hallelujah!* However, this story exemplifies the importance of putting the right ingredients into our physical cravings. But how much more should we pay attention to our spiritual life?

In Acts 2:42, the Bible gives us the ingredients of the early churches success. The Bibles says, *"They devoted themselves to the apostles teachings, to fellowship, to the breaking of bread and to prayer."* We have to mix all four of these into our bowl if we want to be spiritually healthy and strong. Which of the four is missing from your recipe? Reading and listening to the word, spending time with other believers, personal communion with Christ or prayer? If you strengthen your weakest link, its inevitable, God will strengthen your life.

In the passage above, you'll see these 4 ingredients caused a 7-Fold Increase for the early church. The increase came in the area of miracles, unity, giving, generosity, joy, favor and salvations. *I call this the 7-Fold Increase.* What God did for the disciples in their day, God will do for you today. The only stipulation? You have to use the right ingredients!

<u>Step to Start Strong:</u>

Apply Acts 2:42

FEBRUARY 27

Front End Alignment.

"Trust in the Lord with all your heart and lean not on your own understanding; in all your ways submit to him, and he will make your paths straight."

Proverbs 3:5-6

Before I bought the last set of tires for my Tahoe, I took it to the mechanic to have my front end aligned. It cost me but why did I do it? Its simple, I didn't want to *"wear out"* my brand new tires because tires aren't cheap! When you align the front end of your car with your tires, the car will drive in a straight line. If the tires are out of line, its easier to deviate off course without even realizing it. Aligning your front-end will not only make your car go straight but it will take any shake out of the steering wheel. Ultimately, the life of your tire will be significantly longer, not to mention a more comfortable ride along the way.

It's the same when you're striving to fulfill your purpose in life. The Bible says, *"In all your ways acknowledge the Lord and He will make your paths straight."* You have to make sure your life is aligned with God's plan. If not, you'll waste time, energy and resources and ultimately end up in a place of confusion. I charge you; Stay true to your calling. Don't deviate from your dream. Keep moving forward.

Meditate on this thought today: *"Consistency is the key to unlock the door to your destiny."*

God spoke to me and said, *"If you start our straight with me and stay true to your calling, you'll end up right where you need to be;* In the center of My will." This is the revelation: How you spend the front-end of your day will determine your final destination.

Isaiah 46:10 says,*"God declares the end from the beginning so that His purposes will be established."*

May God establish your steps today. May He make your paths straight in Jesus name. Don't wear yourself out.

Align your life with the Lord.

Step to Start Strong:

Alignment Yourself with the Lord

FEBRUARY 28

Divine Healing

Jesus said to them, "A prophet is not without honor except in his hometown and among his own relatives and in his own household." And He could do no miracles there except that He laid His hands on a few sick people and healed them. And He wondered at their unbelief as He was going around the villages teaching."

Mark 6:4-6

Jesus, the Son of God, stepped off His throne and into a sin-sick world. He was stripped of His divinity as He stepped into our humanity. Indeed, Jesus is the Greatest Evangelist who ever walked the world. In Mark 6, we see clearly the compassion Jesus had for His community. He laid His life down to help those who were drowning in sin and suffering. However, those who knew Him in His hometown didn't want anything to do with Him. *How could this be?* The people in this community thought they knew who He was. In reality they only knew Him as the Son of Joseph but we know He was the Son of God. Here's my point: You must first believe in Jesus if you want to receive His benefits.

The scripture of the day doesn't say, Jesus would not do any miracles among friends and family in His hometown. It says, *"He could not."* This is an interesting thought? Why is this so? It doesn't say this anywhere else in the text. In every other city, the Bible says, *"He healed everyone who was sick and diseased.* (Matthew 9:35)" What was the difference? One word; *"Unbelief."* Some people believe and receive the divine benefits of the Kingdom and others don't. I've had countless individuals ask me the question, *"Is it God's will to heal?"* And the answer is always a resounding yes, yes, yes! It is God's will to heal! Now, when and how He heals is another study for another day. However, the starting point for your faith must rest in the realization that your God is Jehovah Rapha. This means *"He is the God who will heal thee."* Whenever you hear people pray the word if, you know this person doesn't have faith in divine healing. They may say, *"God, if it is your will to heal my sick son please touch Him now."* If, is an implication that says, I don't know what God wants to do? In fact, God has already made up His mind about sickness. The question is, *"Have you made up your mind to believe in His will to heal."* If so, we need to remove *"if"* from your prayer life. If releases doubt and uncertainly into your circumstance but the will of God releases faith. Romans 10:17 says, *"Faith cometh by hearing and hearing the word of God."* The Psalmist said, *"Bless the Lord Oh my soul and forget not His benefits. He cleanses me from all of my sins and He heals me of all of my diseases."* You receive healing the same way you receive salvation; By believing the word of God by faith. Sadly, the people of Nazareth didn't believe so Jesus couldn't do what He wanted to do.

Step to Start Strong:

Believe & Receive the Benefits of the Bible

MARCH 1

Fear Not!

"So do not fear, for I am with you; do not be dismayed, for I am your God. I will strengthen you and help you; I will uphold you with my righteous right hand."

Isaiah 41:10

Some scholars say the phrase, *"Do not fear and Do not be afraid"* are found 365 times in the Bible. One for everyday of the year, including leap year so relax God's got you covered.

This tells me, every morning when you roll out of bed, you can envision this scripture above the doorpost of your front door before you leave the house. This is good news! You don't have to be afraid today! Why? Because God is with you and that's the truth.

Every time God speaks of this principle, He chooses to couple it with His promise; *"Don't be afraid because I am with you."* Think about it; Whenever God says something once its important but when He says something over and over again, it's an imperative. Why would He drill us with this declaration dozens of times?

I think the answer is found in the fact that the #1 weapon of Satan is fear. Fear is the opposite of faith and fear paralyzes God's people. Fear prevented a whole generation from entering the promise land and fear will you keep you from your promises too if you let it. So, let faith arise inside of your soul today! If God be for you, who in the world can be against you? Don't let the Spirit of fear keep you from following Jesus to the fullest.

With some research, I found out there are countless fears and phobias around the world. However, the top 3 in America were: The Fear of a Man-Made Disaster such as terrorism or a suicide bomber, #2 The Fear of Government Corruption, and #3 The Fear of Cyber-Crime relating to people stealing your identity and personal information. This may be scary for some but for those who are called by His name we know we overcome. You and I have no reason to fear!

It amazes me that fear has been around since the beginning of time but Satan has not changed his tactics. He will do whatever it takes to cripple you from fulfilling your calling.

Satan is the Father of Lies but Jesus is the Author and the Finisher of your faith. The Spirit of Fear says, *"Stop"* but The Spirit of Faith says, *"Keep moving Forward!"*

Step to Start Strong:

Let Faith Arise!

MARCH 2

WAITING ON THE LORD

"Those who wait on the Lord will renew their strength. They will soar on wings like eagles; they will run and not grow weary, they will walk and not be faint."

Isaiah 40:31

Have you ever felt like you were waiting on the Lord? Sure you have! It seems we spend most of spiritual lives waiting on the next promise to be fulfilled. Maybe you're waiting on the Lord to bring peace and restoration for your family? Someone else may be waiting on the Lord to completely heal their broken heart? The next person may be waiting on the news that they will be having a baby? You may be waiting on a promotion, salvation for a family member or clarity for a business decision? Whatever describes your situation, just know that the waiting rooms for the righteous maybe full but sooner or later God is going to call your name.

The word for *"wait"* in this famous verse, doesn't mean you sit around with your legs crossed and wait for God to answer your last prayer. The word wait actually takes on the connotation of a waiter in a restaurant. What does a waiter do in this setting? He serves the people sitting at in his designated section. So When God says, *"Those who wait on the Lord they shall renew their strength."* What He actually means by waiting is serving the Savior and the people assigned to your area of influence. By doing this, a new-found strength will surge inside of your soul.

The best antidote for an answer prayer is to be an answer to prayer to someone else's prayer. It's amazing to me, when I help other people with their problems I quickly forget about my own. Humility coupled with servanthood will release the favor of God upon your life which will ultimately bring strength.

Are you weak today? Are you worried? Are you waiting on the Lord? If so, keep serving and keep showing up! You are about to be seated in a section of divine strength. Go ahead and take a praise break and keep worshipping while you wait! You will run and not grow weary, you will walk and not faint! May God bless you as you wait!

Step to Start Strong:

Worship while you Wait

MARCH 3

Have Faith in God

"Now faith is the substance of things hoped for and the evidence of things not seen."

Hebrews 11:1

Listen to me: No matter what you are facing today, there is hope. Faith is the substance of the things hoped for and the evidence of things not yet seen. What are the *"things"* you are hoping for this year? What do you desire to see God do?

With these things in mind, you need to know *"Faith"* is the evidence that these things are going to happen! If you believe in the Lord Jesus Christ and have Faith in His word, *"Nothing is impossible for you!"* Faith in your Heavenly Father is the evidence that something good is going to happen to you this year.

Don't let the Devil lie to you. Keep fighting the good fight of faith. The day to day battles you and your family are facing, are all centered on the destruction of your faith. Why is this so? Because the devil knows if He can deter you from the faith, He can ultimately destroy your hope. And pity the man who has no hope. If you or someone you know has lost their hope, it shows they are losing their faith. Keep fighting for faith and keep holding on to hope! Our God is not a God who can lie, He will always do what He says He will do! Usually a struggle is a sure sign that you are about to make it to the other side. It's always darkest right before the dawn. The Son is about to rise with healing in His wings.

1st Corinthians 13:13 says, *"Now these 3 remain: Faith, Hope and Love but Love is the greatest."*

1st Thessalonians 1:3 also says, *"We remember, your work produced by faith, your labor prompted by love, and your endurance inspired by hope in our Lord Jesus Christ."*

Step to Start Strong:

Keep Fighting the Good Fight of Faith

MARCH 4

The Best is for Now!

"Everyone brings out the choice wine first and then the cheaper wine after the guests have had too much to drink; but you have saved the best till now."

John 2:10

This is one of the most misquoted verses in the Bible. Most people say, God has saved the best for last and this could very well be true but this is not what the scripture says. John writes, *"God has saved the best for now!"*

I believe time is one of the greatest enemies against the church. Why do you say so? Well, we rush here and we rush there and we say, *"I don't have enough time."* How many times have you said that recently?

Indeed, time is a precious commodity. We can make more money but we can't make more time. Time is valuable and the enemy knows how to play this hand against us. We put off prayer, priorities and even people because we run out of time during the day. We live our lives searching for the next best thing when God has promised to store up treasure for us in Heavenly places.

I wanna say, *"Don't settle for God's second best when you can have God's best."* The enemy will distract you by saying, one day you can witness to your family or someday you can start exercising. Always pushing off the promises of salvation, health and healing. Why should this be when God says, *"He has saved the best for now!"* In fact, Today is the day of salvation, not tomorrow! Do you believe this? This year is going to be your greatest year, not next year!

Let's look at the word NOW spelled backwards. What does it say? It says, Won! I believe when you live your life in the here and now, you'll begin to win the war against your enemy.

Don't procrastinate your God-given purposes! I feel an urgency in my spirit today. It's not Now or Later. It's Now or Never! Some supernatural doors only stay open for a second. Its time to turn the knob and take a step through the door of your destiny!

Furthermore, in this story, this was the beginning of miracles for the ministry of Jesus. His time had come and He almost allowed the spirit of delay to keep him from destiny. However, His mother pushed Him into His purpose when He turned water into wine. She remembered the words of Gabriel and she knew it was time for God to be glorified. With this in mind, allow the Holy Spirit to move in you and through you today. Whatever God has been calling you to do, Just do it NOW! The battle has already been won!

Step to Start Strong:

Win the Battle by Being Obedient.

MARCH 5

The Power of a Made-up Mind

"Daniel resolved not to defile himself with the royal food and wine."

Daniel 1:8

Daniel was a young lad when he was exiled into Babylon. This city could be compared to the Las Vegas of our day. The area was infested with debauchery, perversion and homosexuality. It wasn't a pleasant, peaceful place for God's people to dwell. In fact, fear gripped their heart as they wondered what would happen to them next. Life as they knew was changed in an instant.

Have you ever felt this way before? Suddenly something changes within your family and you wonder what will happen next? This is what happened to Daniel. However, despite Daniel's circumstances, the favor of God followed Him. Daniel was one of the Hebrew boys that was chosen to train in the royal palace with the King. However, the purpose of this process was to brainwash God's people. The King wanted them to forget where they came from and ultimately, the God in whom they served. The King changed their culture, he changed their name and now he was trying to change their customs. At this point in the story, Daniel stood up in His spirit and said, *"Enough is enough!"* I resolve in my heart not to defile myself with the delicacies of the King. Certainly, a big stand for a small boy!

Having resolve simply means you make up your mind. You don't have to be loud or rebellious to do this. All you have to do is say, *"As for me and my house we're going to serve the Lord!"* I call it quiet strength. Just like Jesus, He was silent but strong as they led him to the slaughter. Indeed, He possessed the power of a made-up mind.

What are you facing today? Are you single minded or double-minded? Are you one way today and another way tomorrow? If so, take some time to make up your mind concerning the matter. Sit down and lay a solid bedrock foundation of faith so you can move the mountain before you and ultimately, move forward.

A wise man once said, *"It's hard to change a made-up mind."* Daniel made-up his mind that he was not going to be moved! This is the kind of spirit we need if we're going to turn this nation around. Go ahead and make up your mind to save money and not spend so much money. Get on the same page with your spouse when you disciplining your kids. Make up your mind from this day forward, I'm going to tithe. If Daniel was single-minded at 17, you can be too!

Put a plan in place & release the power your made-up mind!

<u>Step to Start Strong:</u>

Be Single Minded

MARCH 6

70 TIMES 7

"Then Peter came and said to Him, 'Lord, how often shall my brother sin against me and I forgive him? Up to seven times?" Jesus said to him, "I do not say to you, up to seven times, but up to seventy times seven."

Matthew 18:21-22

I wonder if you're holding a grudge against anyone? Is there any dissension between you and your family? How about an old friend? Maybe your spouse? Your pastor? Your co-worker? Or Maybe even your Boss?

If you're not sure, a sure sign is the sensation you feel when you see this person. Your soul will always speak through your emotions even though nobody else may hear it. Listen to this indicator. If you find yourselves talking about people behind their back or dodging people in your path, there's a good chance there's probably bitterness in your heart.

The longest 18 inches in the world is from your head to your heart. If confronted, you would probably say you're ok but deep down in your heart are you really? My pastor use to say, *"We need to do a check-up from the neck-up!"* This means, we should examine ourselves honestly on a regular basis.

This was Peter's intention when He ask Jesus this question. So, Go ahead and ask Jesus today, *"Do I need to forgive anyone?"* Go to God first and if He releases you, go to that person and make things right. Forgiveness is a choice. Follow the example of Christ today and Choose to Forgive 70 times 7.

<u>Step to Live Strong:</u>

Forgive those who have Hurt you

MARCH 7

Prayer-Walking

"Seek the peace and prosperity of the city. Pray to God for it! If the city prospers you will prosper."

Jeremiah 29:7

Prayer-walking is simple. You pray while you walk. Everybody can participate in this principle! The Apostle Paul gave us the exhortation to *"pray without ceasing"* and my first thought was how could I ever do this? His implication gives us some insight on prayer-walking. Prayer is an attitude of the heart. You can live your life in a posture of prayer when you go about the duties of your day.

As much as we would like to, we can't stay in our prayer closet 24 hours a day. We have to be good stewards of what God has set us over but I've got good news, wherever we go so goes God! We can stay in constant communication with the Holy Spirit throughout every situation of the day. This is why they call it a *"personal relationship with God."* He wants to be intimate with you.

So, I challenge you today. Commune with Christ between your business endeavors. Talk to God as you walk, as you wait and as you work. He promises to speak if you will set your affections on Him.

My prayer for you is that God would give you insight on-sight as you walk in the power of the Holy Spirit today. Be intentional with your prayers and defeat the spiritual warfare that is setting itself against you.

Step to Start Strong:

Take a Prayer-Walk

MARCH 8

J.O.Y

"Nehemiah said, 'Go and enjoy choice food and sweet drinks, and send some to those who have nothing prepared. This day is holy to our Lord. Do not be grieve, for the joy of the Lord is your strength."

Nehemiah 8:10

An acronym to help you remember the pathway to pure joy would be Jesus first, Others second and Yourself last. If you live by these things in increasing measure, you will tap into a spring of living water. At least, this is what happened in this story.

Nehemiah chapter 8 writes the history of Ezra reading and teaching the Israelites the meaning of the scripture. As he was reading, the people starting weeping. They had never heard the word like this before. It touched them so deeply that they began to repent and return to God. If you read the word, it has a way of totally transforming your world.

The Word made them weep but afterwards, it made them leap for everlasting joy. True conviction will always bring a conversion in your heart. It reminds me of the scripture, *"Weeping may endure for a night but joy cometh in the morning."* If you will endure the seasons of weeping in your life, they will be followed by a season of divine strength. The weeping waters the seed of strength in your soul.

The prophet said, God has heard your cry! No more mourning! Go enjoy a nice dinner out on the town but make sure you give something to the poor. I love this Biblical principle!

Seek God first, Give to others in need and enjoy the rest for yourself! There's plenty for you to enjoy, all you need to do is change your perspective. In order to be happy, something has to happen but Joy is different. Joy comes from Jesus. Joy is a fruit of the spirit. Spiritual Gifts are given but the Fruit of the Spirit is grown.

How do you grow a garden of Joy? Love the Lord your God with all your soul and Love your neighbor as yourself. By loving like this, your joy will be complete which will ultimately usher in God's perfect peace. It's His process; Love, Joy and Peace can be yours today in Jesus name!

Remember, The Joy of the Lord is your strength!

Step to Start Strong:

Rejoice!

MARCH 9

EASTER

"He is not here; he has risen!" Hallelujah!

Matthew 28:6

There were 2 types of anointing at the tomb on Easter Sunday morning. In Luke 24:1-3, we read about the original spice girls, *"On the first day of the week, very early in the morning, the women took the spices they had prepared and went to the tomb. They found the stone rolled away from the tomb, but when they entered, they did not find the body of the Lord Jesus Christ."* Two anointings with two different results. The spice girls believed in Jesus but they didn't believe in His promises. The scripture prophesied after 3 days He would be raised from the dead. So why bring spices? Our indication is these women were going to anoint Jesus' body that day. Myrrh was used for embalming fluid so the spice girls were trying to cover up the stench and the blood stain body. My point is, many times we try to embalm our problems and cover them up the best we can. We don't want to bother anyone and we certainly don't want anyone to notice our struggle so we maintain the issue when no one else is around. This was the action taken by Mary Magdalene and the gang. Let's embalm Him. The second anointing was supernatural. I can only imagine what all of creation experienced at sunrise on Easter morning. My first thought is, *"O Death, where is your sting?"* For the former things have passed away and in the moment, grace was awakened at the dawn of a new day. The tables turned and what Satan meant for ever, God used for the good and the saving of many lives from this moment forward. This was the anointing of the Holy Spirit. In fact, the anointing of the Holy Spirit is releasing resurrection power today to lift anything that has been holding you down. The same anointing that raised Jesus Christ from the grave lives inside of you. (Romans 8:11) This was and is the second anointing! One was used to embalm the body and the other was used to awaken the body so we could bounce back from any obstacle! What I hear the Lord saying this morning is, *"The anointing of the Holy Spirit will roll your stone away."* The stone represents anything that is hindering your relationship with the Lord right now. The stone separates you from seeing the Lord with the right perspective. Moses wrote the law on tablets of stone. What does this mean? When Jesus was raised from the dead, the law was replaced by grace. What a revelation for the church today! No longer do we have to live by a checklist in order to approach and please God. We can come into His presence today by the precious blood of Jesus Christ! No more religion! Just a right relationship! Ask yourself this question: What does the stone represent for me? Say, In Jesus name, I pray you would roll this stone away. Don't Embalm it. Extract it! Remove the limits off of my life today and release resurrection power in my midst! In Jesus Name!

Step to Live Strong:

Celebrate the Risen King!

MARCH 10

A Personal Pit-Stop

"When he was at the table with them, he took bread, gave thanks, broke it and began to give it to them. Then their eyes were opened and they recognized him, and he disappeared from their sight. They asked each other, "Were not our hearts burning within us while he talked with us on the road and opened the Scriptures to us?"

Luke 24:30-32

After Jesus conquered the grave, He appeared to His disciples for a period of 40 days. He made a pit-stop on the earth to personally greet these men face-to-face. The first encounter happened on the way to Emmaus which was 7 miles west of Jerusalem. As Jesus walked and talked with Peter and John the scripture says, *"Their hearts burned within them."* This was a case I like to call, *"Holy Heart Burn!"* The word of God is like a fire. It has the power to rekindle the flame inside of your spirit, body and soul.

After the death of Jesus, the disciples were heart-broken. They had forsaken everything to follow Jesus and suddenly Jesus was gone. They were more than disappointed. They were utterly devastated.

In Proverbs 13:12 we read, *"Hope deferred makes the heart sick."* These men were so sad, they were sick. Have you ever been there before? You placed your hope in something or someone and the story took an unexpected turn? Times like these have the power to suck the life right out of you. I am thankful this is not the end of the story.

Jesus couldn't stand the thought of going to Heaven without first paying Peter and the others a personal revelation of who He really was. As they were walking away from Jerusalem, Jesus encouraged them with the word of God. The word of God breathes life back into us. It gives us hope to take another lap around the race track. Just a little time spent with Jesus can re-fuel us so we can endure yet another day. If you are walking away from a hurtful situation, call on His name today. He is just a whisper way. Set your affections on Him and He will set your soul on fire. May your heart burn for Him both now and forevermore. This is why the original disciples all served the ascended Christ even to their death. Sometimes all we need is a Pitstop; a chance to catch our breath.

<u>Step to Start Strong:</u>

Take a Personal Pit-Stop

MARCH 11.

I'll Be Back!

"Then Simon Peter came and went into the tomb; and he saw the linen cloths lying there, and the handkerchief that had been around His head, not lying with the linen cloths, but folded together in a place by itself."

John 20:6-7

The Gospel of John tells us that the cloth which had been placed over Jesus' face was not just thrown aside, but was neatly folded. Why?

According to the tradition of that day, after a servant set the dinner table, he or she would wait, just out of sight, until the family had finished eating. When a person was finished, they would rise, wad up the napkin and toss it onto the table. A clear sign to come and clean up their setting. However, if they got up from the table, folded their napkin and set it beside their plate, the message was, *"I'm not finished yet. I'll be back!"*

It's amazing to me how much you can say by not saying anything at all. Your mannerisms, attitude and actions hold great weight throughout the day. When Jesus folded the linen cloth wrapped around His body, He was sending a sure sign to the church. What was His message? No need to worry. I'm coming back soon! Who is He coming back for? His body! A pure and spotless bride of course…

Luke 21:25-28 says, *"There will be signs in the Heavens by way of the sun, moon and stars. On the earth, nations will be in anguish and perplexed at the roaring and tossing of the sea. People will faint from terror, apprehensive of what is happening on the earth. At that time they will see the Son of Man coming in a cloud with power and great glory. When these things begin to take place, stand up, lift up your head and rejoice, because your redemption is drawing near."*

The signs of the times are certainly all around us. There is no need to be afraid church. Just be aware. The scripture is clear; *"Stand up! Lift up your head! and Rejoice! For your redemption is drawing near!* Indeed, Jesus is coming back soon!

<u>Step to Start Strong:</u>

Stand up, Lift up your head, and Rejoice.

MARCH 12.

THE 11TH COMMANDMENT

"Be still and know that I am God."

Psalm 46:10

Psalm 46:10 is certainly easy to remember but not so easy to implement into our personal lives. Being still is not popular. It seems to impede our progress. When we take time to sit, at least in the American culture, we feel like we're wasting our time. But I have found out, time is not wasted when we use it to be with the Lord. If anything our time is redeemed.

This reminds me of the children of Israel. They wandered in the desert for 40 years trying to make it to the Promised Land. Many Historians say, it took them 40 years to walk 250 miles. What took them half their life would only take us a few weeks. This is absurd! Why did it take them so long to get to their final destination? The scripture says, *"Because they rushed right pass the report of the Lord."*

This proves the point that not all movement is progress. Just because you are busy doesn't mean you are moving forward. The children of Israel were walking but they were walking in circles! Have you ever felt like you weren't gaining any ground? You seem to face the same old problems of struggle and strife. You may say, *"How many more times do I have to deal with this situation!"*

If so, I have some pastoral advise for you today. If you want to experience something you've never experienced before, you may have to do something you've never done before. Stop doing the same old stuff expecting a different result. Try doing something different. Be intentional. Be still and seek wisdom from the Holy Spirit. Ask Him for advise and wait for a response. I would refuse to go through another day in the wrong direction. Let's be willing to be still and know that He is God today. I call it, *The 11th Commandment.*

Step to Start Strong:

Be Still before the Lord

MARCH 13.

A Glutton for God

"Blessed are those who hunger and thirst after righteousness for they shall be filled."

Matthew 5:6

In the natural, you get hungry by not eating. When you miss a meal, it doesn't take very long for your stomach to start crying out, *"Give me something to eat!"* However, in the supernatural, you develop a spiritual appetite by ingesting the things of God. What do I mean? When God touches you or speaks to you, it creates a hunger on the inside of you for more of Him. A Holy Hunger if you will.

Psalm 34:8 says, *"Taste and see that the Lord is good."* When you get a double dose of the Holy Ghost, it spurs your spiritual appetite for another experience. You become gluttonous for God. The reality is our God is a jealous God and He wants you to seek after Him. He wants you to hunger and thirst after His righteousness which means right-living.

When you live this way, you soon realize you can never get enough of God! The more you get, the more you want! The facets of His majesty are infinite and everlasting. Do you want more? Are you hungry for more of Him? May this word whet your appetite to keep seeking wholeheartedly after Him. Someone used the terminology "that *your faith can pull on Heaven."* This is God's ultimate goal, *"That His kingdom would be established on the earth."* Are you hungry for more of Him? If so, get ready. You will be filled! God bless you!

Step to Start Strong:

Stay Hungry and Thirsty for More of Heaven!

MARCH 14.

THE SIFTING PROCESS

"And the Lord said, 'Simon, Simon! Indeed, Satan has asked for you, that he may sift you as wheat. But I have prayed for you, that your faith should not fail; and when you have returned to Me, strengthen your brethren."

Luke 5:31-32

Jesus prophesies Peter's backslide. Anytime you read a name stated back to back in the Bible, this means God is trying to get your attention intimately. Jesus speaks to Simon Peter and tells Him what is happening behind the scenes spiritually. Satan is approaching the throne of God asking to sift this man as wheat.

The process of sifting happens when you examine something thoroughly to isolate the most important or useful part. You filter the lumps and large particles in order to have a purified substance. This is the Lord's intention when you endure all types of suffering. Everything unimportant is removed when you go through times of sifting. Ultimately, God is drawing you back to your first love during these times.

The Apostle Paul said, *"I want to know Him by the power of His resurrection and the fellowship of His suffering."* The process of sifting goes hand in hand with power. You cannot have one without the other. If He suffered, we will suffer. If He was resurrected from the grave. We will do the same.

If you faithfully follow after Jesus Christ, power and suffering will follow you. Therefore, I have great news, *"Your current condition is not your permanent position!"* Embrace the process. Sifting will ratify your ministry. It will create compassion in your heart toward God's people. It will also, give you great influence. People will wonder how you made it through the battle? Your answer will be, *"It's All because of Jesus Christ and His sacrifice!"* Take up your cross and follow after Him today.

Step to Start Strong:

Don't Backslide. Slide Forward.

MARCH 15.

Double Edged Sword

"For the word of God is alive and powerful. It is sharper than the sharpest two-edged sword, cutting between soul and spirit, between joint and marrow. It exposes our innermost thoughts and desires."

Hebrews 4:12

The word is God is compared to a double-edged sword in scripture. *What does a double-edged sword do?* It cuts in and it cuts out. When Simon Peter stood up and preached on the day of Pentecost, the Bible says, the people present were cut to the heart. *What caused this cutting conviction?* The anointing of the Word of God! It's cuts both ways! It causes change when I speak it to others and it does the same when someone speaks it to me!

The Double-edged sword also speaks of the Old Testament and New Testament coming together for one point of purpose. *What's the purpose?* To reveal Jesus Christ as Savior of the world. The Old testament is Jesus Christ concealed and the New Testament is

Jesus Christ revealed. Yes, the scripture is all about our Savior. If you look long enough, you can find Jesus in every story.

Lastly, the double-edged sword is our weapon of warfare. You can withstand the attacks of the enemy by swinging this sword. *How do you swing the sword?* By speaking the word out loud! Most people think about the word with great intention but never move forward with action. We have get over ourselves and speak the word with boldness! Faith will come when you hear yourself speak the word even when you don't feel like it. I'm talking about feelings. I'm talking about faith. Faith says, *I will overcome every obstacle that the enemy puts in my way!* Do you believe this today?

If you will read the word of God when you don't need it; The Holy Spirit will bring it to remembrance when you do need it! It's called your double-edged sword!

Step to Start Strong:

Use your Sword

MARCH 16.

E FOR ENTERTAINMENT

"Knowing their thoughts, Jesus said, 'Why do you entertain evil thoughts in your hearts?"

Matthew 9:4

First of all, its beyond my comprehension how God can discern the thoughts of mankind. Psalm 139:2 says, *"God perceives our thoughts from afar."* He not only knows what you're doing right now, He knows what you're thinking right now. Absolutely amazing huh?

Jesus used this gifting quite often as He interacted with others in ministry. Many times, the scripture says, *"Jesus knew their thoughts"* so He addressed their thought processes head on. Jesus never avoided problems; if anything, He attacked them. Why? Because...

Man's biggest battlefield is in the mind. In this story, Jesus encounters the mind of a religious person. The Pharisees had looked at the God of Law so long they couldn't understand to see the other side of Grace. So, He addresses their misunderstanding with a question. *"Why do you entertain evil thoughts?"* Now, when God asked you a question, He already knows the answer! He's usually pointing to the problem! He sees what you don't see.

God knows whether or not you are entertaining evil thoughts from day to day. You have thousands of thoughts a day but you have the choice to meditate on the ones you want. You can either guard the doorway to your heart or you can invite evil in to entertain him. Try thinking about, what you're thinking about today and see if you notice what God already knows about you.

Let's apply 2nd Corinthians 10:3-5 in closing:

> *"For though we live in the world, we do not wage war as the world does. The weapons we fight with are not the weapons of the world. On the contrary, they have divine power to demolish strongholds. We demolish arguments and every pretension that sets itself up against the knowledge of God, and we take captive every thought to make it obedient to Christ."*

May we e*ntertain the Holy Spirit today!*

Step to Start Strong:

Take every thought Captive!

MARCH 17.

In the Beginning...

"In my former book, Theophilus, I wrote about all that Jesus began to do and to teach."

Acts 1:1

In the beginning God created the Heavens and the Earth. It was perfect until He created people. Adam and Eve took grace for granted and sinned which opened the door to death and eternal separation from God. In this moment, the plan of redemption was put in place and for this reason, God sent His son to die in our place. What a perfect plan! What a perfect God! Certainly, perfect peace for you and me.

This was God's plan but what was Jesus' purpose? Matthew 4:23 says, *"Jesus went about teaching in the synagogue, preaching the Kingdom of Heaven, and healing all kinds of sicknesses and diseases among the people."* Jesus was a teacher, a preacher and a miracle worker! He backed up His words with the way He lived His life. The Bible says in John 21:25, *"that Jesus did many other things while He was on earth. If every one of them were written down, I suppose that even the whole world would not have room for the books that would be written.*" Wow! We only have The 4 Gospels but there were so many other things left out! Jesus accomplished so much while He was on earth. You wanna know the best part? This was just the beginning...

In Acts 1:1, we read the account of "*everything that Jesus <u>began to do and teach</u>.*" Over 2,000 years ago, Jesus was just getting started. The God who worked miracles way back when is the God who still works miracles today! Our God is not a God that He should lie. He has never changed! He still sets the captive free! He still heals sick bodies and He still has the power to save sinners. All we have to do is call on the name of Jesus and He will finish what He started! He's alive and He is the same yesterday, today and forevermore! Indeed, it's the beginning of a brand new day! I wonder what He wants to do through you this week?

<u>Step to Start Strong:</u>

Believe the God of the Bible!

MARCH 18.

The Tower of Babel

"Then they said, 'Come, let us build ourselves a city, with a tower that reaches to the heavens, so that we may make a name for ourselves; otherwise we will be scattered over the face of the whole earth."

Genesis 11:4

On the way home from India one year, our crusade team had the honor to stop by in Dubai for 26 hours. God opened a door for us to minister to a Southeast Asian congregation the only night we were there. The timing was absolutely perfect! Like always, we blew in, blew up and blew out! It was the first time we ministered in the Middle East but certainly not the last. Dubai is a very special place. It's one of the richest cities in the world with architecture that you can barely believe with your own eyes. The city is home to the largest mall in the world, indoor ski resorts located in the middle of the desert heat and many other man-made must-sees. However, the grandiose of all sites is the tallest building in the world. This centerpiece is named after the President of UAE, The Burj Khalifa. This steel structure was completed in 2010 with a whopping 163 floors that reach 2,722 feet in the sky. The god-like monument only cost 1.5 billion to build? We took a trip to the top and my heart couldn't help but think of The Tower of Babel.

This isn't the first time a group of people built a building in the Middle East trying to get to Heaven. In Genesis 11, we read the account of this endeavor. The scripture says, *"These men were trying to make a name for themselves by building something everyone could see."* Are we guilty of doing the same thing? *Are we building our own kingdom's on the earth or are we building the kingdom of God? W*hat is the motive behind everything we do? Do we need to be seen and recognized in order to feel accomplished? Or is the approval of God more than enough?

The Burj Khalifa cannot be avoided. You can easily see it as you are flying into the city. It gets your attention from a great distance. Do you know what gets the attention of God? It's not how good you are but how great He is. It's not how high you can go but how low you can go. Frank Bartleman, an intercessor for the Famous Azusa Street Revival said, "*The height of your revival depends upon the depth of your repentance.*" If you want to build something that will last. Build God an altar and watch God show up and show off. The Tower of Babel represents our own self-centeredness. It signifies what we can do in our own strength. We can never get to Heaven without Him and we will never have His approval apart from Him...It doesn't matter what everybody else says about you. Only what He sees in you. So, let's tear down our own personal Tower of Babels today, before He has to.

Step to Live Strong:

Don't Babel. Build an Altar.

MARCH 19.

Buy the Field

"The kingdom of heaven is like treasure hidden in a field. When a man found it, he hid it again, and then in his joy went and sold all he had and bought that field."

Matthew 13:44

This parable is a passage spoken in a simile. Jesus compares one thing, with another thing, in order to make His point more emphatic and powerful.

He teaches us that the Kingdom of Heaven is "like" a treasure hidden in a field. When a man found it, he hid it again and then in his joy went and sold all he had to buy the field.

This is a perfect picture of our redemption. One day our eyes were enlightened to the understanding of our sinful nature so what did we do? We repented and turned to God. We found Him in the field of this world. He became *our treasure* in earthen vessels as we buried Him in the depths of our soul. With this in mind, the Holy Spirit has now filled us with everlasting joy. Why?

Because true joy is found in a relationship with Jesus Christ! The paradox of this experience should provoke us to our purpose.

Can you relate to the man in this story? Have you sold everything to buy the field if you will? This comparison speaks of sacrifice. In America, many have settled into what I call, *Comfortable Christianity.* We only want to do what we want to do within the Kingdom. Many worship God with their lips but their hearts are far from Him.

And Yes, we certainly possess the treasure but are we fulfilling our purpose? Ask yourself this question: *Am I holding anything back from God?* If so, the solution is simple; Pray this prayer:

God, *"restore unto me the joy of thy salvation."* Do you remember how it felt when you first got saved? If you can cultivate that emotion in your heart on a daily basis you will be overwhelmed with a fresh adoration toward your King. What we need is to get the Joy of our Salvation back! Joy will cause you to lay down anything for Him because He laid down everything for you.

Go ahead. Sell everything and buy the field! What this really means is, *"Deny yourself, Take up your cross and Follow Him daily."*

Step to Start Strong:

Buy the Field

MARCH 20.

One Life to Love

"Because your love is better than life, my lips will glorify you."

Psalm 63:3

One Life to Live was a famous soap opera series that aired on ABC for over 40 years. The broadcast was a dynamic daytime drama that focused on the issues within The Lord Family. It was a Hollywood Hit in its day!

However, just like this show came to a conclusion, our life will one day come to an end as well. We only have one life to live. How will we live it? Instead of just living a mediocre life, my hope is that all of us would live a life of meaning, a life of love.

We only have one life to love. Here's a provoking thought for every person: *"Is your presence helping or hurting the people God has put in your path?"*

If you say, you are apart of The Lord's Family, you should be loving others with no strings attached. We've all got issues and if you say you don't have issues, then that's your issue!

God's love is unconditional. It's not based upon our behavior. If it was, we would be required to act a certain way and look a certain way in order to experience His love and acceptance. He loves us so much but He loves us enough to not leave us the same. His love changes us.

Think about it: Conditional love says, do something for me and I will do something for you. Unconditional love says, I don't care what you do, I'll never stop loving you. This is the kind of love that attracts people to the Lord! We can love others no matter what because He first loved us.

Apply this principle to the relationship with your spouse. Start showing your kids and co-workers the unconditional love of the Lord! No matter what you are facing today: Remember, Love conquers all things! Don't kill anyone with kindness. Just lavish them with the love of the Lord! You've only got one life to live so use your life to love. Let's be laid-down lovers amen?

<u>Step to Start Strong:</u>

Live a Life of True Love

MARCH 21.

VICTORY VERSE

"The Word of God is alive!"

Hebrews 4:12

Do you have a Victory Verse? A scripture that describes the details of what God has done for you? If not, I am challenging you to take ownership of one and memorize it. You may have one in mind already. It would be the verse that gives you victory when you call to mind the goodness of God! Some call it a Life Verse. I say, Victory Verse because I love Victory! Whatever you say, just know this verse is something substantial to anchor your spirit to in the storms of life.

As for me, while reading the Bible one day in 2003 when I first got saved, I came across my victory verse. I knew God had done for me what I was now reading early. It seemed like the Lord had written these words just for me.

Psalm 40:1-3 says, "*I waited patiently on the Lord and He turned to me and heard my cry. He lifted me out of the mud and the mire and He set my feet on a rock. He gave me a firm place to stand. He put a new song in my heart. A hymn of praise to my God. Many shall see and hear and put their trust in the Lord.*"

This verse fulfills the legacy of my life. The Hoy Spirit picked me up, turned me around and set my feet on solid ground! Yes! Jesus delivered me from a disastrous bed of drug and alcohol addiction! But the key is in verse 3; *"Many shall see and put their trust in the Lord."* This is my hope. This is why I get out of bed every morning; to comfort others with the same comfort that I have been comforted with.

Seek the scriptures and ask the Holy Spirit to give you a Now Word. A word that will get you through the day or even through the year. This is the victory that has overcome the world: even our faith in God's word. So, whatever you do. Find a Victory Verse!

Step to Start Strong:

Memorize your Victory Verse

MARCH 22.

FLYING UNITED

"Oh, How good and how pleasant it is when God's people live together in unity!"

Psalm 133:1

Fly United: These 2 words reminded me of the day of Pentecost when the early church was in the Upper Room praying for a fresh baptism in the Holy Spirit. This account is found in Acts Chapter 2. The Bible says, *"They were all in one place and in one accord."* These passionate praying people were all unified up under the umbrella of Jesus Christ. This was the intention of Jesus' prayer in John Chapter 17. He prayed, *"May they be one, as The Father and I are one."*

If we are going to finish the race and go the distance in our family and ministry, this component of cooperate unity has to be set in place. We cannot serve the Lord in discord! I'm going to say that again, *"As a cooperate body of believers, We cannot serve the Lord in discord."*

When you hear someone strumming the guitar, it releases a beautiful melody unto the Lord. However, when one string is out of key, the whole song doesn't sound the same. This shows us the importance of taking the time to spiritually tune ourselves with the Holy Spirit. One string out of key can ruin the rest. We have to unify ourselves with the Lord and with those around us.

What melody do you make under the roof of your house? What does the Lord hear in the depths of your heart?

In order for us to go on to higher heights we must FLY UNITED with the Lord. We must FLY UNITED with our family. And we must FLY UNITED in the church. The Unity in the Spirit unleashes the leverage that we need to tread upon head of Satan and his serpents.

Typically, we never Fly United but we did on our way back from California. As I was boarding the United Airlines 747 Jet, I could almost hear the Lord say in my spirit, *"You're FLYING UNITED on the way Home."* In fact, we're all headed home and from now on the best way to Fly is United. *Are you with me?*

<u>Step to Start Strong:</u>

Live your Life in Unity: *FLY UNITED*

MARCH 23.

DIE DAILY

"I die everyday!"

1st Corinthians 15:31

What did the Apostle Paul mean when He wrote these 3 words to the First Corinthian Community Church?

He wasn't alluding to natural death here because it is appointed unto man *"once"* to die and then the judgement. So this leaves us with two choices if we use the process of elimination. We have A, a soul or B, a spirit. Well, the spirit never dies so surely He must be speaking about His soul. The soul relates to our mind, will and emotions.

What does this mean? Our will, our way of doing things and our stinking thinking must die everyday! Why? So the Will of God can live and manifest in the life of every believer. This is not a one time prayer we pray in the altar of a church. It's not a flippant decision we make in the moment. This way of living is a continual sacrifice offered to God everyday.

Sacrifice speaks of surrender.

It's easy to surrender your sin to God but it is a very hard thing to sacrifice yourself on the altar of God. Yes, we confess our sin but we can't stop with confession. We must sacrifice ourselves on a day to day basis.

Many people make Christ their Savior but very few make Him Lord of their lives. We confess our sins to make Him our Savior but we have to sacrifice ourselves to make Him our Lord.

Dying Daily is a weighty word but it must be done if we want to dwell in the fullness of God. The reality is Jesus wants more of you! He wants your sins, your self, and your service. *Have you surrendered your sin? How about yourself? How about your service?*

According to scripture, we must die everyday!

Step to Start Strong:

Die Daily!

MARCH 24.

THE LATTER GLORY!

"The latter glory of this house shall be greater than the former!"

Haggai 2:9

Bill Johnson made this statement: *"It's hard to have the same fruit of the early church, when we value a book they didn't have over the Holy Spirit that they did have."*

His point: The Bible wasn't canonized until the beginning of the 5th Century. It's easy to forget the Bible we read didn't exist during the day of the disciples. So, what did they depend upon for their strength? I would say three things: 1) The Old Testament Scripture 2) The Testimony and the Example of Jesus 3) & The Precious Holy Spirit.

With these three things, the Bible says, *"They turned the world upside down."* (Acts 17:6)

With all of the knowledge and technology of the 21st Century, we have to wonder why don't we see the same results as the early church? I believe this is a key: Yes, we know Jesus and yes, we have a plethora of information about the Bible at our fingertips but we are missing this one important and vital component: *"Knowing how to submit and follow leading of the Holy Spirit."* This is the unchangeable key to supernatural signs and wonders.

Many leaders and church attenders in our day do not know how to do this. We've received salvation and yes, we have a knowledge of the word but we are missing this key ingredient.

We have to honor the Holy Spirit like we honor the written word of God. Jack Taylor addresses the issue like this: *"It's not The Father, The Son & The Holy Bible. It's the Father, The Son and The Holy Spirit!"* In fact, the Holy Spirit is the one who inspired The Bible!

I warn you, do not listen to anyone who devalues the Word of God but also, steer clear of anyone who mocks and makes fun of the manifestations of the Holy Spirit. This quote is a fun way to illustrate this point: Someone once said, *"Too much word and you're dry up. Too much spirit and you'll blow up but when you combine the word and the spirit, you'll grow up."* By living your life in the Word and by the Spirit, you will have a great spiritual advantage. Maybe this is why God said, *"The latter glory of this house will be greater than the former?"* The Glory is yours, says the Lord!

Step to Start Strong:

Honor the Holy Spirit

MARCH 25.

THE 1,000 FOLD INCREASE!

"May the LORD, the God of your fathers, increase you a thousand-fold more than you are and bless you, just as He has promised you!"

Deuteronomy 1:11

As Moses prayed this prayer over His people so I declare it over you this day. *"May the LORD, the God of your fathers, increase you a thousand-fold more than you are today and bless you, just as He has promised!"* As I read through the scripture, I see a common theme. We serve a God who loves increase. He loves to make something out of nothing. You don't think you have much to offer? Guess again! If you take what you have and give it to God, He will multiply it! This is His promise!

Watch this: The Children of Israel were in bondage for 400 years in Egypt. They didn't know God. The only stories they had heard were the stories from their ancestors about Abraham, Isaac and Jacob. As far as they knew, He was the God of not enough. They were slaves and they worked by the sweat of their brow everyday making bricks. Why should we follow God?

However, God raised up a humble man by the name of Moses and they followed Him out of Egypt into the desert by the Spirit. The familiar system of being a slave was gradually destroyed. God started providing for them supernaturally by raining manna and quail from the sky. During this season, God was trying to develop their trust and dependency upon Him on a *"daily basis."* (Remember, The Father's Prayer: "Give us this day our daily bread:) It's the same way for us today. God is teaching us to trust Him in times of scarcity so we want buckle in times of blessing. In this season, God goes from the God of not enough, to the God of just enough.

When we taste and see that the Lord is good, we tend to forsake our ways and keep following the Lord into unfamiliar places. This is God's Goal. He is a Good, Good Father. If we pass the test, we prove to Him that He can trust us with more. We now move from the God of just enough, to the God of more than enough. This is when we come into the Promise Land. It's a land flowing with milk and honey representing His bountiful provision. God's word says, *"He is a Promise Keeper so this makes us Promise-Reapers!* " Are you ready to reap the promises of God?

Just one of these promises is found in Deuteronomy 1:11.

God wants to bring the blessing of a 1,000 fold increase to you and your family today. I don't know how He's going to do it but He said it! I believe it! and that settles it, in Jesus name

<u>Step to Start Strong:</u>

Receive the 1,000 Fold Blessing!

MARCH 26.

THE SHADOW OF DEATH

"Even though I walk through the valley of the Shadow of Death, I will fear no evil."

Psalm 23:4

While running along the coastline of California the Lord gave me this revelation. Many times, we feel like we are in a spiritual valley but in reality its just a temporary plateau.

This particular morning, I grabbed a quick cup of coffee and threw on my running shoes to take a jog down the boardwalk to hear from God and get some fresh air. As I ran a few miles, the path I followed took me took me to the end of the cove and headed up a mountain. The steps were steep but every few minutes the ground would level off and I would have the opportunity to catch my breathe as I continued climbing. Before long, I patted myself on the back, as I stood on the pinnacle of a hidden overlook that allowed me to see for miles down the beach. It was picture perfect! However, on the way back to the hotel, God gave me insight into Psalm 23. See, the valley of the shadow of death is not a physical place. It's a spiritual attack from the Shadow of the Spirit of Death.

Think about this way: You love Jesus and you serve Him with your whole heart. Many times, you are running hard after Him and you encounter a divine divide. Something the opposition tries to break your determination from moving forward so you can experience the view from the top. These hindrances are demonic forces that pass you by and their shadow tries to hinder you by darkening your days. So I ask you, *"What has been hindering you lately?"*

As believers, we are not called to go down. The only time we should go down is to bow our knee and pray. I charge you: Don't back down today! Rise up and take your rightful place!

Remember, when the Shadow of Death passes you by, this is God's cue to drive you back to your knees. The dark seasons in life have a way of stripping us of things that are less important. Your relationship with the Lord and your family are the two most important things in your life. Get some rest and refocus your life. If you are having a tough time today, use the plateau to get some proper rest and spiritual nourishment. You will need it if you want to finish the race. So, don't give up now. You've come way too far! Why would you want to miss the amazing view from the top? In fact, you are the brink of a beautiful new horizon.

"Its easy to gain spiritual revelation but extremely hard to correctly communicate." I hope you can "see" what I said this morning. Your life is broken up into segments. We can't always be going up but we should never go down. Surrender is never plausible unless you are giving into the Lord. So don't worry, you're not going down, you're just getting ready to go back up again! The Shadow of Death may be passing you by but the Spirit of Life is all around you.

Step to Start Strong:

Get Some Rest

MARCH 27.

STRONGHOLDS

"The name of the Lord is a strong tower. The righteous run to it and they are safe."

Proverbs 18:10

A strong hold is anything people trust in other than God. People tend to trust man, money and materialism more than they trust God. Whenever the enemy sees someone trusting in something other than God, he has legal access to come into their soul and set up a strong hold. He hides in the darkness by deceiving them from living in the fullness of God. The Apostle Paul put it this way: *"Do not give the devil a foot hold!"*

Proverbs 21:22 gives us some insight into this subject: It says,*"One who is wise can go up against the city and pull down the stronghold in which they trust."* Wisdom will show you what is of God and what is not. When God gives you the wisdom to see an area of misplaced trust, you can pull down these strongholds in praying specifically.

Have you been depending upon people for your overall joy and peace? Are you trusting in your money to bring you security and satisfaction? What strongholds are holding you back from experiencing true freedom in Christ? Ask God for wisdom right now and pull them down in Jesus name! Trust is an expression of faith. If you have faith in the Lord Jesus Christ, you can fully trust Him today. Go ahead and run to Him and rest assure you will be safe.

Step to Start Strong:

Pull Down Every Stronghold in Prayer

MARCH 28.

THE ROCK OF REVELATION

"When Jesus came to the region of Caesarea Philippi, he asked his disciples, 'Who do people say the Son of Man is?" They replied, "Some say John the Baptist; others say Elijah; and still others, Jeremiah or one of the prophets. "But what about you?" he asked. "Who do you say I am?" Simon Peter answered, "You are the Messiah, the Son of the living God." Jesus replied, "Blessed are you, Simon son of Jonah, for this was not revealed to you by flesh and blood, but by my Father in heaven. And I tell you that you are Peter, and on this rock I will build my church, and the gates of Hell will not overcome it."

Matthew 16:30-18

When Simon Peter first met Christ by the Sea of Galilee in John Chapter 1, Jesus said to Him, *"You are Simon but you will be called Cephas which is translated Peter."* We see clearly the Grace of God in this story. Jesus accepted Simon just the way he was but He refused to leave him that way. Jesus not only changed his name but He changed his whole way of thinking, the way he dealt with people and the way he worshipped. If you don't know: *"Jesus will change everything for you if you will let Him."*

We see the outward manifestation of an inward change when Jesus asked Peter a question that day. He said, *"Who do you say that I am?"* It was in this moment that Peter professed Christ as the Son of the Living God. Up until this moment, I believe Simon Peter really wrestled with who Jesus was. He said He believed with His mouth but if the truth be told, his heart had some catching up to do. This man was just like us. We say we believe certain characteristics about God but deep inside we struggle to walk them out by faith. It's a trust issue. For Peter, this was a valley of decision and his answer ultimately changed his destiny.

His break-out session with Jesus started with this statement: *"Upon this rock I shall build my church and the gates of Hell shall not prevail against it!"* The rock represents revelation. What was his revelation? That Jesus Christ was the rock of his salvation! His answered revolutionized His relationship with Jesus and instantly rerouted His life. The prophetic word spoken over His life was fulfilled and his name was changed from Simon to Peter which means, *"little rock."* You could say, Peter was a chip off the old block.

So my question for you today is: *'Who do you say that Christ is?"* Is He your Savior? Your Deliverer? Your Healer? You answer the question. I know what God has done for me but what has He done for you? Go ahead and thank God this morning for being everything to you. He alone is worthy! Build your house on the Rock!

Step to Start Strong:

Build your House on the Rock

MARCH 29.

NOT MY WILL

"Father, if you are willing, take this cup from me; yet not my will, but yours be done."

Luke 22:42

This was the first and only time Jesus ever asked to do something that was contrary to His Father's will? We have to ask the question why? His whole life had been spent in perfect union and submission to His Father in prayer. Only in this moment did He hesitate and ask for a way out. He could had rebelled, resisted and ran from the will of God but instead, He embraced the decision of something He did not want to endure.

Sure we could say the cup of suffering was the sacrifice He was about to endure for the sins of the world. But I think it was much, much deeper. We have to remember, Jesus had *"never"* been separated from His Father. The Trinity had always been intimately intact. From the beginning of time up until this moment, the Father had always been securely by the His son's side.

The scripture says, *"He who knew no sin 'became sin" so that you and I could "become" the righteousness of God."* Jesus became sin and we know sin separates people from God. The cup of suffering He spoke of represented the three day separation of the Son from His Father. Now we know why He cried out, *"Father, Father! Why have you forsaken me!"* This is why He asked for the cup of suffering to be passed. However, His separation provided our salvation.

How do we apply this principle? I would say, *"Everyone wants God's will but not everybody is willing to take His route."* Are you willing to be obedient even to the point of death? Even when you don't understand? Even when you're standing alone and no one agrees?

Let's pray this prayer today: *"Not our will, but your will be done." In Jesus Name, Amen.*

<u>Step to Start Strong:</u>

Be Obedient even when you Don't Understand

MARCH 30.

28 Seasons.

Ecclesiastes 3:1-8

To everything there is a season,
A time for every purpose under heaven:
A time to be born,
And a time to die;
A time to plant,
And a time to pluck what is planted;
A time to kill,
And a time to heal;
A time to break down,
And a time to build up;
A time to weep,
And a time to laugh;
A time to mourn,
And a time to dance;
A time to cast away stones,
And a time to gather stones;
A time to embrace,
And a time to refrain from embracing;

A time to gain,
And a time to lose;
A time to keep,
And a time to throw away;
A time to tear,
And a time to sew;
A time to keep silence,
And a time to speak;
A time to love,
And a time to hate;
A time of war and a time of peace."

There is a time and a season for every activity under the sun. God gives us an exhausted list of 28 seasons we could find ourselves in at any given time. Despite all the day to day activities, Here's what I want you to see in this scripture: *"There is never a time or a season to quit!"*

"We do not belong to those who shrink back and are destroyed, but we belong to those who have faith and are saved." (Hebrews 10:39)

"So, do not grow weary in doing good, for in due season you will reap a harvest if you do not give up." (Galatians 6:9)

Don't give up on your family, don't give up on the church and definitely, don't give up on Jesus! He promises to leave you and never give up on you! Remember, it's always darkest right before the dawn. Whatever you do: Don't give up today.

<u>Step to Start Strong:</u>

Don't Give up!

MARCH 31.

REBOUNDING

"Rejoice not over me, My enemy! When I fall, I shall rise!"

Micah 7:8

If you understand the sport of basketball, you understand the importance of rebounding. Even the best teams in the NBA only shoot slightly above 40%. In college, the average field goal percentage drops to 30% and it's even lower for high school players. What does this tell us? We miss more shots than we take! With this in mind, we better learn how to rebound. This technique teaches us to correctly position ourselves to get a second chance at a shot before our time runs out. It's the same way in everyday life.

Proverbs 24:16 says, *"For though a righteous man falls seven times, He gets back up."* Did you read that right? Can a righteous man fall? Yes, he can fall but more importantly, he can rebound from a missed opportunity. The only difference between a righteous man and an unrighteous man is he gets back up. Rebounding is a fundamental key for righteousness. If you missed it yesterday, get back in the game today and give it another try. Micheal Jordan put it this way: *"You will miss 100% of the shots you never take."* If you want to succeed you have to bold in the area of rebounding.

If you're anything like me, you're not satisfied with just being on the team. You want the ball and you want to win! So, talk to Jesus Christ, your Life Coach today and ask Him to put you back in the game of life. If you don't know how to do anything else, just box out your opponent and get the rebound! As Christians, we don't want to live our lives on the defensive but rather the offensive. For the Kingdom of God suffers violence but the violent take it by force!

Step to Start Strong:

Get Back in the Game!

APRIL 1.

PRAISE PHRASE

"Faith comes by hearing and hearing the word of God."

Romans 10:17

God has given great gifts to the body of Christ and one of my all-time favorites is the gift of preaching. Nothing moves you more than the anointing of a powerful preacher. It can literally raise you up out of your seat and get you going in the right direction. But what do you do when you're down and there's no preacher to be found? I'll tell you what you can do: You can preach to yourself. You can have a conversation within your spirit. Some of the best sermons I have ever heard were the exhortations from my own lips to my own soul. King David put it this way, *"I have learned to stir myself up in the spirit."* This is a spiritual secret. I release you today, *"It's ok to preach to yourself."*

I call these private conversations, *"Praise Phrases!"* When the enemy comes in like a flood, I open up my mouth and begin to praise the Lord and sometimes, I preach to myself. Why do I do this? Because the Bible says, *"Faith comes by hearing and hearing the word of God."* When you audibly speak the word of God, your spirit hears the word of God and in this moment, faith is created inside of you to overcome whatever you are facing. We have to use this weapon of warfare called words. Thinking good thoughts is only half the battle. To completely conquer our conquest, We have to open up our mouths and speak, sing and sometimes, shout! I have found out, your words will create your world. So, I'm asking you today, *"What do you say when you preach to yourself?"* Can somebody say, *"Preach!"*

Step to Live Strong:

Stir Yourself up in the Spirit

APRIL 2.

THE TRAVELING PSALM

"I lift up my eyes to the hills—where does my help come from? My help comes from the Lord, the Maker of heaven and earth. He will not let your foot slip—He who watches over you will not slumber. Indeed, He who watches over Israel will neither slumber nor sleep. The Lord watches over you—The Lord is your shade at your right hand; the sun will not harm you by day, nor the moon by night. The Lord will keep you from all harm—He will watch over your life; the Lord will watch over your coming and going both now and forevermore."

Psalm 121

This passage is often called, *The Traveling Psalm.* Notice how the Lord says, *"He will watch over you five different times is these few verses."* He's stressing the fact that He forever sees you and He will never forget about you. You are the apple of His eye. He heroically holds you in the palm of His hand. Nothing can separate you from His endless love. If you ever lose sight of this truth, all you have to do is lift your eyes unto the hills and you will see Him looking back down on you. He is the one who is watching over you every moment of every day. This should bring you great courage and comfort to keep looking to Him for your strength and safety. What better bodyguard than the God Most High?

A matter of fact, you are surrounded by angels on every side. As you travel to and fro, keep singing this psalm, *"My God is with me and He is watching over me."*

(Our family reads this Psalm and prays before every trip)

Step to Start Strong:

Pray the Traveling Psalm as you Travel

APRIL 3.

SET UNDER AUTHORITY

"And He replied, "I am a man under authority.""

Matthew 8:9

God is the author of authority. The enemy of authority is me, myself and I. In the beginning, Adam and Eve was deceived. They followed after Satan, their Step-Father and rebelled against the authority of God. They stepped out from under the protection, position and perfection of God. Ultimately, this opened the doorway to death.

Authority is like an umbrella. *We have to get under, what God has put over us, if we ever want to get over, what God wants to put under us.* We can't step out from under authority and expect to be a blessed believer. God has a job description for His body in the New Testament. It consists of 2 things: *Sacrifice and Submission.* Anything with two heads is a freak and anything with no head is dead if you know what I mean.

1st Corinthians 11:3 says, "*Now, I want you to know that the head of every man is Christ.*" Jesus Christ, the word of God, is our final authority. We can't pick and choose what we want to do and who we want to follow. We have to be Umbrella Fella's. We have to remain under the authority God has placed over us if we want to prosper to full potential. People who are not under authority have no authority. Think about it.

Therefore, realign yourself with your parents, your pastor, your spouse and your employer. By doing so, you're setting yourself up for great success. You can trust this principle: Set yourself under authority and watch God give you authority.

Step to Start Strong:

Submit to Governing Authorities.

APRIL 4.

The Characteristic of an Overcomer

"I discipline my body like an athlete, training it to do what it should. Otherwise, I fear that after preaching to others, I myself might be disqualified."

1st Corinthians 9:27

True character is who you are when no one else is around. Do we live different lives in the dark than we do in the daylight? Sadly, many christians are carnal and they live one way on Sunday and another way the rest of the week. This should not be so.

True character is a vital component if you want to live an overcoming life in Christ Jesus. What you practice in private will always be brought out in public. It's just a matter of time. What if your current lifestyle was laid out for everyone to see. Would you be really embarrassed or very well-pleased?

If you want to be an overcomer, you must pay attention to your daily disciplines. You are the sum of every choice you have ever made. If you desire a better life, start making better decisions. Discipline your body and train it to do what it should be doing. By doing so, you'll slowly see the tides turn. Rise to the occasion today and overcome your obstacles! This is your objective: "Your Character."

True Character is the Characteristic of an Overcomer!

Step to Start Strong:

Be a person of True Character

APRIL 5.

Hosting the Holy Ghost

"My soul thirsts for God, for the living God. When can I go and meet with God?"

Psalm 42:2

What if Billy Graham's personal assistant called you today and said, *"Do you mind meeting with Reverend Graham tonight for dinner?"* He would like to give you a few hours of his time if you are available. What would you say? I know what I would say: *"Absolutely! Just tell me when and where and I'll be there! What an opportunity! But why would he want to meet with me?"*

Now, surely you wouldn't show up late and lazy looking. You would be there on-time and dressed to impress. Ready to receive whatever He had for you. The worse thing you could do is say you're coming and not show up or fall asleep during your conversation with him.

Along the same lines, any time we treat our relationship with the Lord this way. We forget we have the amazing opportunity to meet with the most important person in the world everyday. His name is not Billy Graham but the Lord God Almighty! I would say He is a pretty important person to meet with wouldn't you? Certainly, well worth a few minutes of your time.

David asked this question in the Old Testament, "*When can I go and meet with God*?" Now, in this Psalm He was thinking about his past worship experiences in the temple. He longed to be back in God's presence to encounter His power.

For you and I, we have this treasure in our earthen vessels called *"The Holy Spirit."* He is willing to personally meet with you anywhere at anytime. There's always room at His table. The light is always left on for you. You can literally *Host the Holy Ghost* on a daily basis. In the midst of your busy life, don't forget to incorporate the presence of Jesus. When you wake up say, "*Good Morning Holy Spirit*." Let's do life together. What do you want me to do today? My body, soul and spirit is yours. Be a Good Host for the Holy Ghost today. He wants to spend some time with you.

Step to Start Strong:

Host the Holy Ghost

APRIL 6.

VICTORY IN THE VALLEY

"But thou art holy, and you inhabit the praises of your people."

Psalm 22:3

In Ancient Israel, the leaders in the surrounding nations were always fighting over land. People and property were an answer to how much power and prestige a particular King had in his back pocket. When two opposing armies were at the brink of going into battle, one army would station themselves on one side of a mountain and the other army would do the same on the other side with the valley separating the two. Battles were never fought on mountaintops. Battles were fought in the valley. The army who overcame in the valley was the army who won the victory.

The spiritual battle we fight on a daily basis is operated the same way. Your enemy loves to attack you when you are in the valley. When you are down on yourself and discouraged in life. In fact, things seem a lot larger than they really are when you find yourself in a valley. The truth is the mountains that are surrounding you today are not near as big as they seem. So, don't give up so easy. It's not as bad as you think.

This reminds me of the scripture that says, *"He inhabits the praises of His people."* Jesus was born in Bethlehem in the Land of Judah and Judah means praise so it's safe to say, Jesus was birthed in praise. He had the attention of Heaven and all the angels rejoiced at His arrival. Furthermore, Jesus loves the praises of His people! It's His favorite part of the day. When you find yourself in a valley, all you have to do is praise the name of Jesus and He will fill the valley that you find yourself in. The low place will overflow with the presence of God when your mouth is filled with praise. Don't run from your enemy. Stand still today and see the salvation of the Lord!

This valley is for your benefit. Nothing grows on-top of the mountain, only in the valley. Don't miss your opportunity to grow. Don't miss your opportunity to know God on a deeper level of intimacy. Luke 3:5 says, *"Every valley shall be filled in and every mountain made low."*

There is Victory in the Valley says The Lord!

Step to Start Strong:

Take a Praise Break!

APRIL 7

Rise & Shine!

"Arise and Shine! For your light has come! And the Glory of the Lord is risen upon you."

Isaiah 60:1

If you will take the time to read the scripture, you'll see many metaphoric terms we use in everyday life. For instance, when you were young, your mom used to walk in the room, open the blinds and say with her sweet southern voice, *"Rise & shine sweetheart!"* Its time to go to school. At least this is the way it was in my world. Little did I know, Isaiah 60 was being spoken into my spirit and I didn't even know it. So, what does these words mean?

When you rise and shine, you wake up every morning desperately desiring to do your best for God. People notice when you live your life this way. They will wonder what makes you different from every other person. Your countenance and character will set you apart. You will be like a city set on a hill, shining for all to see. A beacon of hope for your surrounding community.

When you rise and shine, the spirit of excellence will rest upon you. People shine when they are doing what they were created to do. If you sing? Sing with all your heart. If you serve? Do it with sincerity of heart. If you are a stay at home mom? Raise your kids to shine like the stars in the sky! Whatever you do, "*Find your groove and give it all you've got!*"

What will happen when you Rise and Shine? The Glory of God will give you great favor. He will light up your world and you will see where to go and exactly what to do. Don't waste your life trying to live somebody else's dream. By doing this, you won't shine. You'll fall short. Just be you. In reality, nobody can be you better than you.

Someone said, *"your light will shine the brightest in the darkest places."* Don't be afraid. Just rise and shine! Your light will dispel the darkness and the glory of God will arise all around you.

Step to Live Strong:

Rise & Shine!

APRIL 8.

The Ultimate Art of War

"Next to him was Shammah. When the Philistines banded together at a place where there was a field full of lentils, Israel's troops fled from them. But Shammah took his stand in the middle of the field. He defended it and struck the Philistines down, and the Lord brought about a great victory."

2nd Samuel 23:11-12

One of my favorite characters in the Bible is Shammah. He was one of King David's top three mighty men. When David first met him, he was in debt and in great distress. Has anybody ever felt this way before? However, in his desperation, He followed the King into a cave. (1st Samuel 22:2) This was the beginning of His journey of faith. Over time, the Spirit of God molded him into a reliable and powerful individual. Here's his story:

> *"Shammah owned a pea patch on the outside of town. Many people would say it wasn't much but to Shammah it was everything and more. It represented everything He worked hard for. One day, the Philistine Army marched over the hill and everyone fled except him.*

> *They demanded that he hand over His property and here's what I want you to see; Shammah did not negotiate with the enemy. He took his stand in the middle of the field, ready to defend and willing to destroy any adversary that threatened his family or property.* This man was brutal with sin! He gave the army an ultimatum. You either leave or die! He was willing to lay down His life to guard what God had entrusted unto Him.

Can I ask you a question: What has God entrusted to you? Whatever it is, don't take your position lightly. Small oversights have huge ramifications in the spirit.

I charge you: Fight for your family. Fight for your future. If anything, Fight for what's right!

The Ultimate Art of War is to win without a fight. When Satan shows up to steal something from you, he would love for you to lose heart and just give up and give him what he wants. He is wise, patient and cunning. He will overpower you with fear to paralyze your faith. He knows without faith, you can't finish the race. By faith, Shammah stood his ground on the outside of town. The enemy will also try to attack you in areas you care least about. His assignment was on the outside of town. It wasn't in the heart of where everybody else wanted to be. However, it was still significant to him. He did not let doubt strip him from his destiny. He was faithful even in the small assignments. This story is the epitome of who you and I are called to be. Be brutal with sin. Be brutal with unbelief. Mind in the beginning, what you want to be in the end. Guard your pea-patch! If you are faithful with little, God can give you more. This is the Art of War.

Step to Start Strong:

Guard what God had given you.

APRIL 9.

Here I Am Send Me!

"Then I heard the voice of the Lord saying, 'Whom shall I send? And who will go for us?" And I said, "Here am I. Send me!"

Isaiah 6:1-8

Notice how something had to die for Isaiah to have his a life-changing experience with the Lord. What is getting in the way of your breakthrough? Pride? People? Worry? Work? Whatever it is, put it to the side today and allow the Lord to give you fresh revelation.

Isaiah's revelation radically revolutionized his life. In this passage, Isaiah looked up and saw the Lord sitting on His throne. His holiness compelled Him to look in to see His sin. His immediate conviction caused him to cry out for forgiveness! After this, He looked out and heard the voice of the Lord saying, *"Who shall I send?"* And He gave a great shout, *"Here I am Lord, Send me."*

My story looks a lot like this. When I first got saved, I prayed this prayer repetitiously: *"If you can use anyone Lord, you can use me. Touch my hands Lord & my feet. Touch my heart Lord, speak through me. If you can use anyone Lord, you can use me!"* Little did I know, God was going to answer this prayer over and over again. And the Good News? He wants to use you too!

We've all been commissioned just like Isaiah. Yes, we need to go into all the world to share the Gospel. But more importantly, we need to go into *"our world"* and share the Gospel. The word *"Go"* in the Greek, literally means, *"as you are going."* You don't have to go to the other side of the world to be a witness. You can share Christ with others as you are going about your daily activities. This makes the mandate a lot more manageable. We are witnesses in our world.

Someone once said, *"The greatest missionary journey you can take is across the street."* Wherever you go, just go for God!

Do you want to be used by God? If so, I challenge you: *Ask the Lord to use you to lead someone to the Lord this year.* If you accept the challenge, Pray this Prayer: *"If you can use anyone Lord, you can use me." Here I am Lord, Send Me!*

Step to Start Strong:

Say everyday: Send ME.

APRIL 10.

The Formula for Success

"In the beginning, God."

Genesis 1:1

The Formula for Success is strategically placed within the binding of the Bible. Just think about the first four words of Genesis Chapter 1. They say, *"In the Beginning, God!"* Wow! What a way to start strong! Why begin the whole redemption story with these words? I believe God wanted us to know, before there was anything, there was God. So, before we do anything, we should acknowledge God. Let me say it this way: *"If you want to live a successful Christian life, you must learn to incorporate God at the beginning of everything you do."* In the spiritual realm, this is the Formula for Success.

Matthew 6:33 puts it this way; *"Seek ye first the Kingdom of God and His righteousness and everything else will be added unto you."* The cross of Jesus Christ is not a subtraction symbol. It is a plus sign for every individual!

If you will put God first, He will add so much to your life. He will add love, joy, peace, patience and so much more! You'll experience His presence, and He presence will pave the way for supernatural peace and even prosperity! It's a win, win situation. You get God and all of His benefits. (Psalm 103:1-3) So, Go ahead, put God to the test! Put the best at the beginning of everything you. It's the Formula for Great Success; *"In the beginning, God!"*

Step to Live Strong:

Put God First

APRIL 11.

TODAY MATTERS

"This is the day the Lord has made; Let us rejoice and be glad in it!"

Psalm 118:24

A few years ago, I came across this prayer:

> Dear Lord, *"So far I've done all right. I haven't gossiped. I haven't lost my temper. I haven't been greedy, grumpy, nasty, selfish, or over-indulgent. I'm really doing good. But in a few minutes, I'm going to get out of bed and I'm really going to need your help!"*

God loves honestly, transparency and authenticity. He knows you better than you know yourself. Why not be brutally honest with Him? Life may not always be easy but you can always find something good in everything you go through.

John Wooden said, *"Things turn out best for those who make the best of how things turned out."* Don't allow what has happened in your past to dictate your future. If something or someone is controlling the way you live your life, you may not be in total submission to the Holy Spirit. Ask God why you really struggle with those situations when you get out of bed? When He answers you, don't be hasty. Listen to his instructions. God speaks to be heard but more importantly, He speaks to be obeyed.

May we stop trying to finish in the flesh what we started in the Spirit.

Step to Start Strong:

Be Honest and Transparent before the Lord.

APRIL 12.

The Roman Road

The Roman Road is a collection of verses in Paul's Epistle to the Romans that offers a clear and concise path to the grace found in Jesus Christ. Although many people believe they will go to heaven because they have lived a good life, been baptized as a child, served in the church, or treated others fairly, the Bible declares that none of us can live up to God's standards of righteousness. Therefore, we need an inroad to God that doesn't rely on anything we do, but rather, depends upon what He has done for us. In fact, this reality sets Christianity apart from every other religion in the world. Furthermore, the Roman Road provides a detailed map for our salvation and eternal fellowship with God. Follow these steps to a secured salvation:

1. We must acknowledge God as the Creator of everything.

    Romans 1:20-21 "For since the creation of the world His invisible attributes are clearly seen, being understood by the things that are made, even His eternal power and Godhead, so that they are without excuse, because, although they knew God, they did not glorify Him as God, nor were thankful, but became futile in their thoughts, and their foolish hearts were darkened."

2. We must realize that we are sinners and that we need forgiveness.

   Romans 3:23 "For all have sinned, and fall short of the glory of God."

3. God gave us the way to be forgiven of our sins.

   Romans 5:8 "But God demonstrates His love toward us, in that, while we were still sinners, Christ died for us."

4. If we remain sinners, we will die. However, if we repent of our sins, and accept Jesus Christ as our Lord and Savior, we will have eternal life.

   Romans 6:23 "For the wages of sin is death, but the gift of God is eternal life in Christ Jesus our Lord."

5. Confess that Jesus Christ is Lord and believe in your heart that God raised Him from the dead and you will be saved!

   Romans 10:9-10 "That if you confess with your mouth the Lord Jesus and believe in your heart that God has raised Him from the dead, you will be saved. For with the heart one believes unto righteousness, and with the mouth confession is made unto salvation."

6. There are no other religious formulas or rituals. Just call upon the name of the Lord and you will be saved!

   Romans 10:13 "For whoever calls on the name of the LORD shall be saved!"

This is the way to salvation. This is The Roman Road!

Step to Start Strong:

Memorize the Roman Road

APRIL 13.

MAMA MADE THE DIFFERENCE!

"In her deep anguish Hannah prayed to the LORD."

1st Samuel 1:10

You can search the scripture but you will not find a prayer prayed by a mother that wasn't answered concerning her children. Supernatural power is released when a mother cries out on behalf of a child. It can't be explained. There's just a divine connection between the two.

Hannah interceded for the Prophet Samuel, Elizabeth believed for her son John the Baptist and Mary treasured many things in her heart for Jesus. Many times, when you see an influential person, you will find praying parents behind the scenes. Prayer makes the difference. The best thing we could ever do for our family is pray for them on a consistent basis.

To all the Mother's Today, we want to honor you. Thank you for bringing us into this world, believing in us and fighting the battles of life beside us. I believe all of us would agree, *"Mama made the difference."* May her children rise up and call her blessed today! God, we thank you for our mother's. We wouldn't be here without them.

Deuteronomy 5:16 *"Give honor to your father and your mother, as you have been ordered by the Lord your God; so that your life may be long and all may be well for you in the land which the Lord your God is giving you."*

Step to Start Strong:

Honor your Mother and Father

APRIL 14.

POWER RELATIONSHIPS

"Two are better than one, because they have a good return for their labor."

Ecclesiastes 4:9

People are like elevators. They will take you up or they will take you down. This statement is tested and true; *"You are who you hang out with."* My Father's words have not failed after all these years.

Who you hang around is a vital piece to your personal success. *"Show me your five best friends and I will show you what your life will look like in ten years."* Take a moment and think about who you spend most of your time with?

My Guidance Counselor in college shared a bit of wisdom with me one day that I will never forget. He said, *"Son, you never want to be the big fish in the little pond for too long. It's always better to be the little fish in a big pond.* What did he mean?

Many times, we like to stay in the cool, calm waters of the comfortable instead of placing ourselves around power people who will teach us and provoke us to grow. It's always easier being in a relationship with people who think the same way you think. The Apostle Paul didn't say, *"I have the mind of Christ."* He said, *"We"* have the mind of Christ. We, as the Body of Believers are always better together.

The more a muscle can stretch, the more it can grow. God's ultimate goal is for us to grow! Go ahead and step into situations where God can stretch you. The Psalmist said, *"One can put a 1,000 to flight but two can put 10,000 to flight."* This means there is exponential power when we come together for the sake of the Gospel. Ask God to put you in the right place for a Power Relationship! The Right People can produce the Right Plan. Can I get an Amen?

Who do you open most of your with and what difference are they making in your life?

<u>Step to Start Strong:</u>

Stay Teachable

APRIL 15.

ABC's

"The secret things belong to God and God alone."

Deuteronomy 29:29

Just because you've never seen something supernatural doesn't make it superficial or fictitious. As Christians, we should never reduce our theology to our own level of personal experience with God. The sum of our encounters with Christ are only a drop of his infinite power and capability. A matter of fact, the majority of our mind should be reserved for the things we do not know about God. Class is always in session when it comes to knowing more about the Lord. Don't lean upon your own understanding. Depend upon the Holy Spirit. Here's why:

Psalm 147:5 says, *"Great is our God, abundant in power; his understanding is beyond measure."*

Isaiah 55:8 says, *"For my thoughts are not your thoughts, neither are your ways my ways, declares the Lord. For as the heavens are higher than* *the earth, so are my ways higher than your ways and my thoughts than your thoughts.*"

1st Corinthians 1:27 says, *"For the foolishness of God is wiser than human wisdom, and the weakness of God is stronger than human strength.*"

The underlining theme in our life should be, *"Let God be God and every other thing a Liar!"* It's the 1st Order of Theology: There is a God and I am not Him. This is the work He has called us do, *"Just Believe."* Theoretically, This is our ABC's! Its simple and its not a secret. He's the Alpha and the Omega. You can trust Him both now and forevermore.

Step to Start Strong

Just Believe

APRIL 16.

BUILDING BLOCKS

"Therefore everyone who hears these words of mine and puts them into practice is like a wise man who built his house on the rock. The rain came down, the streams rose, and the winds blew and beat against that house; yet it did not fall, because it had its foundation on the rock. But everyone who hears these words of mine and does not put them into practice is like a foolish man who built his house on sand. The rain came down, the streams rose, and the winds blew and beat against that house, and it fell with a great crash."

Matthew 7:24-27

Look at the similarities in this story. There were two men who heard the same word from God. They both decided they needed to do something so they built a house. Somewhere along the way they endured a severe storm which threatened the very work of their hands. One house was swept away on the sand and the other house remained on the rock. *What made the difference?* One man heard the Word of God and put it into practice and the other saved it for a rainy day but sad to say, *"It was too late!"* The damage was already done.

James 1:22 says, *"Do not merely listen to the word, and so deceive yourselves. Do what it says."*

As believers, most of us already know what to do.

Putting God's word into practice is the building blocks for our faith. Practice doesn't make perfect. Practice makes permanent. This is why the wise man's house withstood the test. He worked God's word and guess what? It worked for Him! So this means it will work for you too!

Step to Start Strong:

Put God's word into practice

APRIL 17.

I Believe I Can Fly

"You yourself have seen what I did to Egypt, and how I carried you on eagles' wings and brought you to myself."

Exodus 19:4

There are two types of people who need wings. People who find themselves in devastation and people who are fighting for their dreams. Both need to spread their wings and fly!

Are you in despair? Crushed under the rocks of discouragement? If so, I want you to know we've all been there. However, there is always hope.

"If you wait upon the Lord, He will renew your strength." This is a powerful promise. Wait on the wind of God's spirit, spread your wings in prayer and He will take you onto higher heights in Jesus Name! Just wait and see!

Secondly, are you fighting for your dreams? Are you finding it hard to get your goals off the ground? If so, I want you to know we've all been there before too! So, how do we get wings on our dreams? The secret is consistency. You can give up, give in or give it all you've got! I say, *"Let's give it all we've got for God!"*

I believe with all of my heart that God wants to give us more. More of His love, More of His power, More of His mercy! Now is the time to spread your wings and soar! May God grant you deliverance from despair and dynamite power for your dreams! I believe its time to fly.

Step to Start Strong:

Spread your Wings & Fly

APRIL 18.

Grand Central Station

"For though we live in the world, we do not wage war as the world does. 4 The weapons we fight with are not the weapons of the world. On the contrary, they have divine power to demolish strongholds. 5 We demolish arguments and every pretension that sets itself up against the knowledge of God, and we take captive every thought to make it obedient to Christ."

2nd Corinthians 10:3-5

The battlefield for a believer begins in the mind. Unfortunately, weapons of mass destruction cannot shut the mouth of the devil. If so, he would no longer be a threat to us. He is unharmed by our physical retaliation. So, their must be another way to overcome his schemes and strategies. Have you ever thought, how can we win the war over our adversary?

The scripture says, *"We disarm the devil when we take every thought captive and bring it under the obedience of Christ."* We win the war when we watch over our thought life. Our mind is like Grand

Central Station. All day long, we have dozens and even hundreds of thoughts traveling through our mind at a rapid pace. What train we decide to board will ultimately determine our final destination.

Let's train our thoughts to think like Christ. When a train pulls up trying to lead you down the wrong track, turn your back and clear your mind. Don't lose you train of thought today. Keep your mind focused on Christ. It's going to be a great day! All aboard!

Step to Start Strong:

Stay on Track

APRIL 19.

A WORD TO THE WISE

"The proverbs of Solomon, the son of David, were written to know wisdom and instruction, To perceive the words of understanding and To receive the instruction of knowledge."

Proverbs 1:1-3

The scripture says, *"Solomon was the wisest man that has ever lived."* Over the course of his life, he penned these priceless precepts that are applicable for every culture in history. We call these writings, *"The Proverbs."* The Proverbs were written to help men make wise decisions.

We gain this kind of wisdom in one of two ways: *Through mentors and through mistakes.* Unfortunately, most of us learn through making mistakes which the world coined *"life lessons."* How many of you wish you knew what you know when you were in your teens and twenty's?" All of us do! This is why I love the Proverbs! They keep us from making unwise decisions. In fact, they teach us a better way.

There are 31 chapters in the Book of Proverbs; One for every day of the month. Try reading a chapter once a day that corresponds to the current date. It's easy to keep up with this reading plan this way.

Do you desire wisdom? Do you desire understanding and insight? Here's a word to the wise: *Read a proverb everyday or even one a week.*

Knowledge is knowing but wisdom is applying what you know. There's a big difference!

Here's my prayer for you today: *"May the Lord crown you with wisdom, understanding and insight in all situations that arise in your life, both now and forevermore, in Jesus Name!*

Step to Start Strong:

Read a Proverb Everyday

APRIL 20.

The Running Man

"Therefore we also, since we are surrounded by so great a cloud of witnesses, let us lay aside every weight, and the sin which so easily ensnares us, and let us run with endurance the race that is set before us."

Hebrews 12:1

In 2008, I boarded a plane and flew to Cape Town, South Africa for my first international mission opportunity. These two weeks of ministry drastically changed the trajectory of my life. I saw God perform signs, miracles and wonders right before my eyes. It was in this moment that I knew I was called to be a Missionary Evangelist.

If you know me, you know I love to run. I enjoy running for a few different reasons: Of course, it's good for my health but it's also easier to see the city and countrysides of the places we travel too. But there's another reason why I run and its really the most important; I tend to hear the Lord's voice when I'm outdoors.

It was on this African excursion that I rolled out of bed one morning and slid on my sneakers to go away for an early run. I began to go along the beautiful bay that day and suddenly, God gave me a vision of a man carrying a torch. I'll never forget it. It was a picture of a man on fire carrying the fire of the Hoy Spirit. I said with my whole being, *"God, I want to be that man."* A man of fire! A man running with a torch to touch the nations with the power of God. This vision has never left me and it has been fulfilled over and over again over the years.

In fact, this is why we chose to create the Running Man Logo for Chance Walters Ministries. It's a picture of the people of God going from here to there across the globe carrying the Good News of the Gospel of Jesus Christ. As the church, *"We exist to Spark Revival Worldwide!"*

Someone ask John Wesley one day, *"How do you attract such large crowds at your meetings?"* He answered, *"I just set myself on fire and people come to watch me burn!"* Let's pick up the victory torch today and burn ever so brightly for the world to see. Take up the torch and go touch somebody with the fire of God. I encourage you, keep running and keep burning! Why? Because Jesus is running with you and He's coming back soon!

Step to Start Strong:

Keep Running & Keep Burning.

APRIL 21.

Holy Habits

"This has become mine, That I observe Your precepts."

Psalm 119:56

Aristotle said, "We *are what we repeatedly do. Therefore, excellence is not an act but a habit."* It has been taught, if you want to form a healthy habit, do that very thing over and over again for 21 days. Daily disciplines determine the reality of your destiny.

What does your daily routine look like? Most of us march to the rhythm of a beat all day every day. Think about the things you do everyday.

What we do is who we are.

Whether you know it or not, you are a leader. The question is what direction are you leading people? With this in mind, may we make sure we are leading people in the right direction and of course, in the right way. A recent study suggest that even the most introverted individuals influence at least 20,000 people in their lifetime meaning your life has great influence. According to John Maxwell, this is the definition of a leader; influence.

Who are you influencing and who is influencing you?

John Maxwell says, *"A leader is one who knows the way, goes the way, and shows the way."*

<u>Step to Start Strong:</u>

Lead others Well

APRIL 22.

The Gender Reveal

"So God created man in His own image; in the image of God He created him; male and female...

Genesis 1:27

Is God male or female? This is a great theological question. Remember, the Bible should always interpret the Bible. So, God gives us some insight into this question in Galatians 3:28. It says, *"There is neither Jew nor Greek, slave nor free, nor male or female; for you are all one in Christ Jesus."* Jesus became a Jewish man by His own free will when He came to earth but in His glorified body, He is God Almighty. God is a spirit who has eternal attributes of both male and female. God has no gender, race or social class. God is God and He is everything to everyone who believes in His supremacy and sovereignty.

As for us, things are slightly different. We are created in His image just as He designed us to be. At this moment, Kacie and I are at the halfway mark of having our second child. Tuesday afternoon, we had our third doctor's appointment to discover the gender of our child. The first two appointments were unsuccessful as the baby refused to uncross its legs for the reveal. We prayed and thought we would go back one more time to see if we could get a clear picture of the anatomy. With great anticipation, we have been celebrating the future birth of another beautiful baby girl. Yes! We are having another Baby GIRL! Victory will be a big sister and daddy will be smitten for a second time. We are happy and mama is healthy. What else could we ask for? God chooses the gender of a child. According to His will, He creates children in His own image (Psalm 139).

Step to Start Strong:

Be Fruitful & Multiply

APRIL 23.

THE PRINCIPLE OF MULTIPLICATION

"Then God blessed them, and said, "Be fruitful and multiply; fill the earth and subdue it."

Genesis 1:28

These were the first words human ears had ever heard in the earth from their Heavenly Father. God said, *"I bless you! Be fruitful and multiply!"* There's something in the scripture called, The Law of First Mention. The first time a word is mentioned lays a foundation for how God will use it later within the content and context of a book. This Bible study tool is used as a key to help you understand and unlock some of the deep things of God.

Consequently, in the mathematical world, addition is beneficial but multiplication is better. You can increase with both, but in the spirit, *2 is always better than 1.* When Jesus fed the 5,000 with 5 loaves of bread and two fish, the Bible says, *"Jesus lifted up the substance and asked God to bless it."* If you're going to have a ministry of multiplication, you must give what you have to God and ask Him to bless it. Once Jesus blessed the bread, He gave it back to His disciples and they willingly and generously gave it to those who were in need. Notice, the bread didn't multiply in God's hands but it multiplied in their hands. The miracle manifested as they let go of what God blessed them with. You and I have been blessed to be a blessing. We have freely received, therefore we should freely give.

Proverbs 11:24 says, *"One person gives freely, yet gains even more; another withholds grudgingly but comes to poverty."*

How is this so? Because God is the one who brings the increase! We operate on His terms and on His timeline. We can give freely and we can do it cheerfully. We can trust our substance in the hands of an all-sufficient Savior. *"If you cast your bread upon the water, in many days it will come back to you."* (Ecclesiastes 11:1) It's called a miracle. It's called multiplication.

God, I pray you would multiply our ministry in the mighty name of Jesus. May we be able to do more with less! So I ask you, *Bless this week with your bounty, in Jesus Name!*

Step to Start Strong:

Give God your Best

APRIL 24.

The Greatest of All-Time

"Blessed are the poor in spirit, for theirs is the kingdom of heaven."

Matthew 5:3

After a 32-year battle with Parkinson's disease, Muhammad Ali passed away at the age of 74 on Friday, June 3rd. This 3-Time World Heavyweight Champion boxer impacted the world in a profound way. He left us with so many memorable moments, quotes and stories.

One of my favorites is a story about Ali flying on an airplane. As the plane ascended into the skies the pilot directed everyone to remain seated with their seat-belts buckled because of the strong turbulence. The stewardess came down the aisle to make sure everyone was in compliance with the captain and she soon noticed the Big Boxer was still unbuckled. She asked him politely to buckle his seat-belt and he angrily answered, *"Superman doesn't need a seatbelt!"* Without skipping a beat she firmly fired back, *"You're right and Superman didn't need an airplane either."* I need you to buckle up now sir!

Muhammed Ali was named Cassius Clay at birth but He renounced this label when he converted to Islam at 22 years of age. He considered it his *"slave name"* and said from this point forward he would be called Muhammad Ali. He adopted this name from the founder of Islam, Elijah Muhammad.

He declared, dozens and dozens of times, that He was The Greatest of All-Time and He was certainly great but not the greatest of all-time. If He could speak to us today, I believe He would say, *"Great is the Lord and may His name be greatly praised!"* (Psalm 145:3) Muhammed met his maker and if his biography describes the reality of his heart, it was a rude awakening. Death has a way of waking up even with strongest willed individuals. The Bible says, *"It is appointed unto man once to die and then the judgment."* Indeed, the death rate is one per person.

The scripture goes on to say, *"Every knee shall bow and every tongue shall confess that Jesus Christ is Lord."* It's either bow now or bow later. Let's bow our hearts in humble adoration to God today. He is the Greatest of All-Time and He always will be no matter how great we think we are.

Step to Start Strong:

Humble our Hearts to Him

APRIL 25.

THE CHRISTIAN CRISIS

"This is why it is said: 'Wake up, sleeper, rise from the dead, and Christ will shine on you."

Ephesians 5:18

Crisis has historically led so many people to cry out for more of God. What is a crisis? It could be anything from a global tragedy to a personal disaster. However, for me personally, this drive I am trying to describe comes from the gaping chasm between personal reality and scriptural reality. What we see and experience on a daily basis and what is Biblically available are two different things. Throughout the ages, their have been those who refused to conform to the status quo of what was normal and visible and what was commonly understood. The exploits and examples date back to the early disciples. The persecution they experienced broken them out of the religious system of their day. Many men and women have paid the price for us to have the history and understanding of scripture that we have as a church.

This crisis of faith pushed them past lukewarm Christianity and catapulted them into a dangerous depth of an unknown spirituality. This crisis is not dangerous because it is heretical or unscriptural, it is dangerous because it challenges the way things have always been done. This type of crisis challenges the people who have grown cold and comfortable in their Christian faith. However, God will use those who have laid their whole life on the altar of God. In fact, in these last days, God is raising up reformational voices in the earth who are hungry and thirsty for more of God. Do you believe there is more to experience in your relationship with God? Do you believe there are facets of faith you have not tapped into? If so, I pray you would begin to put feet to your faith and begin to believe in the Supernatural God of the Bible. By doing this, nothing will be impossible for you and me.

I can almost hear the voice of the Lord right now saying, *"Awake O' Sleeper and rise from dead and Christ will shine upon you!"* Let's begin to call forth the visible realities of Heaven to confront the unbiblical realities on earth. We need a mighty move of God in America to defeat the present principalities of darkness. I believe our best days are ahead as the Bride of Jesus Christ. May His Kingdom come and may His will be done today! If you believe it shout, "Amen!"

May this Christian Crisis be a Catalyst to Call many to the Cross of Jesus Christ!

Step to Start Strong:

Don't conform. Be transformed.

APRIL 26.

The 4th Dimension

"The God who gives life to the dead and calls those things which do not exist as if they did."

Romans 4:17

Believe it or not, there is a 4th Dimension in the world we live in. It is the spiritual world in which we cannot see with our natural eyes of understanding. There is a God and there are celestial beings who work behind the scenes to govern the supernatural world. Our goal as Christians is to understand that what we see temporarily doesn't have to be the end of the story.

Early this morning, I was reminded of the early days of Dr. Yonggi Cho, the Pastor of Prayer Mountain in Seoul, South Korea. When He planted his church and began his ministry in 1958, he only had 5 people in his congregation as they gathered in a pop-up tent at the edge of town every Sunday morning. The story goes on to say, He prayed around 5 hours a day, not because he was super spiritual but because he didn't have anything else to do. One day during his prayer time, he closed his eyes and God gave him a vision of 3,000 people in his church pews. He opened his eyes, obviously shaken by the revelation and wondered what it would be like to pastor so many people. It was in this moment that Dr. Cho became pregnant with a vision of reaching thousands of people in South Korea.

The following Sunday He preached to the 5 people in his congregation as if he were preaching to 3,000. Afterwards, the people said, *"Why did you shout today and speak so passionately?"* Why? Because He was pregnant with a vision! From this point forward, *"He called the things that were not as if they were."* The story says, He would close his eyes and preach as if he were preaching to thousands of people. He was tapping into the 4th Dimension. He didn't place his faith in something he could see, touch, taste or hear. He placed his faith in the Holy Spirit and the seed that was planted in his soul during his time of prayer.

Today, Dr. Yonggi Cho has the largest church in the world with over a million in his congregation. How did he do it? He started callings the things that were not as if they were. He spoke to the 5 as if they were 5,000 and the 5,000 as if they were 500,000. When he began to do this, He was tapping into the 4th Dimensional World and His words ultimately developed His world.

What you see shouldn't determine what you believe. What you believe should determine what you see. Begin to confess what you see in the spirit and you will see God move in a mighty way. I pray you have a 4th Dimensional Day in Jesus name!

Step to Start Strong:

Pray until you get Pregnant with Vision.

APRIL 27.

RISEN

"He is not here. He has RISEN! Come and see the place where He lay."

Matthew 28:6

We just got around to watching the 2016 Easter release of the movie Risen. It's a must-see for the 21st century church. Any opportunity to see a reenactment of the scripture is certainly a night well spent. This particular movie portrays a different vantage point from the common Gospel accounts. It gives us the angle of the unbeliever in Jesus' day. This perspective is important if we are going to reach those who seem to be unreachable.

Proverbs 11:30 says, *"He who wins souls is wise."* If we are going to be effective in winning the lost, we need a healthy dose of wisdom to do so. How do they think? What do they believe? How were they raised? All these are valid questions we need to ask ourselves when approaching a lost person. When we know their perspective, we can speak more pertinent to their problems.

My second thought while watching this movie was most people need to see the proof of God's power before they place their life in His hands. Thats why the Apostle Paul said, "*My message and my preaching were not with wise and persuasive words, but with a demonstration of the Spirit's power, so that your faith might not rest on human wisdom, but on God's power alone.*"

Where's the proof? The proof is in the church. You are the Trophy of God's Grace and you are the proof of God's power. To reiterate this point, one of the soldiers made this statement at the end of the movie; *"I have seen 2 things that I cannot reconcile: A dead man without question and that same man alive again."* Without a doubt, it is my life-changing belief that Jesus Christ is alive. In fact, the greatest miracle anyone could ever receive is the miracle of salvation! When this occurs, the same power that raised Jesus from the dead lives comes on the inside of you. (Romans 8:11) This is why, you are the proof of His power! Since He lives, you will live too! May the Church ARISE and be what God intended it to be; proof of His power!

Step to Start Strong:

Rise up & Be Living Proof of God's Power!

APRIL 28.

PAGE 23 VISION

"Where there is no vision, the people perish."

Proverbs 29:18

It was a night I'll never forget as I watched people from every nation, tribe and tongue touch Heaven with the passion of their prayers. Yes, it was a Tuesday Night Prayer Meeting and the place was packed with 1,000's of people from around the world. Who goes to church on a week night just to pray anyway? The Brooklyn Tabernacle Church in New York does that's who:) Our mission team had always heard about the Famous Brooklyn Tabernacle Choir so we thought we would stop by to see what their church was all about. Well, it didn't take us long to figure things out. We soon discovered the Tuesday Night Prayer Meeting released the power to move that music ministry around the world. As a church, we already know this but why don't we do this: *Why don't we give the best hours of our day in prayer.?*

When we returned to North Carolina, I was intrigued with this ministry so I bought the book, *"Fresh Wind, Fresh Fire."* A best seller and great read that tells the history about how this church got started. If you want to know more, buy the book because all I want to do is tell you about what's on page 23.

Jim Cymbala, the Senior Pastor, made a statement on page 23 that drives me even today. In the early days, this small struggling church used to meet on Sunday nights with a few people to pray. One particular night, the Holy Spirit moved in an unprecedented way and shook Pastor Jim deep in his spirit. It was in this moment that he said these words with all of his heart and I call it, *"The Page 23 Vision."* He said, "I despaired at the thought that my life might slip by without seeing God show himself mightily on our behalf." You may want to marinate on the full meaning of this thought. Don't miss it this morning. He said and we should agree, "*I despaired at the thought that our lives might slip by without seeing God show himself mightily on our behalf.*" My thought is, we all experience despair on different days but the greatest despair is the thought of missing out on all the power, presence and provision God has in store for us as a church. I don't know about you but my prayer for the past few years has been, *"God, help me to not miss it and help me not to mess it up!"* Let's begin to pray until God gives us a clear vision and then let's keep praying so we can accomplish it. If we do these two things with all diligence, God will be mighty in our midst. My prayer is that God would send us a Fresh Wind and a Fresh Fire in our church services this year. Let's refuse to let our lives slip by without seeing God show Himself mightily on our behalf! May God bless you with a Page 23 Vision.

Step to Start Strong:

Don't let your Life Slip you By

APRIL 29.

A Fixed Rate

"*Fix your* eyes on Jesus, the author and the perfecter of your faith."

Hebrews 12:2

A fixed interest rate loan is a loan where the interest rate doesn't fluctuate during the period of the fixed rate. This allows the borrower to accurately predict their future payments on their new home. By fixing the rate, the payments remain the same. This reminds me of God's way of doing things.

The word "Fix" in Hebrews 12:2 means, *"a continual gaze."* As mature believer's, we should never take our eyes off Jesus. This is true because our eyes are the gateway to our soul's satisfaction.

This principle reminds me of the story when Simon Peter walked on water one day. His venture was a great success until he shifted his focus from the word to the waves. (Matthew 14:30) Jesus beckoned Him to get out of the boat with the comfortable christians and walk on water. What a miracle! Jesus said, *"Come"* and he literally walked on the word. However, somewhere in the story, he took his eyes off of His Savior and placed them on the storm. This principle proves a powerful point:

"The key to conquering any circumstance or situation is the ongoing ability to keep your eyes off of your surroundings and on your Savior." The waves of the world are constantly crashing against our dreams and destinies. If we are going to fulfill the call of God upon our personal and cooperate lives, we are going to need the courage to not only take the first step but to discipline ourselves to keep our eyes on God. If we adopt these two principles, our faith will not fail and fear will always be under our feet. Let's call out for courage today and most importantly, let's fix our eyes on Jesus the author and the perfecter of our faith. I feel confident in this very thing, that He who began a good work in you will bring it to completion on the day of Jesus Christ.

Step to Start Strong:

Fix your Eyes on Jesus

APRIL 30.

A PRAYER PARTNER

"I thank my God every time I think of you, offering every prayer of mine with joy [and with specific requests] for all of you, [thanking God] for your participation and partnership [both your comforting fellowship and gracious contributions] in [advancing] the good news [regarding salvation] from the first day until now."

Philippians 1:3-5

If I desire more insight on a particular passage of scripture, I always go to the Amplified Version of the Bible. It has a way of opening my eyes and broadening my perspective to see what God is saying a bit more clearly. Many people argue and debate over what version of the Bible to use but my answer is always this: *"Just use the one you read the most."* Amen? So, let's look at this passage: The Apostle Paul was thanking God for his partners in the Gospel. *What exactly is a partner?* A parter is someone who takes part in the undertaking of any endeavor. For our sake, we are partaking in the Father's Business which is establishing The Kingdom of God on the earth by way of evangelism and discipleship. If you are a born-again believer, you are a part of the body of Christ & *"you"* have a *"part"* to play, no matter how big or how small you think it is. 1st Corinthians 12:27 says, *"Now you are the body of Christ, and each one of you are a part of it."*

One of the easiest ways to partner with us at Chance Walters Ministries is to pray. When we pioneered this ministry almost 3 years ago, God spoke to me very clearly and said for us, *"To pray for our partners everyday."* By my conviction, I've done my best to pray for every one of you who play a part in our ministries success. How do I do this? I simply say repetitiously, *"God bless all of our ministry partners."* You told Abraham in Genesis 12, that you would bless those who bless us and we have been blessed beyond measure so by faith I ask you to bless all our partners in Jesus Name! At this time, God will place certain faces in my spirit and I will call out your name and needs if I know them. Whenever you mail in a seed offering, I will sit in my car outside the post office and prayer a blessing over your sacrifice before I pull away. *Why do I do this?* Because we believe in the Power of Partnership. When we both play our part with all of our hearts, there is a special blessing that is released into the Body of Christ. Unity is the understanding that we need one another to have maximized success. The Apostle Paul understood this principle and this verse conveys a clear message. In order for the Good News to go forward, we must stand together. (Psalm 133) So, let's pause for 60 seconds today and pray for one another. Prayers cross geographical divides. We can unify ourselves in the spirit today by simply believing by faith. We become partners when we pray for one another. We all have a part to play. Let's pray!

Step to Start Strong:

Find a Prayer Partner

MAY 1.

The Joy of the Lord!

"Though you have not seen him, you love him; and even though you do not see him now, you believe in him and you are filled with joy unspeakable and full of Glory. For you are receiving, the end result of your faith."

1st Peter 1:8-9

"Joy is the settled assurance that God is in control of all the details of your life, the quiet confidence that everything is going to be all right, and the courageous choice to praise God in every circumstance."

Do you have a reason to rejoice this morning?

Luke 10:20 says, *"Rejoice, for your name is written in the Lamb's Book of Life."* If you're saved, you should take a praise break everyday and thank God for His forgiveness and grace in your life.

Why? Because your daily celebration is a demonstration of your revelation.

2nd Chronicles 20:15 says, *"The Battle is not yours, it belongs to the Lord!"*

Say this with me: *"The Battle belongs to the Lord and the Victory belongs to me."*

God's fights the war for your when you faithfully worship and obey His word.

The Notable Author & Poet, C.S. Lewis said, *"Joy is the serious business of God."*

Do you want to take care of some serious business?
Love, Laugh, and Live a Little.
Enjoy everyday.
It's really hard to endure something you don't enjoy.
So, no matter what you're facing today,
Ask God to fill your cup with the Fruit of JOY!
1st Peter 1:8 says, *"That this Joy is full of Glory!"*
Do you want to experience the Glory of God?
When you enjoy Jesus on an everyday basis, it releases you into another Realm of the Spirit.

Practice what the Apostle Paul preached: He said, "*Rejoice in the Lord always! Again I say, Rejoice!*" (Phil 4:4)

<u>Step to Start Strong</u>:

Fix your Eyes on Jesus

MAY 2.

FATHER'S DAY!

"The godly walk with integrity; Blessed are their children who follow them."

Proverbs 20:7

In the last 20 years there has been a 550% increase in violent crimes, 400% increase in illegitimate births, 2000% increase in teen pregnancy, 300% increase in teen suicide. And listen to this; 70% of the people in jail come from fatherless homes! Yes, 70% of the prisoners in the United States grew up with an absentee father, and 79% of people addicted to drugs came from a fatherless home! These statistics are astonishing.

In the beginning, God created marriage between male and female and this covenantal relationship was never intended to be broken. Sadly, the divorce rate in America is over 50%. To take it a step further, it's the same in the church as it is outside the church. This should not be so. This issue alone is the reason for so many of our struggles. In fact, many call the Millennial's, the Fatherless Generation. So, what does this have to do with Father's Day? Everything.

During the three years of Jesus' earthly ministry, His Father spoke to Him from Heaven three times. On the day He was baptized, on the Mount of Transfiguration and the day before He was crucified. All three times, His Father spoke words of affirmation and approval. These words permeated His soul and proved two things: *The Father's Love and The Father's Presence.* This is what children need the most.

Therefore, to all the Father's who have loved their families unconditionally over the years, we want to say thank you for defying the odds. You are making a difference in the world but more importantly, you are making a difference in your family. Keep fighting the good fight of faith! It will be worth it all in the end.

I can almost hear the words of your Heavenly Father this morning saying, "*Well done, thy good and thy faithful servant.*"

<u>Step to Start Strong</u>:

Be Faithful to your Family

MAY 3.

THE RIGHT TOUCH

"A large crowd followed and pressed around him. And a woman was there who had been subject to bleeding for twelve years. She had suffered a great deal under the care of many doctors and had spent all she had, yet instead of getting better she grew worse. When she heard about Jesus, she came up behind him in the crowd and touched his cloak, because she thought, "If I just touch his clothes, I will be healed." Immediately her bleeding stopped and she felt in her body that she was freed from her suffering.

Mark 5:25-34

At once Jesus realized that power had gone out from him. He turned around in the crowd and asked, *"Who touched my clothes?" "You see the people crowding against you,"* his disciples answered, *and yet you can ask, 'Who touched me?'* But Jesus kept looking around to see who it was. Then the woman, knowing what had happened to her, came and fell at his feet and, trembling with fear and told him the whole truth. He said to her, *"Daughter, your faith has healed you. Go in peace and be freed from your suffering."*

The elements of seeing something supernatural captivates you and takes you to place of curiosity where you live and long to see it again. For this purpose, the people followed the Son of God to see His power.

The crowds pushed and pried just to touch Jesus and to be by His side. In fact, there were 3three types of touches. There were people who followed Him because He was famous. There were others who bumped into Him accidentally because there was so many people surrounding him. But lastly, there were a few who touched him because if they didn't they were going to die. This type of touch apprehended the attention of God. So it was for this woman who had been hemorrhaging for 12 years. She risked her life to get to Jesus. According to the Law, she was considered unclean for her condition but she didn't care if they stoned her in the public square. She knew if she could just touch the hem of His garments, she would be freed from her suffering. This is the type of faith that moves mountains.

Step to Start Strong:

Reach out and Touch Him by Faith.

MAY 4.

SEED-TIME & HARVEST

"As long as the earth endures, seedtime and harvest, cold and heat, summer and winter, day and night will never cease."

Genesis 8:22

On Father's Day afternoon, we drove down to my parents house for dinner and dessert. Before we ate, my dad walked me around the house to show me how good his garden was doing. This year He planted watermelon, squash, lettuce and potatoes just to name a few. However, when we got to the tomato plants, he shared an interesting story.

A family in Siler City has a long-line of tomato seeds that they have been passing down for over 100 years. The tomatoes were so healthy and hearty, the ancestors would keep the seeds and sow them year after year because the harvest was so appetizing. Recently, my dad was given some of the seeds so He planted them hoping for the same result.

Think with me: The Bible says, *"As long as the earth endures; seed, time and harvest will never cease."* On the day of Pentecost, the seed of the Holy Spirit was planted into 120 people in the Upper Room. These men and women have literally turned the world upside down. (Acts 17:6) There are more Christians in the world today than any other time in the history. Even today, the Kingdom of Heaven is still suffering violence but the violent are taking it by force! (Matt. 11:12) This is the Good News!

Christianity is the fastest growing religion in the world! In fact, its Harvest Time ladies and gentlemen! The hearts of mankind have been plowed with pain and persecution, the seeds of the Holy Spirit have been past down throughout all generations, therefore, all we have to do is swing the sickle which is the Word of God! Indeed, we are in the Last Days and the Time is Now to Reap the Rewards of Righteousness.

Here's the Key: *"Everything you do in life is like sowing seed."* All day, everyday you are planting seeds in the souls of mankind. Your words and your worship. Your gratitude and good deeds. Your smile and service. All these things are considered seeds! I don't know about you but I want to leave a generational blessing behind for my family and ministry. Just like The Family in Siler City.

Its Harvest-Time!

Step to Start Strong:

Go Sow some Seed

MAY 5.

The Key to Overcoming Temptation

"Then Jesus was led by the Spirit into the wilderness to be tempted by the devil. After fasting forty days and forty nights, he was hungry. The tempter came to him and said, "If you are the Son of God, tell these stones to become bread." Jesus answered, "It is written: 'Man shall not live on bread alone, but on every word that comes from the mouth of God."

Matthew 4:1-11

If Jesus was tempted by the devil, you can assure yourself, He's going to tempt you too. The essence of temptation is someone trying to fulfill their own desires. James 1:14 says, *"But each person is tempted when they are dragged away by their own evil desire and enticed by the devil."* By doing this, you become the leader of your own life instead of depending upon and following the will of the Lord. The spiritual attack exemplified in this Temptation of Christ reveals to us the 3 major categories of temptation. Jesus was enticed by the enemy in the area of provision, the area of protection and the area of power. All of Satan's tricks and schemes fall under these 3 categories. So how do we overcome temptation? Well, let's look at the life of Jesus: Jesus was tempted in every area in life yet He was without sin. *How did He pass the test?*

In this story, we hear Jesus repeating these 3 words every time He was tempted, He said, *"It is written! It is written! It is written!"* This proves a powerful point: *The Word of God is our Greatest Weapon of Warfare!* If it was good enough for Jesus, its good enough of me! This shows us the importance of studying to show ourselves approved.

Lastly, let's look at the enemy's approach. Satan loves to use seeds of doubt to lure us away from dependency upon God. *"IF"* is His favorite word. He will whisper lies to you. He will say, *"If you are a son or a daughter of God? If you are saved? If it's not too late?"* All these questions leave us questioning God? In the beginning, Satan played the doubt card to Eve, *"Did God really say?"* These fiery darts of doubt are aimed to distract us from who God is and who we are in Christ. Ultimately, The enemy is attacking our identity. Again, this shows us the importance of becoming one with the Bible. James says, *"The Bible is like a mirror."* It shows us who we are and it shows us who we are not. Sadly, many christians are suffering from an Identity Crisis. They know who He is but they don't know who they are. How do get help? Open your mouth and say, It is Written! The word really does work! This is the Key to "Overcome Temptation."

Step to Start Strong:

Quote the Word

MAY 6.

THE TURN-AROUND ANOINTING

"And Elisha the prophet called one of the sons of the prophets, and said to him, "Get yourself ready, take this flask of oil in your hand, and go to Ramoth Gilead. 2 Now when you arrive at that place, look there for Jehu the son of Jehoshaphat, the son of Nimshi, and go in and make him rise up from among his associates, and take him to an inner room. 3 Then take the flask of oil, and pour it on his head, and say, 'Thus says the Lord: "I have anointed you king over Israel."

<u>2nd Kings 9:1-3</u>

Lucifer was the Choir Director of Heaven. You can read his life story in Isaiah 14 and Ezekiel 36. The scripture says, *"He was the anointed cherub."* He led all the Angels in worship. He was perfect in beauty and blameless in all of his ways until sin entered his heart one day. Pride caused him to lose his position, power and prestige. He was cast out of Heaven for everyone to see.

It's interesting to read how 1/3 of the angels turned from worshipping God to follow Satan. This explains how people get drunk on deception and end up in dire situations. He makes people think that what they are doing is ok until its too late. The anointing he carries is counterfeit. He tries to turn people around from following after the one true God.

The story in 2nd Kings gives us a clear picture of this anointing. Jehu received a word from the prophet that he was going to be the next King over Israel. All he had was a word from the Lord and the anointing of the Holy Spirit and let me say this is all you need.

After the anointing was applied upon his life in private, God began to move in his public life. This anointing caused 5 people to Turn Around in this story. (2nd Kings 9:1-35) However, every time Jehu took a step of faith, the enemy sent a wave of opposition to try and turn him around. But Here's the Good News: *"Greater is He that lives in me than He that lives in the world!"* Instead of the enemy turning Jehu around, He turned the enemy around! How did he do it? By believing the word of the Lord and depending upon Holy Spirit to do what He said He was going to do. In fact, the anointing of the Holy Spirit makes all the difference.

Let's spend some time in the inner chambers away from the world this year. What we do in private is more important than what we do in public. It's in this place that He pours His oil on us. Everyone wants a powerful anointing but not everyone wants to pay the price for it. May we crucify the flesh and consecrate ourselves from the counterfeit today. There is something called, The Turn Around Anointing!

Step to Start Strong:

Consecrate yourself from the Counterfeit

MAY 7.

The Apple of His Eye

"In a desert land he found him, in a barren and howling waste. He circled him and cared for him; he guarded him as the apple of His eye."

Deuteronomy 32:10

You are the Apple of God's eye. He knows your name and He knows your pain. In fact, He knows you better than you know yourself. He is familiar with all of your ways. Before a word is on your tongue, He already knows what it will be. Such information is too lofty for me to fathom but not for God. He is omniscient. He knows *"everything."* Yes, Everything!

Think about this for a moment: God has His eye on you. This principle should bring us perfect peace. *"While we were yet sinners, Christ died for us."* He knew we were going to fail before we failed but yet and still He sent His Son to die for us. This is why they call it amazing grace! His eye has been you since the beginning when you took your first breath.

The scripture of the day describes God's heart toward mankind. God found us, He circled around us, He cared for us and He guarded us as *The Apple of His Eye*. We are the centerpiece of all creation. He has His eye on you. The question is: *"Are your eyes on Him?"*

2 Chronicles 16:9 says, *"The eyes of the Lord search the whole earth to strengthen those who are fully committed unto Him."*

Do you need strength today?

You can commit yourself to Him because He is fully committed to you.

May we *"Keep Him as the Apple of our Eye."* (Psalm 17:5)

I believe an Apple a day will keep the devil away.

Step to Start Strong:

Keep Christ in the Center

MAY 8.

The "U" in Church

"And let us not neglect our meeting together, as some people do, but encourage one another, especially now that the day of his return is drawing near."

Hebrews 10:25

Church is not a church without "U." If you are not apart of the church the church is missing something valuable. The word *"church"* literally means the *"called out ones."* When Jesus called you out of the crowd, He set you apart with other people called the church. The church is not a place, it's a people. Jesus said, *"Where two or three are gathered in my name, there I AM in the mist of them."* The church doors are open when people open their hearts in fellowship with one another. Sunday, is not the only day we can go to church but its a day set aside in our culture where many go to church.

The scripture says, *"Therefore, let us not neglect our meeting together as some people do but let us encourage one another especially now that the day of his return is drawing near."* The purpose of church is to encourage one another. Do you need encouragement today? If so, "U" should go to church. It's the birthplace of the blessing. How do we know? A man by the name of Jacob encountered God in Genesis 28 where He saw a stairway leading up to Heaven with angels ascending and descending upon it. When He woke up, He named the place Bethel meaning, *"House of God."* I believe when we worship with other believers we create an atmosphere where angels can move about freely to bring the blessing. Here's where we get the phrase, *"The praises go up and blessings come down."* In fact, today is a great day to worship God! Who knows He may relent and leave behind a blessing? We'll never know until we go!

Let's put the "U" in its proper place today so the church can be all God intended it to be.

Step to Start Strong:

Fellowship with other Believers

MAY 9.

Ask, Seek & Knock

"Jesus said to them, 'Suppose you have a friend, and you go to him at midnight and say, 'Friend, lend me three loaves of bread; a friend of mine on a journey has come to me, and I have no food to offer him. And suppose the one inside answers, 'Don't bother me. The door is already locked, and my children and I are in bed. I can't get up and give you anything. I tell you, even though he will not get up and give you the bread because of friendship, because of your boldness, he will eventually get up and give you as much as you need."

Luke 11:5-8

This passage is speaking about persistence in prayer. How many times do people stand in need without kneeling in prayer? The Bible says, *"When you pray say!"* (Matthew 6:9) Your faith is activated when you speak what's in your spirit. Hebrews 10:6 says, *"Faith cometh by hearing and hearing the word of God."* We have to take what's in our spirit and speak it into existence. *How do we do this?*

Well, Jesus tells us a short story about a man in need of some bread. In the mist of his need, he goes to a friend in the midnight hour who neglects to help him. However, the Lord gives us a key to unlock the door of provision; It's called persistence.

This man had the option to quit, feel sorry for himself or make an excuse. But what did he do? Despite receiving the alternate answer, he kept knocking on the door with boldness. The greek word boldness means, *"shameless persistence."* This key turned His friends heart and eventually, he changed his mind and gave him as much as he needed.

Let me say this: we have a friend in Jesus and we all stand in need of something this morning. The distinguishing mark that makes a man or breaks a man is the ability to stay persistent in dire situations.

This man was waking up His neighbors in the middle of the night because He was desperate. Many times, we keep our need to ourselves because we don't want to bother anybody else. By doing this, we miss out on the bread that God wants to put on the table. If it matters to you, it matters to God. "*Let us go to His throne of grace with boldness so that we can receive mercy to help us in our time of need.*"

What do you need God to do for you this week? Whatever it is, open your mouth right now and ask Him with you whole heart to do a miracle. "*We have not because we ask not.*" If you don't have something you need, it may be because you haven't asked. Let's be persistent in prayer.

Step to Start Strong:

Ask, Seek and Knock

MAY 10.

Now Faith Is...

"Now faith is confidence for what we hope for and the assurance of what we do not see."

Hebrews 11:1

The word faith is very familiar in Christian circles. What does it mean? Hebrews 11:1 makes it real clear: *"Now, Faith is confidence for what we hope for and the assurance of what we do not see."* When you come to Christ, you have to come by faith. There's no other way. We are saved by grace through faith and it is a gift from God. (Eph. 2:8) Even though you do not see God, you love God and even though you do not see God you believe in God by faith. (1st Peter 1:8) If you are a child of God you have been given a measure of faith. (Romans 12:3) As you grow in your relationship with God, His righteousness is revealed to you from faith to faith. (Romans 1:17) The same faith that saved me years ago is the same faith that is keeping me today and my hope is that it will continue to grow even till the end.

So how do you grow in faith? Its simple. You grow in faith by applying Biblical principles in your everyday life. When you apply the word, God proves to you that the word really does work! Therefore, the fruit of faith always leads to a deeper dependence upon God. If God did it once, He can do it again.

We've learned a lot about faith in full-time evangelistic ministry. Back in the beginning, God made it real easy for me to understand. I don't know about you but I tend to over complicate things. I can rationalize my way right out of a spiritual blessing. So, God spoke one word to me so I wouldn't get confused. He just said, *"GO!"* That's it, *Just GO!* I said, *"Yes sir"* and we have been walking by faith ever since. He's taught us so much about living a life of faith.

Faith says, it not what you see, it's what God said. If you can see it, it's not faith. Faith sees something that other people cannot see. Faith sees into the spirit.

Can I ask you a question? What do you see today? Do you see pain or promises? Do you see burden or breakthrough? Do you see opposition or opportunity? It all boils down to this one word: FAITH.

Do you desire more faith? *"Faith comes by hearing and hearing the word of God."* Whose words are you listening to today? This is the answer if you want to grow from faith to faith and glory to glory. Faith is always NOW! Let's have a Faith-Filled Day in Jesus Name!

Step to Start Strong:

Fuel your Faith

MAY 11.

A Limited Time Only

"According to your faith may it be unto you."

Matthew 9:29

What if God has limited His unlimited powers on the earth according to our faith? I think so. This is deep but it's worth discussing.

Since the beginning, God has chosen to use man as a conduit of His power to accomplish His kingdom purposes. God is all-sufficient meaning He doesn't need you and I to be sustained. In His supremacy, He can do anything at anytime but in his sovereignty, He has made up His mind to use the hands of man on the earth. But even this is for a limited time only.

Think with me: If God has the power, all we need is faith. Faith is the economy of Heaven. What if I pulled up into the convenience store to pump some gas to get me down the road but didn't have any money? How many of you know I wouldn't get very far! It's the same way in our spiritual life. When we approach the spiritual filling station, we need faith if we want to receive anything from the God. Without faith, it is impossible to please God. However, through faith in the finished work of Jesus Christ, we have access to every spiritual blessing in the heavenly places. Faith is the invisible substance that authorizes a divine transaction.

Many times when we read about the miracles in the life of Jesus, we see these words, *"According to your faith may it be unto you."* What did he mean? Jesus is teaching us that He is willing if we will believe what He said. The scripture says, *"Nothing is possible if a person believes."* We know that nothing is possible with God and we know that all power and authority is in His hand but what we fail to see is the second part of the verse, *"if a person believes."* Yes, *Anything is possible if you believe*. This is the key: Do you believe? Do you really believe the Word of God? If so, nothing is possible for you. According to your faith may it be done to you.

Rod Parsley said, *"The atmosphere of expectancy is the breeding ground for miracles."* Faith mixed with expectation is a powerful combination! Let's rely on the power of the Holy Spirit today. *This opportunity is For a Limited Time Only*. Jesus is coming back real soon.

Step to Start Strong:

Mix your Faith with Expectation

MAY 12.

THE PROCEEDING WORD

"It is written, Man shall not live by bread alone but by every word that proceeds out of the mouth of God."

Mathew 4:4

In the English language, some of our words are similar in sound but different in context. For instance, the word precede means *"to go before"* but the word proceed means *"to go after."* In this verse, God says, we should live by both: The preceding word and The proceeding word.

What is the preceding word: The preceding word is the written word of God. God spoke it and they wrote it; Forty authors over a period of 1,500 years to be exact. The Holy Bible contains 66 books, 1,899 chapters and 31,103 verses. That's a mouth full of words, literally. The Bible is the Best-selling book in the history of the world and as believers, we know why. It's the bread that Jesus said, *no one should live without!* Why? Because The Word of God strengthens us spiritually and builds us up emotionally and better rest, it has the power to save our souls. *"If you want to hear the preceding word of God on a daily basis, all you have to do is open God's mouth."* His mouthpiece is His manuscript by which we call the Bible.

But what about the proceeding word? The proceeding word is a word that God is speaks into your spirit. One is the written word and the other is the spoken word. The second is equally important than the first. Its imperative that we ask ourselves this question everyday: *What is God saying to me today? In this moment? What does He want me to do today? In this hour?*

If we neglect the proceeding word, we can sink into complacency and cause ourselves to grow cold spiritually. We need to read but we also need the word that proceeds from the mouth of God today. This is the fresh manna God was talking about that falls from Heavens to the doorway of our soul.

Matthew 4:4, in the Message Translation puts it this way, *"It takes more than bread to stay alive. It takes a steady stream of words from God's mouth."* God has something to say to you today. Ask yourself, *What is God saying to me today? What does He want me to do?* This is Good News. May a steady stream of God's word prepare your way today. Go ahead; Say, Speak Lord, I'm Listening.

Step to Start Strong:

Open God's Mouth

MAY 13.

20/20 Vision

"Where there is no vision, people perish."

Proverbs 29:18

What's your vision? Where are you going? What do you want to do this year? How about the next 5 years or 10 years? It's vital for every believer to have a vision! Why is this so? Because the Bible says, *"where there is no vision, people perish."* Meaning *"if you don't have a vision, you feel empty, unoccupied and even lifeless at times."* I believe this is the root of complacency in the church. When we fail to cast vision, we ultimately sit around and look at each other and how many of you know a church that is inward oriented will eventually implode. When we fix our eyes on ourselves, all we see is our sin and struggle. On the other hand, if we focus on our vision, we will ultimately see what God sees; our destiny.

The psalmist said, *"O' Come Magnify the Lord with me!"* What are you magnifying this morning? Let's magnify the Lord. Let's enlarge our vision. Let's focus on the future!

If don't know where you're going, you'll probably end up there. This phrase is cliche but very common among christians circles. *Why is this so?* A recent study shows that over 70% of Americans dread waking up to go to work. Why would you live your only life doing something that you really don't enjoy. The Bible says that Jesus Christ came to give us life *and life more abundantly*. When we seek Him with our whole heart, we find out who we are in Him. When we find out who we are in Him, we can discover what we're supposed to do for Him.

I challenge you: Write a 20/20 Vision. If the Lord tarries, where do you want to be? What do you want to be doing? Let me put it this way: If money wasn't an issue. What would you do? This is a good place to start.

Is your spiritual eye-sight 20/20? If you don't know, it may be time for a check-up.

Step to Start Strong:

Write down your Vision

MAY 14

Good, Good Father

"How much more will the Heavenly Father give the Holy Spirit to those who ask him!"

Luke 11:13

There's a popular song on the radio right now entitled, *Good, Good Father.* Most people think Chris Tomlin wrote the song because he sings it so well and he has written so many other christian hits. However, to the world's surprise, a small band from Mid-town Atlanta who call themselves, House-fires actually wrote the lyrics. Why am I telling you this? Because there really is a God in Heaven who loves you with a radical love and He's a Good, Good Father!

When Jesus gave us the model for prayer in Matthew 6, He said, "*When you pray, pray this way: "Our Father who art in Heaven, hallowed be thy name*!" Now to us it may sound cliche but to those who heard this teaching for the first time were challenged in their thinking. Did He just say Father? Our Father who art in Heaven?

For so long, the children of Israel had to approach God through ritual, ceremony and sacrifice. Jesus destroyed this doctrine with one word. We went from a *form* of worship to a Heavenly Father, a pattern for people to follow to a personal relationship with God! This is so good!

It's interesting to look at the Greek word here for *Father.* The original language reads *"Abba"* which literally means, *"Daddy."* Jesus said, *"When you pray, pray this way: "Our Daddy who lives in Heaven."* Some people have a skewed perspective about who God really is so they have a hard time with this thought. They think God sits in Heaven just waiting for them to mess up so He can swing his hammer of discipline and judgment. This couldn't be farther from the truth. The scripture says, *"God is compassionate and gracious, slow to get angry and abounding in loving-kindness."* (Psalm 103:8) I really like the slow to get anger part don't you? These 4 characteristics are coupled together 7 different times in the Bible. This should tell us something about our daddy.

If our earthy Father's know how to give good gifts to their children, how much more does our Heavenly Father give us good, good gifts. As a Father, I would lay my life down for my kids but how much more has God done for His children worldwide. He's our God but He's also our Abba, Father. You don't have to do anything to earn your Father's love and acceptance. He's on your side and He always will be. *He's a Good, Good Father.* May Daddy bless you today!

Step to Start Strong:

Take a Moment to Think about God as your Father

MAY 15.

GIVE THANKS

"Give thanks to the Lord, for he is good; his love endures forever."

1st Chronicles 16:34

Thanksgiving is the seed for God to give you more. If we're not thankful for what God has already given us, why should we expect God to give us more to murmur about? Lets count our blessing today and not our burdens. *What are you thankful for today?* The best way to overcome your obstacles is to get something in your life bigger than your obstacles. This pillar of thanksgiving will always keep our lives in proper perspective.

Thanksgiving should be a lifestyle. It's not just a day set aside for us to meet and eat with our family. Thanksgiving is an attitude of the heart. It didn't originate with the Pilgrims, it originated with the people of God.

What if all you had tomorrow was what you thanked God for today? So I thought for a few moments this morning, we should pause and pray to thank God for being so good to us over the years. Start with something small and keep thanking him as long as you can. This is a great way to jumpstart your day with Jesus. Let's be a thankful people. Indeed, we have a lot to be thankful for wouldn't you agree?

1st Thessalonians 5:18 "Give thanks in all circumstances; for this is God's will for you in Christ Jesus."

Step to Start Strong:

Pray a Prayer of Thanksgiving

MAY 16.

More Than These

"When they had finished eating, Jesus said to Simon Peter, "Simon son of John, do you love me more than these?" "Yes, Lord," he said, "you know that I love you." Jesus said, "Feed my lambs."

John 21:15

Jesus asked Simon Peter this question three times before He ascended to Heaven; *"Do you love me more than these?"* Do you love me more than ministry? Do you love me more than money? How about more than the multitudes? I wonder what these things represent in your life? What gets in the way of your love & relationship for the Lord?

Think of it this way: No one ever starts out serving the Lord with the intention of failing in the public eye. Sometimes, the scheme of Satan is to keep your sin silent. He wounds you and then waits patiently why you accumulate influence. He knows the begetting sins will eventually cause you to self destruct. So that when you fail, He'll not only destroys you but those who follow you as well.

God showed me this as I read an article about the crumbling of a Christian Empire that had great influence in the earth. This ministry was massive in every way until subtle sins began to seep their way into the lives of the leadership. We've all heard the stories. Megachurch pastors who submit to sexual immortality. Other laity who are lured away and enticed with embezzlement. The list goes on and on.

However, this particular article made a statement that I think will speak to us today: It said, "*We have created a monster that God was unwilling to feed, so we had to feed the monster ourselves.*" The rest was history. Ultimately, the ministry was completely destroyed and doesn't exist till this day.

Don't miss this: *"God promises to provide for everything that He has asked you to do."* The question is, *"What has God asked you to do?" In this case, this ministry was participating in things that were ungodly which took their eyes off their love for God.* The same happened in Simon Peter's story. What about your story? What has God asked you to do? He told Simon Peter to Feed my lambs. I think the statement remains the same today. Let's show the world how much we love the Lord. Do you love Him more than these?

<u>Step to Start Strong</u>:

Feed the Sheep in your Field of Influence

MAY 17.

FAITH IN THE FIRE

"When you walk through the fire, you will not be burned; the flames will not set you ablaze."

Isaiah 43:2

If fire represents trial and tribulation, *How can you walk through the fire and not be burned?* Here's a clue: Fire cannot consume fire. He who walks through the fire will not be burned if He is already on fire for God. The second fire will just intensify the first.

So what's the purpose for the fire? Fire refines our relationship with the Lord. Notice, we walk *"through"* the fire. The fiery trial that you are experiencing this morning isn't a final destination. It's not even a pitstop. It's just a scene in a real life motion picture in which God reveals His grace and glory. The greatness of God covers us so even our enemies that oppose us will ultimately work for our good. So don't flinch is the face of this fiery furnace. Stay strong and persistent. Keep your eyes on the prize which is in heavenly places with Christ Jesus.

The real question is: *Are you on fire?* If so, I pray this fiery attack would intensity your love of the Lord and refine your relationship with God and others.

When you exit the other side, the smell of smoke will not even be on your clothes. In fact, your inner resolve will be stronger than ever. This fire will prove the point. So be encouraged with the words of 1st Peter 4:12-13 today:

> *"Beloved, do not be surprised at the fiery trial that has come upon you, as though something strangewere happening to you. But rejoice that you share in the sufferings of Christ, so that you may be overjoyed at the revelation of His glory."*

Do you want a greater measure of God's glory? If so,*"keep your faith in the fire."* The scripture says, "*You are going from faith to faith and glory to glory.*"

Step to Start Strong:

Be a Fiery Faith Individual.

MAY 18.

THE PRAYER OF JABEZ

"Jabez was more honorable than his brothers, and his mother named him Jabez saying," Because I bore him with pain." Now Jabez called on the God of Israel, saying, "Oh that You would bless me indeed and enlarge my territory, and that Your hand might be with me, and that You would keep me from harm that I may be free from pain!" And God granted his request."

1st Chronicles 4:9-10

The first eight chapters of 1st Chronicles is dedicated to the historical account of the 12 tribes of Israel. If you want to practice your Hebrew syllables or you're having a hard time going to sleep, this is a great place to start. God gives us an extensive list of genealogy from the beginning of time. We read line by line as He describes the family tree of every generation from Adam to Abraham.

It's interesting to see that 99% of the list is just names with no detailed information about the individual. However, as you're reading through chapter 4, you'll notice how God stops when He gets to the birth of Jabez and then He dedicates two verses to His life. *Why is Jabez so special?* What did He do that set Him apart? I'll tell you what He did; He prayed with purity and passion!

So, what did He pray? He prayed 4 specific things: *"Jabez, cried out to the God of Israel: O' that you would bless me and enlarge my territory, that your hand might be upon me and that you would keep me from harm so that I may free from pain."*

Jabez petitioned for supernatural blessing, prosperity, presence and protection. His prayer with filled with purpose.

Therefore, I challenge you to memorize this prayer and pray it everyday. Pray it over your children and your church. Pray it over your family and your finances. *Pray it with passion!*

You may be asking why? Well, I believe this prayer has the power to change every aspect of your life. This prayer will not only change your circumstances but consequently it will change you.

Jabez left a legacy in the history of His nation. How did He do it? *By prayer!* Let's be a people of passionate prayer who leave another line or two for people to talk about. Let's be like Jabez. He began his life in pain but He ended it with prayer. Let's cry out to the God of Israel in the days ahead!

(For additional Reading: The Prayer of Jabez by Bruce Wilkinson.)

Step to Start Strong:

Memorize and Pray the Prayer of Jabez

MAY 19.

Who's the Author?

"And they were astonished at his teaching, for he taught them as one who had authority, not as the scribes."

Mark 1:22

What was the difference between the teaching styles of Jesus and the scribes? The answer is one word: *"Authority."*

Let's look at the 2 styles: A scribe is one who copies information from one scroll to another. They passed down the oral traditions by transferring the Old Testament words to plant called papyrus. It was the note book paper of their day.

So, who is Jesus? Jesus is the Word. He is the author of what the scribes were writing about. The scribes spoke out of their assumption but Jesus spoke from His authority. *See the difference?* The root word for authority is author. He is the author of all things.

Now knowing this: *Why would you listen to what the world has to say about you or anything else?* Jesus is the way, the truth and the life. Everything else is counterfeit. Allow the Holy Spirit to teach you and guide you down paths of righteousness. Whatever you do, don't forsake the plan that God has placed in your heart. It will come to pass if you place your trust in the one who wrote the words on your heart. He is the author of the Bible but He is also the author of your faith. Keep trusting Him today. You don't want to miss the ending. It's the Grand Finale!

Step to Start Strong:

Give God the Authority to Write your Story

MAY 20.

TRUE IDENTITY

"For no matter how many promises God has made, they are "Yes" in Christ. And so through him the "Amen" is spoken by us to the glory of God."

2 Corinthians 1:20

At 5 o'clock am on August 31st in 2007, a man was found behind a dumpster in Richmond Hill, Georgia beaten to a state of unconsciousness. Someone mugged this guy and left him for dead. When the employer found him, he was barely alive so they rushed him to the hospital with the hope of nursing him back to health. Weeks later, this mystery man survived but was left with a severe case of amnesia. He didn't know who he was and he didn't know who he belonged too.

The FBI took fingerprints as they partnered with local authorities to try and solve the crime for this man's sake. Sadly, no one knew his name and he couldn't remember anything. The investigation continued for many months when Dr. Phil picked up on the story and brought this man on the stage of National TV. Everyone hoped that someone would step forward with vital information to help this man find his home. *The end result?* No name, no identity and no one to go home to. He didn't know who he was and he didn't know who he belonged to.

What if this happened to you? Well, spiritually speaking it happens to individuals everyday. The devil works overtime to distort and disguise the true identity of God's kids. Many people don't know who they are and they don't know who they belong to. Their personal perception is skewed and they don't have a clue why they're here on the earth.

Do you know who you are in Christ? If you need to be reminded the words "*In Christ*" are written well over 140 times in the scripture. Most of these references give a characteristic of what it means to a child of God. *You are chosen, accepted, loved, forgiven and valuable just to name a few.* This is your true identity when you give your life to Christ.

It's important to note that everyone was created by God but not everyone is a child of God. In order to be a child of God, you have to choose Christ and this will determine who you belong.

Just last year, after 11 years of not knowing who he was, Benjamin Kyle finally rediscovered his identity through a well known forensic genealogist agency. He never lost hope. May we never lose our hope, not only for ourselves but for those who live in the world as well.

Step to Start Strong:

Walk in your True Identity

MAY 21.

MERCY IN THE MIDDLE

"Because of the Lord's great love we are not consumed, for his mercies never fail. They are new every morning; great is your faithfulness!"

Lamentations 3:22-23

MERCY IS AMAZING. It's actually new every morning. This means everyday you have a fresh start, a new beginning and another chance to be and all that God created you to be. Yesterday is a cashed check and tomorrow is a promissory note but we do have today. *That's why its called, a present!* It's His mercy and its always in the middle of who God is and what He does.

Grace happens when *"God gives you what you do not deserve"* but Mercy manifests when *"God doesn't give you what you do deserve."* Do you see the difference? I don't know about you but I'm eternally grateful for God's amazing grace and mercy. Today, God is not going to give us what we deserve.On the contrary, He is going to give us full access to His throne of grace knowing that we can obtain mercy to help us in our time of need. (Hebrews 4:16)

With this is mind, let us put mercy in the middle of everything we do. Let's show mercy knowing we are receiving mercy. It will never fail! May your day start strong as you walk with the Lord within His mercy and grace.

Micah 6:8 reiterates this idea, *"So, what does the Lord require of you? To act justly and to love mercy and to walk humbly with your God.*

Step to Start Strong:

Show Mercy

MAY 22.

The Name of Jesus!

"Therefore God exalted Him to the highest place and gave Him the name that is above every name, that at the name of Jesus every knee should bow, in heaven and on earth and under the earth."

Philippians 2:9-10

Why do we pray in Jesus name? Have you ever asked yourself this question? Why do most people end their prayer with this blessed benediction? Let's take a look.

First of all, I want to call your attention to the authority of the name of Jesus. *"God has given Him the name that is above every name."* The name of Jesus literally means, *"He Saves."* This implies that He can save anyone or anything from anyone or anything. He has all power and authority in Heaven and on earth. The scripture goes on to say that, *"Demons tremble at the name of Jesus."* Why? Because they know he can torture them before their time. (Matthew 8:29) And we should be tender to the same reverent fear that cries in the heart of creation. Yes, perfect love cast out all fear but we should never lose our reverence before the Lord.

Secondly, I want you to see the unity within the word Jesus. If we all gathered in a group today and shouted our first name in unison, it would be very chaotic and confusing. No one could hear what the other person was saying. This is equally true in the church: *"We cannot serve the Lord in discord!"* However, if we all shout the name of Jesus at the same time, we can hear the clarity and unity that God so desires for His body. Jesus is the bridegroom which unifies His bride. Therefore, when we pray in the name of Jesus, we manifest His authority but we also unify ourselves. The Apostle Paul said it this way, it's the Name *"of whom the whole family of God in heaven and on earth is named."* (Eph. 3:15) Yes, we bare His image and His nature but we also bare His name. Which brings me to my last point: When we are born into the family of God, we inherit our Father's name; His name is our name because we become sons and daughters of God. (2nd Corinthians 6:18) When we pray in the name of Jesus, we are praying our family name. His name gives us full access to every spiritual blessing in the Heavenly places. (Eph.1:3) For example: When Kacie and I got married a few years ago, she inherited my last name. Her name is now, Kacie Hyatt Walters. When she signs a check, she signs her new name because we share a joint banking account. If she walked into the bank this morning and asked the teller to withdraw all of our personal assets, she would not be turned away. Why? Because she is my wife and we are one. It's the same way with a child of God. Being that we bare his name, we have the privilege to call out on the Name of Jesus for every need that comes our way. As the old song says, "When you don't know what else to say, just say His name." It's the Name that is above every name! His name is Jesus and He still saves.

Step to Start Strong:

Pray in Jesus Name

MAY 23.

THE VIA DOLOROSA

"Carrying His own cross, He went out to The Place of the Skulls."

John 19:17

The Day Jesus was crucified, He carried His cross from Pilate's Praetorian all the way down the Via Dolorosa. The Via Dolorosa was a street in the Old City of Jerusalem that stretched about 2,000 feet. It wasn't a backstreet on the other side of the tracks. It was the business district in the center of commerce. Indeed, it was the heart of Jerusalem.

Why did Christ choose this path to carry His cross? I believe it was to make this powerful point to us today. *We have enough crosses in the church.* What we need is more crosses in the center of commerce! We need men, women and children alike to deny themselves and to take up their crosses and follow Him daily!

The Cross represents purpose. The Cross; the purpose of Christ was pointed with passion to fulfill His ultimate purpose which is salvation for all people. May we follow faithfully in His footsteps today. Let's take the cross from the church when we leave on Sunday and take to the center of commerce in all of our cities! From the private places to public places! Let's rise up and take salvation down main street for everyone to see. This is the only Hope for the world! This is the pathway to purpose!

It's called The Via Dolorosa! It's the pathway to Victory!

<u>Step to Start Strong</u>:

Carry your Cross outside the Church

MAY 24.

LIVING IN THE LIGHT

"Therefore confess your sins to one another and pray for one another so that you may be healed. The prayer of a righteous person is powerful and effective."

James 5:16

The Bible is clear. We go to God for forgiveness but we go to one another for help and healing.

One day, we hosted a Teen Challenge graduate in our chapel who was celebrating one year of sobriety. Over the past 12 months, He has been walking with the Lord and living in the light. However, during his testimony, He shared the darkest day of his journey with Jesus. He made this statement and I want to share it with you today: He said, *"the night before I entered Teen Challenge, I was in a hotel room all by myself and I had planned to end my life. I was helpless and hopeless and even though I desired healing, I felt like there was no way out. I loaded my pistol and pulled it out as I had planned and all of sudden, my cell phone vibrated in my pocket. I looked down and guess who it was? It was my pastor calling me to check in. Little did He know, I was seconds from committing suicide. He said, "whatever you do, don't lose hope for tomorrow your life will never be the same."* Divine intervention saved this man's life and His pastor didn't even know it until He shared the story this week. It was a very moving moment for all of us to hear this testimony. What can we learn from this story? First and foremost, I want you to see that the enemy operates in darkness but the Lord lives in the light. Whenever we confess our sins and struggles to one another, we dismantle the powers of darkness. When a born again believer lives in the light, the shadow of the enemy disappears. One of the worse things we can do is suppress our problems and expect them to go away.

What is the one thing that is holding you down today? Pause with me for a minute. Confess it before God right now. Give it to Him with the best of your ability. Say it two or three times. We are children of the light, therefore let's walk in the light. Speak the word in your spirit so your flesh can hear it. Let faith arise this morning. You will be victorious. The prayer of a righteous person is powerful and effective.

Step to Start Strong:

Live your Life in the Light

MAY 25.

THE EXTRA DEGREE

"Whatever your hand finds to do, do it with all your might."

Ecclesiastes 9:10

At 211 degrees, water is hot. However, at 212 degrees water is boiling. *What's the difference? Just one degree!* Boiling water creates steam and how many of you know that steam can move a locomotive. One degree of difference can release a force of power to move a machine. It's the same way with the way you live your life. Small decisions have huge ramifications in the spirit.

So, what's the extra degree? Let's call it *"Additional Effort."* The extra degree can bring you exponential results in anything you do. In what area of your life do you need to add some *"Additional Effort?"*

Reading your Bible, losing weight or saving money? Additional effort to spend quality time with your family or finish a degree? Whatever your hand finds to do, apply the extra degree. It will make a big difference. It's your life. Its time to turn up the heat.

Vince Lombardi said that, *"inches make the champion."* Thomas Edison said, *"many of life's failures come from people who did not realize how close they were to success when they gave up."* God reiterated this idea when He said, *"the race is not given to the swift, nor the battle to the strong but the race is given to those who endure to the end!"* (Eccl. 9:11)

Therefore, apply the extra degree today. Let's give off some supernatural steam! Remember, courage is fear holding on for one more minute. Don't quit now! You've come way to far! Let's go the extra degree in everything we do.

Step to Start Strong:

Apply the Extra Degree

MAY 26.

God's Garden

I call these the *'Lettuce Passages.*" We all need a well-balanced diet for our physical health but we also need to do our best to maintain our spiritual well-being. How do we do this? One of the easiest ways is by ingesting the Word of God daily. The scripture will give your soul the strength to endure yet another day. In the Book of Hebrews, there are 13 chapters that represent the "*Let us Statements.*" Notice the charge doesn't say, *"Let me."* God doesn't have any favorites. God's best work is started and finished through unity. Let us meditate upon these precepts for a few minutes.

Hebrews 4:1 "Therefore, since a promise remains of entering His rest, let us be careful that none of you be found to have fallen short of it."

Hebrews 4:11 *"Let us, therefore be diligent to enter that rest, lest anyone fall according to the same example of disobedience."*

Hebrews 4:14 *"Seeing then that we have a great High Priest who has passed through the heavens, Jesus the Son of God, let us hold firmly to the faith that we profess."*

Hebrews 4:16 "Let us therefore come boldly to the throne of grace, that we may obtain mercy and find grace to help in time of need."

Hebrews 6:1 *"Therefore, leaving the discussion of the elementary principles of Christ, let us go on to perfection, not laying again the foundation of repentance from dead works and of faith toward God."*

Hebrews 10:22 *"Let us draw near with a true heart in full assurance of faith, having our hearts sprinkled from an evil conscience and our bodies washed with pure water."*

Hebrews 10:23 *"Let us hold fast the confession of our hope without wavering, for He who promised is faithful."*

Hebrews 10:24 *"And let us consider one another in order to stir up love and good works."*

Hebrew 11:1 "Therefore we also, since we are surrounded by so great a cloud of witnesses, let us lay aside every weight, and the sin which so easily ensnares us and let us run with endurance the race that is set before us."

Hebrews 12:28 *"Therefore, since we are receiving a kingdom which cannot be shaken, let us have grace, by which we may serve God acceptably with reverence and godly fear."*

Hebrews 13:13 *"Therefore let us go forth to Him, outside the camp, bearing His reproach."*

Hebrews 13:15 *"Therefore by Him let us continually offer the sacrifice of praise to God, that is, the fruit of our lips, giving thanks to His name."*

Step to Start Strong:

Eat your Lettuce

MAY 27.

The Naba Flow

"May my lips overflow with praise, for you teach me your decrees."

Psalm 119:117

The Hebrew word *"Naba"* is mentioned 11 times in the Old Testament. This word contains the idea of *"a continual flow."* All the references refer to the words we speak as believers. We have a continual flow of righteousness or a continual flow of unrighteousness. The choice is ours. We can speak words of life or we can speak words of death.

Its the Naba Flow. When we tap into the well-spring of life which is found in Christ Jesus, there will be a bubbling brook of boldness that the Holy Spirit will manifest in our mouth. This is the river that Jesus spoke about that flows out of the believers belly. Revelation 22 and Ezekiel 37 speaks of the River of God that flows from the Throne of God. The River of Righteousness lives in you and He desires to speak through you.

David said, *"I set a guard over my mouth to watch over the door of my lips."* (Psalm 141:3) We should practice this principle. Let's keep watch over the words that we speak. Some of us need to build a dam to stop the flow of negativity that spews from our lips. The old saying is true, *"If you don't have anything good to say, don't say anything at all."* Lets flow in faithfulness and truth today. Let's speak words of life over ourselves and others. One word spoken under the anointing of the Holy Spirit can change someones circumstance. Let the Naba Flow.

Step to Start Strong:

Be Careful not to Speak Careless Words

MAY 28.

Real Repentance

"There is joy in the presence of God's angels over one sinner who repents."

Luke 15:10

Why do the angels rejoice when one person repents from his or her sins? Because they are the ones who drag them to the fiery flames of Hell. At of all the angelic duties, this is the one thing that they dread. Dragging the souls of unrepentant people to the dark dungeons of the deep. They resemble the heart of our Heavenly Father because, *"He is patient with us, not wanting anyone to perish, but everyone to come to a place of repentance."* This is why they rejoice, because of real repentance. This type of repentance is genuine. It means to turn from your sins.

William Booth, the founder of the Salvation Army, understood this principle and prophesied a warning for modern day America: He said, "*The chief danger of the 20th century will be religion without the Holy Spirit, Christianity without Christ, forgiveness without repentance, salvation without regeneration, politics without God, and heaven without hell.*"

May this statement cut us to the heart: Repentance is still a relevant term. As a whole, we need to turn! We need turn from our sins and we need to turn to Him! He is the only one who can save both body and soul from the fiery flames of Hell. Let's give the angels a reason to rejoice today! Let's lead by example and lead a life of real repentance. By doing so, who knows? Others may follow in our footsteps.

Step to Start Strong:

Live a Lifestyle of Repentance

MAY 29.

What is it?

"I am the living bread that came down from heaven."

John 6:51

Every morning, fresh manna miraculously appeared to provide for God's people. Manna is a symbol of Jesus leaving Heaven to come to a needy world. Just like manna came to the Israelites doorstep, Jesus comes to the doorstep of our heart. We don't have to work to get to Him. He willfully comes to us. The manna was small and sweet like honey. Jesus came as a babe wrapped in swaddling clothing. The manna fell in pleasant places which represents the boundary lines within the Word of God. It's in His presence where we find fullness of Joy. It's in Him where we find the desires of our heart.

However, somewhere along the way the Israelites slipped into a spirit of complaint. (Exodus 16) One person became ungrateful and the other people agreed. This caused the whole community to grumble. They screamed, *"Moses why did you bring us out here to die?"* But it's interesting to see how the manna fell from the sky while they were sleeping. They didn't have to worry or fear for their next meal. Their only requirement was to wake up and walk by faith as a child of God. The cloud by day and the fire by night was a sure guide to provide. The blessing was proportional to meet everyones need. This was their daily bread.

So, What's your need? What is it? What do you need God to do for you? God has promised to meet all of your need according to His riches which is in Christ Jesus our Lord. Don't worry. The word of God is true. If you will be still, you will see the salvation of the Lord. Don't complain. When we complain, we're saying, *Jesus you're not enough.* The Israelites murmured about the manna meaning, God, your Son is not enough. If Jesus is all you have, don't you have all you need?

My prayer is that manna would fall all around you this morning. His presence is sweet and His promises are powerful. Be reminded of this very thing, *He didn't part the Red Sea for you to die in the desert.* Provision is already in the pipeline. *What is it?* It's the Living Bread that comes down from Heaven everyday if you will look for it and be grateful. God bless you!

Step to Start Strong:

Thank God for your Daily Bread.

MAY 30.

The Hallel Songs

"When they had sung a hymn, they went out to the Mount of Olive."

Matthew 26:30

The word *"Hallel"* means praise. When you shout, *Hallelujah!*What you are saying is, *"Praise be to God!"* Out of the 150 Psalms in scripture, the 113th through the 118th chapters are called the *"Hallel Psalms."* These songs were sung by the Hebrew people at times of celebration. During the Passover, Pentecost and Harvest Festivals, they would gather and sing these verses to the Glory of God. The reason for the singing was to return thanks to the God who saved, healed and delivered them from the land of Egypt and hand of Pharaoh.

The essence of all these exaltations were all wrapped around blessing. God blessed His children so in return the children blessed His name in praise and worship. The word *blessed* means happy, increase and abundance but on the contrary, the word cursed means decrease and lack. Here's the Good News; *God wants to save you, heal you and deliver you! He wants to bless you!* The old song is true, "*The praises go up and the blessing comes down.*"

May our mouth be filled with praise today.

Take time to read the *"Hallel Psalms"* for your scriptural reading today and think about what Christ has done for you. Psalm 113 through Psalm 118 will touch your heart as you focus on salvation, deliverance, healing and blessing.

Step to Start Strong:

Read the Hallel Songs

MAY 31.

MARANATHA!

"Men of Galilee, "Why do you stand here looking into the sky? This same Jesus, who has been taken from you into heaven, will come back in the same way you have seen him go into heaven."

Acts 1:11

When I was at Lee University in Bible School, a young asian girl used to greet everyone on the sidewalk with these words, *"Jesus is coming soon."* It's the only words I ever heard her speak and to be quite honest, it kinda freaked me out a little bit. She would pass by and whisper those words in such an eerie tone. However, thinking back on the reality of this statement she couldn't be more right. *Jesus is coming back soon.*

In the early church, born-again believers used to greet one another with the same words. The Greek word used was *"maranatha"* meaning, *"The Lord is coming back soon."* It was their hello if you will. A way to distinguish one another when walking down the street.

If this event was close over 2,000 years ago, how much closer is the hour of Christ's coming today? You can look at the signs of the times and see the fulfillment of scripture happening right before our very eyes. (See Matthew 24 and Luke 21) As these things come to pass, we shouldn't look down and get discouraged. In fact, the scripture says, *"to look up and rejoice because our redemption is drawing near!"* (Luke 21:28) The angels are setting the table for the greatest celebration in all of world's history. The Wedding Supper of the Lamb! So, let us not forget why we are here. We are here to know Him and make Him known. May we live our life in the light of eternity because we are living in the last seconds of the last days.

In closing, let's read the words of the Apostle Paul in 1st Thessalonians 4:16-18, "*For the Lord Himself will come down from heaven with a shout of command, with the voice of the archangel and with the [blast of the] trumpet of God, and the dead in Christ will rise first. Then we who are alive and remain [on the earth] will simultaneously be caught up (raptured) together with them [the resurrected ones] in the clouds to meet the Lord in the air, and so we will always be with the Lord! Therefore, comfort and encourage one another with these words [concerning our reunion with believers who have died].*

Maranatha my friends! May your day be filled with God's manifest presence, peace and power, in Jesus Name!

<u>Step to Start Strong</u>:

Life your Life in Light of Eternity

JUNE 1.

MAKE UP YOUR MIND

"You will decide on a matter, and it will be established for you, and light will shine on your ways."

Job 22:28

The Word of God is called the incorruptible seed in scripture. Once you sow it in your soul, you cannot get it out. It will never wither or waste away. I'm always reminded of this truth when a word is quickened in my mind at a random time during the day.

This morning, Job 22:28 came to me immediately so I know this verse is for someone specifically. The Bible says, *"You will decide on a matter and it will be established for you and light will shine on your ways."*

The word decide in Hebrew means *"to cut off."* When you make a concrete decision, you are cutting off the other option. There's no wrestling within yourself what you're supposed to do. It's a done deal. So I ask you, *"What decision have you been procrastinating or putting off?"* No decision is actually making the wrong decision. You have to choose?

When we make godly decisions, we give God the freedom to fulfill His promises in our life. He will establish our steps when we Iive our life with a single-mind with the things of the Spirit. James 1:8 says, *"a double-minded man is unstable in all of His ways."* This man goes back and forth when making decisions. He's unstable and unpredictable. He has a hard time living up to his on word but more importantly, He has a harder time living up to God's word. Therefore, God can't plant Him and bring forth the righteous fruit that He so desires because he is indecisive.

With this in mind: *What decision needs to be made today to bring you a brighter tomorrow?* Once you find the answer, cut off the other option. When you do this, God's light will shine on all your ways!

<u>Step to Start Strong</u>:

Make up your Mind

JUNE 2.

THE GOD OF ALL COMFORT

"But when the Comforter comes, the Holy Spirit, whom the Father will send in My name, He will teach you all things, and bring to your remembrance all things that I said to you."

John 14:26

The Holy Spirit is commonly called the comforter in scripture. One of His attributes is to comfort believers because many times, He will call us into uncomfortable situations. Has anybody ever been uncomfortable before? In fact, the Spirit of the Lord will never take you to a place where your flesh is comfortable. God isn't overly concerned with our comfort level. On the contrary, He desires intimacy in the innermost parts of our heart. Let me say it another way, *God is more concerned with your final destination than your current situation.* Comfort gives birth to complacency but intimacy gives birth to expectancy. (John 3:6) So, this is why He calls Himself the Comforter.

With this in mind, I love our big, fluffy comforter on my bed. It helps me rest and relax so I can wake up refreshed. In the same way, we need to rest and relax in our relationship with the Lord. When we abide in His presence, we walk in His refreshment.

Whatever you do, don't rebel against the Spirit's leading. Jesus was directed into a desert experience but when He finally came out, He was full of the Holy Spirit's power. God will use every pain for His overall purpose. Let's change our perspective today and let any discomfort drive us to the God of all comfort.

1st Corinthians 1:3 *"Praise be to the God and Father of our Lord Jesus Christ, the Father of compassion and the God of all comfort, who comforts us in all our troubles, so that we can comfort those in any trouble with the comfort we ourselves receive from God. For just as we share abundantly in the sufferings of Christ, so also our comfort abounds through Christ."*

Step to Start Strong:

Find Comfort in Christ

JUNE 3.

The Promises of God

"Therefore, [inheriting] the promise depends entirely on faith [that is, confident trust in the unseen God], in order that it may be given as an act of grace [His unmerited favor and mercy], so that the promise will be [legally] guaranteed to all the descendants [of Abraham]—not only for those [Jewish believers] who keep the Law, but also for those [Gentile believers] who share the faith of Abraham, who is the [spiritual] father of us all— 17 (as it is written [in Scripture], "I have made you a father of many nations") in the sight of Him in whom he believed, that is, God who gives life to the dead and calls into being that which does not exist. 18 In hope against hope Abraham believed that he would become a father of many nations, as he had been promised [by God]: "So [numberless] shall your descendants be." 19 Without becoming weak in faith he considered his own body, now as good as dead [for producing children] since he was about a hundred years old, and [he considered]

the deadness of Sarah's womb. 20 But he did not doubt or waver in unbelief concerning the promise of God, but he grew strong and empowered by faith, giving glory to God, 21 being fully convinced that God had the power to do what He had promised. 22 Therefore his faith was credited to him as righteousness (right standing with God)."

Romans 4:16-22

Some scholars say, there are over 5,000 promises within the pages of the Bible. A promise is a binding declaration made by God for something to be done or given for our benefit. The best news? *"God is not human, that he should lie, nor a son of man, that he should change his mind. Does he ever speak and not act? Does he make promises and not fulfill them?"* (Numbers 23:19) If this is true and I believe it is, this makes God a Promise-Keeper and His children, Promise-Reapers. What has God promised you? Have you searched the scripture to see what He has to say? As the old song says, *"We should stand on the promises that cannot fail, When the howling storms of doubt and fear assail, By the living Word of God we shall prevail. Why? Because we are "Standing on the promises of God!"*

Abraham, the Father of our Faith, stood on the promises of God. God spoke to Him when He was 70 years old and said, *"Sarah was going to have a son and their descendants would be as numerous as the stars in the sky."* (Genesis 18) How long did He stand on this promise from God? For 30 long years, yet He did not waiver in unbelief. He waited for the word of God to be fulfilled. What word are you standing on? What promise has God spoken over your life? Take a second to remember the revelation? Now, read Romans 4:16-22 again with *"your"* promise in mind.

Step to Start Strong:

Stand on the Promises of God

JUNE 4.

PUTTING FEET TO YOUR FAITH

"And how will anyone go and tell them without being sent? That is why the Scriptures say, "How beautiful are the feet of messengers who bring good news!"

Romans 10:15

Recently, *over 100,000 people gathered for the specific purpose of prayer and fasting for another Great Awakening in our nation. It was a day we will never forget as we celebrated the 110th Anniversary of the Azusa Street Outpouring led by William J. Seymour. Why 110 years? What was the significance and why was this day special?*

History tells there were multiple prophecies spoken by different individuals that 100 years after this rain of revival another rain would come with greater intensity; a latter rain. *This movement wouldn't come at one place with one person but it would be poured out all over the world for a remnant of believers who desire revival.* This describes you and me. This is our hearts desire; *"to see souls saved!"* We don't want to miss this moment. This is our hour in history to rise up and be apart of this great end-time harvest of souls. It's happening right before our eyes. Right now, more souls are being saved than any other time in history! The harvest is ripe but the scripture says, *"the laborers are few."* This means God wants to use you! Let's put feet to our faith today and walk out the word for the world to see.

The early rain of revival started pouring on the Day of Pentecost in Acts Chapter two. The latter rain of revival is falling now! Prayer this prayer; Holy Spirit, rain down on me now, in Jesus Name!

Step to Start Strong:

Ask for the Rains of Revival

JUNE 5.

Buy the Field

"The Kingdom of Heaven is like treasure hidden in a field. When a man found it, he hid it again, and then in his joy went and sold all he had and bought that field!"

Matthew 13:44

One summer, I was sitting on the front row in a conference while the speaker was sharing the word of the Lord. To my surprise, in the middle of the service, he suddenly stopped speaking and walked over to me with smile on his face. Feeling a bit uncomfortable, I sort of smiled back and waited for a reply as blood began to rushed to my face. With what seemed to be eternity, He finally proceeded to tell me 3 specific things over the microphone, despite the fact that we had never met or spoken before. He said, *"you're in full-time evangelistic ministry."* I nodded my head, yessir. In the midst of this transition, *"you have bought the field."* Now immediately, I knew what this meant. Buying the field means forsaking everything to follow Jesus. And lastly, He said, *"but you need a bigger net!"* After these words, he walked away and finished his message as tears filled my eyes. The Bible says, *"to test the spirit and weigh the words spoken by men to see if they are from the Spirit of God."* (1st Corinthians 14:29) So this is exactly what I did. Since this encounter, I have asked myself over and over again; *"How do I build a bigger net?"*

As I meditated upon this one sentence, it dawned on me. The most common use for a net in scripture is for fishing. Peter and the crew caught 153 fish on the Sea of Galilee early one morning because they worked together to cast the net. *This word has changed the way I work*. Our ministry needs a bigger net so we can catch more souls for the Kingdom of Christ. We need more people involved. We need to expand our borders and create a bigger vision so we can impact more people. So this is where we spend our energies One pastor said, *"I've never been interested in numbers!"* But I beg to differ! Numbers represent individual people and I care about people which means I should care about the numbers. Some call it *"net worth."* Every number represents an asset in God's eyes. Ultimately, the net represents unity. It speaks of the ability to reach our capacity within our call as a ministry. In other words, we need you take your part of the Gospel net and help us cast it in every country across the world. The most popular net in Jesus' day was the drag net. The crew threw the net over board and everyone pulled simultaneously to bring in the big catch. As we cast and drag the net, I believe we'll catch so many fish off the bottom of the sea. It's a great honor to do this together. Let's buy the field, build a bigger net and evangelize the earth!

Step to Start Strong:

Build a Bigger Net

JUNE 6.

FORGIVEN

"Therefore the kingdom of heaven is like a king who wished to settle accounts with his slaves. When he began the accounting, one who owed him 10,000 talents was brought to him. 'But because he could not repay, his master ordered him to be sold, with his wife and his children and everything that he possessed, and payment to be made. So the slave fell on his knees and begged him, saying, 'Have patience with me and I will repay you everything. And his master's heart was moved with compassion and he released him and forgave him [canceling] the debt. But that same slave went out and found one of his fellow slaves who owed him a hundred denarii; and he seized him and began choking him, saying, 'Pay what you owe!' So his fellow slave fell on his knees and begged him earnestly, 'Have patience with me and I will repay you. But he was unwilling and he went and had him thrown in prison until he paid back the debt. When his fellow slaves saw what had happened, they were deeply grieved and they went and reported to their master [with clarity and in detail] everything that had taken

place. Then his master called him and said to him, 'You wicked and contemptible slave, I forgave all that [great] debt of yours because you begged me. Should you not have had mercy on your fellow slave [who owed you little by comparison], as I had mercy on you? And in wrath his master turned him over to the torturers (jailers) until he paid all that he owed. My heavenly Father will also do the same to [every one of] you, if each of you does not forgive his brother from your heart."

Matthew 18:23-35

The farthest 18 inches in the world is from your head to your heart. You may know to do something in your mind but to walk it out in the world takes the help of the Spirit of God. So it is with the subject of forgiveness. What do you do when you're having a hard time forgiving someone? Try thinking about how much you have been forgiven of. This is a game-changer.

The Bible says, *"Blessed are the merciful, for they will be shown mercy."* Do you need mercy? Try giving mercy. We reap what we sow even with this subject. If you are a man of mercy, man will show you mercy. Don't fall into the trap of abhorring offenses. Unforgiveness leads to the root bitterness and bitterness blocks the blessing of God.

You may need to forgive yourself. Don't take yourself to seriously. You may need to forgive God. He's full of grace and mercy. You may need to forgive someone individually. If so, do it quickly! It will be well worth it.

Step to Start Strong:

Give the Gift of Forgiveness

JUNE 7.

Love thy Neighbor

"Love the Lord your God with all your heart and with all your soul and with all your mind and with all your strength. The second is this: Love your neighbor as yourself. There is no commandment greater than these."

Mark 12:30-31

The Hebrew word for shekinah means *"neighbor."* The greek word for neighbor in the New Testament means *"nearest one."* When God says, *"to love your neighbor as yourself,"* He's not exactly referring to the people across the street. He's challenging you to pay attention to the people who are in your path everyday. It's a proximity issue. Who will you come in contact with today? Tomorrow? At home or at work? Others you meet on the street? Who exactly are they? According to the greatest commandment in scripture, they are your neighbor; Your nearest one.

So what does it look like to love your neighbor? When God gives us instruction, He's always thinking with the end in mind. If His love abides in us, we are called to be instruments of righteousness in the earth; The fragrance of Christ for our communities. We do this by freely giving what we have freely received. What have we received? The Love of God! The Greatest Gift! The Gift of His presence!

When we release the love that has been poured into us by the Holy Spirit, we cancel the assignment of the enemy. Hate seems to be running rampant in the earth but God's Love is the strongest force in the universe. It melts the heart of a sinner, restores the life of a backslider and empowers those who desperately desire to do right. The source of this love comes from the Shekinah. He is the nearest one. Let His love fill your life today and overflow into others along the way. Think of the end in mind. What difference has He made in your life? What difference will you make in others?

Step to Start Strong:

Love Your Neighbor as Yourself

JUNE 8.

The Glory of God

"Then Moses said, "Show us your Glory."

Exodus 33:18

We are in dire need of the Glory of God. The Apostle Paul put it this way, *"So all of us, who have had that veil removed can see and reflect the glory of God. And the Lord--who is the Spirit--makes us more and more like him as we are changed into his glorious image."* So comes the phrase, *"we go from glory to glory."* (2nd Cor. 3:18)

The glory is different from the anointing. The anointing of the Holy Spirit brings the power to accomplish a specific purpose but the Glory of God brings repentance. As I was praying in the spirit a few mornings ago, God gave me this revelation. What we need in our nation is a mighty move of the Glory of God! This was the heart cry of Moses as He was leading the nation of Israel. He knew the only thing that would distinguish His land from all the other lands of the earth was the manifest presence of God, otherwise known as His Glory.

The Glory of God is the weight of who He really is showing up in a room. It shifts the atmosphere if you've ever experienced it. People can't stand or speak. They stand in awe of His might and power. People weep and lay prostrate on the floor speechless; all because of His majesty and goodness. I can feel Him right now as I type this devotional. When the Glory of God comes in it's fullness, *"everything"* else gets out of the way; Worry, sin and sickness has to go when the King of Glory comes in! No one wants to move or mess it up. Its pure perfection and peaceful. This kind of presence brings men, women and children to their knees.

Moses understood the glory better than anybody else in history because He dwelled in it for 40 years. Everyday he woke up under a cloud by day and fell asleep under the fire by night. This Glory brought provision by way of manna, direction by signs in the sky and overall, nothing died before its time. The children of Israel were supernaturally sustained by this glorious atmosphere. In fact, their shoes and clothes lasted for years on end.

To those who will allow it, God is bringing His manifest presence back to the church worldwide in these last days. For the prophet said, *"the Glory of this present house will be greater than the Glory of the former house."*(Haggai 2:9) So, I speak into your spirit this morning, *"Get ready for the Glory!"* Ask His manifest presence to fill your house! Ask God to send His Glory wherever you go! I love the anointing but before we are used in power, we need to position ourselves under the Glory! In closing, pray this prayer with me: *"God, Show <u>us</u> your Glory!"*

<u>Step to Start Strong</u>:

Give God the Glory

JUNE 9.

Fox Hole Prayers

"Do not be anxious about anything, but in every situation, by prayer and petition, with thanksgiving, present your requests to God."

Philippians 4:6

Billy Kim, the well-known Youth for Christ evangelist, tells the story of an American soldier hiding in a foxhole during the Korean War. When his commander-in-chief ordered him to go rescue his wounded mates on the front lines, the soldier took a long look at his watch to stall until his authority was out of sight. All alone, a fear gripped him so deeply that he couldn't move. After several minutes of sitting still a colleague reminded him of his rescue assignment. Again he looked at his watch and delayed. Finally, after several more minutes, he leaped out of the bunker and fearlessly carried all of his companions to safety.

At the end of the day, a friend asked him to explain his actions. *Why did you wait so long to go help your friends? And why were you staring at your watch?* The soldier stated with great honesty, *"In the moment, I was so scared because I knew I wasn't ready to die. I hate to wait until my fear subsided— knowing that at a certain time, on every hour, my mother had said she would be praying for me. Then I knew as the clock struck the high hour, no matter what awaited me on the other side of that bunker, I could face it because my mother was bombarding Heaven with her prayers."*

This moves me knowing the battle we live in as born-again believers. I have to ask: Who has your back in prayer? And Secondly, who are you praying for?

What is one of the greatest gifts we could give our kids, co-workers and family members for generations to come? The confidence in knowing that our hearts are bowed in humble adoration to the God of the Universe on their behalf. *For the fervent prayer of a righteous person is powerful and effective!* Our passion for prayer can change the course of history.

"So, Don't be anxious about anything, but in every situation, by prayer and petition, with thanksgiving, present your request to God." Even in a Fox Hole, He will be faithful and true.

"We pray for you everyday."

<u>Step to Start Strong</u>:

Pray for your Family and Friends

JUNE 10.

Whatever It Takes

"The race is not given to the swift nor the battle to the strong."

Ecclesiastes 9:11

Many years ago in the midst of my addiction, I didn't know what to do. At times I wanted to die but sadly even death would not have me. Other times, I wanted to live but peace was so unfamiliar I couldn't protect it. My self-pity and shame always sucked me back down the drain. What did I do? The only thing I knew to do: I began to drink and drug, fuss and cuss, smoke and chew and hang out with girls that do! But gratefully, one day, things began to change.

God showed me a better way. He spoke repetitiously through my family. In fact, I'll never forget my father giving me a gift one day. It was one of those seasons where all of our resources were exhausted and we didn't know what to do. The gift was a small coin that had these 3 words written on it, "*Whatever It Takes*."

He told me to put this coin in my pocket and carry it with me, wherever I went, as a reminder that I could do whatever I set my mind to. If temptation or depression seemed to get the best of me, I could symbolically reach down into my pocket and recollect the promise that God was with me. And if God be with me, who or what could be against me! These words have never left me and they never will.

Sadly, I lost the coin but gratefully, I gained Christ. The same can be true for you; If you're facing insurmountable odds this morning, Remember 911. The 9th Chapter of Ecclesiastes verse 11 says, "*The race is not given to the swift nor the battle to the strong but it is given to those who endure to the end.*" Don't give up today and whatever you do don't give in! If God be for you, who can be against you? Sometimes, we need to get out of the way, so God can be God. This is a powerful promise. You can do whatever you put your mind to from the word of our Father. Amen.

Step to Start Strong:

Do Whatever It Takes

JUNE 11.

PEOPLE OF PRESENCE

"You make known to me the path of life; in your presence there is fullness of joy; at your right hand are pleasures forevermore."

Psalm 16:11

Life is so good. God has given us life and life more abundantly through a relationship with His son, Jesus Christ. Of all the luxuries and blessings, He so lavishly and freely gives us, there is one that towers above them all; *It's His presence.* God's presence is the most sacred, safe and soothing place you could ever pursue. The best part? His presence is all around you!

Jacob was reminded of this truth when God's presence surrounded him on every side. He woke up from a dream and screamed! *"Surely, the presence of the Lord was in this place and I didn't even know it!"* (Genesis 28:16) This sounds like some of us during the busyness of our day; we forget that God's presence is a whisper away.

From here forward, let's practice being presence driven people instead of performance driven. Performance says, *I have to work my way into His presence,* when in all actuality, Emmanuel is already among you. The scripture says that, *"We have this treasure in our earthen vessels "to show" that this all-surpassing power is nor from us."* It's His presence!(2nd Cor. 4:7)

The reason I write the words to you is simple. This morning, I woke up, stumbled to the coffee maker, only to go sit at the kitchen table and gaze across the front lawn. As I enjoyed my Java, I was reminded of how good God has been to me and my family. This thankfulness provoked me to lift my hands and call on the name of Jesus. Almost instantly, His presence fell on me like rain. It ran down my body and refreshed me like nothing this world has to offer. He is so tangible and so true.

What he does for me, He will do for you. So, enjoy His presence today. Shift your perspective to the person of the Holy Spirit and call on the name of the Jesus. Let's be *"People of Presence."*

Step to Start Strong:

Acknowledge God's Presence

JUNE 12.

Extreme Epidemic

"Now the works of the flesh are evident, which are: adultery, fornication, uncleanness, lewdness, idolatry, sorcery, hatred, contentions, jealousies, outbursts of wrath, selfish ambitions, dissensions, heresies, envy, murders, drunkenness, revelries, and the like; of which I tell you beforehand, just as I also told you in time past, that those who practice such things will not inherit the kingdom of God."

Galatians 5:19-21

The Greek word *"pharmakia"* means pharmacy. This word appears five times in the New Testament: in Gal 5:20, Rev 9:21, 18:23, 21:8, and 22:15. "Pharmakia" translated into our English Bible is *"witchcraft" or "sorcery."* Pharmaceutical drugs are an epidemic in our nation. Over 75% of the men that enter the Teen Challenge Program are addicted to prescription pills and many end up heroine addicts because heroine is much cheaper on the streets. However, drug abuse isn't something new. This practice has been around since ancient times.

Pagan priests used to mix a potion with root and wine that made their routine worshippers high for an extended amount of time. People would come to pay tithes at the temple and the sorcerers would give them their fix so they would keep coming back. The drug and the drink was said to open up doors in the spirit world to give the participants power. They would hallucinate and hear voices from evil spirits. Drug addicts in our day deal with the same issues. Drugs give you a false sense of power and control. The root of the ancient organization was to make money and the issue is still true today. Doctors flippantly prescribe pills to hurting people, drug dealers hustle to help others form a habit and many times, the family pays the price. So, what do we do? What's the answer? How do we fight against pharmakia?

We keep telling the truth. We can't save everyone but we can save someone. We can keep changing the world one soul at a time! So, who do you know that needs to be set free from this spirit? Take a moment & think; Immediately, someone came to your mind. This is the person that you need to pray for everyday.

Over the years, we've seen hundreds of addicts set free by the power of the Gospel of Jesus Christ. However, I've noticed something. As we pray for people, many times their situation gets worse before it gets better. Rest assure, this is a sign that the Holy Spirit is moving in their life. When the personal pain gets bad enough, people are more apt to change. So, be encouraged if things seem to be falling apart in that special someones life. It could be all apart of God's radical plan of redemption. Keep a fortified front against the dark spirit of pharmakia! Cut him off of your family tree!

Step to Start Strong:

Pray for the Addicted

JUNE 13.

SHAKE IT OFF!

"But Paul shook the snake off into the fire and suffered no harm."

Acts 28:5

Back in December 2012, I traveled to India for the very first time with Pastor Mati Joseph, my faithful pastor friend from New York City. The night before our departure, I had to officiate a wedding so I arrived home late, only to rush and pack my suitcase for our 10 day journey. However, what happened next, almost scarred me for life. My suitcase was stored in the hall coat closet so I snatched it up and hastily threw it in the middle of the living floor so I could pack and get some last minute sleep. To my surprise, as I unzipped my suitcase and flipped it open, a snake suddenly snapped out at my face. For lack of better language, *I screamed like a school girl and darted down the hall!*

Now thankfully, this happened before Kacie & I got married, otherwise the story would have taken a different turn. However, being all by myself, I mustered up enough courage to come out of hiding and kill the copperhead curled up under my couch. Yes, you read that last sentence right; a copperhead was hibernating in my suitcase for the winter but I am proud to say, He never saw the warmth of spring. I shook him off and like the Apostle Paul, I suffered no harm.

Out of this startling storyline, the Lord taught me a valuable lesson. Any time, you rise up to do something great for God, you will suffer spiritual attack and persecution from people. So go ahead and get ready for it. Paul put it this way, *"I do not want you to be ignorant of the devil schemes."* (2 Cor. 2:11) For me, I have been taught by adversity and tested by fire! I almost expect it to come now but it doesn't distract me because I know the truth. The truth is *"the level of the spiritual attack is directly proportioned to the level of spiritual blessing that is coming our way."* This is why Satan is coming against you because God is about to bless you! A matter of fact, *"I see a great and effective door opening for you in the spirit but there are many who oppose you."* So, stand strong today. Don't let what others say, close the gate to God's will for your life.

In conclusion, after I settled myself that night, I journaled the spiritual attacks that tried to keep me from getting on that plane the next day. If I had time, I would tell you in detail, the opposition we faced for this particular trip. It was the one of the greatest battles we ever fought in the spirit but thankfully, God delivered us from it all! Every attack fell impotent in the face of an all-powerful God! We pursued God's plan and traveled around the globe, only to see countless miracles that drastically changed my relationship with the Lord. All because I shook off the fiery darts of the devil that tried to change the direction of my destiny.

<u>Step to Start Strong</u>:

Shake off every Opposition!

JUNE 14.

10 Ways to Release God's Healing Power

#1 Through the presence of the Spiritual Gift of Healing:

> **1st Cor. 12:4-11** "There are diversities of gifts, but the same Spirit. There are differences of ministries, but the same Lord. And there are diversities of activities, but it is the same God who works all in all. But the manifestation of the Spirit is given to each one for the profit of all: for to one is given the word of wisdom through the Spirit, to another the word of knowledge through the same Spirit, to another faith by the same Spirit, to another gifts of healing by the same Spirit."

#2 Through the laying of Hands: *Mark 16:18 "They shall lay hands on the sick, and they shall recover."*

#3 Through the Elders prayer & Anointing Oil: *James 5:14 "Is anyone among you sick? Let him call for the elders of the church,* *and let them pray over him, anointing him with oil in the name of the Lord. And the prayer of faith will save the sick, and the Lord will raise him up."*

#4 Through speaking the word to your sickness: *Mark 11:23 "For assuredly, I say to you, whoever says to this mountain, 'Be removed and be cast into the sea,' and does not doubt in his heart, but believes that those things he says will be done, he will have whatever he says."*

#5 Through the Power of Agreement: *Matthew 18:19-20 "Again I say to you that if two of you agree on earth concerning anything that they ask, it will be done for them by My Father in heaven. For where two or three are gathered together in My name, I am there in the midst of them."*

#6 Through your own Faith: *Mark 11:24 "Therefore I say to you, whatever things you ask when you pray, believe that you receive them, and you will have them."*

#7 By the Name of Jesus: John 14:13-14 *"And whatever you ask in My name, that I will do, that the Father may be glorified in the Son. If you ask anything in My name, I'll do it."*

#8 By Praying for Others: Job 42:10 "And the Lord restored Job's losses, when he prayed for his friends. Indeed the Lord gave Job twice as much as he had before."

#9 Through the Faith of Others: *Mark 2:5-11 "When Jesus saw their faith, He said to the paralytic, "Son, your sins are forgiven you."*

#10 Through the Modern Day Miracle of Medicine: *Matthew 9:12 "When Jesus heard that, He said to them, "Those who are well have no need of a physician, but those who are sick do."*

Step to Start Strong:

Walk in Divine Health

JUNE 15.

DIVINE HEALING

"God anointed Jesus of Nazareth with the Holy Spirit and with power and He went about doing good and healing all who were oppressed by the devil, for God was with Him."

Acts 10:38

If I've heard it once, I've heard it 1,000 times; Pastor Chance, *"Is it God's will to heal?"*

So here's a good place to start with this subject, *"What has God really saved us from?"* The greek word for salvation is *"sozo"* meaning body, soul and spirit. It's a 3-part salvation. When you received Christ as your Lord and Savior, He not only saved you from the fiery flames of Hell, but He saved you from Hell on earth! Many believers have never heard this. Jesus came to seek and save that which was lost. What is *"that?"* It's your body, soul and spirit. Therefore, we have to know its God's will to heal.

Because if its God's will that none should perish and all should inherit eternal life. It's equally so that God desires to deliver the soul and heal the broken body. It's the definition of *"sozo"* and it's all for you and me. This point poses the next question, *"When will God heal?"'* Now, As one who loves to pray of the sick, I always believe God is going to do it right now! Therefore, when I pray for the sick, I always believe it will happen instantaneously. However, and I say it humbly, it doesn't always happen that way. Sometimes, I pray and nothing happens but this will never keep me from praying for the next person. Oral Roberts, the great healing evangelist, used to call this process *"wenting."* The scripture says, *"as they <u>went</u> they were healed."* We may not always witness the miracle with our own eyes but something happens in the spirit when we pray for the sick. Therefore, many times the healing will manifest at a later date. Who are we to doubt what Christ finished on the cross when all He called us to do is pray according to His will and His word. So, this is what we do; *"We call the things that are not as if they were, in Jesus Name."* Lastly, we need to ask *"How"* will they be healed? It's also interesting to see that Jesus never healed anyone the same way twice. He always did exactly what His Heavenly Father said to do and each scenario was different. Why is this so? I believe our Heavenly Father didn't want us to lean on a formula when ministering by faith. This type of faith requires a keen sensitivity to the Holy Spirit. I have found out that sometimes you have to look ridiculous in order to be victorious when praying of the sick. God will ask you to do something out of your comfort zone or understanding. So, don't look for a formula. Look to your Heavenly Father. He is the source of your salvation. He is the same yesterday, today and forevermore!

He still saves, He still sets people free and He still heals the sick! Take God at His word. It's His will to heal.

Step to Start Strong:

Pray for the Sick

JUNE 16.

SABBATH REST

"'Observe the sabbath day to keep it holy, as the LORD your God commanded you. 'Six days you shall labor and do all your work, but the seventh day is a sabbath of the LORD your God."

Deuteronomy 5:12

One of the *most spiritual things you can do is take a nap!* Maybe not everyday but according to scripture we are commanded to rest. Years ago, I heard a man share on the 7-7-7 principle. Here's what He had to say, *"Every week, take a day to rest. Every 7 weeks, take a weekend away and every 7 months, take a full week sabbatical."* Now, you may not follow this suggestion to the day but it's not a bad idea to implement into your yearly schedule.

The word Sabbath means *"stop."* Sometimes, we just need to stop and rest. A matter of fact, today would be a great day to unplug and to do something fun if you can. Call an old friend or family member and meet up. Go to lunch with a couple from church.

Grab a book and fall asleep reading on the couch. Whatever comes to mind, go for it! You will accomplish more in 6 days, if you will just take one day to rest. People will like you more too!

"Therefore, If you have no time to rest. It's exactly the right time." So let the words of Christ saturate your dry and thirsty soul; He said, *"Come unto me, all who are weary and heavy burdened and I will give you rest."* Go ahead and get some rest. You're going to need it for the next season of life.

Step to Start Strong:

Get Some R & R

JUNE 17.

THE BEMA SEAT

"For we must all appear before the judgment seat of Christ, that each one may receive the things done in the body, according to what he has done, whether good or bad."

2 Corinthians 5:10

During the Olympic Games, in ancient Greece, there was an elevated seat on the track and field finish line to give sight to who won the race. It was in this place that they awarded the victor's crown to these hard-working competitors. This area was called, *"The Bema Seat."*

Later, courtrooms adopted this arrangement to host arguments in the mist of the judge and jurors so everyone could see and hear what was happening. Again, it was an elevated seat for people to sit.

Also, you may have seen this type of seat in old church cathedrals as priest would climb the stairs up to the podium to address the congregation. Again, it was an area set aside for the sole purpose of one persons presence. *Otherwise, known as, the Bema Seat.*

According to scripture, every believer will face the *Bema Seat of Christ.* One day you will appear before God all by yourself and He will reward you for the things you have done. Everyday we are preparing to present ourselves before our King. Everything we do and everything we say is being recorded by the scribes of Heaven and one day, we will give account for all of it. You may think the world is getting away with what is being done in secret but there is one who is watching. His name is Jesus and He is the righteous judge.

My challenge to you is to *"Live your life in light of eternity."*Think with the end in mind. What you do now, really does affect eternity. Our goal would be to stand before the *"Bema Seat of Christ"* with our head held high knowing we have done all that we could do to be hard-working committed people who have defended the Gospel with all diligence and might. Our hope is for Him to say,*"Well done, thy good and faithful servant!"* No words would be greater. Come now, enter into eternal rest.

1st Corinthians 3:11-15 *"For no one can lay any foundation other than the one already laid, which is Jesus Christ. If anyone builds on this foundation using gold, silver, costly stones, wood, hay or straw, their work will be shown for what it is, because the Day will bring it to light. It will be revealed with fire, and the fire will test the quality of each person's work. If what has been built survives, the builder will receive a reward. If it is burned up, the builder will suffer loss <u>but yet will be saved</u>—even though only as one escaping through the flames."*

<u>Step to Start Strong</u>:

Be Ready for the Bema Seat

JUNE 18.

All Things

"Beloved, I pray that you may prosper in all things and be in health, just as your soul prospers."

3 John 1:2

Third John is the shortest epistle in the New Testament with only 13 verses. However, when we take the time to meditate upon it's precepts, we sense the weight of God's promise for those who would live by it.

"Notice your financial and physical health is directly tied to your spiritual well-being in verse two." If you feed the flesh, the flesh will subdue the spirit. If you feed the spirit man, the spirit will prevail and you will prosper in all things. Yes, your Heavenly Father is in the Blessing Business! He wants you to prosper in all areas of your life.

You may ask, *"How do I start the process of prosperity in my soul?"* The word soul here translates as *"psyche."* It means the whole being of a person. The same word is used in reference to the life of Jesus in John 10:15 and I quote; *"Just as I know the Father and the Father knows me, I lay my life down or soul down for my sheep."* Now, this is deep!

Yes, Jesus laid His physical life down for you and me but literally, He laid down His *"whole being also."* His submitted His mind, will and emotions to His Heavenly Father so we could prosper in all things.

The definition of true spiritual health is walking in the truth. Jesus said, *"you will know the truth and the truth will set you free!"* Free from what? Free from the curse of sin and all things that come along with it! What's the opposite of the curse? *You can call it Blessing or Heavenly Prosperity!* This is the pathway to inherit all the promises of God: *Walking in truth and love.* By these things, you will prosper in all the promises of God!

Step to Start Strong:

Walk in Truth and Love

JUNE 19.

God of the Gates

"The LORD loves the gates of Zion more than all the other dwellings of Jacob."

Psalm 82:7

God loves the *Gates!* Genesis 22:17 says, *"you will possess the gates of your enemies."* Isaiah 28:6 says, *"The Lord will be a source of strength for those who turn back the battle at the gates."* Even the Holy City of Jerusalem has 12 gates that are named after the 12 Apostles. *So, why does God place so much emphasis on the gates?*

A gate is a *hinged barrier* that is used to close an opening in a wall or fence. The main purpose is to *"let people in or let people out"*. With this in mind, the gate represents free will. God lets us choose what we let in and what we let out including Himself. God is love, therefore God gives us a choice. Joshua said, *"As for me and my house, we will serve the Lord!"* We choose to go to church! We choose to worship! We choose to be the Gatekeepers over our own lives.

Many years ago, when I served on staff at Sandhills Teen Challenge, God spoke this word to me. One of my daily duties was to walk down the long driveway at 5:00am and open the gate for our hours of operation. Early one morning, as I was opening the gate with sleep still in my eye, the Lord said, *"You're a Gatekeeper." A Gatekeeper*? At this time, I'd never heard this terminology, but I found out later this was a person who served in the temple and their job qualifications were quite interesting. Gatekeepers were called to prepare the grounds so others could come in and experience the presence of the Lord. They controlled the gate so that they and others could experience the fullness and excellency of the King.

You also are called to be a Gatekeeper. You prepare yourselves on a daily basis to host His presence so others can experience the God of the Gates. You are also an ambassadors for the King. The word ambassador means messenger but in its literal form it means hinge. God spoke to me and said, *"We are called to be the hinge to open the gate so that the King of Glory can come into dark, empty souls of mankind."* You have a part to play. The doorway of destiny cannot open without the Hinge of the Holy Spirit.

Do you need to oil your hinges this morning? Allow the Holy Spirit to pour His presence on you before you go out and fulfill your daily duties. He will show you who needs to be let in and who needs to be let out. He will also show you what needs to come in and what needs to come out! Jesus said, *"broad is the gate that leads to destruction but narrow is the one that leads to life!"* So, Go ahead and enter His gates with thanksgiving and come in His courts with praise today! Be a Gatekeeper because God loves the Gates!

Step to Start Strong:

Guard the Gate of your Soul

JUNE 20.

Stir up the Spirit

"Stir thyself up in the Spirit."

Psalm 35:23

Notice David's direction: He was stirring himself *"up"* in the Spirit! Not down in the depths of depression! So many people worry themselves right out of the will of God. How about we learn to turn our negative energy around and worship our way through the weakness that tends to overbear us. It works both ways!

If David knew how to do anything, he understood that God's presence was of utmost importance. David was a man just like us. He faced so many obstacles and disappointments. However, he discovered a secret. How to stir himself up in the spirit.

Grandparents, parents, pastors can't always do it for you. *The purpose of godly discipline is to get you to a place of self-discipline.* Spiritual maturity says, I know what to do now. I've been tried by adversity and tested by fire! I know I can reach inside of myself and pull out the answer because He lives in me! We honor men but not above God. Sometimes men will pull you down but God will always lift you up!

Let's stir ourselves up today! I'm reminded of what David prayed in Psalm 37:4, *"This One thing I ask of the Lord and this one thing I will seek this week; That I may dwell in the House of the Lord, all the days of my life, just to gaze upon the beauty of the Lord and to inquire upon His precepts. For better is one day in His house than a thousand elsewhere!"*

Step to Start Strong:

Stir Yourself up in the Lord

JUNE 21.

PARTAKERS OF HIS GRACE

"Ye are all partakers of my grace."

Philippians 1:7

All of us have been given a measure of grace according to the gift of God. (Ephesians 4:7) By this, we are constantly building a reservoir of this grace and favor to be released. I believe this is what the Apostle Paul meant when He said, *"I have been made a minister, according to the gift of grace that was given to me." (Ephesians 3:7)* The grace to be a minister was given to Him so he could freely release this grace to others. So it says,*"freely give because you have freely received." (Matthew 10:8)* Yes, we go to the throne of grace to receive mercy in *"our time of need"* but we also, go to the throne of grace so we can release the reservoir of grace that lives inside us.

Simon Peter builds on this thought as He writes, *"As every man has received the gift of grace, even so minister the same one to another, as good stewards of the manifold grace of God."* (1 Peter 4:10) Are you a good steward of the grace of God? God gives us grace so we can give it away. As John said, "*Out of his fullness we have all received grace in place of grace already given.*" (John 1:16) So, let's be good ministers of the manifold grace of God today? Let it flow freely. Release the reservoir of favor that abides on the inside of you. Be a partaker of God's grace.

Acts 20:32 *"And now I commend you to God and to the word of His grace, which is able to build you up and to give you the inheritance among all those who are sanctified."*

Step to Start Strong:

Partake of His Grace

JUNE 22.

A Sovereign Savior

*"The steps of a good man are ordered by the Lord,
And He delights in his way."*

Psalm 37:23

One weekend, I sat on the front row of Evangel Temple in Jacksonville Florida, to hear Evangelist Reinhart Bonnke share the word of God. For those of you who don't know him, listen to this statement carefully; *"God has used this man to lead more souls into the Kingdom than any other man in history."* Yes, a weighty word but absolutely true! Over 76 million decision cards have been filled out in His 42 years of ministry and they're still counting. He shared his story recently and I want to share it with you. Here's how he started his ministry: After graduating Bible school in Wales, Reinhart decided to spend one day sight-seeing in London before He headed home to Germany for the summer. All he had was a few coins as He got off the train so He walked around downtown to see what he could see for free. Toward the end of the day, He lost his sense of direction and ended up in a residential community. As he approached a particular intersection, He looked above the doorway of a house and saw the words, *"Home of George Jeffrey's."* He thought, *"this can't be the home of the Great UK Revivalist could it?"* As he kept walking, something urged him to turn back and knock on the door. So curiously, He slowly strolled down the ole pathway and gave a hard knock on the front door. Almost instantly, an elderly lady answered, so He said, *"Is this the home of Reverend George Jeffrey's?"* To his surprise she said, *"yes it is." "How can I help you?"* Wild eyed Reinhart quickly said, *"Would it be a bother to come in and see him?"* But she hastily said, *"Absolutely not!"* However, George heard the knock from up stairs and said with a deep, demanding voice, *"Let the boy come in, I've been waiting on him!"* Wow! What a moment this must have been! As the old man walked in frailty down the stairs, young Reinhart walked in the front door. Now after a cordial and respectful introduction, Reinhart talked and talked and talked out of anxiousness until George finally said, *"shall we step into a private room to pray?"* As they fell on their faces that day, this powerful hell-destroying patriarch laid hands on this young lad, to do what? To impart a supernatural blessing for his upcoming life of ministry. At the time, no one knew Reinhart would shake the nations with the Gospel from this point forward? But God did. Also, what was the chances of Reinhart stumbling upon the home of the great revivalist? A very slim chance but not to a sovereign Savior! The scripture says, *"the steps of a good man are ordered by the Lord!"* God ordained Reinhart Bonnke's steps to the door step of this man's humble abode. Why is this so? As Reinhart said on Sunday, *"to pass the flaming torch of the Gospel to the next generation!"* This is our call as Christians. To impart the imperishable truth of the grace of God to those around us. Can you believe Reverend George Jeffrey's went home to be with the Lord just a few days after this encounter? True Story. I charge you: Listen to the leading of God's voice. He's a Sovereign Savior. Whatever you do, *"Don't miss your moment."* Where would 76 million people be if Reinhart Bonnke didn't turn around?

<u>Step to Start Strong</u>:

Read the Autobiographies of Early Church Leaders

JUNE 23.

UNWHOLESOME TALK

"Do not let any unwholesome talk come out of your mouths, but only what is helpful for building others up according to their needs, that it may benefit those who listen."

Ephesians 4:29

Unwholesome Talk? King David understood this principle because He prayed in Psalm 141:3, *"Set a guard over my mouth O' God and keep watch over the doorway of my lips!"* *"For the one who guards his lips, preserves his life."* (Prov.13:3) Yes, the words we speak on a daily basis determines the outcome of our destiny.

Let me put it this way: *"Do you desire a brighter future?"* If so, watch the words that flippantly fly out of your mouth! Every person is a personal prophet over their own life! If you say, you're old; you'll start acting like an old person! If you say, you'll always be broke, you might as well get used to it! *"For Death and life are in the power of the tongue and those who love it will eat of its fruit."* (Proverbs

18:21) Love what? For those who love to talk will eat its fruit. What fruit? The fruit of what your words produce.

So, I ask you: "*What do your words produce*?" Think about your consistent conversation. What does your tone sound like? Is it rooted and grounded in love? Do you speak words of faith or fear? Your words ultimately create your world.

Therefore, I charge you: Watch your words and do a cross-examination at the end of the day. The word says, Don't let any unwholesome talk "*come out of your mouth*!" Just because something passes through your mind doesn't mean it has to come out of your mouth! Try taking "*every thought captive by making it obey your Lord and Savior Jesus Christ.*" (2nd Cor. 10:4-5) The word works!

Step to Start Strong:

Speak Wholesome Words

JUNE 24.

Spiritual Fitness

"Physical training is good, but training for godliness is much better, promising benefits in this life and in the life to come."

1st Timothy 4:8

The Bible is simple, relevant and applicable in all areas of life. Even in the avenue of physical fitness. The Apostle Paul exhorts young Timothy *"to take care of his temple"* because his body is the dwelling place of the Holy Spirit. This type of training is good but training in godliness is so much better. We need both.

The Greek word for discipline is *"gymnadzo"* from which we get our word gymnasium. It derived from another word meaning *"naked."* What's the correlation? When Greek athletes would gather in a gym to compete athletically, they would strip off their clothing so they wouldn't be hindered for the purpose of winning their event. Here was Paul's point; *"if we are going to train ourselves in godliness, we have to strip off everything that hinders us as Christians."*

Otherwise, we will be weighted down with the worries of this life and ultimately, lose ground against Satan.

1st Corinthians 9:24 says, "*Do you not know that in a race all the runners run, but only one receives the prize? Run in such a way as to win the prize! Everyone who competes in a game trains with strict discipline.*"

Therefore, I charge you to *"say no to the things that hinder God's plan and purposes for you life!"* Above all else, protect the call of God that has been placed inside your soul! Don't be distracted by the devil and His schemes! Let's strive for godliness! Physical training feels good now but godliness brings benefit both in this life and in the life to come! We need both!

May we be physical, emotionally and spiritually fit to do, whatever God calls us to do, with *excellence.*

Step to Start Strong:

Get Fit

JUNE 25.

GET OUT OF JAIL FREE!

"It is for freedom that Christ has set us free. Stand firm, then, and do not let yourselves be burdened again by a yoke of slavery."

Galatians 5:1

Jesus Christ came to set the captive free. On the contrary, Satan came to steal, kill and destroy. This is the altercation of the ages; *Satan induces the yoke of slavery but Christ sets the captives free.* The yoke the scripture speaks of is a wooden beam normally used between a pair of oxen to enable them to pull a heavy load especially when they are working harmoniously. The task-master would place this weighted scale on their backs to control which way the animal would go. He would then unyieldingly whip them and scream laborious commands all day long just to make sure he met his goal. *This symbolizes the yoke of bondage.* Many people wake up every morning with a yoke around their neck. Satan tells them what they can do and what they can't do. He whips them with worry and fear all throughout the year. He shouts commands of confusion and lies to lure them farther and farther away from the Lord. This is his ultimate goal. If He can't keep you out of Heaven, He will do He best to make you unfruitful on the earth.

If you find yourself under the yoke of yesterdays guilt and shame; Be of good cheer! If God set you free one time, He can set you free a second time! Many people give grace to the sinner but they have no mercy for the saint. They love salvation but they are impatient with people when it comes to sanctification. *This is not so with your Savior.* He is full of grace and compassion and He is slow to become angry. (Psalm 145:8) You can always go to God because God will always understand. Listen to what Isaiah 10:27 says, "And it shall come to pass in that day, that the burden shall be taken off his shoulders, and the yoke from around his neck, and the yoke shall be destroyed <u>because of the anointing</u>." In other words, "There is no chain too big for God to break!" All we have to do is call on His name! Jesus is still saying, "Come to me, all who are weary and heavy burdened, and I will give you rest. <u>Take my yoke</u> upon you and learn from me, for I am gentle and humble in heart, and you will find rest for your souls. For <u>my yoke</u> is easy and my burden is light." The world thinks the yoke of Christ is dominating and daunting but they couldn't be more deceived. The yoke of Christ is liberating. He loves you and He would never do anything to hurt or harm you. His ultimate goal is to give you rest in your soul. Therefore, Go ahead and walk out from up under the yoke of bondage that is holding you back. He holds the keys to death, hell and the grave! *"We all get out of jail for free!"* All you have to do is believe!

<u>Step to Start Strong</u>:

Be Equally Yoked with the Lord

JUNE 26.

Crown Me!

"He redeems me from death and crowns me with love and compassion!"

Psalm 103:4

The Bible speaks of 5 different crowns that will be given to people in Heaven according to how they lived their life on earth. Jesus Christ Himself will award us publicly for every good deed in that day and O' what a day it will be for those who have been faithful. What crowns do you desire?

1. The Crown of Righteousness:

Timothy 4:7-8 "*I have fought the good fight, I have finished the race, I have kept the faith. Finally, there is laid up for me the CROWN OF RIGHTEOUSNESS, which the Lord, the righteous Judge, will give to me on that Day, and not to me only but also to all who have loved His appearing.*"

<u>2. The Imperishable Crown: (The Victor's Crown)</u>

1 Corinthians 9:24-27 *"Do you not know that those who run in a race all run, but one receives the prize? Run in such a way that you may obtain it. And everyone who competes for the prize is temperate in all things. Now they do it to obtain a perishable crown, but we for an IMPERISHABLE CROWN. Therefore I run thus: not with uncertainty. Thus I fight: not as one who beats the air. But I discipline my body and bring it into subjection, lest, when I have preached to others, I myself should become disqualified."*

<u>3. The Crown of Life: (The Martyr's Crown)</u>

<u>Revelation 2:10</u> *"Do not fear any of those things which you are about to suffer. Indeed, the devil is about to throw some of you into prison, that you may be tested, and you will have tribulation ten days. Be faithful until death, and I will give you the CROWN OF LIFE."*

<u>4. The Crown of Rejoicing: (Soul-Winner's Crown:)</u>

1 Thessalonians 2:19-20 *"For what is our hope, or joy, or CROWN OF REJOICING? Is it not even you in the presence of our Lord Jesus Christ at His coming? For you are our glory and joy."*

<u>5. The Crown of Glory:</u>

1 Peter 5:1-4 *"The elders who are among you I exhort, I who am a fellow elder and a witness of the sufferings of Christ, and also a partaker of the glory that will be revealed. SHEPHERD THE FLOCK OF GOD which is among you, serving as overseers, not by constraint but willingly, not for dishonest gain but eagerly; nor as being lords over those entrusted to you, but* *being examples to the flock; and when the Chief Shepherd appears, you will receive the* CROWN OF GLORY *that does not fade away."*

Step to Start Strong:

Crown Him King of your Heart

JUNE 27.

THE GIFT OF GOD

"I know that there is nothing better for people, than to be happy and to do good while they live. That each of them may eat and drink, and find satisfaction in all their toil—for this is the gift of God."

Ecclesiastes 3:12-13

JESUS CHRIST CAME to redeem us from the curse of sin. Sin is the root cause that makes everything so complicated. Someone said, *"there are 7 deadly sins"* but I say, *"all sin is deadly."* They all lead to death! Just ask Adam & Eve.

In Genesis 3, we read the curse that was pronounced upon man after he sinned; God said, *"Cursed is the ground because of you; through painful toil you will eat food from it all the days of your life. It will produce thorns and thistles for you, and you will eat the plants of the field. By the sweat of your brow you will eat your food until you return to the ground, since from it you were taken; for dust you are and to dust you will return." Adam's hands was greatly effected by the curse of sin. His disobedience opened the doorway of damnation to come upon all people. Man was formed from the dust of the earth so God cursed the whole earth too! Instead of easily yielding the blessing, it would painfully produce thorns and thistles by the sweat of man's brow. No more fulfilling work, man would have to toil just to make ends meet. Does this sound like anybody's week? Watch this:*

Galatians 3:13 says, *"Christ redeemed us from the curse of sin by becoming a curse for us. For it is written: "Cursed is everyone who is hung on a tree."* Yes, Jesus Christ became sin so that you and I could be redeemed from sin and all of its benefits! Including the curse against our work! Hell can't stop the work of our hands! *Do you know why?* First, when we see Christ fully entering into the work of redemption, we are told that He sweat great drops of blood in the Garden of Gethsemane. Matthew Henry's Commentary puts it this way, "Sweat came in with sin and became a branch of the curse. However, when Christ was made sin for us, He underwent a grievous sweat, so that the curse of sin could leave our lives forever." In the words of Sinclair Ferguson, "Jesus undid everything Adam did and did everything Adam failed to do." What a beautiful picture of redemption! Secondly, Jesus wore the crown of thorns on the cross as a symbol of the curse in the garden. This is a powerful picture of Him becoming the sin-bearing, curse-removing Second Adam. Again, Matthew Henry wrote: "*Thorns came in with sin, but they went out with salvation because his sufferings became our grace and glory."* The point of the story? We don't have to work alone. We can be co-laborers with Jesus Christ! He wants to work with you to get the job done! No more meaningless duties from day to day. Your life is making a difference because you have been redeemed!

Step to Start Strong:

Work as unto the Lord

JUNE 28.

WORK IT OUT!

"For we are God's workmanship, created in Christ Jesus to do good works, which God prepared in advance for us to do."

Ephesians 2:10

When God created you, He didn't say, *"Oh my, I think I made a terrible mistake! What in the world am I going to do now?"* No! When God create you, He had a very specific plan and purpose for you to pursue. The God of the universe wired you for His good work. This should excite you! You are God's masterpiece.

This word *"masterpiece or workmanship"* in the Greek is *poiema*, which is the word where we get poem or poetry. This means you are the poem that God wanted to write when He gave you life. As He redeems you, you become *"His word made flesh."* His handiwork for the world to see!

With this in mind, I declare that, *"Now is the time for you to rise and shine for God's glory is among you."* You already know what to do! Just do it whole-heartedly! You were born with the burden to do what you love and it will never leave you. The gifts of God are irrevocable and without repentance! What God created you for will never crumble! His purposes were prepared for you in advance! They abide on the inside of you. All you have to do is, *"Work it out!'*

Ask God today: What am I supposed to be doing? When He speaks, Jump and don't ever look back. It's going to be exceeding and abundantly better than you could ever ask or think.

Step to Start Strong:

Work it out!

JUNE 29.

LEAD WITH LOVE

"So when you, pass judgment on others, yet do the same things, do you think you will escape God's judgment? Or do you disregard the riches of His kindness, tolerance, and patience, not realizing that God's kindness leads you to repentance?"

Romans 2:3-4

In one of our previous Leadership Conferences in Southeast Asia, my Father made a statement in his teaching that stuck with me: He said, *"we judge others by their behavior but we tend to judge ourselves by our intentions."* Such a convicting thought when fully considered.

It's so easy to pass judgment onto others without ever turning the sword of self-examination on ourselves. The Word of God should cut both ways. It should convict others when we speak it but more importantly, it should convict us when we hear it. King David understood this principle as He prayed this prayer in Psalm 139; He said, *"search me and know me O'God to see if there be any wicked way within me."* We could see our sin more clearly before we came to Christ but now we have to be more intentional about our seasons of personal soul-searching. Don't succumb to the temptation of judging others. Judge yourself first.

"Because t*here is only one Lawgiver and Judge, and He is the one who is able to save and destroy. But you—who are you to judge your neighbor?*" (James 4:12) Don't be judgmental. Just love Jesus. It's the loving-kindness of the Lord that *"leads people to repentance."* Let's Lead with Love because *"Mercy Triumphs over Judgment." In fact, may we adopt Micah 6:8 as our life verse:*

"He has shown you, O man, what is good;
And what does the Lord require of you
But to do justly,
To love mercy,
And to walk humbly with your God?

Step to Start Strong:

Judge Not!

JUNE 30.

KINGDOM AUTHORITY

"He appointed twelve that they might be with him and that he might send them out to preach and to have authority to drive out demons."

Mark 3:14-15

Notice the 3 directives for the 12 apostles when they were appointed into public ministry. Their number one priority was to simply *"be with Jesus."* This idea is a conflict with popular church opinion. Many believers think they have to start the day doing something in order to be in right standing with Him. He didn't say, Do. He simply said, Be with me. There's a big difference.

"In fact, the moment you stop thinking about self and what you have to do while praying and worshipping, at last you are praying and worshipping." This sacred act of enjoying the presence of Jesus should be held at our highest regard. Never forget the fact that you have an all-access pass to the throne room of grace not because of what you do but because of who He is.

Only when we internalize this idea can we fully proclaim the power and majesty of directive number two; which is to preach. Now, the word preach means to proclaim but this means much more than preachers just standing behind a pulpit. You can proclaim from a social media platform or to a stranger on the street. This is the type of ministry that Jesus is calling us to. Ministry shouldn't be something we do. Rather, it should be who we are. Our love for people should be an overflow from our time spent with the Lord. Try to remove busy and tired from your vocabulary. We're not called to be busy while running ourselves ragged. We're called to rest in our relationship with God and be fruitful.

When these two manifest, the devil has to flee which is directive number 3: When you walk in Kingdom Authority. Think about it? You're saturated in the Holy Spirit from spending time with Jesus, you know who you are because you've heard him speak to your heart and now, you're boldly proclaiming what He spoke to you in your spirit! The end result of this instruction? Nothing less than *"turning the world upside down!"* And this is the fullness that God is calling us to, *"3 in 1: Kingdom Authority."*

Step to Start Strong:

Be with Jesus

JULY 1.

Focus your Faith

"So we fix our eyes not on what is seen, but on what is unseen. For what is seen is temporary, but what is unseen is eternal."

2nd Corinthians 4:18

Faith comes by what you hear, not by what you see. What you hear from Heaven is always more important than what you see in a situation. This is the way you have to think if you are going to walk by faith.

Consider Abraham, the Father of our Faith in Hebrews 11:8, *"For by faith, when called to go to a place he would later receive as his inheritance, He obeyed and went, even though he did not know where he was going!"* This is a sure sign of faith! His sight screamed, No! But Heaven whispered, Go! Have you ever been there before? You didn't know what to do and you didn't know which way to go? If so, be sure not to neglect that still small voice in your spirit! This whisper will be the voice behind you saying, *"This is the way; walk in it!"*

In fact, faith says, *"what you hope for will actually happen."* So, whatever you do, don't lose your hope. Hope means to, *"Have Only Positive Expectations!"* You'll never hear Heaven speak doubt, defeat or discouragement. If you feel this way, you need to focus your faith. How do you do it? By fixing your eyes not on what is seen but what is unseen. What is unseen? Your unanswered prayers and unfulfilled promises! Its time to focus your faith on what God said, not what you see. Make this a daily discipline. It will bring you an abundance of peace and joy no matter what you're walking through.

Step to Start Strong:

Focus your Faith

JULY 2.

FOLLOW ME

"We must pay careful attention to what we have heard, so that we do not drift away. How shall we escape if we ignore so great a salvation? This salvation, which was first announced by the Lord, was confirmed to us by those who heard him. God also testified to it by signs, wonders and various miracles and by gifts of the Holy Spirit distributed according to His will."

Hebrews 2:1-4

JESUS DID NOT perform miracles to show us what God can do. We all know God can do whatever He wants to do! On the contrary, miracles followed Jesus' ministry because God wanted to "*show us what we could do, if we would live a life fully submitted to the Holy Spirit.*" Over and over again, the scripture calls Christ, *"the Son of Man."* This simply means that Jesus was stripped of His divinity so He could pick up His humanity and "*show us how to live out a supernatural lifestyle.*"

If Jesus performed miracles as God, I am impressed but I am not beckoned to follow him and do what He did because He was God. However, if Jesus performed miracles as a mere man, this truth challenges me to conform to His example in all things. How did He do it? Acts 2:22 says, "*Jesus of Nazareth was a man accredited by God to you by miracles, wonders and signs, which God did among you through him, as you yourselves know.*" Who did it? God did it through His Son. With this in mind, I've got Good News for you; you also are Sons and Daughters of the God Most High. So I have to ask: When was the last time you experienced something supernatural? Did it leave you *"wondering"* how in the world did this happen? If so, this was God's intention. A sign of a miracle leaves us in wonder which leads us down a path of right-living for His Name's sake. I guess what I'm trying to say is, "*God wants to use you.*" Yes, you!

Do we follow Jesus in word only and not in deed? If He was our example, *"Our life should be a living replica of His righteousness in all things."* I can almost hear Him saying this morning, *"Come, Follow Me."* I want to teach you a new thing. Just trust me.

Step to Start Strong:

Follow in the Footsteps of Jesus

JULY 3.

THE KEY TO SUCCESS

"Be strong and very courageous. Be careful to obey all the law my servant Moses gave you; do not turn from it to the right or to the left, that you may be successful wherever you go. Keep this Book of the Law always on your lips; meditate on it day and night, so that you may be careful to do everything written in it. Then you will be prosperous and successful."

Joshua 1:7-8

Joshua 1 is the only chapter that mentions the word success in scripture. *The Good News?* Joshua won the war! He successfully killed 31 Kings to step into his destiny and ultimately lead God people into the Promised Land. How did he do it? Don't miss this: "*By meditating on the Word of God!*"

Meditation did not originate with eastern religion as some may think. Meditation originated with God. This teaching shows us *"meditation will ultimately manifest obedience in the heart of man."* This scripture rings true: *"As a man thinks in his heart so is he."*

So, what determines our ongoing success spiritually speaking? Our lingering thoughts and the words on your lips.

Mahatma Ghandi said,

> *Your thoughts become your words.*
> *Your words become your behavior.*
> *Your behavior become your habits.*
> *Your habits become your values.*
> *Your values become your destiny.*

Let me ask you a question: If your mind was a garden, *"What would be irrigating your imagination?"* The upcoming election? The bottom line on your bank account? Your past pains and present problems? You tell me? Who or what holds you attention?

If I've learned anything while walking with God, it is this: *"If I will give God my attention, He will always exceed my expectation and ultimately grant me great success."* This is an Ancient KEY, I call Meditation.

<u>Step to Start Strong</u>:

Meditate upon the goodness of God

JULY 4.

FIREWORKS!

"Our God is a consuming FIRE."

Hebrews 12:29

The 4th of July Weekend is one of the most popular holidays on the calendar because it's the weekend we celebrate our freedom and commemorate those who fought to obtain our privilege. To be festive, people decorate, make their favorites desserts and do their best to have fun in the sun with those they love. Many of you do the same thing every year as we do. We always enjoy our time with family and friends out at Masonboro Inlet between Wrightsville Beach and Carolina Beach. It has been a family tradition for years now. Our family does a lot of things but one thing we don't do is shoot fireworks. Don't get me wrong, we love watching fireworks but we don't buy fireworks. How about you?

The Bible teaches us that the Fire Works. Fire burns away impurities, Fire gives us light to our surroundings and Fire provides warmth for many people around the world. The properties of fire seem infinite and interesting to study but heres my favorite.

Unlike any other element, fire does not exist in a natural state. Fire can only form or manifest by consuming other matter. Fire converts the energy of other objects into different physical states. In essence, Fire is a transformer. It changes things. I believe this is the purpose of the Holy Spirit when He comes to dwell inside of a person. Speaking of Jesus, John the Baptist said, *"He will baptize you with the Holy Spirit and Fire."* (Matthew 3:11) Jesus will purify you, provide for you, and be light for your path but He will also transform you into a different person. To those of you who have been walking with the Lord for any amount of time, you know this Fire-really-works.

The scripture says, *"Our God is an all-consuming fire."* Father, we pray that your fire would fall afresh on us this week to consume us and convert us into your love and power. May your love purify us, provide for us, light our path and make us into the people that you want us to be in the mighty name of Jesus, Amen! Let the Fire-Work!

Happy 4th of July!

Step to Start Strong:

Celebrate your Freedom in Christ Jesus.

JULY 5.

The Sword of the Lord

"Coming out of his mouth is a sharp sword with which to strike down the nations. 'He will rule them with an iron scepter.'"

Revelation 19:15

D. L. Moody was one of the greatest evangelist of all time. In a 40-year period he won a million souls, founded three Christian schools, launched a great Christian publishing agency, established a world-renowned Christian conference center, and inspired literally thousands of preachers to win souls and conduct revivals. He traveled across the American continent and through Great Britain with some of the greatest and most successful evangelistic meetings the world has ever known. It was Henry Varley who said, "*It remains to be seen what God will do with a man who gives himself up wholly to Him.*" And Moody endeavored to be, under God, that man; and the world did marvel to see how wonderfully God used him.

This beckons the question: *"What does our nation really need?"* I'll tell you what we need: *"We need another wave of radical revivalists to emerge on the scene!"* Do you need to be revived? If so, take time to read the autobiographies and writings of those who left a footprint in history because of their faith. Nothing can stir you up the spirit better than a testimony of what God did in someone else's life

In the past, I've read books on Kathryn Kuhlman, John G. Lake, David Wilkerson and more! What are you reading? I've learned: *if you want to be a leader, you have to be a reader!* Here's a key; If you read a chapter a day before you go to bed, you can read over 2 dozen books a year with ease.

So it was with D.L. Moody. He was *"The Sword of the Lord"* for His generation and you can be one in yours too! *"For it remains to be seen what God will do with a man who gives himself up wholly to Him."* Only time will tell just who is that man. Let it be you and let it be me.

<u>Step to Start Strong</u>:

Be the Sword of the Lord

JULY 6.

A Time of Restore

"After Job had prayed for his friends, the Lord restored his fortunes and gave him twice as much as he had before."

Job 42:10

Job literally lost everything but His own life and his wife. Out of the blue, things took a sudden turn and suddenly He found himself laying in the dust in total devastation. In the moment, everyone expected Him *"to curse God and die"* but what did He do? The scripture says, *"He fell down and worshipped by saying, "The Lord giveth and the Lord taketh away but may the name of the Lord be forever praised!"*

Nobody knew God was going to restore his fortunes and give him twice as much as he had before. What the devil meant for evil, God turned around for the good of Job's behalf. But notice when it happened: *The substance of restoration wasn't released until Job began to pray for His friends.* This reaffirms a passage found in Ephesians 6:8 that promises, *"what you do for others God will do for you."* Absolutely amazing! You can work for God and God will work for you!

Job experienced the miraculous restoration when He became a beacon of light to his brothers. Afterwards, what did God do? God ministered through him but He also ministered to Him. This is a powerful principle in scripture.

Most people sit around and wait for God to answer their prayers instead of giving God an opportunity to use them to be an answer to prayer! When you begin to live your life as a minister of reconciliation, God will begin to reconcile and restore the broken pieces in your path. We have to crucify the mentality of my four and no more. God has so much in store for you if you will not let the pains our your past dictate your future.

Go ahead, pray for somebody today. Get your eyes off your problems and help somebody else navigate through their problems. By doing this, your problems will minimize and God's promises will be maximized in your mind. God wants to do for you, what you cannot do for yourself! Now, is the time to restore.

Step to Start Strong:

Be a Minister of Reconciliation

JULY 7.

Real Resolution

"Let us hold fast the confession of our hope without wavering, for he who promised is faithful."

Hebrews 10:23

William Carey is known to many as *"The Father of Modern Missions."* This man could not be silenced and his fire to reach the heathen with the Gospel could not be put out. The list of what he accomplished in his life is staggering. Just to name a few, he planted and pastored a church, translated the Bible into 37 different dialects and some say, he impacted India more than any other man in history. This is why I love William. He was truly a General in God's Army.

With this in mind, is their anybody out there who is willing to carry this torch into the 21 Century by proclaiming to every person that Jesus Christ is Lord and Savior of All? If God is speaking to you: "*Will you accept the call?*"

If so, adopt William Carey's acclaimed quote into your ministry today, *"If you Expect great things from God, you will Attempt great things from God."* Don't draw back from your dream. Remember, God wants to fulfill the desires in your heart more so than you do.

In conclusion, Carefully read the *"11 Resolutions"* that were implemented into William Carey's *"Missional Community"* in India that changed so many lives. My prayer is that God will use us to change our culture, cities and communities in the same measure. Will you go for God?

MAY WE STRIVE:

1. To set an infinite value on men's souls
2. To acquaint ourselves with the snares which hold the minds of the people
3. To abstain from whatever deepens our prejudice against the Gospel
4. To watch for every chance of doing the people good
5. To preach "Christ crucified" as the grand means of conversion
6. To esteem and treat people always as our equals
7. To guard and build up "the hosts that they may be gathered"
8. To cultivate their spiritual gifts, ever pressing upon them from
9. their missionary obligation, since Indians only can win India for Christ
10. To labor unceasingly in biblical translation

11. To be instant in the nurture of personal religion
12. To give ourselves without reserve to the Cause, "not counting even the clothes we wear our own"

Step to Start Strong:

Expect Great Things from God.

JULY 8.

A Beautiful Mind

"Let this mind be in you, which was also in Christ Jesus."

Philippians 2:5

The Holy Spirit is a person. If you don't see Him as a person, it will be very hard to develop a personal relationship with Him. In my many years of ministry, I've noticed in some Christian circles the Holy Spirit is never mentioned. People speak of God the Father & God the Son but the Bible teaches us there is another person in the Trinity and He is God the Holy Spirit. To some, He is the God they never knew. If He is a person, we have to believe that He has a mind, will and emotions. Your mind allows you to think, your will guides your desires and your emotions release what we call feelings. Now pay close attention to this: *"Is it possible that the Holy Spirit wants to teach us how to think, what to desire and how to feel what God feels? I think so.*

John 16:13 says, *"But when He, the Spirit of Truth comes, He will guide you into all the truth. He will not speak on his own; He will speak only what he hears, and He will tell you what is yet to come."* Our God is omniscient meaning He is all-knowing. A matter of fact, God can never think of something He has never thought of before. Why? Because He knows everything and He wants to guide you into all truth.

Think of it this way: You have somebody who knows everything about everything living on the inside of you and He is committed to be your teacher. If you don't understand something or you need an answer for a certain area in your life, just ask Him. Many times, *"we have not because we ask not."* Go ahead; open your mouth and ask God for the solution you have been worrying about! You may be surprised at how quickly He answers. He's done this for me so many times. Its like suddenly the answer is downloaded into the hard-drive of my heart and I say, *"where did this come from?"* Answers come from The Holy Spirit.

My prayer is that,*"this mind be in you, which was also in Christ Jesus."* What mind? The Beautiful Mind of Jesus Christ. May you think, desire and feel like Him forevermore.

<u>Step to Start Strong</u>:

Embrace the Person of the Holy Spirit

JULY 9.

Open Heavens

"Jesus came from Galilee to John at the Jordan to be baptized by him. And John tried to prevent Him, saying, "I need to be baptized by You, but You coming to me?" But Jesus answered and said to him, "Permit it to be so now, for thus it is fitting for us to fulfill all righteousness." Then he allowed Him. When He had been baptized, Jesus came up immediately from the water; and Behold the Heavens were opened to Him, and He saw the Spirit of God descending like a dove and remaining upon Him. And suddenly a voice came from heaven, saying, "This is My beloved Son, in whom I am well pleased."

Matthew 3:13-16

John the Baptist felt unworthy to baptize Jesus and rightfully so. However, I also understand, *"Being willing to do what you are not qualified to do is sometimes what qualifies you."* John's obedience to

Jesus changed everything. All of Heaven stood at attention as they heard the Father's heart declare to the son, *"I am so pleased with you."* No one expected this: Heaven invaded earth by the humility of a man. This was the answered prayer from all the prophets of old! God, *"why don't you rend the Heavens and come down?"* (Isaiah 64:1) This had been the invitation for a divine visitation for so long and suddenly God showed up like a dove descending upon His Son with the Holy Spirit of God.

In this moment, The Heavens were *"opened."* This word means to tear or to split. It's the same word in Matthew 27:51 that teaches us, *"the veil of the temple was torn in two from the top to the bottom; the earth shook and the rocks split."* If we pay attention to the story, it was a combination of grace and glory! The torn veil represents the fulfillment of the law which occurred by the sinless life of Jesus Christ. The splitting of the rock begs the question: *"Is anything to hard for God?"* and lastly, The Heavens were opened to prove to the prince and the power of the air that the enemy had been stripped of his authority once and for all.

The Best News? The Heavens are still open! Every believer has an Open Heaven over their head. For those who don't; The Closed Heaven is between their own ears. I used to pray this way, *"God rend the Heavens and come down"* but I later found out, He's already accomplished this act. We don't have to content for Him to come! Here's here and He's with till the end!

The Open Heaven gives us a full access pass to a personal relationship with God which includes every spiritual blessing in Heavenly places. Can I ask you a question: If the Heavens are opened; *"Why do we live our lives like they are closed?"* May we pray this way: *"Our Father, who art in Heaven. Hallowed be thy name. Thy Kingdom Come. Thy will be done. On earth* *as it is in Heaven, In Jesus Name, Amen.*

Step to Start Strong:

Envision an Open Heaven

JULY 10.

POISON

"Jesus came from Galilee to John at the Jordan to be baptized by him. And John tried to prevent Him, saying, "I need to be baptized by You, but You coming to me?" But Jesus answered and said to him, "Permit it to be so now, for thus it is fitting for us to fulfill all righteousness."Then he allowed Him. When He had been baptized, Jesus came up immediately from the water; and Behold the Heavens were opened to Him, and He saw the Spirit of God descending like a dove and remaining upon Him. And suddenly a voice *came* from heaven, saying, "This is My beloved Son, in whom I am well pleased."

Matthew 3:13-16

The older I get the less complicated I become. You may ask why? Because I have learned as a child of God, I have to be cautious and careful if I want to fulfill the call that has been placed upon my life. It takes years to build credibility but only one choice to cause it all to crumble. Think about it; All the blood, sweat and tears that have been shed during your years, wasted because you made a flippant decision. The quote, *"Rome wasn't built in a day"* teaches us the best way to grow is steady and sure. This sheds light on the vitality for each of us to *"guard our anointing"* as my pastor's wife used to say. Nothing is more important than protecting our the call that the Lord Jesus Christ has place upon our lives.

Ultimately, people fall because they don't protect the call. Satan loves to poison the potential of God's people to keep them from their purpose. For example: Have you ever said, *"that person has so much potential."* What did you really mean? You meant if they will ever get it together God will use them! This is not a compliment for a christian; it's a way to say, they are wasting their life. May it not be said for this remnant of believers. Yes, as we go to different levels, we will fight different devils but the Bible is still true. *"Greater is He that lives in me that He that lives in the world! This is the victory that has overcome the world; our faith in our Heavenly Father!"*

By living with this mind-set, we will maximize our potential. So I ask you: What has been poisoning your potential and paralyzing you purpose? Dump it down the drain today, in Jesus Name. Its poison!

Step to Start Strong:

Protect the Call of God

JULY 11.

A Sure Salvation

"Salvation is found in no one else, for there is no other name under heaven given to mankind by which we must be saved."

Acts 4:12

A few years ago, a very influential talk show host made a bold statement on National TV that she believed, *"there were many roads to Heaven."* As an evangelist, I beg to differ because the Bible teaches something different. The Highway to Hell may have many roads but the Free-way to Heaven has only one! Jesus Christ, the Gateway to God!

This may help you: One day, not too long ago, we were in a foreign country eating at a restaurant after one of our revival services. Like always, I was starving because I don't like to eat before I preach. As I meandered through the menu, I was clueless because I couldn't read the language and the pictures were few. The waiter finally arrived to take our order and when it came to my turn, I pointed at a dish that sounded delicious and said, *"I'll take this!"* He said, I am so sorry Sir; we are completely sold out of that option this evening. Can I help you find something else? Well, first of all, I'm not upset because I didn't even know what it was anyway! So, I went on to ask Him, what the restaurant was known for to make my choice a bit easier. After my request, His countenance rose like the sun as He went on to say, *"Sir, there is a dish that people drive for many miles to come eat and it's absolutely amazing. It's our families personal favorite and it has made us famous in the city."* Sold! I said, *"I'll take it!"* And all of sudden, he understood his mistake; *"I'm so sorry Sir; we've sold out of that dish tonight as well."* You've got to be kidding me right?

After I finished sulking, the Lord spoke to me, and I learned a valuable that day: *"You cannot give what you do not have!"* This is why Jesus Christ is the way, the truth and the life because Jesus Christ is the only one that has paid the ultimate price for your sins. He died a sinners death so that you and I could be made righteous in His sight! Yes, the pathway to the foot of the cross may look different for each individual but the way to Heaven all looks the same because salvation cannot be found in any other name.

Therefore, you can place all of your trust in the fact that His salvation is sure. Don't be distracted with side dishes or deceived with worldly desires. Hunger after His holiness because His salvation is sure!

Step to Start Strong:

Go to God First and Foremost

JULY 12.

The Cry of Creation

"Ask the animals, and they will teach you or ask the birds in the sky, and they will tell you who I am."

Job 12:7

Has God ever used nature to speak to you? Romans 1:20 says, *"Since the creation of the world, God's invisible qualities—his eternal power and divine nature—have been clearly seen, being understood from what has been made, so that people are without excuse."* The Psalmist spoke a powerful truth as He said, *"The Heavens declare the Glory of God."* Indeed, nature is a great evangelist for God.

Now don't miss this: Man's glory comes through manufacturing but God's glory comes through what He created. If you will take time to pay attention to what created, He will speak to you. Their have been countless times over the years, where I have had a tugging in my heart to get away from the worries of the world, just to take a walk and get alone with Jesus. In the mist of this, my mind will clear and I will hear the still small voice of the Holy Spirit.

These moments are the most meaningful; God will illuminate a thing that surrounds me and all of a sudden, everything makes sense.

Isaiah understood this as He said, *"Look up into the heavens. Who created all the stars? He brings them out like an army, one after another, calling each by its name. Because of his great power and incomparable strength, not a single one is missing. O Jacob, how can you say the LORD does not see your troubles? O Israel, how can you say God ignores your rights? Have you never heard? Have you never understood? The LORD is the everlasting God, the Creator of all the earth. He never grows weak or weary. No one can measure the depths of his understanding. He gives power to the weak and strength to the powerless." (Chapter 40:26-29)*

The Bible teaches us that God is sovereign over nature. With this in mind, be watchful as He uses it for an illustrated sermon just for you to see. It's the Cry of Creation. He created you and He knows how to get your attention.

Step to Start Strong:

Pay Attention to the Cry of Creation

JULY 13.

EXCITED ANYONE?

"Clap your hands, all ye people; shout unto God with the voice of triumph."

Psalm 47:1

God has been speaking to me about enthusiasm and how important it is the life of a believer. The Greek word for God is *"theos,"* and theos is a part in the word, *"enthusiasm."* This means, real, genuine enthusiasm was birthed within God Himself. His presence carries a tangible feeling of energy and excitement for those who desire to tap into it. Do you get excited when you talk about God? I sure hope so because enthusiasm for God is contagious. The people you hang around will either give you a kick-start or they will kill you battery. Choose to do life with people who pick you up instead of pull you down. I've noticed so many people are satisfied with being apart of the Church of the Frozen Chosen with Pastor Pillow and Sister Sheets as they sing, *"O' Lay me down to sleep."* How can this be? We are living in the most exciting times in history. These are the days the prophets spoke about in scripture and you and I get to experience the signs of the times first-hand.

If you've been a spectator in the stands, its time to walk by faith onto the field. I can almost hear the Saints of God lifting their voices and clapping their hands in the Grandstand of Heaven as we stir ourselves up in the spirit this morning! Indeed,*"This is the day that the Lord has made and we will rejoice and be glad in it!"* Implementing this principle is half the battle. Get excited about God! God is not dead and He's definitely not boring! Anyone excited?

Step to Start Strong:

Be Enthusiastic!

JULY 14.

In His Sight

"Precious in the sight of the Lord is the death of His saints."

Psalm 116:15

Yesterday afternoon, I had the honor and privilege to facilitate a memorial service for a man who lost his life last week due to drug addiction and depression. The old country Chapel was full of family and friends who were seeking comfort from one another and ultimately from God. So, what did I do? The only thing I know how to do! I preached a simple but powerful message about the grace found in the Gospel of Jesus Christ! Do you wanna know what happened? A multitude of people got saved that's what! It never ceases to amaze me just how ripe the harvest is really is! Aways remember, as the world gets darker and darker, our platform to preach gets brighter and brighter!

I encouraged you today; God's word is true. He will take what the devil meant for evil and turn it around for your good. He still saves. He still sets the addict free and He still heals sick bodies for those who believe. No one knows the day or the hour in which we will meet the Lord. But all I can say is this; *Now is not the time to be playing games with God.* The enemy is running rampant in the earth because He knows his time is short. It always grieves my heart to see so many hurting and harassed by the devils schemes. The apostle Paul said, *"to HATE what is evil and to cling to what is GOOD."* Over the years, I have developed a deep desire to come against addiction and what it does to so many people and their families. This is the driving force in our ministry; *"To rescue those who are being led forth to death and To hold back those who are staggering toward the slaughter."* (Prov. 24:11)

Therefore, here is my personalized prayer for each of us this morning: *"Far be the Spirit of Bondage from me and my family O' God. May we walk in freedom the rest of our days as we grow in godliness from generation to generation to reach the nations for your glory. From this day forward, I take hold of all of your promises and I shall not be moved. As for me and my house will serve you and you alone, in Jesus Name, Amen.*

Step to Start Strong:

Hate what is Evil and Cling to what is Good

JULY 15.

THE SPIRIT OF DELAY

"But I the Lord will speak what I will, and it shall be fulfilled without delay."

Ezekiel 12:25

In different seasons in life, we can come into constant contact with dark spirits that will do their best to delay our God-given destiny. These attacks will come in all types of shapes and sizes. They can come in the form of distractions, deterrences or anything else that impede the progress we have been making in our walk with the Lord. In light of these things, *"we can't be ignorant of the devils schemes"* He shows interests in your destiny but He will never urge you to do anything about it today. He will always encourage you to do tomorrow what God wants you to do today. This is the Spirit of Delay.

The word delay means: *"To put something off that could have happened now or to put someone off that could have been helped today; including yourself."* Think about this with me: *"What have you been putting off that the Holy Spirit wants you to do either now or in this season of your life? What have you been procrastinating or postponing?"*

Hebrews 10:39 says, "We don't belong to those who shrink back and are destroyed, but we belong to those who have faith and are being saved."

So, don't lose your life by serving the Spirit of Delay today. Its time to rise up and allow the word of the Lord to be fulfilled by faith.

Abraham, Isaac and Jacob all encountered this Spirit in their journey in life. May we learn from their mistakes.

Step to Start Strong:

Don't Delay. Fast Forward

JULY 16.

A Space for Grace

"Seek the LORD while He may be found; Call upon Him while He is near. Let the wicked forsake his way and the unrighteous man his thoughts; And let him return to the LORD and He will have compassion on him."

Isaiah 55:6-7

Conviction is a sure sign of the Holy Spirit's work inside the soul of a man. It's different from condemnation. Condemnation comes from Satan with the ultimate goal to push us farther from our Heavenly Father. On the other hand, Biblical conviction comes laced with compassion to ultimately draw you back to Him. The fruit of godly conviction is called genuine repentance.

Isaiah 42:3 puts it this way; "*He will not cry out or raise His voice, Nor make His voice heard in the street. A bruised reed and a smoldering wick He will not snuff out until He brings forth justice in the* nations." What does this mean? It means the Lord is long-suffering with the children of men.

Over the years, I have learned this from the Lord: He loves to leave a *"Space for Grace"* to give us time to repent for our sins. Despite what your guilt and shame may say; God doesn't sit around in Heaven with a long leather belt waiting for us to fall short so He can release His flame and fury upon us. If anything, *"He desperately desires for us to repent so He can leave behind a blessing for us."* (Joel 2:14) But sadly, this doesn't always happen. Many keep crossing the red tape of redemption to keep doing what they what to do despite what the Holy Spirit is speaking to their heart.

However, there will come a time when the payment of sin will be brought to unrepentant people. You can choose the sin but you cannot choose the consequences. In regard to this: All I can say is, *Woe to those who have the lost the sensitivity of the Holy Spirit.* Callused hearts cannot feel conviction; but those who hide the word of God in their hearts will not sin against thee.

My prayer is that we would leave a space for grace in the lives of other people but we would also be a partaker of God's grace in our own lives.

Step to Start Strong:

Leave a Space for Grace

JULY 17.

The 80/20 Rule

"No soldier gets entangled in civilian pursuits, since his aim is to please the one who enlisted him."

2nd Timothy 2:4

The main thing is to keep the main thing the main thing. As a soldier in the Army of the Lord, we have to stay away from distractions and do our best to stay in our strength zone. More than any time in history, we must go overboard when it comes to guarding our priorities and protecting our calling. It's so easy to lose focus on the eternal matters at hand. *So, how can we be sure to do this on a daily basis?*

Here's one idea: Make a list of the top 10 things you need to get done today and number them according to their importance. If you accomplish the Top 2; Researches say, you will get an 80% return on your labor. However, if you ignore the top 2 and accomplish the last 8; you'll only receive a 20% return. *It's called the 80/20 Rule.* It's the recipe for real success and it will come naturally when you prioritize the top 20%.

Don't fall into the deception that you have to know everything. I've learned its better to surround yourself with others who are experts in their field than to try and figure out the field. You don't have to be a now-it-all. Stay within your strengths and delegate your weaknesses. Take charge of your time and give attention to what matters most.

It's not old-fashioned. I make a list everyday and I do my best to accomplish the top two. It will work if you make the most of your time.

So, what do you need to do today? I encourage you to walk by faith and do what God has placed in your heart. Don't involve yourself in civilian affairs, Don't let your life pass you by and don't let the devil rob you of what matter most.

Step to Start Strong:

Make a to do List

JULY 18.

This is My Story

" Enter his gates with thanksgiving and into His courts with praise; Give thanks to him and praise His holy name."

Psalm 100:4

These are the words of Fanny Crosby in the ole song; *"This is my story, This is my song, Praising my Savior, All the day long!"* With this in mind, the overflow of thanksgiving and praise should be woven into the fabric of our everyday life. This principle sends a sobering message to the soul that God is ultimately in control.

Let me ask you a question: *"What if all you had tomorrow was what you thanked God for today?"* This alone could change your attitude and posture of praise. St. Ambrose, an Italian Bishop in the 4 Century, understood this act of surrender as He said, *"No duty is more urgent than that of returning thanks."*

One of my mentors conveyed this message to me at a very young age; He used to say, *"It's never too late to give thanks by saying, "Thank you or writing a Thank You note."* It's true. In the midst of pressing times, we have to take time to express our gratitude toward God and our appreciation toward other people. Especially to those who are in the household of faith.

Let me ask you another question: Do those around you really know how much you love and care about them? Sometimes we assume they do but do they? At times talk is cheap but time is the greatest commodity. I challenge you; Make sure people know how much you care. One act of kindness can change the trajectory of someones day and even the course of their life. Let's learn to live a life of thankfulness.

"This is our story, This is our song, Praising our Savior, All the day long!"

<u>Step to Start Strong</u>:

Write a Thank you Note

JULY 19.

Sharing is Caring

"We are Christ's ambassadors, as though God were making his appeal through us. Therefore, we implore you on Christ's behalf: Be reconciled to God."

2 Corinthians 5:20

Have you ever felt the impression that you were supposed to share your faith with somebody but for whatever reason you didn't? If you're honest, the answer would be yes because we've all done this a time or two. But I wonder if this act of disobedience to the Holy Spirit is sin? I think so.

In scripture, we see 2 different categories of sin: There's the Sin of Commission and the Sin of Omission. You know the difference right? The sin of commission refers to the moment *"when you do what you know you're not supposed to do."* You openly and willingly committed the sin. However, on the other hand, you have the sin of omission. This is *"when you don't do what you know you're supposed to do."* James 4:17 puts it this way; *"To him who knows to do good but does not do it. To him, it is sin."*

Let's compare it to sharing our faith; What if you were walking down the street and suddenly, you saw a house on fire with violent screams coming from the inside. Obviously it would alarm you and catch your attention. However, you may not be a superhero and kick down the front door and drag everyone to safety but the least you could do is call 911 to try and get them some help. To keep walking and act like you saw nothing would be cold-hearted and even criminal.

It's the same way in the spiritual world. We have the life-saving power of the Holy Spirit living on the inside of us and we come in contact with people who are on the pathway to Hell everyday. To not share the love of God with them in anyway *"when prompted by the Holy Spirit"* is considered disobedience; Otherwise known as sin.

Let me ask you a serious question: "*Do you care that people are dying and going to Hell everyday*? If so, let me ask you another question: "*When was the last time you shared your faith*?" It's not a condemning question; just thought provoking. All evangelism begins with a burden. If you really care, you will really share. So, be on the look out for an open door to share your faith with someone today. Jesus didn't call us to The Great Omission but the Great Commission. It's the churches only mission.

Step to Start Strong:

Listen to the promptings of the Holy Spirit

JULY 20.

The Marks of Jesus

"From now on, let no one cause me trouble, for I bear on my body the marks of Jesus. The grace of our Lord Jesus Christ be with your spirit, brothers and sisters. Amen."

Galatians 6:17-18

The critical theological truth in the Book of Galatians is both practical and extremely powerful. The Apostle Paul continually reiterates the importance of living a life by faith instead of living life by the Old Testament law. We hear his sincerity of heart when he says, "*this is why I am writing you with such large letters from my own hand. You cannot finish in the flesh what you started in the spirit.*" We are made righteous in the sight of God by faith in the Son of God but we also receive other spiritual inheritance from Him the same way. This directly opposed the thought processes of the religious people in their day. In the past, people had to live by the 613 traditional commandments in order to be in right standing with God and man. Today, we simply place our faith in Christ Jesus.

He fulfilled the law by living a sinless life, now we who believe are positioned to receive all of His promises. This is Good News.

However, salvation is free but the marks of a true disciple are costly. Following Christ will cost you something. In Biblical days, the Pharisees did not want to suffer and it tends to be the same way today. The Apostle Paul said, *"Do you want to now who the real disciples are? Have everyone take their shirts off?"*The Pharisees will have a smooth back but the backs of the disciples will be marked with scars and suffering? These men paid a price for the freedom that we have today. May we maintain it by being men and women of the word. If we want to know God, we must know the word of God. If we want to please God, we must obey God even when it hurts and nobody else understands.

What scars do you have for the sake of the Gospel? What marks do you bare on your back which speaks of your past? The Apostle Paul personalized this book to the church in Galatia and it still speaks to us today. May we count the cost for the cause of Christ. We cannot finish in the flesh what we started in the spirit.

Step to Start Strong:

Bare the Marks of Christ in your Life

JULY 21.

Vitamin B

"and God revealed Himself to Samuel through His word."

1st Samuel 3:21

As a youth Pastor, I used to say this phrase weekly, *"if you want to hear from God; all you have to do is open His mouth."* God is always speaking and one the most consistent ways to hear His voice is through the scripture. Over the years, I have developed a self-discipline to read the word of God everyday.

For illustration purposes, I am sitting in the bay window of my house right now with a cup of coffee and my Bible. There's some soft worship music playing in the background as my family is still sleeping because its very early this morning. This is my quite time with Jesus and what I consider the most important part of my day. Ministry should always be an overflow of who we are and not just something we do. I've discovered if I don"t feed myself in the morning, it becomes hard to help other people throughout the day. We all need our Vitamin B Gos-pill in order to maintain a healthy christian diet.

So what do we do? We read a little bit of the Bible everyday. Don't focus on quantity. It's not about how much your read but more importantly, remembering and applying what you read. On any given day, I will read one chapter and a psalm depending on where the Holy Spirit leads me. Usually in the midst of my reading, the Lord will speak something soft in my spirit, which sends me off into prayer and worship for the remainder of the time. To be honest, the duration of my devotion is not too long; maybe 10 to 20 or at most 30 minutes in the morning. The most important thing is that we're plugging ourselves into the source of power that will sustain us throughout the rest of the day. The key is to start the life-giving flow of the Holy Spirit in the beginning of the day and keep the connection until we go back to bed. This is vital for our personal and cooperate victory. We must start and stop with Jesus. Just a little bit can go a long way when God is in it. We call it, Vitamin B.

Step to Start Strong:

Take your Vitamin B Gos-pill

JULY 22.

Top Shelf

"Heaven and earth will pass away, but my words will never pass away."

Luke 21:33

Harry Truman said, *"Not all readers are leaders but all leaders are readers."* Growing up, I really disliked the idea of sitting down to read but today, it's one of my favorite things to do. In reality, reading can do a lot of you:

1) Reading can help you relax.

It's something about losing yourself within a storyline that takes your mind off what's really going on at work, at home or in your checkbook. For me, it's the best way to take a step back so I can see the forest instead of the trees. Overall, a great way to relax. Go ahead give it a try.

2) Secondly, Reading can remind you.

There are certain books that I revisit almost every year because the content challenges me in a profound way. This is one reason why we read the Bible everyday. We are forever changing but the Bible remains the same. God's word speaks to us right where we are in life. John the Beloved said it best when He repeated Himself over and over again in his letters. He knew we already knew what to do so he kept reminding us of certain truths. Therefore, I release you to read and say things twice. I do.

3) Lastly, Reading can revitalize your relationships.
Almost everyday, I share publicly what I've been reading privately. Whether it be in a meeting, counseling session or small talk conversation. Any relevant information is fuel for your relationships. This is why we should read up on a variety of topics and authors to broaden our perspective. So, how do we grow in knowledge and understanding? By living a life of continual learning; Gandhi put it this way; "*Live like you would die tomorrow but learn like you were to live forever.*" This will deepen your level of relationships but also widen your influence of discipleship.

Step to Start Strong:

Read, Read, Read

JULY 23.

PEOPLE GROUPS

"He said to them, "Go into all the world and preach the gospel to all nations."

Mark 16:15

What did Jesus mean when He said, *"Go into all the world and preach the Gospel to all nations?"* Understanding who He was referring to will help us gain a deeper revelation of who He was speaking to. The word nation derives from the word *"ethne,"* which literally means; people groups. A people group is a category of people who identify with each other based on similarities, such as common language, social, cultural and economic status. According to the Joshua Project, there are over 16,500 people groups on the planet. When combined, we find our world's total population at 7.38 billion and counting. But there's more: Out of the 16,500+ people groups, there are 6,668 that are considered unreached. An unreached people group (UPG) is a community where there are too few professing Christians that are able to engage the city with church planting. Technically speaking, the percentage of evangelical Christians within an unreached group is less than 2 percent. Here's the alarming statistic: Unreached people groups make up 42% of our worlds population. That's 3.11 billion people. Yes, you read that right. Almost half of the world has never heard of Jesus Christ. They are "unreached."

It's amazing to me; with all the technology, internet and social media outlets, that there are still so many that are dead in their transgressions and sins. This is why it makes perfect sense for Jesus to still be screaming, *"Go!"* It's two-thirds of God's name! Go, Go, Go! The command remains the same; Oswald Smith said it best; *"Many talk of the Second Coming but half the world has never heard of the first."* We can't reach everyone but we can reach someone. Each of us have a responsibility to reach out. Lets go until we can't go any longer.

Step to Start Strong:

Go into All Nations

JULY 24.

The Mount of Transfiguration

"After six days, Jesus took with him Peter, James and John and led them up a high mountain by themselves. There he was transfigured before them. His face shone like the sun, and his clothes became as white as the light. Just then there appeared before them Moses and Elijah, talking with Jesus. Peter said to Jesus, "Lord, it is good for us to be here. If you wish, I will put up three shelters—one for you, one for Moses and one for Elijah."

Mark 16:15

Jesus sends out a personal invitation to Peter, James and John to go see what no man has ever seen; The transfiguration of the Son of God into His glorified body. When Moses the priest and Elijah the prophet meet with Jesus in this moment, I want you to see the first response of the flesh. Peter quickly makes 2 statements: *"Lord, is it good for us to be here? And if you want me to; I will build you 3 shelters?"*

When I read this, God showed me the insecurity of the soul which leads us to an improper perspective within our relationship with Jesus. Peter's first response was, "*Lord, is it good for us to be here*?" We see how Peter felt *"unworthy"* to be in the presence of the Lord. How could this be? When Jesus invited Him into this life-changing experience in the first place. What do you mean, *"is it good to be with God?"* We need to stop second guessing the goodness of God and all of His benefits. He wants to take all of His children to the mountaintop to behold the beauty of the Lord and show them something new about Himself.

Secondly, Peter said, *"Can I build you a shelter?"* Not only do people tend to feel unworthy in the presence the Lord but their first response is work. These 2 elements can stunt your spiritual experience. Listen up: You are worthy and you don't have to work your way into His presence. He invites you today. It's ok. We don't work for the cross but we do work from the cross.

This reminds me of the seraphim that are described in Isaiah Chapter 6; The Bible says, "*with four wings they cover their faces and with two wings they fly around the throne, singing; Holy, Holy, Holy is the Lord God Almighty!*" This reminds me of worship and work. We should be worshipping twice as hard as we work. When we put this element in it's rightful place, we will see radical results and real life transfiguration. Don't waste your days by waking up to rush off to work. Choose the latter and lay on the Mountaintop where miracles manifest. You are worthy to be in His presence because of the blood of Christ Jesus.

Step to Start Strong:

Climb the Mountain of Transfiguration

JULY 25.

GRADUATION DAY

"The race is not to the swift nor the battle to the strong."

Ecclesiastes 9:11

One of my favorite moments in ministry is to witness a student graduate Teen Challenge. Every program is a little bit different but one truth remains the same: God is still using Teen Challenge to change lives and we just watched another family get restored right before our very eyes. It never gets old and it never will. We still shout and we still cry. Do you know why? Because another soul has been rescued from the clutches of Satan. Literally, thousands of people have found set freedom through the ministry of Teen Challenge. The statement released at our 50th Anniversary years ago is so true; They said, *"Freedom is found here! Hope lives here! Changed lives leave here!"* This couldn't be more true.

At one of these graduations, I had the honor to be the graduation speaker and these were my 3 exhortations to the family:

Sir Winston Churchill, the late Prime Minister of England, once spoke at a commencement service as everyone sat on the edge of their seat waiting for the wisdom that would flow from his lips. As he approached the podium, he stared into everyone's eye and said, these 3 words with piercing passion: *"Don't ever, ever, ever give up!"* and He went and sat back down. Everyone was appalled and astonished. These 3 words hold so much weight. We can't give up on God, we can't give up on ourselves, we can't give up on our friends and family and we certainly should never give up on our destiny. God has a plan and quitting is never an option. Mulhammond Ali also spoke to a crowd at Harvard many years ago in 1975. It was the same situation as the house was packed full of people waiting to hear this world champion boxer encourage them with words. What did he say? Everyone was surprised when He stood to say two words before he took his seat. What were the words? He said, *"Me. We."* His message was one of unity. Scripture is clear. God has not only called us to be committed christians but he has also called us to community. Psalm 133 says, *"Oh how good and how pleasant it is for brothers to dwell together in unity." For in the place of unity, God commands the blessing life forever."* We find new life in Jesus Christ but we find out who we really are when we're with others. So, don't forsake the assembly of the saints. We need God and we need one another.

Lastly, I wanted to top the other two with a shorter graduation speech so I boiled all of my wisdom down to one word. This one word says it all. This word is actually the name that is above every name. It's the only name on earth by which we can be saved. It's the name that causes sick bodies to be healed. This name causes demons to tremble. It's the name that breaks the bondage of addiction and sets the captive free. It's a powerful name but it's also the sweetest name I know. If you don't remember anything else I say today, "Don't forget this name!" His name is JESUS!

Step to Start Strong:

Shout Jesus

JULY 26.

The Laying on of Hands

"Do not neglect the gift you have, which was given to you by prophecy when the council of elders laid their hands on you."

1st Timothy 4:14

Scripture is clear about the Doctrine of the Laying on of Hands. The Apostle Paul speaks the most on the subject because He knew personally the importance of spiritual impartation. He shares some insight in Romans 1:11 by saying, *"I long to see you so that I may impart to you some spiritual gift to make you strong."* Impartation means to freely give what you have freely received. To give a share of your spiritual inheritance to someone else. How do you think you got where you are today? This Gospel has been passed down from person to person from the very beginning and this is why we still stand strong today; not because of our own wisdom or wit, but because of the ripple effect of righteousness throughout the ages.

One way to impart spiritual gifts is through the laying on of hands and prayer. Out of the 5 senses, there's something special and even supernatural about a touch. Think of the feeling you receive when you get a hug or a hearty handshake. Physical touch effects the soul but it can also make or break the spirit of a man.

The Bible references this idea quite frequently: For Jesus took children in His arms and began to bless them by laying His hands on them. (Mark 10:16) After the church at Antioch had fasted and prayed, they laid their hands on Barnabas and Saul and sent them on their away. (Acts 13:3) While the sun was setting, all those who had any who were sick with various diseases brought them to Him; and laid His hands on each one of them for He was healing them. (Luke 4:40) Is anyone among you sick? Let them call for the elders of the church to pray over them and anoint them with oil in the name of the Lord and the prayer offered in faith will cause the sick to recover." (James 5:14) "For this reason I remind you to rekindle the gift of God which is in you through the laying on of my hands." (2nd Timothy 1:6) What do these scriptures mean? They mean the anointing that you have received from the Holy One is transferable by physical touch. Next time you have the opportunity; Hold hands with your wife and pray. Lay hands on you kids and release a supernatural blessing. Anoint your friend that is sick with oil and lay your hands on them and command the sickness to flee. Ask your co-workers or Sunday School class to join hands by point of contact before you pray. This is the signature of agreement. Do you believe? If you do, obey the promoting of the Holy Spirit today. Go ahead and reach out and touch somebody by faith. When you do this, His Holy Hands will come upon your hands and something of substance will be released.

Step to Start Strong:

Make a Point of Contact

JULY 27.

The Kingdom of God

"For the kingdom of God is not eating and drinking, but righteousness and peace and joy in the Holy Spirit."

Romans 14:17

Righteousness, peace and joy in the Holy Ghost is the evidence of the Kingdom of God in the life of a believer. What is righteousness? Righteousness means you are in right standing with God. When you receive Christ you are made perfect in your position because of what He accomplished on the cross. His righteousness has been imputed to you. What's peace? An old Jewish Rabbi told me, peace is *"Nothing missing, Nothing broken."* When you have the piece of peace implemented into your soul, you are completely satisfied. What's joy in the Holy Ghost? God spoke to me and said, *"Righteousness + peace = The Joy of Jesus.* If you are in right standing with God and people, the peace of God that surpasses all understanding will guard your hearts and minds in Christ Jesus.

When these two ingredients are mixed with purity and prayer, the manifestation of joy will come from the Holy Spirit. It's unstoppable. However, if there is a breach in any of your relationships, you can't experience perfect piece and perfected joy will be far from you.

So my question is: Are you in right standing with God? Are you in right standing with people? If so, peace shall be prevalent and joy will be your best friend. If not, repent today. Make the relationship right and times of refreshing will come from the Lord. It's that easy. It's the Kingdom Connection.

Therefore, I pray that this would be the status of your soul: *"For Joy is the settled assurance that God is in control of all the details of my life, the quiet confidence that ultimately everything is going to be all right, and the determined choice to praise God in every situation."*

Step to Start Strong:

Be Kingdom Minded

JULY 28.

FINISH THE JOB

"David ran and stood over him. He took hold of the Philistine's sword and drew it from the sheath. After he killed him, he cut off his head with the sword. When the Philistines saw that their hero was dead, they turned and ran."

1st Samuel 17:51

King David not only killed the Giant Goliath but He cut His head off. Go with me for a minute: For 40 days and 40 nights, this unruly Philistine taunted the Armies of Israel in the Valley of Elah. One army camped out on one side of the mountain as the opposing army gazed across the great divide. When the oversized enemy screamed, every soldier shook in fear. What do you do in this case? King Saul said, *"For any man who will rise up to shut the mouth of this man, I will lavishly give him great riches, my daughters hand in marriage and he will never have to pay taxes."* Not a bad deal. However, nobody moved. Have you ever been so gripped with fear that nothing could motivate you? This was the situation at hand. Nobody knew what to do? Until David showed up on the scene.

David put the promises of God to the test by making a public spectacle of the power of God there that day. He boldly accepted the challenge and said, *"you come at me with a spear and a sword but I come to you in the name of the Lord! For the same God who delivered me from the paw of the bear and the mouth of the lion will show up and deliver me in your midst!"* Can you sense the faith in this sentence? His implication was: *"If God did it one time, He can do it again!"* It's amazing to me that David placed the rock, which represents Jesus Christ, in his sling and He hurled it under the anointing Holy Spirit and guess what happened? God guided this small, smooth stone to hit the devil right between the eyes. Saul's faith slain a 1,000 but David's faith slew 10,000! But He didn't stop there.

As he stood in the valley with everyone watching; He took the dead soldiers sword and he completely cut off the head of Goliath. By one man's obedience, the whole nation celebrated a corporate victory that day. But here's what God showed me: The scripture says, *"After these things, David impelled Goliath's head on a stick and took it back home and placed it in his tent."* He was going to make sure he didn't forget who gave him the victory. Many people win the battle in the church world while losing their family at home. David understood this principle. He knew private victory was more important than public victory. What you do for everyone else is nullified if you lose your own family in the process. Therefore, I encourage you to keep fighting the good fight of faith and finish the job. It all starts at home.

<u>Step to Start Strong</u>:

Finish what you Started

JULY 29.

Second Chances

"But you, Lord, are a compassionate and gracious God, slow to anger, abounding in love and faithfulness."

Psalm 86:15

The Webster's definition of a *"chance"* makes me laugh. A chance means, *"there's a possibility that something is about to happen!"* With this in mind, I want to say, *"We serve the God of Second Chances."*

Where sin abounds, grace abounds that much more. He who has been forgiven much, in the end; will love much. Have you been given second chances? If so, I know that the grace and peace of God has been multiplied unto you.

If we set up too many man-made rules and regulations within our church, people will never associate it as a family. By doing this, you want get any Judas' but you want get a Simon Peter's either. When you give people chances, from time to time, you'll come across a traitor and a thief but unless you are willing to take a risk, you will never discover the other eleven who will become faithful fighters of the faith. Thats why we should give second chances. Because where would we be without them?

1st Corinthians 1:26-31 says, *"Take a good look at who you were when you got called into this life. I don't see many of "the brightest and the best" among you, not many influential, not many from high-society families. Isn't it obvious that God deliberately chose men and women that the culture overlooks and exploits and abuses, chose these "nobodies" to expose the hollow pretensions of the "somebodies"? That makes it quite clear that none of you can get by with blowing your own horn before God. Everything that we have—right thinking and right living, a clean slate and a fresh start—comes from God by way of Jesus Christ."*

Here's a good principle to live by: *"Try to out-give the second chances that you have received from the Grace of God to the world."* If you're like me; It would probably take a life-time.

Step to Start Strong:

Give other People a Chance

JULY 30.

TRUE WORSHIPERS

"Yet a time is coming and has now come when the true worshipers will worship the Father in the Spirit and in truth, for they are the kind of worshipers the Father seeks. God is spirit, and his worshipers must worship in the Spirit and in truth."

John 4:23-24

God doesn't seek worship; He's not insecure and needy. However, he does seek worshippers. Even still, He seeks people with child-like faith that would wholeheartedly seek his face. This kind of worship doesn't remind God of who He is but it definitely reminds us in whom He is. You always become like the one you worship. In our case, when we gaze upon the beauty of the Lord, we become more like His Son Jesus Christ. His love keeps compelling us to righteousness because His loving-kindness leads us to repentance. Can God really be this gracious? Love gives the best. Knowing this, God created us with a God shaped hole in our heart that only He can fill. When He fills it with His spirit, we get the greatest gift; we get HIM. The only thing greater than a man being in right standing with his Heavenly Father is a man who is willing to fall on His face daily to worship His Heavenly Father. Worship is not something you do; it's a Lifestyle. Let's worship our way through the week.

1st Chronicles 16:23-31 *"Sing to the LORD, all the earth; proclaim his salvation day after day. Declare his glory among the nations, his marvelous deeds among all peoples. For great is the LORD and most worthy of praise; he is to be feared above all gods. For all the gods of the nations are idols, but the LORD made the heavens. Splendor and majesty are before him; strength and joy are in his dwelling place. Ascribe to the LORD, all you families of nations, ascribe to the LORD glory and strength. Ascribe to the LORD the glory due his name; bring an offering and come before him. Worship the LORD in the splendor of his holiness. Tremble before him, all the earth! The world is firmly established; it cannot be moved.* Let the heavens rejoice, let the earth be glad; let them say among the nations, "The LORD reigns!"

Step to Start Strong:

Worship God in Spirit and in Truth

JULY 31.

A FEEL FOR THE REAL

"I am the good shepherd. I know My sheep and My sheep know Me." - Jesus

John 10:14

The Fraud Department for the United States Treasury has an interesting way to train their new employees. With all the modern technologies, you could imagine how difficult it would be to track criminals who infiltrate our economy with fake money. Where do you start? People in this field *"get a feel for the real."* All day-everyday, they handle, stare, study and flip through countless pieces of printed currency. In order to quickly catch a counterfeit, they must over-familiarize themselves with the authentic.

Spiritually speaking: Jesus put it this way, *"I know my sheep and my sheep know me."* Do you really "know" the Lord? Do know how to discern what God wants you to do and what He doesn't want you to do? Can you discern His voice? His presence? How about the promptings of the Holy Spirit?

As people who are known by the Lord, we should be so sensitive to the Spirit that we can hear Him in a crowded room. Even within uneasy circumstances, the whisper of His words should shake our inner soul. Without a doubt, the devil comes to steal, kill and destroy but the real deal; Jesus Christ has come to give us life.

How do you develop a feel for the real? One word; *Repetition.* Repetitiously, read the Word of God over and over and over again. Passionately pray to your Heavenly Father and listen for His voice. Meditate upon His precepts and put them into practice. Day after day, year after year and before long, the real deal will be so deeply engrained into who you are, you'll forget who you were and the world is all about. Friends, don't fall for the counterfeit. Keep following Jesus Christ.

Step to Start Strong:

Sow, Reap & Repeat.

AUGUST 1.

PERFECT PRAISE

"The children were shouting in the temple courts, *"Hosanna to the Son of David,"* and the religious leaders were indignant. "Do you hear what these children are saying?" they asked him. "Yes," Jesus replied, "Have you never read, *"From the lips of children and infants you have ordained perfect praise."*

Matthew 21:16

With small children in the house right now, this scripture couldn't be more true. As my eyes gaze upon my kids, I am captivated by the great love of the Lord. Only He could create something out of nothing and more importantly, sustain what we call life in her mortal body. It's absolutely astonishing! *"For in Him, we live and move and have our being.* (Acts 17:18) *and By Him, all things are held together."* (Colossians 1:17)

This principle is easily understood while watching a newborn. A baby is totally dependent upon the parents. Twenty-four hours a day, seven days a week, we are attentive to this child. Even while trying to sleep with one eye open; Why is this so? Because with blessing comes responsibility but the work is far worth the reward. As children grow and mature, we watch them fulfill the purpose God had planned for them before time began. Until then, we will keep watch over their souls and pray for them everyday.

For God says, "*Out of the mouths of babes, you have ordained perfect praise*!" When children cry out to Jesus, they give God the highest praise. With this in mind, I feel it is our greatest responsibility as Christ-followers to pass the flame of Heaven to the next generation. King David put it this way in Psalm 71:18, *"Do not forsake me, O' God, until I declare your power to the next generation, your mighty acts to all who come."*

My prayer is that we, as the body of Christ, would make sure that the children in our spheres of influence would *"know God"* above all things. It doesn't matter if we succeed in everything else when we fail in this is one. If we neglect the next generation, we will cripple the church. Our kids, grandkids and next of kins must be baptized in the Holy Spirit. They must be familiar with prayer and presence. This is our hope and the hope of the world. May their lips sing perfect praise to the Kings of Kings. However, it starts with you and me.

Step to Start Strong:

Pour your Prayers into the Next Generation

AUGUST 2.

Cast your Cares

"Casting all your care on Him, because He cares about you."

1st Peter 5:7

Early one morning, I had the privilege to spend some time with a TBN Recording Artist. All looked well on the outside but what many people don't know is his wife is suffering from terminal cancer on the inside. In these type settings, I know everything I need to know about myself, so I ask questions and sit still and try to heed the voice of the Lord. As we sat and discussed different scenarios, His heart opened up to what was really happening at home. Suddenly, I felt a strong sense of the Holy Spirit and I knew He was above to speak. For confidentiality purposes, I can't share certain things but I do believe the Lord wants me to share this one provoking thought:

God has called us *"to cast all of our cares upon Him because He cares for us."* What does this mean? It means, we don't have to carry cancer, debt, depression and discouragement that seems to bombard our day. In fact, whatever you are carrying this morning, you can cast the weight upon the shoulders of the Lord and He will carry it for you. He wants to be your burden bearer but you have to be willing to hand it over to Him.

With the reality of what this man and his family were fighting, this verse made so much sense. He said, *"my wife and I have never experienced this much peace in all of our lives. We just know everything is going to be all right."* Now, you may be thinking; How can He say this knowing the circumstances at stake? I'll tell you how; He knows that God's word always trumps any trial. His assurance is found in the revelation that God really does care about Him and His families future. Knowing this, He can cast all of His cares upon Him.

Will do the same thing this morning? What has been stressing you out? What are you and your family fighting at home? What do you know that nobody else knows? Whatever it is, big or small, place it upon the shoulders of the one who can carry the weight of the whole world. You are not a beast of burden. You are a Child of God. Cast your cares upon Him.

Step to Start Strong:

Cast your Cares upon Christ

AUGUST 3.

GLIMPSES OF GLORY

"And my God will supply all your needs according to His riches in glory in Christ Jesus."

Philippians 4:19

Has God ever spoken something to you but your circumstances said, *it will never happen?* This has occurred so many times in my life and ministry. For example, listen to this story and learn from my example: Many years ago, God placed a desire in my heart to go to Brazil. Without a doubt, I knew one day I would go. *Why Brazil?* I have no clue; I just knew. Therefore, it didn't surprise me when one day someone invited me to go. The Bible says, *"God does nothing without first speaking it to the prophets."* If you will take time to listen, the Lord will show you things to come. I call them *Glimpses of Glory*. However, I let the opportunity pass me bye? Why? To be quite honest, because of my bank account. There was a great and effective door before me but the thing that opposed me was money.

Here's a life lesson: Your personal finances should never be the deciding factor for something that God has called you do. Where God guides, He always provides. But The crippling part: The person who asked me to go to Brazil was going to sponsor me if I had first agreed. However, I didn't know this until the team got back from Brazil. God taught me a very valuable lesson through this experience: *Never again will I allow finances determine my future.*

Many years later, another opportunity came my way to go to Brazil. What did I do? I paid the $2,000 upfront by faith and said, I'm not going to miss this boat. The 8 day trip was life-changing for me but when I got back; guess what was in my PO Box? A check for exactly $2,000 from a donor that has never given to our ministry nor never sense. A miracle? It was for me.

Through this process, God was proving his provisional power and building my faith for where we are doing today. We are going from faith to faith and glory to glory.

Never again will I let natural circumstances tell me what God has called me to do. How about you? What has God called you to do? Now, is the time to lean in and listen to the leading of the still small voice of the Holy Spirit. If He says, Go. Just go. If He says, do it. Just do it. You can analyze yourself right into anxiety. So, don't overthink the opportunity. Keep it simple and let God be God. Some doors may never open again. The question remains: Is it you Lord? If so, I say, Go for it!

Step to Start Strong:

Don't miss your Moment

AUGUST 4.

EVEN SO

"He which testifieth these things saith, Surely I am coming quickly. Even so, come, Lord Jesus."

Revelation 22:20

One of my favorite ways to getaway with God is to go jogging. Sometimes, I run down the greenway in Greensboro, other days, I park downtown and run the busy city blocks. When I travel across state lines and even abroad, I always try to get up early so I can slip away to spend some quite time with Jesus. This is one of the ways He speaks to me. *How does God speak to you?* Where is your favorite place to getaway with God? For Jesus, it was the Garden of Gethsemane. For Peter, it was His boat. But how about you? Where's your special place? Wherever it is, you need to *"schedule"* times of seclusion. By doing this, you'll be more sensitive to the Holy Spirit.

Recently, I was out running at Southwest Guilford Park and this is what the Lord spoke to me: *"Even now, think bigger but think it all the way through."* If you really trust my word, you will not only cast the net into the world but you will cast the net into your own soul. Man's word will let us down but my word will never fail you. It will stand the test of time. Even now."

The second from the last verse in the Bible says, *"Even so, Come Lord Jesus come."* John the Beloved penned these words on the Island of Patmos near the end of his life. So Yes, Jesus is certainly coming back sooner than later but what I want you to see is Jesus wants to send His Spirit now. Don't wait to rejoice on that day, for no one knows the day or the hour in which he will come. *Rejoice today!* Don't wait to work on your wildest dreams next year! Go hard after God right now and watch Him meet you there! Don't think small and short! Think big and broader, but think it all the way through. Your greatest enemy and critic is you. God wants you to fulfill His will more than you do. Getaway away with God and pray; *"Even so, Come Lord Jesus Come. Come now because we need you now than ever!"*

Step to Start Strong:

Get Away with God.

AUGUST 5.

LOVE VS. FEAR

"There is no fear in love. But perfect love drives out fear, because fear has to do with punishment. The one who fears is not made perfect in love."

1st John 4:18

When you trace the motive for every willful act and decision that you make every day, you'll see that the reason why you did it was for one of two reasons; *Love or Fear.* Every person is motivated by love or moved by fear. This is profound but also very powerful. What we do is one thing but why we do it is more important. I live my life with great passion to preach and teach Biblical principles. This is what I do but why do I do it? It has to be to see the captive set free. Period! This is what motivates me.

So how about you? You know what you do but have you ever asked yourself, *"why do you do it?"* This one question can revolutionize your life. The gifts and calling of God are irrevocable and without repentance. You have many gifts (plural) but you have one calling (singular). What are you called to do? But more importantly, why do you want to do it? Take some time and think it through. You've got one life. Make it count church.

Whatever you do, be motivated and moved by love because perfect love casts out all fear. Don't work because you are afraid of being poor. Do something fulfilling and satisfying. Don't pray because you are afraid of going hell. Pray because you want to hear your Heavenly Father's voice. Don't obey your authority because you have to but because you want to. See the difference. What we do and why we do it should all be infused with the love of Jesus Christ. Fear has no place in the church; Just the Love of Jesus.

Step to Start Strong:

Be Motivated by Love

AUGUST 6.

SPEAK, LORD! I'M LISTENING.

"So Eli told Samuel, "Go and lie down, and if He calls you, say, 'Speak, LORD, for your servant is listening.'" So Samuel went and lay down in his place."

1st Samuel 3:9

We should all settle down in a certain place to seek the face of the Lord everyday. This is a discipline many Christians call Quiet Time and it's called this for a reason. Praying is a two-way street. It's you talking to God but it's also you taking time to listen. Don't miss this: *"You haven't finished praying until you take time to listen."* He wants to speak to you but how desperate are you to hear from Him?

Do you need His direction? How about His affirmation or confirmation? If so, slow down. Take a deep breath. Fix your affection on Him and begin to worship. Open your mouth and begin to bless His Holy name. It may take a few minutes but eventually, you should get settled in your spirit. His presence will begin permeate your innermost being. This inner calm is a channel for you to hear from Him. When He speaks, you'll know it. For His thoughts are not your thoughts and His ways are higher than yours.

This principle reminds me of the story of Jesus on the Mount of Transfiguration when He was transformed into His glorified body. In this climatic moment, God the Father spoke this charge from the clouds to Peter, James and John. He could have said anything in this moment but He decided to day, *"This is my Son, whom I have chosen; Listen to Him!"* Why would He say these words? Because He knew our tendency would be to talk too much! But He also knew we would be tempted to rush out of His presence! These words still ring true today. We need to talk less and listen more but we also need to wait on Him more which will cause us to work less.

I challenge you; wait for the still small voice of the Holy Spirit. When He speaks; place your faith in what He said because it alone will give you the victory in your circumstance. Why does He whisper His words? Because in order to hear a whisper, you have to be in close proximity to the person. Let's put these words into practice today. Go ahead and say, *"Speak Lord, I'm listening!"* I can't wait to hear what He has to say.

Step to Start Strong:

Listen to the Lord!

AUGUST 7.

THE ARMY OF THE LORD

"So Eli told Samuel, "Go and lie down, and if He calls you, say, 'Speak, LORD, for your servant is listening.''' So Samuel went and lay down in his place."

1st Samuel 3:9

When I graduated from Teen Challenge in April 2004, the student body marched into the auditorium singing this ole song; *"I hear the sound of the army of the Lord! It's a song of praise! It's a song of war! I hear the sound of the Army of the Lord!* These lyrics seem to be prophetic as our nation heads down a road that is bringing more division than genuine repentance. Does this bother you? If so, don't be discouraged when you watch the news and hear a message of doom and gloom. All you have to do is; *Believe the Bible.*

During the days of Elijah, God spoke a word that said, *"I have reserved a remnant of righteous believers in the center of this sinful society."* Is our society sinful? Certainly, to say the least, but if we could somehow see all the Christian soldiers scattered across the nation right now, I believe that faith would arise in our soul.

Statistics say, there are 2.2 billion believers (31%) in the world and according to Barna's Research, 73% of Americans profess to have faith in Christ. Now these numbers are probably skewed but here's my point: Jesus said, *"Upon this Rock I shall build my church and the gates of Hell shall not prevail against it! What's the rock?* The rock is the revelation that Jesus Christ is Lord of all making Him the Commander-in-chief of the Army of the Lord. Troops, we still have a lot of work to do but there's more mighty men and women of God out their than you think. This remnant will usher in a great end-time revival not only in the world but right here in America.

John Newton, the author of Amazing Grace, assured us of such victory;

> *"The Lord has chosen, called and armed us for the fight; and shall we wish to be excused? Shall we not rather rejoice that we have the honor to appear in such a cause, under such a Captain, such a banner and in such company? A complete suit of armor is provided, weapons not to be resisted, and precious balm to heal us if we receive a wound, and precious ointment to revive us when we are close to fainting."*

Be revived mighty warrior! You were made for war! We are all apart of the Army of the Lord! Never forget; Today we carry a cross. Tomorrow we will wear a crown. Keep fighting the good fight of faith my friend. He will be faithful to the end.

Step to Start Strong:

Keep Marching Mighty Warrior

AUGUST 8.

LUCIFER'S FALL

"Jesus replied, "I saw Satan fall like lightning from Heaven."

Luke 10:18

Isaiah gives us the account of Lucifer's Fall in Chapter 14 verses 12-15. Notice the repetitive use of the word "I."

"How you are fallen from heaven,
O Lucifer, son of the morning!
How you are cut down to the ground,
You who weakened the nations!
For you have said in your heart:
'I will ascend into heaven,
I will exalt my throne above the stars of God;
I will also sit on the mount of the congregation
On the farthest sides of the north;
I will ascend above the heights of the clouds,
I will be like the Most High.'

> *Yet you shall be brought down to Sheol,*
> *To the lowest depths of the Pit."*

The Heart of SIN and PRIDE is me, myself & I; Just look at the middle letter of both. In fact, when Satan sinned, one translation says, *"He was kicked out of Heaven by the Finger of God."* I like to think it was his pinky finger! Regardless of your perspective, we have to remember it is *"not about you and me. It's all about him."*

Ezekiel 28:14-18 gives us another look at the first sin:

> *"You were the anointed cherub who covers; I established you; You were on the holy mountain of God; You walked back and forth in the midst of fiery stones. You were perfect in your ways from the day you were created, Till iniquity was found in you. "By the abundance of your trading, You became filled with violence within, And you sinned; Therefore I cast you as a profane thing Out of the mountain of God; And I destroyed you, O covering cherub, From the midst of the fiery stones."Your heart was lifted up because of your beauty; You corrupted your wisdom for the sake of your splendor; I cast you to the ground, I laid you before kings, That they might gaze at you. You defiled your sanctuaries By the multitude of your iniquities, By the iniquity of your trading; Therefore I brought fire from your midst; It devoured you, And I turned you to ashes upon the earth In the sight of all who saw you."*

Proverbs 16:18 says, *"Pride comes before a fall."* If it happened to Lucifer in a perfect environment; *"How much more should we hide the word of God in our hearts so that we would not sin against thee?"* May we fall to our knees daily and pray that we will not fall into such sinful disgrace.

Step to Start Strong:

Give God all the Glory

AUGUST 9.

THE STATE OF THE CHURCH

"And I tell you that you are Peter, and on this rock I will build my church, and the gates of Hades will not overcome it."

Matthew 16:18

The Christian church has been a cornerstone of American life for centuries, but sadly much has changed in the last 30 years. Americans are attending church less, and more people are not practicing their faith outside of its four walls. Millennials in particular are coming of age at a time of great skepticism and cynicism toward institutions—particularly the church. Add to this the broader secularizing trend in American culture, and a growing antagonism toward faith, and these are uncertain times for the American Church. Based on a large pool of data collected from the Barna Institute, they conducted an analysis on the state of the church, looking closely at affiliation, attendance and practice to determine the overall health of Christ's Body in America. Debates continue to rage over whether the

United States is a "Christian" nation or not. Some believe the Constitution gives special treatment or preference to Christianity, but others make their claims based on sheer numbers—and they have a point: Most people in this country identify themselves as Christian. Almost three-quarters of Americans (73%) say they are a Christian, while only one-fifth (20%) claim no faith at all (that includes atheists and agnostics). A fraction (6%) identify with faiths like Islam, Buddhism, Judaism or Hinduism, and 1% are unsure. Not only do most Americans identify as Christian, but a similar percentage (73%) also agree that religious faith is very important in their life (52% strongly agree + 21% somewhat agree). Even though a majority of Americans identify themselves as Christian and say religious faith is very important in their life, these huge proportions actually portray a much smaller number of Americans who actually *practice* their faith. When the variable of church attendance is added to the mix, a majority becomes the minority. When a self-identified Christian attends a religious service at least once a month and says their faith is very important in their life, Barna considers that person a "practicing Christian." After applying affiliation and practice, the numbers drop to around one in three U.S. adults (31%) who fall under this classification. Barna researchers argue this represents a more accurate picture of Christian faith in America, one that reflects the reality of a secularizing nation. Another way Barna measures religious decline is through the post-christian metric. If an individual meets 60 percent or more of a set of factors, which includes things like disbelief in God or identifying as atheist or agnostic, and they do not participate in practices such as Bible reading, prayer and church attendance, they are considered post-Christian. Based on this metric, almost half of all American adults (48%) are post-Christian. Post Christianity is the loss of the primacy of the Christian worldview in political affairs, especially where Christianity had previously flourished. This includes personal world views, philosophies, ideologies and movements that are no longer rooted in the language and assumptions of Biblical Christianity. (Excerpt taken from Barna.com)

All I have to say is, "You choose this day in whom you will serve but as for me and my house, we are going to serve the Lord." This is the State of the Church.

Step to Start Strong:

Be the Church

AUGUST 10.

JESUS LOVES ME

"I have loved you with an everlasting & unfailing love."

Jeremiah 31:3

JESUS LOVES ME this I know; For the Bible tells me so. This ole song holds a strong theology. How do we know that we are loved by God? Its simple. Jeremiah 31:3 says, *"I have loved you with an everlasting & unfailing love."* Here are two characteristics of God's love for you. It's unconditional and unending. This is Good News.

Unconditional love means I love you period. Don't put a comma where God's put a period. You can't earn His love. There's nothing you can do to make Him love you any more and more importantly, there's nothing you can do to make Him love you any less. His love for you is steadfast! He doesn't pick the pedals off the flower and say, I love you. I love you not! It's always I love you; every single time of every single day.

Which brings me to my second point: God's love is unending. The Bible says, God is love and He cannot change. If His character can't change His love for you can't either. He's always loved you and He always will. This type of love wants to give you the best. God wants you to have the best and He's the best. His presence is the greatest present! You always become like the one you love and His will is for you to be more like Him. Whatever you do don't resist His loving relationship. Jesus knows you, this I love.

Step to Start Strong:

Ask God for a fresh revelation of His Love

AUGUST 11.

JESUS CHRIST

"Therefore, God exalted him to the highest place and gave him the name that is above every name."

Philippians 2:9

What does the name Jesus mean? We know Him as a person but what is the symbolism and significance of the sweetest name we know? Jesus is the transliteration of the Hebrew word Joshua or Yehoshua. Joshua was a type and shadow of Jesus in the Old Testament as He led the children of Israel completely out of Egypt and into Canaan, the ultimate Promised Land. Joshua was the commander-in-chief of the Armies of Israel but Jesus is the commander-in-chief of the Armies of Heaven. In the Greek, Jesus means, *"Yahweh is Salvation or in a more simplified form; "He Saves."* What does Jesus do? He saves people from sin just like He did for me and you. Indeed, Jesus is our Savior and Lord.

However, in case you didn't know, Christ is not Jesus' last name. Christ is a description of who He is. Just like, Jesus of Nazareth or Jesus, Son of Mary, Jesus Christ was a title given to Him by God. Christ comes from the greek word *"Christos"* meaning *"anointed one"*. Biblically speaking, when someone was anointed with oil in the scripture we know they were set apart for special service. Jesus was anointed with oil three different times in 33 years. Two different women anointed him at two separate times on two separate occasions. However, the first time He was anointed was the most important. This anointing came from Heaven not from man. This happened when Jesus was water baptized by John in the Jordan River. When He came up out of the water the Holy Spirit descended upon Him like a dove and from that time forward He walked in supernatural power. He was no longer called Jesus but called Jesus the Christ. Why? Because He was anointed with the Holy Spirit. Yes, He wants to save you from your sins but secondly, He wants to fill you with the Holy Spirit. This anointing will break the yoke of any enemy and heal all your infirmities. All you have to do is call out the name that is above every name and sin and sickness must flee. His name is Jesus Christ. All of Heaven stands at attention at the mention of His name. What do you need God to do for you today? Just ask Him right now, in Jesus Name! As the ole song says, *"there's something about that name."*

Step to Start Strong:

Ask God to anoint you with the Holy Spirit

AUGUST 12.

MAKING MISTAKES

"The righteous fall seven times, but He gets back up."

Proverbs 24:16

Someone once said, *"Failure is the only way to get to the top."* If you've failed at something recently, don't let the feeling of discouragement settle into your soul. What do you do? Get back up and try again! Just accept the mistake as a price of progress.

Take Simon Peter for example: He walked on water but He made a mistake when He took His eyes off of Jesus. Everyone saw His success but everyone saw His failure. As a leader, you have to learn how to handle both. Your inner resolve must say, no matter what happens; God's hand is always there to pick me up or pat me on the back. Yes, leaders get attention when they make a mistake but they also get applauded with a job well done. How do we distinguish between the two? When you make a mistake; admit it. It's not how many mistakes you make but it's making the same mistakes that will cost you. Your biggest mistake is not asking yourself what mistakes you are making. Scripture is clear when it comes to self-examination. In order to climb the ladder of success, you must slow down and examine yourself. Lack of focus is the breeding ground for failure. Thomas Edison said, *"I haven't failed. I've just found 10,000 ways that won't work*. It's all about perspective.

With this in mind; What can you change today to get a different result tomorrow? Think relationally, financially, emotionally and spiritually? People change for one of two reasons: They have their minds open or their hearts broken. What do you need to do?

Step to Start Strong:

Re-evaluate your Mistakes

AUGUST 13.

MEMORIZE ME.

"May the words of my mouth and the meditation of my heart be holy and pleasing in your sight, O' LORD, my Rock and my Redeemer."

Psalm 19:14

Do you ever run out of words when you pray? If so, let me share a secret with you. The scripture teaches us that, *"God watches over His word to perform it."* Therefore, when you don't know what else to say, pray a passage of scripture. It's the greater way.

Take Psalm 19:14 for example. David understood that there were two things that tend to get us in trouble; Our mouth and our mind. I challenge you; Memorize these 25 words and pray them everyday. If we fully understood the power of the prayers that we offer up by faith, we would live by the mandate *"to pray without ceasing."* Stop listening for a word and start looking for a verse. When you find a scripture that agrees with your need, wield it at the devil as your weapon of warfare. The Word will work when nothing else will. Its God's will. Pray the word everyday.

Start with Psalm 19:14.

"May the words of my mouth and the meditation of my heart be holy and pleasing in your sight, O' LORD, my Rock and my Redeemer."

<u>Step to Start Strong</u>:

Pray the Word

AUGUST 14.

Spiritual Revelation

"I do not cease to give thanks for you, making mention of you in all of my prayers: that the God of our Lord Jesus Christ, the Father of glory, may give to you the spirit of wisdom and revelation in the knowledge of Him, the eyes of your understanding being enlightened; that you may know what is the hope of His calling."

Ephesians 1:16-20

I love revelation and I'm not talking about the Book even though I love it too! What I love the most is when God opens my spiritual eyes of understanding to see something that I've never seen or understood before. This is what the Apostle Paul prayed for the church of Ephesus. He says, "*I consistently intercede to the Father on your behalf; that He would give you the spirit of wisdom and revelation that you may know the hope of your calling.*" Do you have hope? Do you know your calling? If not, I pray God would open your eyes to see the potential that has been present on the inside of you all along. In this moment, something happens. God allows you to see from His perspective. It's called revelation and understanding. Revelation means *"to uncover."* Has God ever opened your heart to see something new in the sphere of the spirit that you have never seen before? If so, remember this is a work of the Holy Spirit. Revelation and understanding are so important for you to grow in spiritual maturity. But there's more; The other side of revelation is a mystery. Things that are true but you don't understand. Let me say it this way; "*What you do not know is just as important as what you do know.*" Perhaps, this is why they call the Bible a Book of Faith and not a Book of Understanding. If you and I understood everything about everything, we would be God. The truth is, we don't understand everything and we never will. Some situations seem unfair but we can't lose our faith. God is always teaching us something new about His faithfulness and love. In fact, God loves to stretch our understanding of who He is and what He is capable of doing. Especially, through our obedience; When God calls us to do something, He expects us to obey. Our obedience doesn't require understanding but it does require faith; certainly more faith now than ever before. However, if we only obey when we understand, we reduce God down to our own finite mind and reason which includes our own revelation. Case and Point: I am not the Lord of my life; He is. Didn't we abandon our will and make a vow of absolute trust to depend upon His power and provision? We cannot sacrifice our understanding of the character and nature of God on the altar of human reasoning. Revelation and understanding are true marks of spiritual maturity but the mystery of the Gospel must be a relentless pursuit for each of us everyday. One is grace and the other is faith. We have to trust and obey, as the ole song says, because there is no other way. What has God asked you to do that you do not understand?

Step to Start Strong:

Seek Revelation & Understanding

AUGUST 15.

GIVE TO GOD

"Ship your grain across the sea and after many days you may receive a return."

Ecclesiastes 11:1

Your motive is wrong when you give something to receive something in return. Giving to get is not God's way of doing things. When you feel led to give; just give and let God bring the increase to your seed. Pray, plant and let God's power produce a harvest of righteousness for you in due time.

Proverbs 19:7 says, *"If you are gracious to a poor man, you lend to the LORD, and He will repay you for your good deed." "Even if you give a cup of cold water to one of the least of these, truly I tell you, you will never lose your reward."* (Matthew 10:42) The Bible is clear; *"God is not unjust. He will not forget your work and the love you have shown as you minister to the saints around the world."* (Hebrews 6:10) *"Keep giving generously to Him, and your heart will not be grieved, because the LORD your God will bless you in all your work and in all your undertakings.*(Deuteronomy 15:10) *„O, How blessed will you be, you who sow beside all waters." (Isaiah 32:20)*

"Whatever you do, don't grow weary in well-doing, for in due time you will reap a harvest, if you do not give up! (Galatians 6:9)

I believe Ecclesiastes 11:1 is a prophetic passage for us this year. We are shipping grain across the sea as we prepare for our next International Gospel Crusades. For our efforts, thousands will be saved and touched by the power of God. God's word never fails! Please stand with us as we *"Ship our grain (representing our time, talent and treasures) across the sea. When we do this, the promise says, "that after many days we will receive a return." As partners with CWMI, you will receive a return! I am personally believing for a Bountiful Harvest for all of you that pray, plant and water the work of our hands!*

Somebody say this with me: God, *"I am shipping my grain across the sea!"* There's power in the seed but the miracle is in the soil! Today, we pray, plant and water the wonderful work you have called us to and we believe by faith that it is "Harvest-Time!" In Jesus Name!

Step to Start Strong:

Sow a Seed in your Time of Need

AUGUST 16.

Good Morning Holy Spirit

"And do not grieve the Holy Spirit of God, with whom you were sealed for the day of redemption."

Ephesians 4:30

Reinhart Bonnke once said, *"without the Church the Holy Spirit is homeless."* He is like Noah's dove that found no resting place away from the ark. When the dove finally came back to the ark it held an olive branch in its mouth symbolizing the anointing of the Holy Spirit. When the anointing comes upon the church, He will rest upon them with mighty power. In this moment in the story, Noah stretched forth His hand by faith and brought the dove back into the ark. God is still calling the church worldwide to receive His promise of power the same way. The Holy Spirit desperately desires to be within the House of God. However, some pastors and leaders send Him away for lack of understanding and sadly for fear of people.

A dove is easily spooked and so is the person of the Holy Spirit. You can grieve Him Oh' so easily. It can happen so subtle with the words you speak and the attitude in which you live. The word grieved means "*to inflict with great sorrow.*" Meaning you can hurt the heart of God especially when you hurt your fellow brother or family member. The way you live your life matters especially to the Holy Spirit. Your choices create an atmosphere that attracts the Holy Spirit or grieves the Holy Spirit. Be a good host for the Holy Ghost this week. Don't leave Him homeless out of your home or your heart. Give Him an invitation for a visitation but when you do; watch out. He will come in all His glory. He will not turn you away for He is your ever-present help in time of need.

Step to Start Strong:

Give the Holy Spirit a Home

AUGUST 17.

THE KNOWLEDGE OF THE GLORY

"For the earth will be filled with the knowledge of the glory of the LORD as the waters cover the sea."

Habakkuk 2:14

Typically, revival doesn't break out during the best of times but Real Revival does break out when the righteous cry out! I don't know exactly what the next great awakening in the world is going to look like but I do know we are on the fringe of something significant in terms of revival. Before every great awakening, history records a great shaking. If the Lord is doing anything, He is getting the churches attention through the immorality and inequity of our nation.

Habakkuk, an Old Testament Prophet, spoke of a day when the Glory of God would cover the earth as the waters cover the sea. He didn't say it will fill our church buildings. He said, *"The Glory of God would fill the Globe!"* The End Time revival won't be contained in a *"church."* This outpouring will flow down every highway and byway; From your House to the Court House and all the way to the White House! No one can escape the great and dreadful Day of the Lord. We'll see high ranking officials profess Christ as their Lord and Savior. From the gutter-most to the utter-most, you might say,

God is going to make America great again! The knowledge of His Glory will stretch across every sea. The whole world will soon know who the King of Glory is? In fact, The Day is quickly approaching. The Spirit and the Bride say, *"Just watch and see."* It's called, The Knowledge of The Glory!

Come Quickly Lord Jesus!

Step to Start Strong:

Contend for Personal and Cooperate Revival

AUGUST 18.

PERSECUTION FOR THE CROSS

"Bless those who persecute you; bless and do not curse."

Romans 12:14

Charles Spurgeon said, *"Never did the church so much prosper and so truly thrive as when she was baptized in the blood. The ship of the church never sails so gloriously along as when the bloody spray of her martyrs falls on her deck. We must suffer and we must die, if we are ever to conquer this world for Christ."*

Persecution causes the church to pray and prayer causes the church to spread. At least this is what History says: In the Book of Acts, we see a cycle; The people of God gathered to pray. The place began to shake as they were endued with the Spirit's power. This power and love flowed through them to their fellow man which brought about great victories in their land. However, this miracle working power created opposition and persecution which eventually pressed God's people back to the place of prayer. Over and over again, we see the same scenario. Prayer, power, miracles and persecution! Why should we expect anything different today?

Martin Luther once said, *"Even the Devil is God's devil!"* Therefore, you don't have to fear when you are on the frontline of being provoked and persecuted by the sons and daughters of disobedience. Why? Because it might be God's way of getting you to pray so that you will be filled with power so you can ultimately fulfill His purpose. Have you ever thought of it this way before?

As the old proverb says, "*The Blood of the Martyr is the Seed of the Church.*" Don't curse your enemies. Pray for them. By doing so, you will obtain the promises of God.

Step to Start Strong:

Bless your Enemies

AUGUST 19.

The Discipline of Drafting

"Follow my example, as I follow the example of Christ."

1st Corinthians 11:1

More people follow Nascar Racing than any other sport in America. It's not a family favorite for me but I can respect the athletic ability of someone who drives over 200 mph in circles for hours on end. The only experience I've ever had within the Nascar World was a night race at Bristol Motor Speedway. Late one Saturday night, a fellow co-worker buzzed my phone in Bible College and asked me if I wanted to take a road trip to watch the race. Our boss' wife was suddenly sent into labor which left someone a free ticket. Being it was up for grabs, fan or no fan, how could I pass up the free opportunity? To be quite honest, it was a day I'll never forget. Bristol is the largest amphitheater in the world and certainly a sight to see.

This is what I learned: Of all strategies on the track, one of the most important is the discipline of drafting. Drafting is when one driver aligns himself behind the driver in front of him for any period of time. The front car cuts the windspeed and resistance for the second car so He can generate greater speed and better fuel efficiency. Over all, drafting creates a current for all other cars to follow during the duration of the race.

Spiritual speaking, this art will work for the church. Whether you know it or not, you are in a race. It's called LIFE. Ecclesiastes 9:11 says, *"the race is not given to the swift nor the battle to the strong but it is given to those who endure to the end."* How do you make sure you endure to the end? Well, one way would be drafting. You draft when you align yourself with biblical principles, purpose and vision. These elements create momentum for you and everyone else to follow. The Apostle Paul modeled this truth for those who lived in the City of Corinth. He understood the importance of mentorship and passing the torch to the next generation. He knew we could draft off each others revelation, understanding and breakthrough. If we stay close and more importantly stay humble, we can all move forward in our cooperate callings and individual commissions. It's not a matter of who finishes first but how many finish at all.

Who are you modeling your life after? Who are you following Spiritually? Are you drafting in the wrong direction?

Here's a wisdom key: Everyone needs a Paul, Barnabas & Timothy. A Paul representing a spiritual father or leader like a pastor or a mentor. A Barnabas who represents a brother or sister in the faith who sticks close and causes you to speak comfortably. Lastly, in order to be complete, everyone needs a Timothy.

Someone you are mentoring or pouring your life, heart and wisdom into. This type of drafting breaks the back of the devil. Choose someone to follow and choose wisely.

Step to Start Strong:

Utilize the Discipline of Drafting

AUGUST 20.

In God We Trust

"It is better to trust in the Lord, than to put confidence in man."

Psalm 118:8

Out of the 23,145 verses in the Bible, Psalm 118 verse 8 falls directly in the middle. I believe this theme is at the heart of scripture because it is one the greatest struggles of man. What's the struggle? *"The daily temptation to depend upon the hand of man rather than the Hand of God."* So the question is: "*Who are you depending upon today*?" Your parents, your 401k, the doctor's report or the President? Whoever or whatever it is, let's look a little deeper into the matter:

God is the source of all things which makes everything else a resource. He will not allow you to depend upon one person or one thing for too long. This includes your spouse, boss, bank account or political party. Your trust in someone or something, should never exceed that of God. God deserves all the glory and He will not yield it to another. (Is. 42:8) In fact, He desires your whole heart and all your adoration. This is the best place to be because God is the greatest. On the other hand, when man lets you down you can rejoice because you know they are not the ones holding you up.

> *"It is truly better to trust in the Lord, than to place your trust in man."*

I've discovered it takes years to build trust but only one mistake to forfeit it all. People make mistakes but God is perfect. You can trust Him with your inner-most thoughts and your most prized possessions. He will always follow through for you with love and faithfulness.

Today, I challenge you; Trust God. Whatever is happening in your heart, put this passage into practice;

> *"Trust in the LORD with all your heart and lean not on your own understanding; in all your ways submit to him, and He will make your paths straight."*

Step to Start Strong:

Trust God

AUGUST 21.

GRACE FOR THE RACE

"May grace and peace be multiplied unto you."

2nd Peter 1:2

Does anybody need Grace for the Race? If so, this is your day; The word grace is mentioned 125 times in the New Testament making it a very important part of our everyday life. Out the 21 epistles, 16 of the books begin with the words, *"Grace be unto you."* Galatians so compassionately calls you into His grace, Ephesians relates to the riches of His grace and Philippians gives us the glory of His grace! If grace were an ocean, the world would be surrounded by grace on every side. Grace is free but it cost Jesus everything. The scripture teaches us 4 types of Grace:

#1 **Saving Grace:** Ephesians 2:8 says, "For by grace you have been saved through faith, and that not of yourselves; it is the gift of God." God's grace saves us, we don't have to earn it or work for it. Its God's unmerited favor.

#2 Justifying Grace: Romans 3:23-24 says, *"for all have sinned and fallen short of the glory of God, being justified freely by His grace through* *the redemption that is in Christ.* If you are a believer, you are justified by grace and you can have peace with God. Justified means, just-if-I'd never sinned. Sometimes we sin; amen? But when we confess our sins, there is a grace of justification that comes over us which keeps us righteous in His sight. Praise God for the Grace of Justification.

#3 Teaching Grace: "The missing message of grace in the church today." **Titus 2:11-12 "**For the grace of God that brings salvation has appeared to all men, teaching us to deny ungodliness and worldly lusts, therefore, we should live soberly, righteously, and godly in this present age." Some people say. I'm under grace therefore I can live anyway I want to. I'm going to Heaven regardless of what I do & what I believe. All I can say is, this is a dangerous place to be. If what you have does not compel you to be more like Jesus, you may not know Jesus. You could just be religious! The Bible says, *"No one who has tasted of His goodness can continue in the error of His way."* You can't live like Hell and expect to go to Heaven. Teaching Grace will change you, transform you and motivate you to live a holy, consecrated and dedicated life.

#4 Enabling Grace: 2nd Cor. 12:7-10 "And lest I should be exalted above measure by the abundance of the revelations, a thorn in the flesh was given to me, a messenger of Satan to buffet me, lest I be exalted above measure. Concerning this thing I pleaded with the Lord three times that it might depart from me. And He said to me, "My grace is sufficient for you, for My strength is made perfect in weakness." Therefore most gladly I will rather boast in my infirmities, that the power of Christ may rest upon me. Therefore I take pleasure in infirmities, in reproaches, in needs, in persecutions, in distresses, for Christ's sake. For when I am weak, then I am strong." Paul took His thorn in the flesh to the Throne of Grace but God didn't remove it, He just gave Him the grace to make it through it. God gave Him grace for the Race! He gave Him the divine enablement to withstand the thorn & in the storm. At times, God will work a miracle in a minute and at other times, there seems to be a season of waiting. Someone said, we live in a microwave generation but we serve a crockpot God. God likes for us to sit back and marinate in His grace no matter what problems we face. What kind of grace do you need for your race today?

Step to Start Strong:

Approach the Throne of Grace

AUGUST 22.

The Heart to Hear

"so prevalent and humbly accept the word planted in you, which can save you."

James 1:21b

The heart to hear the voice of God is much more important than the ability to hear the voice of God. Jesus said, *"My sheep know me and they hear my voice."* God knows how to speak your language and He certainly knows how to get your attention. If you are a born-again believer, hearing the voice of God isn't hard. However, having a heart to hear His voice is a little different.

Luke 11:28 says, *"Blessed are those who hear the word of God and keep it!"*Just to keep it real; With small kids under the roof, I'm already developing the, "*selective hearing syndrome*". Don't act like you don't understand. With silence being a lost art within the season of our home, I just can't answer and engage every conversation and keep my sanity. Yes, I hear the common commotion but sometimes after a long day, I just want to kick back and relax. During these days, I hear the life of my kids but my heart to hear them is dim.

At other times, which are my favorite times, you'll find me on the floor rolling around and laughing at every gesture. What's the difference? They have my full attention and I am quick to do whatever they want me to do. They have my heart and they have my ear. The truth is: God desires the same.

How do we have a heart to hear the voice of God? Through humility. James, the half brother of Jesus said, "*Humbly accept the word of God that is being planted in you.*" Housing the Holy Spirit gives you access to the voice of God but humility allows you to accept. Just because you hear God doesn't mean your heart is in the right place. Hearing Him is good but having a heart to obey is the greatest.

When was the last time you heard God's voice? Did you do what He ask you to do? If not, He may be slow to speak until you obey the last instruction. It's just a thought? Do you wanna be blessed? Its simple; Do what God says to do. If you He hear His words in humility, you'll grow to trust His heart; no matter what.

Lord, we humbly accept your word, your will and your way today, in Jesus Name.

Step to Start Strong:

Develop a Heart to Hear

AUGUST 23.

CHARACTERISTICS OF TRUE REVIVAL

John Wesley was once asked, *"How do you manage to gather such large crowds when you preach?"* His response was immediate: "*I set myself on fire and people come to watch me burn*!" Where does this so-called Holy Fire come from? This kind of flame is only ignited by the burning lamp-stand of fervent intercession. When you willfully sacrifice yourself on the altar of God, the Holy Fire of Heaven will keep falling.

What does fire look like? What are the characteristics of a fire? A fire will warm those around it, brighten the surroundings, and purify whatever is in its path. A spiritual fire works the same way. What does America need more than anything? Revival Fire. Only something that was once alive can be revived. In other words, revival is different from new birth. Yes, we need new converts but for this to happen in large numbers the church needs to wake up and be revived. Isaiah desired this in his day. Listen to His declaration for revival:

> *"Oh, that You would tear open the heavens and come down, That the mountains might quake at Your presence— As fire kindles*

the brushwood, as fire causes water to boil— To make Your name known to Your enemies, That the nations may tremble at Your presence! When You did awesome and amazing things which we did not expect, You came down on Mt. Sinai; the mountains quaked at Your presence." (Is. 64:1-3)

Here are 5 Primary Characteristics of True Revival:

1) A Conviction of Sin
2) A Denunciation of Sin
3) A Revelation of God's Holiness
4) A Deep Awakening of God's Love & Mercy
5) A Heightened Consciousness of Eternity

I challenge you to make a commitment before God and Man to pray for personal revival, cooperate revival and national revival. Prayer is the prerequisite for a powerful move of God's Spirit. Leonard Ravenhill, a 20th Century Revivalist, said, *"At God's counter there are no sale days, for the price of revival remains the same. Revival comes when the church tarry's in prayer."*

Psalm 71:18 has become a life verse for me; It says, "*O'God, Do not forsake me, until I declare your power to the next generation.*"

Will you tarry with me?

Step to Start Strong:

Pray for Revival Rain

AUGUST 24.

BAPTIZED IN SELFLESSNESS

"Now all who believed were together, and had all things in common, and sold their possessions and goods, and divided them among all, as anyone had need."

Acts 2:44-46

The early church was one big community. All the believers were one in heart, body and soul. *No one claimed that any of their possessions was their own, but they shared everything they had.* (Acts 4:32) The Outpouring of the Holy Spirit on the Day of Pentecost brought a fresh Baptism of Selflessness. The only thing worth living for in their world was Christ and Him crucified. The end result was radical abandonment to what was popular or even normal in their day.

This begs the question: What are you living for? Do your possessions own you or do you own your possessions? Are you a consumer or a producer spiritually speaking? David Wilkerson, my Grandfather in the faith once said, *"Do you want to know God's will?" Just find a need a fill it!* God knows all the needs in the world and since the beginning He's decided to use the church to make provision.

True Humility doesn't mean you never think about yourself, it just means you think of your self less. My prayer is that God would Baptize us in Selflessness.

Let us "*Give something away today.*" May we actually love our neighbor as ourselves.

Philippians 2:1-5 *"Therefore, if there is any encouragement in the Messiah, if there is any comfort of love, if there is any fellowship in the Spirit, if there is any compassion and sympathy, then fill me with joy by having the same attitude, sharing the same love, being united in spirit, and keeping one purpose in mind. Do not act out of selfish ambition or conceit, but with humility think of others as being better than yourselves. Do not be concerned about your own interests, but also be concerned about the interests of others. Have the same attitude among yourselves that was also in Christ Jesus."*

Step to Start Strong:

Live Unselfishly

AUGUST 25.

The Silent Years

"For prophecy never had its origin in the human will, but prophets, though human, spoke from God as they were carried along by the Holy Spirit."

2nd Peter 1:21

Theologians call the 400 years between the Old Testament and New Testament, "*The Silent Years.*" Why is this so? The Jewish race had just been released from 70 years of Babylonian captivity when the Prophet Malachi penned His challenge to the church in 430 BC. The purpose of his book was to encourage people to keep God first in their lives no matter what. History tells us why this was such an important prophetic theme spoken by Malachi because little did they know that the Heavens were going to be shut up and silent for the next 400 years. God wanted to make sure His people stayed steadfast and strong through the silent years. During these days, God revealed nothing new to His people. There were no words of prophecy, no manifestations of the Holy Spirit and no miracles, signs and wonders. Just silence.

Have you ever been through a silent season in your walk with God? If so, you know the struggle? So, what do you do when God is silent? *You remember and rely on the unfailing love and faithfulness of God in the past which will always build faith in you for the future.* The truth is, God will never leave you nor forsake you. Even when the Heavens seem like brass, you can know God is watching over His word to fulfill it in your life. If He's silent, you can best bet He's moving behind the scenes setting a stage for you to celebrate.

Is God silent in your situation today? Rest assured, "*The teacher is always silent during the test.*" My motto has always been, "*Do your best and let God do the rest*!" Even when He is silent. He can't hide His presence from you forever! It may feel like 400 years but when He shows up; It will be worth every minute of the wait.

For the children of Israel, John the Baptist showed up on the scene with a fresh word from Heaven. He prepared the way for the coming of the Lord. Silent Seasons are normally followed by a prophetic word that will change the landscape of those who believe it. If you are waiting for a word from God, refuse to change your posture of prayer and praise. Breakthrough is on the way.

Step to Start Strong:

Pass the Test of the Silent Seasons.

AUGUST 26.

Psalm 51

A Psalm of David, which is the record of His repentance of sin regarding the murder of Uriah. This one act was the greatest blemish upon his name and character. All the rest of his faults were nothing when compared to this one outrage. It is said of him in 1st Kings 15:5 that *"He turned not aside from the commandments of the Lord all the days of his life, except only in the matter of Uriah the Hittite."* This prayer exemplifies why David is described as *"a man after God's own heart."* (Acts 13:22) Despite all of David's shortcomings, He always remained dependent of the Lord and repentant toward His sin. Would you not just read these heartfelt words on a page today but pray them from the depths of your soul. May we too but men and women after God's own heart

Psalm 51:

Psalm 51

Have mercy upon me, O God,
According to Your lovingkindness;
According to the multitude of Your tender mercies,
Blot out my transgressions.
Wash me thoroughly from my iniquity,
And cleanse me from my sin.
For I acknowledge my transgressions,
And my sin *is* always before me.
Against You, You only, have I sinned,
And done *this* evil in Your sight—
That You may be found just when You speak,[a]
And blameless when You judge.
Behold, I was brought forth in iniquity,
And in sin my mother conceived me.
Behold, You desire truth in the inward parts,
And in the hidden *part* You will make me to know wisdom.
Purge me with hyssop, and I shall be clean;
Wash me, and I shall be whiter than snow.
Make me hear joy and gladness,
That the bones You have broken may rejoice.
Hide Your face from my sins,
And blot out all my iniquities.
Create in me a clean heart, O God,
And renew a steadfast spirit within me.
Do not cast me away from Your presence,
And do not take Your Holy Spirit from me.
Restore to me the joy of Your salvation,
And uphold me *by Your* generous Spirit.

Then I will teach transgressors Your ways,
And sinners shall be converted to You.
Deliver me from the guilt of bloodshed, O God,
The God of my salvation,
And my tongue shall sing aloud of Your righteousness.
O Lord, open my lips,
And my mouth shall show forth Your praise.
For You do not desire sacrifice, or else I would give *it;*
You do not delight in burnt offering.
The sacrifices of God *are* a broken spirit,
A broken and a contrite heart—
These, O God, You will not despise.
Do good in Your good pleasure to Zion;
Build the walls of Jerusalem.
Then You shall be pleased with the sacrifices of righteousness,
With burnt offering and whole burnt offering;
Then they shall offer bulls on Your altar.

Step to Start Strong:

Be Dependent and Repentant unto God.

AUGUST 27.

H.O.P.E.

"Many are they who say of me, "There is no help for him in God." Selah. But You, O Lord, are a shield for me, My glory and the One who lifts up my head. I cried to the Lord with my voice, And He heard me from His holy hill."

Psalm 3:2-4

Have you ever been overwhelmed with a feeling of hopelessness? Sure you have! If I have gleaned anything while walking with God, I've learned this; *"Life isn't fair."* To put it in the words of Saint Matthew, *"God causes the sun to rise on the good and the evil. He sends the rain on the just and the unjust."* (5:45) This means bad things happen to good people and good things happen to bad people. This is true.

What do you do when life deals you a bad hand? You pray, you seek wise counsel and you do your best to be obedient to God's word. However, at times, your hope is still deferred. Proverbs says, *"Hope deferred makes the heart sick."* Hopelessness can leave you feeling down and even depressed! What do you do now? You do what David did in Psalm 3; *"He cried out to God in the midst of His trouble and what did God do? God lifted His head."*

Here's a word; Don't give up until you get it out! The sacrifices of God are a broken heart and a contrite spirit. Don't let depression get the best of you. Release the overflow of your heart to God in prayer. He can handle your toughest questions and deepest desires. Don't let your past failure determine your future. The pathway of the righteous grows brighter and brighter not darker and darker.

Do you have HOPE? There's always hope even if you can't see it this morning. For these 3 will always remain; *Faith, Hope and Love.* Trust God today. Hope is on the way.

As the acronym says, He. Offers. Peace. Eternally.

Indeed, He is your glory and lifter of your head!

Step to Start Strong:

Don't Lose H.O.P.E.

AUGUST 28.

The Double-Minded Man

"If any of you lacks wisdom, let him ask of God, who gives to all liberally and without reproach, and it will be given to him. 6 But let him ask in faith, with no doubting, for he who doubts is like a wave of the sea driven and tossed by the wind. For let not that man suppose that he will receive anything from the Lord; he is a double-minded man, unstable in all his ways."

James 1:5-8

The Lord has been teaching me about the subject of double-mindedness. The term *double-minded* comes from the Greek word *dipsuchos*, meaning *"a person with two minds or souls."* It's interesting that this word appears only in the book of James. Bible scholars conclude that James might have coined this word. To grasp the full meaning of this word, it is best to understand how it is used within its context.

James writes of the doubting person that he is *"like a wave of the sea, blown and tossed by the wind. That man should not think he will receive anything from the Lord; he is a double-minded man, unstable in all he does."* A doubter is a double-minded man. Jesus had in mind such a man when He spoke of the one who tried to serve two masters in Matthew 6:24. As such, he is *"unstable,"* which comes from a Greek word meaning *"unsteady both his character and in feelings."*

A double-minded man is restless and confused in his thoughts and behavior. This man is constantly in conflict with himself. One torn by inner turmoil who can never stand with confidence in God. Interesting, the term *unstable* is used to describe a drunken man who is unable to walk a straight line, swaying one way and then another. He has no defined direction and as a result, He never gets anywhere! Such a person is *"unstable in all he does"* in which God calls, *"double-mindedness."*

Those who are double-minded do not have the faith spoken of in Hebrews 11:1, *"Now faith is being sure of what we hope for and certain of what we do not see."* We cannot be certain and doubting at the same time like the double-minded man. One part of his mind is sure of something, while the other side doubts. How could this be? This describes a double-minded man.

God cannot grant His blessings upon those who are double-minded. As Jesus declared, *"No one can serve two masters." Either he will hate the one and love the other, or he will be devoted to the one and despise the other."* Those who try to love both God and the world will become unstable in all their ways. God is a jealous God and He will not accept a service that is divided with Satan. Don't be double-minded. Pick a side and watch the words that fly out of your mouth!

<u>Step to Start Strong</u>:

Be Single-Minded

AUGUST 29.

GIVE THANKS

"Now on his way to Jerusalem, Jesus traveled along the border between Samaria and Galilee. As he was going into a village, ten men who had leprosy met him. They stood at a distance and called out in a loud voice, "Jesus, Master, have pity on us!" When he saw them, he said, "Go, show yourselves to the priests." And as they went, they were cleansed. One of them, when he saw he was healed, came back, praising God in a loud voice. He threw himself at Jesus' feet and thanked him—and he was a Samaritan. Jesus asked, "Were not all ten cleansed? Where are the other nine? Has no one returned to give praise to God except this foreigner?" Then he said to him, "Rise and go; your faith has made you well."

Luke 17:11-19

In this story, all ten men were healed but only one came back to *"give thanks."* This happens every day. One of the problems within the American society is that we are blessed in so many ways that we can begin to take the blessings for granted and even develop a sense of entitlement. Ralph Waldo Emerson said, *"if the stars came out only once a year, we would stay up all night to look at them."* He observed that we have seen the stars so often that we don't bother to look at them anymore. It's easy for us to be like this in regard to the blessing of God. We can become so accustomed to the abundance of favor that we receive so freely that we can lose our sense of thankfulness and gratefulness before our Heavenly Father.

May the attitude of entitlement be far from us as the children of God; Just like the one leper, may we be found grateful at the feet of Jesus. All ten reaped the reward but only one came back to worship. Let's us worship our way through everyday with the fruit of giving thanks.

Step to Start Strong:

Sow the Seed of Thanksgiving

AUGUST 30.

God's Will

"Give thanks in all circumstances; for this is God's will for you in Christ Jesus."

1st Thessalonians 5:18

Do you ever wonder what is God's will for your life? If so, scripture gives us an outline to point us in the right direction. This morning let's meditate upon the 4 verses in the New Testament that speak about God's will.

- **Romans 12:2** *"Do not conform to the pattern of this world, but be transformed by the renewing of your mind. Then you* ***will*** *be able to test and approve what God's* ***will*** *is—his good, pleasing and perfect* ***will****."*
- **1st Thessalonians 4:3** *"It is God's* ***will*** *that you should be sanctified: that you should avoid sexual immorality."*
- **1st Thessalonians 5:18** *"Give thanks in all circumstances; for this is God's* ***will*** *for you in Christ Jesus."*

- **<u>1st Peter 2:5</u>** *"For it is God's* ***will*** *that by doing good you should silence the ignorant talk of foolish people."*

These 4 points will help you move forward:

Resist the pattern of this world, stay pure, give thanks in all circumstances and do good to all people. Not a bad place to start! Put these principles into practice and you'll reach your desired destination. God's word is God's will. God bless you!

<u>Step to Start Strong</u>:

Apply God's Word and you will Fulfill God's Will

AUGUST 31.

Be Bold!

"Then Jesus said to them, "Suppose you have a friend, and you go to him at midnight and say, 'Friend, lend me three loaves of bread; a friend of mine on a journey has come to me, and I have no food to offer him.' And suppose the one inside answers, 'Don't bother me. The door is already locked, and my children and I are in bed. I can't get up and give you anything.' I tell you, even though he will not get up and give you the bread because of friendship, yet because of the man's boldness he will surely get up and give you as much as you need."

Luke 11:5-8

The word boldness in verse 8 means, *"shameless persistence or an unashamed attempt."* The early church was baptized in such boldness when the Holy Spirit came upon them on the Day of Pentecost. Before they were full of fear and ran from local authorities but after they shook entire cities and turned the world upside down.

This type of boldness needs to be restored to the church. To be brutally honest, we give up way to easy.

In Luke Chapter 11, Jesus is teaching His disciples the importance of being persistence in prayer. He goes on to say, "*Ask and it will be given to you; seek and you will find; knock and the door will be opened to you. For everyone who asks receives; the one who seeks finds; and to the one who knocks, the door will be opened. (vs.9)* Many times we have not because we ask not, at other times we do not find the answer we are looking for because we neglect the discipline of seeking. Relating to the man in the story, the door was finally opened because of His unashamed boldness to keep on knocking until His friend supplied his need.

Case and point: You can in sit in self-afflicted solitude and struggle in silence or you can humble yourself and approach the Throne of Grace with boldness knowing you are going to receive mercy to help you in your time of need. Be persistent! Don't give up so easy! Keep fighting the good fight of faith! You're closer to your breakthrough than ever before! Remember, the righteous are as bold as a lion! Begin to Roar in this season and watch your enemies be scattered!

Step to Start Strong:

Be BOLD!

SEPTEMBER 1.

NEW BEGINNINGS

"In a great house there are not only vessels of gold and silver but also of wood and earthenware, and some for noble use, some for ignoble. If any one purifies himself from what is ignoble, then he will be a vessel for noble use, consecrated and useful to the master of the house, ready for any good work."

2nd Timothy 2:20

The next time you feel like GOD cannot use you because of your sin, struggles and shortcomings:

Just Remember...

- Noah was an alcoholic...
- Abraham was too old...
- Isaac was a daydreamer...
- Jacob was a liar...
- Leah was an idolator...

- Moses had a speech impediment ...
- Rahab was a prostitute...
- Gideon was full of fear...
- Sampson was a womanizer...
- Ruth was a pagan...
- Jeremiah was too young...
- David had an affair and later killed a man...
- Solomon was a philanderer...
- Elijah was suicidal...
- Jonah ran from God...
- Job went bankrupt...
- The Disciples fell asleep while praying....
- Martha worried about everything...
- The Samaritan woman had five broken marriages...
- Zacchaeus was a swindler...
- Peter denied Christ...
- Paul was a Pharisee...
- Timothy was too timid…
- AND Lazarus, well, Lazarus was dead and God used Him!

Never forget, God can take what the devil meant for evil and turn it around for His glory and the saving of many lives!

(The above reading was written by John Ortberg.)

Step to Start Strong:

Begin Again

SEPTEMBER 2.

THE MACEDONIAN CALL

"During the night Paul had a vision of a man of Macedonia standing and begging him, "Come over to Macedonia and help us.""

Acts 16:9

Almost 3,000 years ago, Joel prophesied that in the last days God would pour out His Spirit upon all flesh. The end result? His sons and daughters would rise up to prophesy as they dreamed dreams and saw visions. (Joel 2) I think it is safe to say that we are living in the last minutes of the last days; meaning men and women alike should prophesy and have a dream that drives them. The world as we know it is coming to a close and the door to the Ark is about to be shut. Are you ready? How about your family? Today is the day to settle this question in your soul. Jesus is coming soon friends. With this in mind, we should be sharing our faith with great urgency because countless individuals find themselves in the valley of decision as their souls are hanging in the balance between Heaven and Hell. Can I ask you a question: Do you have a vision to win the lost?

Here's an example; One day the Apostle Paul heard the Macedonian Call. God spoke to him in the middle of the night by way of vision and what did he see? He saw a man from another country standing before him begging him to come help him. How does this relate to us today?

I believe there are people out their right now crying out to the creator of the universe to send them a sign. Their lonely and confused and there looking for someone who can tell them the truth.

Think of it this way; Someone is calling out to God this morning for help and by the sovereignty of God, only He could direct your steps to the doorposts of this persons heart. All He is looking for is your willingness and availability. May our paths cross intersect with those who are struggling in their faith today. You can do it. Help us to see as you see.

Step to Start Strong:

Ask God for a Dream and Vision.

SEPTEMBER 3.

PREPARE YE THE WAY

"He will turn many of the sons of Israel back [from sin] to [love and serve] the Lord their God. It is he who will go as a forerunner before Him in the spirit and power of Elijah, to turn the hearts of the fathers back to the children, and the disobedient to the attitude of the righteous [which is to seek and submit to the will of God]—in order to make ready a people [perfectly] prepared [spiritually and morally] for the Lord."

Luke 1:16-17

What John the Baptist did for Israel, we can do for others. This man was a forerunner for all of us in the faith. He prepared the way for everyone who would enter into the Kingdom of God during the dispensation of grace. Even Christ said, "*among those born of women, there is no one greater than John.*" (Luke 7:28) Why would Jesus make such a statement? Does God have favorites? Certainly not, what He does for one He will always do for another. By saying this, Jesus was proving a powerful point to the Pharisees of that day. The religious leaders rejected the rhetoric of John and disregarded his doctrine of public baptism and repentance. This is why they pushed him out to preach in the wilderness. He was not welcomed in the sanctuaries and synagogues of the day. Indeed, John had a different way of dress, a different form of diet and a different type of sermon delivery. But we can all agree He was used mightily by God. He challenged the way of the Jew and ultimately prepared the way for Jesus.

How does this relate to you and I today? Well, first and foremost, we can't judge a book by its cover. Just because someone doesn't look like us, sound like us or worship the way we do, doesn't mean we are right and they are wrong. Many times, our perception is skewed by our personal experience and position. Humanity has the tendency to view people through their own religious experience and even social class and culture. When the reality is, God is so much bigger than our capacity to comprehend Him. Here's my point: Many missed what God was doing through John the Baptist because they couldn't see passed His differences. Listen up church: Our dynamic is found in our differences meaning we don't have to have the same perspective to share the same purpose. The world needs some flavor! If everyone was just like me, the world would be boring! Get some people in your life that don't think and act like you do! Ask God to send a John the Baptist into your life to challenge your faith. It's so easy to be lured asleep with all the distractions of our day. What we really need is the anointing to change the direction of a whole generation. John captivated his audience became he was full of the anointing. He didn't care what everyone else thought about him; Just Jesus. Will you be the one to prepare the way for the 2nd Coming of Christ? What John the Baptist did for Israel, we can do for others.

Step to Start Strong:

Prepare the Way of the Lord.

SEPTEMBER 4.

GIANTS IN THE LAND

Finding a Christian in India is kind a like finding a needle in a hay stack. Christians only make up 2.3 percent of its population so as you can see there's a lot of work to be done. The need is so great, it can almost be overwhelming and discouraging from a ministry standpoint.

Before out team departed a few weeks ago, we drove to Raleigh for a prophetic prayer meeting with a small group of people. One word given that night was taken from Numbers Chapter 13 and 14 when a group of men were sent by Moses into Canaan to spy out the Promised Land. Of course, we know that their were two reports that came back after 40 days; 8 of the spies said, *"we can't conquer the land. Giants live there and all the people there are stronger than we are! So these men began to spread a bad report among the people."* (13:32) However, despite a discouraged few, Joshua & Caleb believed a different a report and silenced the people by saying, *"No! God is giving us the land and we should go up and take possession of it; For WE CAN certainly DO IT!"* Two groups, two different reports: One full of fear and the other full of faith. All 10 men visibly and audibly experienced the same situation; so what was the difference? One word; Perspective.

The cowardly Christians said, *"when we compared ourselves to them, we looked like grasshoppers "in our own eyes."* (13:33) These men fell into unbelief because their viewpoint was from their own perspective and not the perspective of God. Instead of looking up, they looked down. Their confidence was birthed on earth and not in Heaven.

It's important to note that God said, over and over and over again, *"I am giving you this land."* The real estate transaction had already been signed and notarized (Psalm 24) but the prospects had the wrong perspective.

Therefore I ask you, what has God promised you? How are you looking at your current situation? Do you see yourself sick or healed? Do you see yourself defeated or victorious? Your viewpoint should come from scripture and scripture alone. God's word is full of promises and all of them are Yes! In Christ Jesus!

This word so greatly encouraged my heart that night as we prepared to enter into India, the Land of Giants. I don't know how God is going to take that 2.3 percent and multiply it but what I do know is this; God is giving us the land. Amen? God's word says, *"The Kingdom of Heaven is at Hand so reach out and take it by faith today in Jesus Name!"*

Step to Start Strong:

Cross into Canaan

SEPTEMBER 5.

TIMES OF TRANSITION

"Have I not commanded you? Be strong and courageous do not be afraid, nor be dismayed, for the Lord your God is with you wherever you go."

Joshua 1:9

The enemy loves to attack you during times of transition. Transition speaks of starting something new. God-given opportunity always brings an air of excitement especially when you have been praying and fasting for breakthrough. On the contrary, Satan loves to take excitement and turn it into anxiety. Anxiety comes when you can't see an expected end but for the Child of God, this is the place we call faith. In fact, this is where Joshua found himself as He led God's people out of complacency and into the Promised Land, the place of destiny. As a spy forty years earlier, Joshua could see the victory in the spirit but everyone else leaned upon their own understanding and forfeited the fight because of their unbelief.

Years later, Joshua was standing on the threshold of what He had been waiting for and what did God say? Of all things to say in this moment, God reiterates 3 defining statement to drill into this military leaders mind. Joshua, *"Don't be afraid! I'm serious! Don't be afraid! Did you hear me, Son? Whatever you do; Don't be afraid!"* The Spirit of Fear was coming at him full throttle to keep Him from stepping into those waters but God knew exactly what He needed; *The Promise of His Presence!*

Some theologians say, the words Do not fear or Do not be afraid are mentioned 365 times in scripture; One for every day of the year. Picture this; every morning when you walk out of your bedroom to face another day. Envision the words, "Do not fear above your doorpost to give you the courage to conquer whatever obstacles stand in the way. Why? Because God did not give you a spirit if fear. He gave you the Spirit of Power, Love and a Sound-mind.

Are you going through times of transition? If so, gravitate toward God's promises today. They will keep you away from fear and keep fill you full of faith. Faith comes when you hear the word of God. Do you hear me? God is with you mighty warrior! Don't worry! Get excited! Don't be anxious! Pray! God's promises are on the way.

Step to Start Strong:

Be Strong and Courageous.

SEPTEMBER 6.

THE PARABLE OF THE MARBLES

"This is why I speak to them in parables: 'Though seeing, they do not see; though hearing, they do not hear or understand."

Matthew 13:13

Once upon a time, there was a foolish boy who had a bag full of beautiful marbles. Now this boy was quite proud of his marbles. In fact, he thought so much of them that he would neither play with them himself nor would he let anyone else play with them. He only took them out of the bag in order to count and admire them; they were never used for their intended purpose. Yet that boy carried that coveted bag of marbles everywhere he went.

Well, there was also a wise boy who wished he could have such a fine bag of marbles. So this boy worked hard and earned money to purchase a nice bag to hold marbles. Even though he had not yet earned enough with which to purchase any marbles, he had faith and purchased the marble bag.

He took special care of the bag and dreamed of the day it would contain marbles with which he could play and share with his friends.

Alas, the foolish boy with all of the marbles didn't take care of the marble bag itself, and one day the bag developed a hole in the bottom seam. Still, he paid no attention and, one by one, the marbles fell out of the bag.

It didn't take long, once the foolish boy's marble bag developed a hole, for the wise boy to begin to find those beautiful marbles, one at a time, lying unnoticed on the ground. And, one by one, he added them to his marble bag. The wise boy thus gained a fine bag full of marbles in no time at all. This boy played with the marbles and shared them with all of his friends. And he always took special care of the bag so he wouldn't lose any. In the end, the foolish boy was selfish and careless, he lost all of his marbles and was left holding an empty bag.

Step to Start Strong:

Be a Good Steward of what God has Given you.

SEPTEMBER 7.

The River of Life

"Jesus answered, 'Everyone who drinks this water will be thirsty again, but whoever drinks the water I give them will never thirst. Indeed, the water I give them will become in them a spring of water welling up to eternal life."

John 4"13-14

Robert Murray McCheyne, an 18th century minister in Scotland, was well aware of the Fountain of Life. He drank from it continually as He wrote these words:

"The Holy Spirit is an imperishable stream, not like those rivers which flow through barren sands till they sink into the earth and disappear. No, the stream of grace that flows from Jesus Christ flows into many a barren heart; but it is never lost there. It appears again—it flows from that heart in rivers of living water. When a soul believes on Jesus, drinks in His Spirit, it becomes as if the Spirit were lost in that soul. The stream flows into such a barren heart and can appear gone; but it is never lost. If you come to

> *Jesus and drink, you shall become a fountain of grace to your family. Through your heart, your words, and through your prayers the stream of grace will flow into other hearts. Those you love best in all the world may in this way receive grace."*

The Holy Spirit lives on the inside of you. Stop holding back the dam of His majesty and glory. Today is the day to let the River flow…

Revelation 22:1-5 "Then the angel showed me the river of the water of life, as clear as crystal, flowing from the throne of God and of the Lamb down the middle of the great street of the city. On each side of the river stood the tree of life, bearing twelve crops of fruit, yielding its fruit every month. And the leaves of the tree are for the healing of the nations. No longer will their be any curse. The throne of God and of the Lamb will be in the city, and his servants will serve him. They will see his face, and his name will be on their foreheads. There will be no more night. They will not need the light of a lamp or the light of the sun, for the Lord God will give them light. And they will reign for ever and ever.

Ezekiel 47:1-5 "The man brought me back to the entrance to the temple, and I saw water coming out from under the threshold of the temple toward the East (for the temple faced east). The water was coming down from under the South side of the temple, south of the altar. He then brought me out through the North gate and led me around the outside to the outer gate facing east, and the water was trickling from the South side. As the man went eastward with a measuring line in his hand, he measured off a thousand cubits and then led me through water that was ankle-deep. He measured off another thousand cubits and led me through water that was knee-deep. He measured off another thousand and led me through water that was up to the waist. He measured off another thousand, but now it was a river that I could not cross, because the water had risen and was deep enough to swim in—a river that no one could cross. He asked me, "Son of man, do you see this?"

<u>Step to Start Strong</u>:

Let the River Flow.

SEPTEMBER 8.

A.S.K.

"Ask and it will be given to you; seek and you will find; knock and the door will be opened to you."

Matthew 7:7

Mark Twain once said, "*He who asks a question is a fool for five minutes but He who does not ask is a fool forever.*" Have you ever hesitated to ask a question in public and pay for it later? We all have! Some questions seem silly and not worth mentioning but if you don't know how to do something or don't know where to go, you better find out who does! We can all save ourselves time and unnecessary heartache by asking simple questions.

King David was full of questions, concern and internal controversy throughout His writings in the Book of Psalms. His heart is an open book for all of us to search and study because He desperately desired to know God and His ways. He asked God tough questions but more importantly He sought God for the answers. Here's where many of us fail? Yes, we have not because we ask not but we also misunderstand God at times because we don't see from His perspective. If you ask the right question, you'll get the right answer but more importantly you'll gain the right perspective in your situation. This is what happens when you ask God questions in prayer. The Holy Spirit will begin to align your heart with the will of God and you'll see something you never saw before. Go ahead; Talk to God openly and ask Him questions but be willing to seek Him for the answer and then get ready for the weight of the revelation. Oliver Holmes once said, "*the mind once stretched by a new idea can never return to its original dimension.*" This is why Jesus told His disciples, "*There is so much more I want to tell you, but you can't bear it right now.*" (John 16:12) God wants to speak to you and stretch you but He will never release His majesty beyond your capacity. (Exodus 33:20) This is why our journey with Jesus goes from faith to faith and glory to glory. We're constantly growing in our knowledge and understanding of Him and He'll keep showing us more and more if we so desire. A matter of fact, you'll be surprised what He tells you this year. Just ask, seek and knock and the door of revelation will be opened unto you.

"O Lord—how long?" (Psalm 6:3) A question of eagerness to see God's plan accomplished.

"What is man that You are mindful of him?" (Psalm 8:4) A question of awe that God even cares about sinful man.

"Why do You hide in times of trouble?" (Psalm 10:1) A question that reveals a longing for God's presence.

"Lord, who may abide in Your tabernacle? Who may dwell in Your holy hill?" (Psalm 15:1) The ultimate question of who may live with God.

<u>Step to Start Strong</u>:

Ask God the Tough Questions

SEPTEMBER 9.

WATCH YOUR MOUTH

"No, the word is very near you; it is in your mouth and in your heart so you may obey it."

Deuteronomy 30:14

Do you want to have a better year than you had last year? If so, *"You better watch your mouth!"* Proverbs 18:21 says, *"Death and life are in the power of the tongue, and those who love it will eat its fruit."* Do you love your life? If so, *"You better watch your mouth!"* According to scripture, your words create your world. Do you desire peace and prosperity from this day forward? If so, *"Say it with me; You better watch your mouth!"* It's true! This is a trustworthy statement that deserves our full attention.

King David said, *"Lord, Set a guard over my mouth and keep watch over the door of my lips!"* (Psalm 141:3) This spiritual spokesman understood the importance of the words He allowed to leave His lips on a daily basis. Why is this so? Because Jesus said at a later date, *"that we would have to give an account for every idle, empty and careless word we speak on earth."* (Matthew 12:36) Every word? Yes, every word.

This thought begs the question: "What have you been saying lately or what have you been saying your whole life that doesn't agree with scripture?" Every word you speak is a seed and it will bear fruit for you. Make sure you're speaking the truth in love everyday of your life.

As one preacher said, *"There's a miracle in your mouth!"* God is watching over His word to fulfill it so hold fast to your confession. Just because you don't see immediate results doesn't mean your miracle won't manifest. Keep speaking the word and the word will eventually make a way. If the word works, you might as well let it work for you.

Pray this with me: *"May the words of my mouth and the meditation of my heart be holy and acceptable in your sight O'God, my Rock and my redeemer."* (Psalm 19:14)

Step to Start Strong:

Watch your Mouth

SEPTEMBER 10.

The Brother's Battle

"Now his older son was in the field. And as he came and drew near to the house, he heard music and dancing. So he called one of the servants and asked what these things meant. And he said to him, 'Your brother has come, and because he has received him safe and sound, your father has killed the fatted calf.' "But he was angry and would not go in."

Luke 15:25-27

In Chapter 15 of the Gospel of Luke, we read 3 parables that pertain to something that was lost. The lost sheep, the lost coin and the lost son. Why did Jesus share these stories back to back? Here my thought: Because the Pharisees were enraged and upset with the message of grace that Jesus was preaching. (Luke 15:1)

In general, *"church people"* rejoice when someone gets saved but very few of them have the grace and mercy to walk someone through a backslidden state. Salvation is always merry but discipleship tends to be messy.

This was the older Brother's Battle in the Parable of the Prodigal Son. He forgot what it was like to be dead in His trespasses and sin. He forgot the stench of the pig pen and He even denied the fact that he had fallen short when He said, *"I have never disobeyed one of your commandments."* (Luke 15:29) This shows that it is possible for a saint to start trusting in themselves rather than depending upon the righteousness of God. In fact, this is the Brother's Battle: *"Self-Righteousness."*

The prophet Isaiah highlighted this condition when He said, *"all of our righteous acts are like filthy rags before the Lord."* (Isaiah 64:6) No matter how much good we do, when we do it apart from Christ, it means nothing and it won't amount to anything. We can't forget who saved us and where we would be without Him. We too were once sinners and the world needs the same Savior.

John Newton, the writer of Amazing Grace, kept this close to his heart when He made this statement late in life: *"Although my memory is fading, I remember two things very clearly: I am a great sinner and Christ is a great Savior."* John fought the Brother's Battle and came out victorious on the other side. How did He do it? He depended upon the finished work of Christ and kept His eyes on God's amazing grace. May we extend the same love to sinners and backslidden sons and daughters today. The Heavenly Father is standing on the front porch of Heaven gazing down the long dusty road waiting for all of them to come home. This is His heart. What's yours?

Step to Start Strong:

Don't Succumb to the Brother's Battle

SEPTEMBER 11.

ARE YOU INTERESTED?

"On the same day, Jesus went out of the house and sat by the sea. And great multitudes were gathered together to Him, so that He got into a boat and sat; and the whole multitude stood on the shore. There He spoke many things to them in parables."

Matthew 13:1-3

Jesus taught in parables. A parable is an earthly story that holds "hidden" spiritual truth. Everyone heard Jesus' teachings in this scripture but not everyone understood. I've always wondered; *"Why would Jesus teach this way if He wanted to reveal Himself to mankind?"* Here's the answer: The multitudes followed Jesus but most of the multitude wanted something free. In order to be a *"disciple"* or student of the word, there is a personal price to be paid. For the first disciples, these men had to leave their nets, businesses and even family to gain the revelation of the realities of Heaven. Regardless of who you are, the price to follow

Jesus and to understand the depths of His teaching is found in this one word: Commitment. Commitment. Commitment. Jesus is seeking a people who are willing to take up their crosses and follow Him. This is why He taught in parables; Because all parables are based upon this one premise: "N*othing is truly yours until you discover it*." If something is free or given to you without a desire, the item tends to be depreciated in your heart because you didn't do anything to obtain it or deserve it. This is so good. Later on in the day, His disciples asked this question in private, "Why do You speak to them in parables? (Matthew 13:10) and He answered them and said, "It has been given to you to know the mysteries of the kingdom of heaven, but to them it has not been given. For whoever has, to him more will be given, and he will have an abundance; but whoever does not have, even what he has will be taken away from him." I want you to add one word in this passage to help you understand what Jesus was really saying and the word is "interest." Read with me; "*For whoever has (interest), to him more will be given, and he will have abundance; but whoever does not have interest, even what he has will be taken away from him. Did that help? The multitudes or most of the world doesn't have an "interest" in Jesus. Therefore, they miss the hidden meanings of the parabolic teachings. To us, who love Jesus, the truths are hidden in plain sight. But to those who are perishing, they are foolish.*" He goes on to say, this is why I speak to them in parables, "*because seeing they do not see, and hearing they do not hear, nor do they understand*." This proves the point that just because someone sees the miraculous and hears the Gospel message doesn't mean they understand it or even desire to. It all comes down to whether or not you are *committed to Christ* and *interested in knowing more about Him*. Yes, we honor the death and burial of Jesus Christ but many neglect the resurrected life that is available on the other side of the grave. This is the journey that Jesus calling us to. Are you Interested? If so, keep seeking and searching!

Step to Start Strong:

Study the Parables

SEPTEMBER 12.

THE FIRST EVANGELISTS

"So it was, when the angels had gone away from them into heaven, that the shepherds said to one another, "Let us now go to Bethlehem and see this thing that has come to pass, which the Lord has made known to us." And they came with haste and found Mary and Joseph, and the Babe lying in a manger. Now when they had seen Him, they made widely known the saying which was told them concerning this Child. And all those who heard it marveled at those things which were told them by the shepherds. But Mary kept all these things and pondered them in her heart. Then the shepherds returned, glorifying and praising God for all the things that they had heard and seen, as it was told them."

Luke 2:15-20

Uneducated, ceremonially unclean and certainly unwanted in ancient society, these shepherd-men received the highest honor to share the story of the ages before anyone else. They were forerunners in the faith; The very First Evangelist. How did it happen? God in His sovereignty could had chosen a King or a Priest to announce His long awaited prophecy. But where did He start? At the very bottom of the socio-economic system. He revealed the birth of His Son to Sheep-herders. They were the first to hear about Jesus after Mary gave birth to her baby. But we have to ask the question; Why Shepherds? Shepherds protected and served the sheep that were used for religious sacrifices in the temple which was a very important duty. No animals meant no sacrifice for sins. When the Angel appeared and proclaimed, *"That the Savior of the world was born in Bethlehem and that He would take away the sins of the world."* He knew a shepherd would not only understand this terminology but know how to correctly articulate the story. In this moment, these men hastily migrated to the manger to worship the one who hung the stars they had stared at for so many years. When they came into His presence, something supernatural happened in their heart. They no longer felt lonely and separated from the rest of society. Instead, unconditional love flooded into their soul for the very first time. What did this love do? It compelled them to make Jesus famous in their surrounding cities and villages. These shepherd-men became the very first evangelists.

What should be our response?
Nothing short of the same; If you've heard the Good News and responded to the love of God, you are called to be a shepherd this year. Your encounter with Christ qualifies you to be a witness to the world. Let's all go tell it on the Mountain! Jesus Christ has come and He is coming back soon to rescue the saints from

a world of sin! You too can be an evangelist in your world. For some maybe the very first evangelist in your family?

Step to Start Strong:

Be like a Shepherd. Share Christ

SEPTEMBER 13.

TALE OF THE TWO LUMBER JACKS

"Take the helmet of salvation and the sword of the Spirit, which is the word of God."

Ephesians 6:17

It was the annual lumberjack competition and the grand finale was between an older, experienced lumberjack and a younger, stronger lumberjack. The rule of the competition was quite simple; who could cut the most trees in a day was the winner.

The younger lumberjack was full of enthusiasm and went off into the woods and began to work right away. He worked all through the day and all through the night. As he worked, he could hear the older lumberjack working in another part of the forest and he felt more and more confident with every tree that he cut down that he would win. At regular intervals throughout the day, the noise of trees falling coming from the other part of the forest would stop. The younger lumberjack took heart from this, knowing that this meant the older lumberjack was taking a rest, whereas he could use his superior youth and strength and stamina to keep going. At the end of the competition, the younger lumberjack felt confident he had won. He looked in front of him at the piles of cut trees that were the result of his superhuman effort. At the medal ceremony, he stood on the podium expecting to be awarded the prize of champion lumberjack. Next to him stood the older lumberjack who looked surprisingly less exhausted than he felt. When the results were read out loud, he was devastated to hear that the older lumberjack had chopped down significantly more trees than he had. He turned to the older lumber jack and said: *"How can this be? What happened? I heard you take a rest every hour and I worked continuously through the night. What's more, I am stronger and fitter than you old man."* The older lumberjack turned to him and said: "This is how; e*very hour, I took a break to rest and sharpen my saw.*"

God help us not rely on mere ability, natural strength and worldly wisdom to maneuver our way through life. We need to hear from the Holy Spirit in order to do what God has chosen us to do. This takes time away from "work" where we can rest in relationship with Jesus Christ and sharpen our sword which represents spiritual disciplines like reading, studying and speaking the Word of God. When you consistently practice this principle, *"The trees that stand in your way will fall in Jesus name!"*

What kind of Lumberjack are you? #1 or #2?

<u>Step to Start Strong:</u>

Take a Break and Sharpen your Saw

SEPTEMBER 14.

STEPS TO A DOUBLE PORTION

"Elijah said to Elisha, "Ask! What may I do for you, before I am taken away from you?" Elisha said, "Please let a double portion of your spirit be upon me."

2 Kings 2:9

The First Place You have to go through in order to receive a Double-Portion is:

1) The Place of Separation

In 2nd Kings, Elisha followed the Prophet Elijah into the city of Gilgal. This area was the operating base for the children of Israel after they crossed into the Promised Land. (Joshua 1) The first thing the Lord had to accomplish in the life of each soldier was circumcision. Circumcision represents covenant and the cutting away of the old man with his past transgression. In order to step into the fullness of God's calling on your life, you have to go through seasons of separation. 2 Timothy 2:22 says, "*to run from anything that stimulates youthful lusts. Pursue righteous living, faithfulness, love, and peace. Enjoy the companionship of those who call on the Lord with pure hearts.*" You can't run with devils and walk with God. 1st Corinthians 2:11 goes on to say, *"and in Him you were also circumcised with a circumcision made without hands, in the removal of the flesh by the circumcision of Christ; having been buried with Him in baptism, you were also raised with Him through faith." You can't be lovers of the world and lovers of God. You have to choose. You can't be double-minded and expect to receive a double-portion of the Holy Spirit. This is the first step and the fist stop.* Have you been to Gilgal? Who do you need to disassociate yourself from this year? What do you need to cut out of your life?

The Second Place You have to go through in order to receive a Double-Portion is:

II. The Place of Transformation

The second stop for Elijah and Elisha was in a city called Bethel. This represents the House of God. (Gen. 28:10-18) When I think about Bethel, I'm reminded about the all-night wrestling match between God and Jacob. This was the place where Jacob's life was changed forever. What made the difference? In desperation, Jacob said, *"I will not let you go until you bless me!"* Jacob possessed a great deal of determination. Determination is doing what you need to do even when you don't feel like doing it. This is the attitude of those who walk under the double-portion of God's Spirit. Elijah told Elisha three times, *"you stay here as I go on to the next city."* Despite the order, the young predecessor knew where the source of power was flowing from and He desired to tap into the same vein so He said, *"As surely as the Lord lives, I will not leave you!"* He was desperate and determined to be transformed. Romans 12:1 says, *"I beseech thee brothers..."do not be conformed to this world, but be transformed by the renewing of your mind."* Beseech means to beg. The Apostle Paul was begging the church to not conform to the world but to be transformed from the inside out. This happens at Bethel. This happens by being apart of a healthy body of believers. Have you been to Bethel? Are you wrestling with God over a situation? Don't give up until God blesses you! Stay desperate and stay determined!

The Thirds and Last Place, You have to go through in order to receive a Double-Portion is:

III. The Place of Occupation: Jericho was the first city the Children of Israel conquered in the Promised Land. Jericho means *"a Place of Fragrance."* It was the beginning of sweet victory for the God's children. Ultimately, the people of Israel conquered 31 cities as they stepped into "all the promises of God." They were no longer slaves. This new generation, who believed the Word of the Lord, crossed over from visitation to habitation. They occupied the land and they still do today all because of faith in the sovereignty and supremacy of God. Have you conquered Jericho? If not, keep marching and keep shouting! The walls will fall down!

Step to Start Strong:

Receive a Double Portion of God's Spirit

SEPTEMBER 15.

A HEAVENLY VISION

"Therefore, King Agrippa, I was not disobedient to the heavenly vision."

Acts 26:19

Countless individuals have written books, stories and even produced movies that revolve around someone's personal experience of a vision of Heaven. John the Beloved had this experienced when the religious leaders exiled him to the island of Patmos, an ancient Alcatraz off the western seaboard of Turkey. It was there that the Spirit of the Lord said to him, *"come up here"* and called him to a higher place called Heaven to show Him what many have never seen this side of the celestial sea. Have you experienced a vision of Heaven? If not, don't be discouraged. There is another type of vision; A Heavenly Vision. This is what the Apostle Paul encountered in Acts Chapter 9.

Saul, before the vision, was a radical religious mass murderer who hunted down converts of Christ. Out of deep hatred, this man was leaving no stone unturned as He believed that the followers of "The Way" were detrimental to the Judaism faith. His core doctrine was driving him until the Holy Spirit literally knocked Him face down on the ground one day. What I love most about this story is Saul wasn't even searching for Jesus but Jesus had His eye on him. When the light of the world shined in His soul, He heard the voice of God say, *"Saul, Saul, Why are you persecuting me? It is useless to fight against my will. Now, get up on your feet! I am sending you to open the eyes of the Gentiles!"* What a turnaround! Within a matter of minutes, this man receives a Heavenly Vision. A mandate with a plain purpose and a specific plan.

With this in mind, What has God asked you to do? The words of the Apostle Paul hold great weight today as He said late in His life, *"The one thing I do; I am forgetting what is behind and I am straining forward to what lies ahead."*

What do you need to let go of or forget from your past?

Many theologians say, for Paul, it was the stoning of Stephen, the first Christian martyr in the New Testament. How about you? What is holding you back from fulfilling your God-given destiny? What is the one thing the Lord has asked you to do from here forward?

The most important thing? Your Heavenly Vision...

May we be able to stand before the King one day and say, *"I have not been disobedient to the "Heavenly Vision."* One encounter with the risen Christ can change your life forever. Just ask Paul. One word from God can drive you into your destiny. Just ask yourself, *"What is God saying to me?"* God, Give me 20/20 Vision! I want to hear and see clearly.

Step to Start Strong:

Don't Be Disobedient to the Heavenly Vision

SEPTEMBER 16.

PSALM ONE-ONE

"Blessed is the one who does not walk in step with the wicked or stand in the way that sinners take or sit in the company of mockers."

Psalm1:1

Notice the great falling away of the man who flirts with sin. It all started when He allowed wickedness to get into his walk. Eventually, the sin caused him to grow complacent so he started standing around. The man who was once very involved in missional living and christian service takes a seat with the mockers. This is the downward progression of sin. It's so subtle but it separates us from what matters most. Our commission is to go and make disciples of all nations.

David Platt, the President of the International Mission Board said, "*We have taken the command of Christ to go, baptize, and teach all nations, and mutated it into a comfortable call to come, be baptized, and sit in one location.*" The sin of pride, fear and selfishness wants you to stop walking with the Lord and pull up a church pew. This is not why Christ saved you. There is so much more in store. Now is the time to stand up, turn around, and start marching Heaven-bound. Don't flirt with sin because sin will win. What is now hidden will one day be brought to the light. Its a downward progression; walk, stand and sit.

Step to Start Strong:

Memorize Psalm 1:1-3

"Blessed is the man who walks not in the counsel of the ungodly, Nor stands in the path of sinners, Nor sits in the seat of the scornful; But his delight is in the law of the Lord, And in His law he meditates day and night. He shall be like a tree planted by the rivers of water, That brings forth its fruit in its season, Whose leaf also shall not wither; And whatever he does shall prosper."

SEPTEMBER 17.

A VOICE FROM HELL

Oh, why am I here in this place of unrest
When others have entered the land of the blest?
God's way of salvation was preached unto men;
I heard it and heard it, again and again.
Why did I not listen and turn from my sin
And open my heart and let Jesus come in?
For vain earthly pleasures my soul did I sell
The way I had chosen has brought me to hell.
I wish I were dreaming, but ah, it is true.
The way to be saved I had heard and I knew;
My time on the earth, so quickly fled by,
How little I thought of the day I would die.
When God's Holy Spirit was pleading with me,
I hardened my heart and I turned from His plea.
The way that was sinful, the path that was wide,
I chose and I walked till the day that I died.
Eternally now, I must dwell in this place.
From my memory I wish I could erase
The thoughts of my past which are haunting me so.

Oh, where is a refuge to which I can go?
This torture and suff'ring, how long can I stand?
For Satan and demons this only was planned.
God's refuge is Jesus, the One that I spurned;
He offered salvation, but from Him I turned.
My brothers and sisters I wish I could warn.
Far better 'twould it be if I had not been born.
The price I must pay is too horrid to tell
My life without God led me directly to Hell.
Oh, soul without Christ, will these words be your cry?
God's Word so declares it that all men must die.
From hell and its terrors, Oh, flee while you may!
So, come to the Savior; He'll save you today!
—Oscar C. Eliason

Step to Start Strong:

Pray thy Kingdom Come, Thy will be done.
On earth as it is in Heaven!

SEPTEMBER 18.

Divine Dreams

"And afterward, I will pour out my Spirit on all people. Your sons and daughters will prophesy, your old men will dream dreams, your young men will see visions."

Joel 2:28

Are you a dreamer? I go through seasons. Most mornings, I arise from my ship and step into the shower and hit the day hard. Other mornings, I wake up and have to wonder, why would I dream such a thing? Just to be clear, I don't believe all dreams are from God and I don't believe all dreams are from the devil. Our sub-conscience minds are always moving but I do believe in divine interruptions from the spiritual world during the night seasons. (Psalm 16:7) With this in mind, we have to weigh the spirits and sometimes ask ourselves; *"Why did I have that dream?"* For example: Last week, I woke up early one morning and when I made it to my study, I immediately recollected my dreams from the night before. This "dream" started at the funeral service of an old friend that had died from a drug overdose. The people who were present were old friends who I used to party with before I gave my life to Christ. Everyone was crying hysterically and drastically upset from the tragic event that had taken place. When the crowd noticed me in the corner, they began to corral around me screaming, *"Why Chance! Why? Why did this have to happen!" Please help us!"* Suddenly, in the natural, my heart was supernaturally burdened for the salvation of their souls. The weight of addiction hit my heart and the spirit of intercession came upon me o' so heavily. By this time, I fully understood why God spoke to me in this dream. He was calling me to intercede on behalf of my drug addicted friend in whom I haven't seen in years. Only Heaven knows what was happening in that moment but all I know is God showed me very specifically that I was supposed to stand in the gap and pray for the spirit of death to pass him over and give him another chance. God has spoken to me many times in the night seasons. If He can't get our attention while we're awake, He will visit us while we are sleeping. Sometimes, I write these dreams down to revisit but this time I shared the story with my wife. The reason for me writing this letter is to awaken your soul to understand the realm of the supernatural. God lured me to His heart that night by curiosity. The dream caused me to see what He was seeing and by faith I began to pray and believe God's will to be done in the situation. This wasn't a bad dream. It was a good dream as long as this dream doesn't come true. I believe God showed me the situation so the burden of addiction and death would be lifted off of this man and even the people at the funeral. The truth is: I don't know where He is and I don't know what He is doing. But by faith, I was being obedient. If I was wrong, what did I lose? If I was right, what did Heaven gain? So I ask you; Are you are dreamer? If so, ask God to give you spiritual insight into certain situations. The first time I traveled to Africa and India on mission trips were all because of a confirmation through a dream. The list goes on and on. Keep dreaming!

Step to Start Strong:

Ask God to Speak to you in the Night Seasons

SEPTEMBER 19.

EARS TO HEAR

"He said to them, 'Do you bring in a lamp to put it under a bowl or a bed? Instead, don't you put it on its stand? For whatever is hidden is meant to be disclosed, and whatever is concealed is meant to be brought out into the open. If anyone has ears to hear, let them hear. "Consider carefully what you hear," he continued. "With the measure you use, it will be measured to you—and even more. Whoever has will be given more; whoever does not have, even what they have will be taken from them."

Mark 4:21-25

Most people have ears but not everyone has ears to hear. Mark goes on to say, "Consider carefully what you hear." Guard your ear gate. Don't allow anything or anyone to come into your heart and make a home. You can't help it if a bird flies over your head but don't allow it to build a nest and make a mess. The Holy Spirit is the overseer of your soul. If He convicts you concerning a conversation with a particular person or TV Show;

Do what David did in Psalm 101; *"Cut it off in the name of the Lord!"* Don't allow worldly words and perspectives to get into your walk. It's not worth it.

Mark concludes with *"the measure that you use, it will be measured back to you and even more!"* The Measure of what? The measure of Hearing your Heavenly Father. Now, God doesn't speak just to be heard, He speaks to be obeyed. When God speaks and all you do is think, I'm not sure if that was God and you never obey because of fear of being wrong. Eventually, what you have will be taken from you and given to somebody else who is willing to respond to His whisper by faith. This is how you multiply your ability to hear in the spirit. You do what God ask you to do and in His sovereignty He gives you more responsibility. Heed the voice of your Heavenly Father. Take what He speaks to you in the quite places of your soul and speak it with authority in public. This is where the ole song says, *"This little light of Mine"* was derived from. Hide it under a bush? Oh Know! May God gives us *"Ears to Hear" & Hearts to Obey, in Jesus Name!"*

Do you have an ear to hear?

Step to Start Strong:

Practice Hearing the Heart of God

SEPTEMBER 20.

Be Like Job

"After Job had prayed for his friends, the Lord restored his fortunes and gave him twice as much as he had before."

Job 42:10

The power of forgiveness restored the fortunes of Job and reconciliation released a double portion of the blessing back into his life. This heartbroken, beat-down individual had the opportunity to grow bitter and say, "*I give up. Why don't everybody just leave me alone.*" But instead He allowed the grace of God to move in His misunderstanding which later compelled him to love those who judged him incorrectly. The unforgiveness that started to grow in His heart was trying to close the window of God's favor that was open over His home. The goal was to drive him in a hole where He would live out the rest of his life in depression and isolation; totally separated from His portion and purpose.

However, Job defied the odds. Instead of backing down, He rose to the occasion and *prayed for His friends. This caused something supernatural to happen in the heaven-lies.* This man didn't care who was right and who was wronged. He set his hurt and his selfish ambition aside and made the first step toward repentance and reconciliation. God met Him in the middle and honored His meekness by relenting judgment upon his friends and releasing supernatural favor back into His life. All this happened after the fact and not a second before. *Forgiveness is always available but pride makes it unattainable for most people.* It took Job 42 Chapters of dialogue to work it out in his own life but eventually He broke-through. The Good News? You can do it too! In light of eternity, nothing is worth holding onto! In light of our sin, nothing is too small to go and make right.

Do you need to pray for a friend that has hurt you? How about a family member? Don't allow unforgiveness to keep you from complete restoration. Start building the bridge of reconciliation. It may take some time but it will be worth every brick when you see the finished work. Be like Job. Make it a priority to pray for your friends and family this week. It will not only restore relationships but it will release a double portion.

Step to Start Strong:

Pray for your Friends

SEPTEMBER 21.

The Little Boy and the Rattlesnake

"No temptation has overtaken you except what is common to mankind. And God is faithful; he will not let you be tempted beyond what you can bear. But when you are tempted, he will also provide a way out so that you can endure it."

1st Corinthians 10:13

There once was a Native American boy who climbed to the top of a very tall mountain. As he stood on the summit, looking around, he heard something slithering at his feet. He jumped back, realizing it was a rattlesnake. Before he could move farther away, the rattlesnake spoke:

"Please, won't you carry me down the mountain? It's cold up here, and I have no food. I don't want to die."

"No," said the boy. *"I know what you are. You're a rattlesnake. You're dangerous to me. If I carry you down the mountain, you'll bite me."*

As the boy started to go down the mountain side, the snake used his sneakiness to make the boy feel sorry for him. *"Please sir, I'm a living creature and you can't just let me die!"*

The boy thought for a moment and said, *"Do you promise not to bite me?"* The snake replied, *"I promise."*

"Well, then, I guess it's okay," said the boy, as he picked up the snake and put it under his shirt. As he hiked down the mountain, the boy could feel the snake getting warmer. It began moving around inside his shirt. *"Remember,"* said the boy, *"you promised not to bite me."*

As they got to the bottom of the mountain, the boy reached into his shirt to put the snake down. Once on the ground, the snake suddenly coiled. Before the boy knew what happened, the snake struck forward and bit him on the leg.

"Why did you do that?" cried the boy. *"You promised you would not bite me!"* As the snake slithered away, leaving the boy to die, it hissed behind him saying, *"You knew what I was when you picked me up."*

Let me say this statement again: *You knew what I was before you picked me up.* If sin could speak, it would say the same thing. Resist temptation today. Look for the way out of ungodly situations. Be vigilant and you will be victorious. Keep watching and praying so that the slyness of sin can't overtake you. Keep standing firm saint and you will see the salvation of your Lord.

Step to Start Strong:

Call a Snake a Snake.
Be Honest with Yourself and Others.

SEPTEMBER 22.

Bitter or Better?

"For I see that you are poisoned by bitterness and bound by iniquity."

Acts 8:23

Bitterness is like cancer. It eats you from the inside out. It comes from unrepentant sin, unforgiveness and long-lived resentment. Eventually, bitterness becomes a part of who you are and you don't even know there's a stranger living in your own house. You co-exist with it and you believe the lie that everything is all right. But there's better way:

It's a place called freedom and God desires for you to dwell there. Many have failed beneath the bitterness of trial and their relationships have suffered even though they know family and friendships are one of the sweetest joys in life...

Next time you see a friend or hear someones name and it immediately causes you pain; there could be a seed of bitterness in your soul. How do you get free from this? By the same way you were forgiven of your sin; confessing you need for help.

Confess your sin and struggle to God and He will answer you by setting you free. Forgiveness does not mean pretending everything is *"OK."* Forgiveness is not forgetting and it's certainly not letting the other party go scot-free. According to St. Augustine, "*forgiveness is simply the act of surrendering our desire for revenge; that is, our desire to hurt someone for having hurt us.*" The fact is; Forgiveness is the gift we give ourselves that enables us to stop drinking poison everyday and expecting the other person to die. You can't control everything but you can allow the Holy Spirit to take control of your will knowing forgiveness is the key that has the power to set the world free.

Ultimately, heart-felt confession removes the root of bitterness and allows us to be healed from our hurt. It can take some time depending upon the situation but if you speak it long enough the freedom will leave your head and get into your heart.

So how do you know when you have been healed? You will be able to talk about it openly and the words will not cause any more pain or displeasure. Yes, scars will exist but the bruises of the past will dissipate. In the words of the Apostle Paul said, "*Let all bitterness, wrath, anger and evil speaking be put away from you.*" You can be bitter or you can get better? The choice is yours.

Step to Start Strong:

Get Better. Don't Be Bitter

SEPTEMBER 23

The Hidden Will of the Lord

"God said, "Take now your son, your only son of promise, whom you love, Isaac, and go to the region of Moriah, and offer him there as a burnt offering on one of the mountains of which I will tell you."

Genesis 22:2

God told Abraham to go sacrifice His son but there were no further instructions. Just go! Why would God give him the direction to the region but no details about the ridge? Its simple; If God were to give us "all" the facts and figures about the journey we wouldn't have to walk by faith. Now without faith, you would say, Ok God, I'll see you at the pearly gates and go through life alone without the need of a close intimate relationship with Him. Walking this way would never please God because God wants to be by your side.

You may not know the outcome of what you are facing today but God does! He knows the end from the beginning and all the content within the book of your life. If you acknowledge Him in all things He will direct you and he will help you to make wise decisions which will ultimately, bring you great success.

By leading us on this level, God increases our spiritual sensitivity to do what nobody else can do without Him. It's not natural because you can't understand it with natural senses. Abraham walked by faith because He heard the whisper of the word; Go. His son, Isaac was walking in obedience to his father but still in the flesh. The flesh will always talk about what it sees, smells and feels despite what God said. God didn't call you to walk by feelings. He called you to walk by faith. This is why the writer of Hebrews coined Abraham as the *"Father of Faith"* because Abraham was tested in every area of faith to give us an example of how we ought to live when we go *"through"* the same things.

What are you going through? Whatever it is, remember the Life of Abraham. He saw, He stepped, He said and He sacrificed what He loved most on the altar of God. God was pleased and blessed his descendants as many as the stars in the sky. Keep your eyes on Christ today. He has a plan for your future. Its called, The Hidden Will of God meaning He will reveal His will along the way.

Step to Start Strong:

Just Go!

SEPTEMBER 24.

THE BLESSING

"So God created man in His own image; in the image of God He created him; male and female He created them. 28 Then God blessed them, and God said to them, "Be fruitful and multiply; fill the earth and subdue it; have dominion over the fish of the sea, over the birds of the air, and over every living thing that moves on the earth."

Genesis 1:27-28

The first words a human ever heard were *"I bless you!"* Adam was created on the sixth day in the Garden of Eden and his freshly formed ears were penetrated with this affirmation from His Heavenly Father as *"The Blessing"* was placed upon his life. Adam woke up and walked under this *"supernatural favor"* that covered every aspect of who he was and what he had authority over. All blessings began to flow from this first blessing.

Adam and Eve was "given" the whole earth to make a home and everything they needed was already thought through by God before they knew they needed it. This was God's original intent until the fall of man. Disobedience opened the door to the curse and the curse cut off the blessing. In this moment, the plan of redemption was catapulted into the first century as the blood of Christ was poured out so that we could be restored back to the blessing. The rest is history. These 3 words are still being whispered from Heaven to the hearts of every human being; *"I want to bless you." Furthermore,* I want to give you everything you need to live a godly life in Christ Jesus. I've already thought your whole life through and everything you need is already stored up in Heavenly places. All you have to do is come into agreement with me and believe and you will find favor to receive the blessing says the Lord!

Yes, *"every good and perfect gift comes from above; health, wealth, peace, prosperity, love, life and longevity of relationships."* God wants to bless you! The curse is canceled by the second Adam that hung on a tree! This year is a year of Victory for you and me! Tap into the truth of God's word and believe! Be fruitful my child and multiply the earth. You have dominion over everything that moves from here to the hills! Speak blessing and receive blessing today in Jesus name! It's the power of the blessing!

Step to Start Strong:

Speak Blessing Over Everybody and Every Thing

SEPTEMBER 25.

Commitment is the Key

"Commit to the LORD whatever you do, and he will establish your plans."

Proverbs 16:3

Commitment is the key. Many men have amazing ideas and greater life goals but very few have the grit to walk it out. Motivation is what gets you started but commitment is what keeps you going; Especially when it comes to the cause of Christ.

The scripture says, *"commit" to the Lord whatever you do and He will establish your plans and bless the work of your hands."* The Lord is committed to you through the new covenant so whatever you do, you should work at it with all of your heart as working for God and not for man. Ask God what needs to be taken off of your plate so you can fully commit and enjoy what He has called you to do. Make a prioritized list of every monthly responsibility and see if anythings needs to be handed to the next person. Many times your disobedience is hindering someone else's growth and you need to get out of the way! You're not God. Jesus is. If you don't have enough time in the day to fulfill your daily duties, you're doing something that you're not supposed to be doing. It's that simple. If you're trying to juggle jobs and hats, you could be opening the door to unneeded stress and worry which can ultimately take years off of your life. You can do more with little when God is in it.

So, what are you fully committed to? Hopefully, your relationship with Christ, your husband or wife, your kids and ministry. What else? Spend the most time on what matters most. Don't do life half-hearted. If so, you should expect half-hearted results. The limit to your impact is determined upon your level of commitment in everything you do.

Will Powell, a friend and a 3-Time Cross Fit Champion of the World says, "*The distance between dreams and reality is called commitment.*" Do you wanna change the world? How about your world? Get motivated and stay committed. It's the key that opens up the doorway to your destiny.

Step to Start Strong:

Commit yourself to the Lord

SEPTEMBER 26.

DEFINING REALITY

"Where there is no vision, the people perish, But happy is he who keeps the law."

Proverbs 29:18

A recent poll suggest that 95% of people don't have a vision for their life. A vision is what you see. What do see your life looking like by the end of this year, 5 years or even 20 years from now? The scripture says, "*God knows the end before the beginning.*" (Is. 46:10) It's called the future perfect tense. We should do our best to live our life the same way. Your vision will determine what you do today if you want to achieve a desired outcome. It's called putting a plan with the purpose. The truth is, it's never too late to lose weight, restore a relationship or even go back to school or birth a new business. You can do anything you put your whole heart to. All visions from God are based upon somebody's need. This is what the vision represents; the unmet need. All great leaders seek to fill the need in their heart and more importantly in the life of others. This is why people become doctors, dentist, teachers and preachers because they want to help people with their problems. You should never stop seeking to fulfill the needs of others.

The late David Wilkerson said, "*Do you want to know the will of God*?" Find a need and fill it. All day everyday; search for hurting people and by God's grace help them with their problems. This is vision. This is reality. Ask yourself; "God, w*hat need do you want me to meet for others*?" When you come to a conclusion, commit the call to Christ and build your whole life around the outcome. If you don't take the risk, nothing will ever happen; Define your reality. Don't allow your life to pass you by. With God's help you can do it!

Step to Start Strong:

Find a Need and Fill it

SEPTEMBER 27.

END TIME INSTRUCTIONS

"Jesus answered, "Be careful that no one misleads you [deceiving you and leading you into error]. For many will come in My name [misusing it, and appropriating the strength of the name which belongs to Me], saying, 'I am the Christ (the Messiah, the Anointed),' and they will mislead many. You will continually hear of wars and rumors of wars. See that you are not frightened, for those things must take place, but that is not yet the end [of the age]. For nation will rise against nation, and kingdom against kingdom, and there will be famines and earthquakes in various places. But all these things are merely the beginning of birth pangs [of the intolerable anguish and the time of unprecedented trouble]. "Then they will hand you over to [endure] tribulation, and will put you to death, and you will be hated by all nations because of My name. At that time many will be offended and repelled [by their association with Me] and many

will fall away [from the One whom they should trust] and will betray one another [handing over believers to their persecutors] and will hate one another. Many false prophets will appear and mislead many. Because lawlessness is increased, the love of most people will grow cold. But the one who endures and bears up [under suffering] to the end will be saved. This good news of the kingdom [the gospel] will be preached throughout the whole world as a testimony to all the nations, and then the end [of the age] will come."

Matthew 24:4-14

Don't panic. God is not nervous. The Bible says, "*when you see these things begin to come to pass, look up and lift up your head! For your redemption draws nigh.*" (Luke 21:28) Don't look down and get depressed! Don't listen to the TV set and get distressed! Fix your affections on the reality of your salvation and the endless joy that is coming your way. You will be in the presence of Jesus, your Savior and friend forever and ever! The catching away of the church is closer than ever before. It's easy to see; The signs of the times say so. Whatever you do, don't allow fear to cause your faith to fall asleep. Wake up and walk out the remainder of your days with great confidence knowing the Bible is true. Jesus loves you and He, Himself is coming back soon! Don't forget; we are not here for ourselves, we are here for Him and to bring him glory. The Grandstands of Heaven are cheering you on today to not only start strong but to finish strong through the fire of the Holy Spirit. Don't think like the world and let your heart wax cold. We are citizens of another Kingdom. It's called the Kingdom of God

What's your End-Time Instruction? Look up & Rejoice! This is a sure sign of your supernatural strength.

Step to Start Strong:

Look up and Rejoice!

SEPTEMBER 28.

Maintaining your Miracle

"What do you conspire against the Lord? He will make an utter end of it. Affliction will not rise up a second time."

Nahum 1:9

Whenever God sows the seed of the miraculous into somebody's life, the enemy will doubtless come and try to steal the seed out of their heart; And he will succeed *if they don't understand it.* (Matthew 13:18) The church has to learn to stand up under the truth of God's word if we want to maintain a life that mirrors the miraculous that God so desires for His children. When the seed of the word of God is sown, it takes some time and effort for the seed to get to a place where it is consistently developing fruit. The initial growth happens underground where no-one else can see or disrupt the process. This represents your heart and the way you live your life in private. The seed sown and received by faith will germinate for God and begin to grow roots of righteousness. *This stage is of utmost importance.* The root system will be the foundation to help you stand in the storms of life. All of this happens way before anyone can see your spiritual success. This is where the miraculous is maintained; In the soil of your soul. *The power is in the seed but the manifestation occurs in the soil.* Is this too deep?

Please understand; The problem isn't with the word of God. The problem is the faith by which we receive. God is the master-planter but the heart of many men is spoiled by what people think and contaminated by the culture of the world. Furthermore, doubt and disbelief can cause us to seek other avenues of security and success when all the time God holds all the answers in His hands. This is called fruit that remains; eternal life with an eternal reward.

So how do you maintain your miracle? By believing, understanding and confessing the Word of God.

Don't let the devil talk you out of your best year yet! Don't listen to the lie that says your health is on a downward slope! Disregard the whisper that says, your struggle will end in financial ruin. Your kids will never serve the Lord! It's all a lie! Stand firm today and believe God! The affliction you are facing will not rise up a second time! God is going to put an utter end to it in Jesus name! If you believe it; Say I receive it!

Step to Start Strong:

Maintain your Miracle.

SEPTEMBER 29.

THE POWER OF PRAYER

"This is the confidence we have in approaching God: that if we ask anything according to his will, he hears us."

1 John 5:14

Prayer matters. Prayer has the power to change things. Prayer changes our situation but more importantly it transforms our perspective. E. M. Bounds, a famous American author said, "*Prayer makes a godly person, and puts within them the mind of Christ, the mind of humility, the mind of self-surrender, service, pity, and prayer. If we really pray, we will become more like God, or else we will quit praying.*"

What does your prayer life look like? Are you discipling anyone in prayer? Do you spend time praying with your family? The gift of prayer is a precious gem from God. In fact, it is the #1 priority for all believers.

Adrian Rogers put it this way, "*The prayer offered to God in the morning during your quiet time is the key that unlocks the door of the day. Any athlete knows that it is the start that ensures a good finish.*"

Do you want to finish well? If so, Start strong in prayer!

Make a prayer list. Take a prayer walk. Start a prayer group. Pray with your spouse before you fall asleep. Whatever it takes; Start today. God will speak in the silence of your heart.

Mother Theresa enlightened us when she said, "*Listening is the beginning of prayer.*" Remove the word "rush" from your relationship with the Lord. Lend Him an ear this year. His voice will keep you from making a world of mistakes. Slow down and seek His face everyday. He knows what you need before you even ask but He wants to hear it come from your mouth. Open your heart today and say, *"I am making a commitment to pray everyday."* It will drastically change the trajectory of your life because there is power, power, wonder-working power in the prayers of the God's people.

"Remember, we pray for our partners everyday."

Step to Start Strong:

Maintain your Miracle

SEPTEMBER 30.

Living a Life of Love

"And now these three remain: faith, hope and love. But the greatest of these is love."

1st Corinthians 13:13

This is a great litmus test to see if you are living a life of love. When you read 1st Corinthians 13, replace the word "love" with your first name. Go ahead and try it! It will speak to your heart and challenge you to *"Love God and Love Others."*

"Love is patient, love is kind. It does not envy, it does not boast, it is not proud. It does not dishonor others, it is not self-seeking, it is not easily angered, it keeps no record of wrongs. Love does not delight in evil but rejoices with the truth. It always protects, always trusts, always hopes, always perseveres. "Love never fails."

But where there are prophecies, they will cease; where there are tongues, they will be stilled; where there is knowledge, it will pass away. For we know in part and we prophesy in part, but when completeness comes what is in part disappears. When I was a child, I talked like a child, I thought like a child,

I reasoned like a child. When I became a man, I put the ways of childhood behind me. For now we see only a reflection as in a mirror; then we shall see face to face.

Now I know in part; then I shall know fully, even as I am fully known. And now these three remain: faith, hope and love. But the greatest of these is love."

What did you find out about yourself?
Are you living a life of love?

Step to Start Strong:

Love God and Love Others

OCTOBER 1.

ONE DAY AT A TIME

"Give us this day our daily bread."

Matthew 6:11

Eleanor Roosevelt said, *"Yesterday is history, tomorrow is a mystery but today is a gift; that's why we call it the present."* Don't allow the devil to rob you from the joys of today by living in past regret. On the other hand; don't be overwhelmed by the doubts and fears of the future. Be present. Live in the moment. God's mercies are anew every morning. He has promised you enough grace to make it through everyday.

During the 40 year journey from Egypt to the Promised Land, God led His children *one day at a time.* They woke up, rolled out of bed and walked outside to receive divine direction. Whenever the cloud moved by day or the fire relocated them by night, they would follow God by faith. Why? Because He was the source of their strength. He gave them their daily bread. In fact, provision miraculously showed up on their front porch every morning. The scripture says, they were protected from the darkness on every side. In His presence, all of their needs were satisfied; each and everyday.

If you were to ask one of them; *"Where are you guys going?"* They would answer quickly; *"The Promised Land!"* You haven't heard? But if you were to ask them; *"How are you going to get there?"* They would look up into the night and say, *"To be quite honest, we really don't know. We're just following the fire one day at a time."*

The point: Don't lose focus. Keep following the fire. God's taking you to a desired destination! Your enemy is already defeated. Daily provision is promised by your Heavenly Father. If God be for you, who can be against you? He will protect you. Keep marching and moving forward. God is the author and perfecter of your faith. It won't look like yesterday. It's gone but it will be a present! Unwrap it with great expectation. God gives the greatest gifts. Believe this: Something good is going to happen to you today!

Step to Start Strong:

Unwrap the Day in Worship!

OCTOBER 2.

WHAT IS YOUR LIFE?

"What is your life? Your life is like the morning fog—
it's here for a little while, then it's gone."

James 4:14

Life is like a parachute jump; you better get it right the first time. How do you get it right? By surrendering your life to Jesus Christ. He can take your mistakes and turn them into ministry opportunities. He alone has the power to make your wrongs right.

Choose today the legacy you want to leave tomorrow. In all honesty, what will you pass to the next generation? If your life was a book; the title would be your name, the preface would be your introductory to the world, and the content within the chapters would be your thoughts, failures and successes. Oh, what a book that would be! If everything were written down for everyone to see. The scripture says, "*For now, we know in part but when the perfect comes, we will be fully known.*"

With this in mind, surrender your pen to the author of your life today. Allow Him to finish the plot of your life according to His perfect will. Charles Ketterling said, "*the best thing you can do for this generation is to lay a few stones for the next to walk on.*" You can do this by being consistent and staying close to biblical conviction. This alone will stand in a world of sinking sand.

If others had to summarize your life with one word; what would that word be? Choose it today and build your life around its beauty. This will be your legacy.

This is your L.I.F.E.

Step to Start Strong:

L. I. F. E. = Living in Freedom Everyday!

OCTOBER 3.

THE MIND OF CHRIST

"Who can know the Lord's thoughts?Who knows enough to teach him? But we understand these things, for we have the mind of Christ."

1st Corinthians 2:16

You were created to have the mind of Christ; to think like He thinks, to know what He wants you to know, to do what He wants you to do and to only say what He wants you to say.

With "*most people*" having over 12 billion brain cells, it's sad to say, most leave their minds unguarded and undisciplined. Here's a thought: *What you put into your mind will eventually come out!* To say it another way; "*Your input determines your output.*" This principle is of utmost importance. What are you listening to? What are you looking at? Who are you imitating? The scripture says, "*Above all things, guard your heart; For it will ultimately guide the course of your life.*" (Proverbs 4:2)

For example: The average American watches 4 to 7 hours of TV a day! Kids from the ages of 5 to 18 watch 16,000 hours of

TV and only spend 13,000 hours in school learning. Now, who is teaching our kids and raising the next generation? The parents or the producers of the movies and TV shows? With Satan being the prince and the power of the air, we have to be vigilant, cautious and intentional when choosing what we allow into our hearts and our homes.

My point: It is utterly impossible to be profoundly influenced by which you do not know. Therefore, build your family and your future around the Word of God and not what the world says. Fix your eyes and Jesus and pray everyday that God would give you the mind of Christ in these last days. We need it! For who can know the thoughts of the Lord? You can! Just lean in and listen. This is a core value.

Step to Start Strong:

Develop the Mind of Christ

OCTOBER 4.

Our Greatest Need

"Whoever wants to be my disciple must deny themselves and take up their cross and follow me."

Matthew 16:24

Jack Hayford, one of the leaders of the Promise Keepers Movement made this statement, *"You cannot disciple a demon and you cannot cast out the flesh."* What did He mean? He alludes to the truth, that what the church needs is deliverance and discipleship. Deliverance sets people free but discipleship gives them the tools to be all they can be.

Without discipleship a recent convert will fall back into their old way of life. A disciple is one who learns from the teachings of someone else. Jesus chose 12 disciples in the beginning who listened and learned from Him for three years and then He released these men to implement His practices to preach, teach and destroy the works of the devil. This model shows us, if you desire to be a great leader, you must first be a good follower. In Matthew 16, Jesus said, *"Whoever wants to be my disciple."* Discipleship is always by choice. You cannot force anyone to follow Jesus. It has to be a work of the Holy Spirit. People will let you down during the discipleship process but you have to remember that they are not forsaking you. They are forsaking you. You're just the facilitator that leads people to the Lord. Ultimately, they are forsaking the ways of the Lord which brings me to my next point: Discipleship must Christ-centered and not man-centered. If we teach others to develop an undivided heart toward God, they will grow in grace and eventually be commissioned into their calling. This is the goal; To nurture new born spiritual converts to a place of biblical maturity so that they will in return; repeat the process. The Great Commission says, *"to Go into All the World" and do what?* Make Disciples. Everyone loves the celebration of a soul-saved and rightfully so but discipleship is a necessity and the undebatable next step. Discipleship isn't easy because it's often dirty. It's getting down in the ditch and helping other people get out of their mess. It's locking arms and saying, I don't care what you do. I'm not giving up on you. This type of love is relying on a power outside of yourself to do what you could not do otherwise. It's a discipline. So, who are you helping? Who are you pouring yourself into? Without Paul, I have to wonder if young Timothy would've remained faithful and finished the race. What about Billy Graham raising young Franklin, the Rebel without a Cause? Just look at the impact He is having in the world today. In the same way, God wants to use the wisdom that you have received to equip the body of Christ to be stronger and ultimately more fruitful. Lastly, Discipleship speaks of the future. Jesus concludes by saying, *"Follow me."* He didn't say, *"If anyone wants to be my disciple, first go and clean up your past."* No! In fact, He says, stop looking in the rearview mirror of your mistakes! I have something so much better in store for you! All you have to do is Follow me. Following Jesus produces Faithfulness and Faithfulness produces Fruit that will remain Forever. The principle is disciples making disciples.

Step to Start Strong:

Be a Disciple. Make a Disciple

OCTOBER 5.

TAKE A STAND

"Finally, be strong in the Lord and in his mighty power. Put on the full armor of God, so that you can take your stand against the devil's schemes. For our struggle is not against flesh and blood, but against the rulers, against the authorities, against the powers of this dark world and against the spiritual forces of evil in the heavenly realms. Therefore put on the full armor of God, so that when the day of evil comes, you may be able to stand your ground, and after you have done everything, to stand. Stand firm then...

Ephesians 6:10-13

Whatever you do; don't back down when the day of evil comes. Humility doesn't mean you are a doormat. The scripture says 4 times in this scripture, "to take a stand!" In the day of evil, despair may say, *"Lie down and die; give it all up."* Cowardice may say, *"Retreat and go back to the worldly way of living. This Christian life is not for you."* This is all a lie. You are surrounded by God's grace on every side. Your knees may be knocking but you better not flee. Square your shoulders, face your fear and keep marching by faith.

This reminds of the Story of Moses of the children of Israel crossing the Red Sea. In the natural, it seemed they were getting ready to die. The Egyptians had them cornered and it looked like they didn't have anywhere to go. There only option was to drown or be dragged back to Egypt. In this moment, they began to scream at Moses, "*why would God bring us this far and leave us to defend for our selves*?" When these words rolled off their lips, all of a sudden, a strong east wind began to blow and it parted the waters of the sea! God miraculously provided a way of safety so that every person could cross over to the other side.

The tendency of the heart is to start complaining in the midst of trouble. Refrain from doubt. God is going to provide a way out for you. Keep watching and praying otherwise this temptation will overcome you.

"Therefore, Do not be afraid. Stand firm and you will see the deliverance the Lord will bring you today. The Egyptians you see today you will never see again. The Lord will fight for you; you need only to be still." (Exodus 14:13-14)

<u>Step to Start Strong</u>:

Take a Stand

OCTOBER 6.

THE FRAGRANCE OF GOD

"Six days before the Passover, Jesus came to Bethany, where Lazarus lived, whom Jesus had raised from the dead. Here a dinner was given in Jesus' honor. Martha served, while Lazarus was among those reclining at the table with him. Then Mary took about a pint of pure nard, an expensive perfume; she poured it on Jesus' feet and wiped his feet with her hair. And the house was filled with the fragrance of the perfume."

John 12"1-3

Honor, service and sacrifice released the presence of the Lord into this living room. Honor opened the house for Jesus to come in, service created a comfortable atmosphere for Him to stay and sacrifice caused Him to manifest His power and glory.

Mary Magdalene, the lady who used to live a life of prostitution, fell at the feet of Jesus and gave him a year's worth of wages. We have to wonder what she did to accumulate this kind of money?

Despite her hurt, pain and public reputation, this lady was ready to put the past behind her. The story of her surrender speaks of salvation. Jesus cast seven demons out of her life at an earlier date so she knew the love of God but now she was willing to make Jesus the Lord of her life. She humbly bowed her heart by faith and anointed the feet of Jesus for His burial. Did she have to give such an extravagant offering for acceptance and forgiveness? Certainly not, but in her eyes, she had been forgiven of so much that she wanted to give God everything and more. In this moment, when she released her offering, the fragrance of the perfume filled the room, representing the presence of God. His presence is attracted to sacrifice and selflessness. Living a lifestyle of repentance creates an atmosphere for Jesus to move freely in the rooms of your heart. For in your weakness, His power is made perfect according to His word.

Honor God today. Serve your Savior with your whole-heart and live a life of sacrifice by walking humbly with the Holy Spirit. *"For we are to God the fragrance of Christ among those who are being saved and among those who are perishing. To the one we are the aroma of death leading to death, and to the other the aroma of life leading to life."* (2nd Corinthians 2:15-16)

Step to Start Strong:

Honor, Serve and Sacrifice

OCTOBER 7.

"Pray also for me, that whenever I open my mouth, words may be given to me so that I will fearlessly make known the mystery of the gospel, for which I am an ambassador in chains. Pray that I may declare it fearlessly, as I should."

Ephesians 6:19-20

Years ago, while fasting and praying during lunch one day, the Lord highlighted these verses in my heart and I will never be the same. It was a rhema word for me and I want to share it with you today. In this verse, the Apostle Paul with his vast education exemplifies his humility to the church in Ephesus by doing what? *By asking others to pray for Him.* Paul was a spiritual giant in His day but He knew the source of His power and how to released it. It wasn't by might, nor by power but God's favor rested upon Him because He was willing to humble himself by praying in the spirit on all occasions with other people.

See, pride will block the blessings of God. Pride says, *I'm independent and I will find a way without you no matter what.* Pride hinders prayer when prayer is our number priority as believers. Do you have a need? Well, I have to ask; Do you pray? Do you pray with other people? The scripture says, *"one can put a 1,000 to flight but two can put 10,000 to flight."* When you join forces in prayer, the supernatural becomes the norm. Angels and anointing begin flow to break the yoke and bring deliverance. Remember, God will never answer a prayer that you don't pray.

Find a prayer partner today. Ask your spouse; "*Will you pray for me*?" Go to the altar this Sunday and pray; not for show but for supernatural strength. The altar is not a one stop cure all. It's a place of habitation where the humble take refuge and find rejuvenation. The words, *"will you pray for me?"* holds endless possibilities. Remember, it's not necessarily how long you pray, it's how quick you believe.

Step to Start Strong:

Make it a habit to ask people to Pray for you

OCTOBER 8.

THE LORD'S PRAYER

"Your will be done, on earth as it is in Heaven."

Matthew 6:10

How do you jumpstart your day with Jesus? One way to awaken your spirit to the greatness of God is to prayer the Lord's Prayer at the beginning of everyday. Joshua received this promise early one morning before He led the Israelites into the Promised Land; *"If this Book of the Law does not depart from your mouth, and you meditate in it day and night, and you observe to do according to all that is written in it. Then you will make your way prosperous, and you will have good success."* (Joshua 1:7-8) What is your part of this promise? Being sure to speak, meditate and obey the Word of God in the morning and in the night. Here's the hope; If you connect with Christ at the beginning of your day and at the end; what happens in the middle is surrounded by truth! And if we know the truth, the truth will set us free from all the devils schemes and distractions. Therefore, *How you start and how you finish are very vital for your overall spiritual health.* Do you want to be successful? We all do! Speak the word and start your day with the Lord's prayer. It will change your life. Go ahead, Give it a try!

While praying this morning the Lord showed me this & I want to pass it on to you. The phrase,*"on earth as it is Heaven"* can also be translated as *"within earth."* You & I are made out of what? The scripture says, *God formed Adam from the dust of the ground.* Therefore, "we *have this treasure, the Holy Spirit, within our earthen vessels to show us that this all-surpassing power is from God and not from us." (2nd Cor. 4:7)*

So as you pray the Lord's prayer from here forward, remember God is using you to advance His Kingdom on earth but He also wants to reveal this power in you (or in earth) during the process. I always say, *"if it's not in Heaven, it should not be in my life."* Yes, we want the Kingdom to come to the earth but we also want the Kingdom to come in the earth also. Let's pray"

"Our Father, who art in Heaven, Hallowed be thy name. Thy Kingdom come, they will be done; on earth & in earth as it is in Heaven. Give us this day, our daily bread and forgive us our trespasses and we forgive those who trespass against us. Lead us not into temptation, but deliver us from evil. For thine in the Kingdom, The power and the glory, Forever and ever, in Jesus Name I pray, Amen."

Step to Start Strong:

Pray the Lord's Prayer Everyday

OCTOBER 9.

ACT LIKE A MAN

"When I was a child, I spoke as a child, I understood as a child, I thought as a child; but when I became a man, I put away childish things."

1st Corinthians 13:11

It's amazing that 90% of the men in the United States say, *"that they believe in God"* and five out of six refer to themselves as *"christians."* However, it's sad to say that only 26% of these men go to church with their wives on Sunday. Think about it: Only one in four women have their husbands by their side worshipping Jesus on a regular basis. The reality is, there is a disconnect between men and church in America. Overall, men would rather be building their house instead of building the House of God. Satan has lured men into leading selfish lives instead being servants of the Most High.

Psalm 127 says, *"unless the Lord builds the house those who build it labor in vain."* America needs a great awakening of mighty men all across our land. 1st Corinthians 16:13-14 says, *"Be watchful, stand firm in the faith, act like men and be strong. Let all that you do be done in love.*" Men need to act like men because real men love Jesus. Men are the priest of the homes. They lead their spouse and children spiritually. They protect and provide to implement peace and security to those in their care. Above all else, men lead in prayer. They don't act like spoiled kids.

The scripture says, *"For when I was a child, I spoke as a child, I understood as a child, I thought as a child; but when I became a man, I put away childish things."* According to this passage, there's a lot of people that need to hit their second "when." Amen?

If you are a man rise up and be a leader in the church. We need you in this hour. If you are a woman pray for us because we need you. May God bless this union, Amen.

Step to Start Strong:

Act Like a Man

OCTOBER 10.

What Happens When Woman Pray?

"The prayer of a righteous person is powerful and effective."

James 5:16

There are times in scripture where men cried out to God and they did not get the answer that they so desired. Moses interceded for his sister Miriam when she was plagued with leprosy for complaining against the Lord? What happened to her? She was cast outside the camp for seven days because she was considered unclean. King David's son was stricken with a fatal illness so he began to fast and pray for his healing. Three days later, he arose form the dust when he heard of his son's death only to go to the temple and worship. Am I saying that God doesn't answer men's prayer? Certainly not! But I am telling you is what I found in the Bible.

You can search the scripture and you will soon discover that there is no prayer offered unto God by a woman that was not answered. Hannah travailed for her son Samuel and God answered her prayer. Rachel, Sarah and Elizabeth all prayed for children and God gave them their hearts desire. My point? There is a special spiritual, emotional and physical connection between a mother and her kids and even a woman with her family. In fact, there is power in the prayer of a woman who sets her affection on high concerning those she loves. Women can change the whole trajectory of a family by fighting the good fight of faith on their knees. I don't know about you but I am eternally grateful for the people who have prayed me into my purpose. If we see further in the spirit it is because we are standing on the shoulders of spiritual giants. Think about: Who has prayed you into your purpose? Maybe your mom? Your grandparents? Your Pastor? Whoever it was say a prayer on their behalf right not.

For there is nothing closer to a woman's heart than their children but I wonder what is close to your heart this morning? The ladies listed above were desperate for God to show up in their circumstance. But I wonder how desperate are you? Jesus said, *"Men out to always pray and faint not."* (Luke 18) Be persistent! Don't give up! Keep praying! Today is a new day. God's favor is falling on your family. If you approach God today in Jesus name, He will not turn you away. Go ahead, Give it a try! This is what will happen if you pray.

Step to Start Strong:

Approach God with Confidence

OCTOBER 11.

A Chain Reaction

"About midnight Paul and Silas were praying and singing hymns to God, and the other prisoners were listening to them."

Acts 16:25

In our day and age, there is always somebody watching. People catch the craziest videos in the midst of triumph and tragedy. Cell phones and internet have drastically changed our culture in so many different ways. It really pays to ponder before you do or say something because you never know who's watching or even listening.

Paul and Silas were the center of attention in Acts Chapter 16 when they were arrested for preaching the Gospel. All eyes and ears were on them because of their boldness. As they began to sing praises unto God, the people in the prison wondered how they could celebrate even though they were bound in chains. What did these men do? They counted it worthy to suffer for the cause of Christ but they didn't stop there! Their faith caused them to mix there suffering with celebration because they knew that deliverance was at the door listening. The scripture says, *"Suddenly about midnight,"* The Holy Spirit manifested Himself in the way of an earthquake and broke down all the doors and set these men free. This act of faith, singing and shouting in the midst of their storm, released a chain reaction. After this, even the jailor and his family got saved.

Don't forget this: There is always somebody listening. I'll never forget standing in a long Starbucks line at the airport early one morning talking to one of our team members about Jesus. We were headed to Asia to host a leadership conference and we were full of joy and expectation to see what God was going to do. When we finally arrived at the register, the lady in front of us turned around and said, *"Order whatever you want. Breakfast is on me this morning."* We smiled and said, *"you don't have to do that ma'am,"* but she insisted and we knew she was serious. Her best friend had past away in Texas a few days earlier and she was flying down to her funeral in great distress. As she listened to us talk about Jesus, hope gripped her heart and tears were streaming down her face. See, somebody is always listening. One of my favorite things to do is to pray in public. Not a lay me down to sleep kind of prayer but an effectual fervent prayer. Not for show but to exemplify the hope that we have in Christ Jesus. People need to know that there is a God who is present and that He is full of power waiting to help us in our time of need. Give it a try! The scripture is true; If you lift up the name of Jesus, The Holy Spirit will draw all men unto you. They're waiting, watching and listening. May a Chain Reaction spread all across America and may it start with the church!

Step to Start Strong:

Cause a Chain Reaction

OCTOBER 12.

LET FREEDOM RING

"Stand fast therefore in the liberty by which Christ has made us free, and do not be entangled again with a yoke of bondage."

Galatians 5:1

The late Dr. Martin Luther King said, *"I have a dream that one day every valley shall be exalted, every hill and mountain shall be made low, the rough places will be made smooth, and the crooked places will be made straight, and the glory of the Lord shall be revealed and all flesh shall see it together!*

This is our hope. This is the faith that I go back to and with this faith we will be able to hew out of the mountain of despair a stone of hope. With this faith we will be able to transform the jangling discords of our nation into a beautiful symphony of brotherhood. With this faith we will be able to work together, to pray together, to struggle together, to go to jail together, to stand up for freedom together knowing that we will be free one day.

This will be the day, this will be the day when all of God's children will be able to sing with new meaning: "My country, 'tis of thee, sweet land of liberty, of thee I sing. Land where my fathers died, land of the pilgrim's pride, from every mountainside, let freedom ring!"

And if America is to be a great nation, this must become true. So let freedom ring from the prodigious hilltops of New Hampshire. Let freedom ring from the mighty mountains of New York. Let freedom ring from the heightening Alleghenies of Pennsylvania. Let freedom ring from the snow-capped Rockies of Colorado. Let freedom ring from the curvaceous slopes of California. But not only that: Let freedom ring from the Stone Mountain of Georgia. Let freedom ring from Lookout Mountain of Tennessee. Let freedom ring from every hill and molehill of Mississippi. From every mountainside, let freedom ring!

And when this happens and when we allow freedom ring, may we let it ring from every village and every hamlet, from every state and every city, we will be able to speed up that day when all of God's children, black men and white men, Jews and Gentiles, Protestants and Catholics, will be able to join hands and sing: "Free at last! Free at last! Thank God Almighty, we are free at last!"

(Excerpt taken from the famous "I have a Dream" speech by Dr. Martin Luther King.)

Have you lost your dream? If so, *"It's time to Dream Again!"* Let the freedom bell ring deep inside of your soul so that you can stand in the liberty by which Christ has made you free.

<u>Step to Start Strong</u>:

Dream Again!

OCTOBER 13.

Jesus - The Great High Priest

"Stephen, full of the Holy Spirit, looked up to heaven and saw the glory of God, and Jesus standing at the right hand of God. "Look," he said, "I see heaven open and the Son of Man standing at the right hand of God." At this they covered their ears and, yelling at the top of their voices, they all rushed at him, dragged him out of the city and began to stone him. Meanwhile, the witnesses laid their coats at the feet of a young man named Saul. While they were stoning him, Stephen prayed, "Lord Jesus, receive my spirit." Then he fell on his knees and cried out, "Lord, do not hold this sin against them." When he had said this, he fell asleep. And Saul approved of their killing him."

Acts 7:54 - 8:1

Stephen, a man full of God's grace and power, was the first Christian martyr in the New Testament Church. You'll notice when the religious leaders were about to kill him, he looked up to Heaven and saw Jesus standing at the right hand of the Father. Later in the Gospel of Mark and in Hebrews we read *"how Jesus ascended into heaven and sat down at the right hand of God."* (Mark 16:19 / Hebrews 10:12) Have you ever wondered why Jesus was standing while Stephen was being stoned? This scene seems to bring Jesus right out of His seat. Does Jesus stand when someone is being stoned or martyred for placing their faith in Him? What is the symbolism or instruction for us to see? In order to do so, we have to understand the duties of a Priest in the Old Testament tabernacle. On the Day of Atonement, the high priest would minister from sunrise to sunset while standing on his feet. He was forbidden by God to sit down. Only when God accepted the sacrifices on behalf of the people could the mediator sit down and rest. While Stephen was being stoned, he cried out with a loud voice, *"Father, lay not this sin to their charge."* Stephen could have died in anger and bitterness of soul but instead he chose to release these men from their sin. This act of grace caused the Great High Priest - Jesus Christ to stand to his feet. Now, the blood was pouring from another man's brow but it was being pumped by the same loving heart; *"Father, Forgive them for they know not what they do."* Sound familiar? This is a picture of redemption that gained all of Heaven's attention. Let's read Hebrews Chapter 4 with this story in mind; *"Therefore, since we have a great high priest who has ascended into heaven, Jesus the Son of God, let us hold firmly to the faith we profess. For we do not have a high priest who is unable to empathize with our weaknesses, but we have one who has been tempted in every way, just as we are—yet he did not sin. Let us then approach God's throne of grace with confidence, so that we may receive mercy and find grace to help us in our time of need."* Indeed, Jesus is our Great High Priest and His love and grace is being poured out on you today. Be sure to share it with others.

<u>Step to Start Strong</u>:

Forgive Those who Hurt You

OCTOBER 14.

No Longer Slaves

"There is no fear in love. But perfect love drives out fear, because fear has to do with punishment. The one who fears is not made perfect in love."

1 John 4:18

There's a popular song in the worship world right now called, *"No Longer Slaves."* It was written by Jonathan Helser, a young man from Randolph County. His parents attend church in Asheboro who had two daughters but never intended to have any more children. A matter of fact, the mother had already scheduled a hysterectomy because the doctor's report showed that she had cancer in her uterus. But God had other plans: One Sunday afternoon, *"the word of the Lord came to this couple"* and said, *"you will have a son and you will name him Jonathan David and he will write songs that will change the course of his generation."* (Not a very believing word considering their circumstance) However, this coupled prayed and believed the word of God and before the scheduled surgery the following week, they asked the doctor to run one more test to confirm the presence of cancer. The Father said in the testimony that, *"it seemed like good news when the doctor came back whistling while walking down the hall."* They ran the test three more times to make sure it was the same woman who was now cancer free! Just a few months later, this couple became pregnant and later bore a son and they named him Johnathon David.

However, he never showed any interest in music. His whole life was consumed with sports but his parents never mentioned the word of the Lord. When he turned 19, Johnathon traveled to England to ministry school and it was there that the prophetic word came to pass in this young man's life. God filled Him with His presence and power and he began to write songs and play the guitar without hindrance.

His hit song says,

"You unravel me with a melody, You surround me with a song, Of deliverance from my enemies, Until all my fears are gone. From my mother's womb, You have chosen me, Love has called my name, I've been born again, Into your family, Your blood flows through my veins, You split the sea, So I could walk right through it, My fears were drowned in perfect love, You rescued me, So I will stand and sing, I am a child of God."

The scripture rings true, "*There is no fear in love. But perfect love drives out all fear, because fear has to do with punishment. The one who fears is not made perfect in love.*" You don't have anything to be afraid today because your Heavenly Father loves you and His love can change anything. Rejoice in this truth today; You are a Child of God!

Step to Start Strong:

Live like a Son and not a Slave

OCTOBER 15.

WHO WILL GO FOR GOD?

"In the year that King Uzziah died, I saw the Lord sitting on a throne—high and lifted up!—and the train of his robe filled the Temple. Angels hovered above him, each with six wings. With two wings they covered their faces, with two their feet, and with two they flew. And they called back and forth one to the other, Holy, Holy, Holy is God-of-the-Angel-Armies. His bright glory fills the whole earth. The foundations trembled at the sound of the angel voices, and then the whole house filled with smoke and I said, "Doom! It's Doomsday! I'm as good as dead! Every word I've ever spoken is tainted and even blasphemous! And the people I live with talk the same way, using words that corrupt and desecrate. And here I've looked God in the face! The King! The God-of-the-Angel-Armies!" Then one of the angels flew to me. He held a live coal that he had taken with tongs from the altar. He touched my mouth with the coal and said, "Look. This coal has touched your lips. Gone is your guilt, and your sins wiped out." And then I heard the

voice of the Master: "Whom shall I send? Who will go for us? I spoke up and said, "I'll go. Send me!"

Isaiah 6:1-8

Where is God sending you today?
What does the Master want you to do?
"Availability is better than ability with God."
Make yourself available to be used by God
and your capabilities are endless.
Will you go for God?

Step to Start Strong:

Heed the Still Small Voice of God

OCTOBER 16.

A STILL SMALL VOICE

"Then He said, "Go out, and stand on the mountain before the Lord." And behold, the Lord passed by, and a great and strong wind tore into the mountains and broke the rocks in pieces before the Lord, but the Lord was not in the wind; and after the wind an earthquake, but the Lord was not in the earthquake; and after the earthquake a fire, but the Lord was not in the fire; and after the fire a still small voice."

1 Kings 19:11-13

Why does God choose to whisper and speak in a still small voice? In order to hear a whisper, you have to be in close proximity to the person; meaning God desires for you to be close by His side. He refuses to battle with the world for your ear and attention. Jesus said, "*My sheep know me and they hear my voice.*"

Do you hear the heart of your Heavenly Father? Do you know His voice? Over the years, I have noticed that *inner calm creates a channel to hear the Holy Spirit.* Quiet your fears, settle your emotions and wait for the still small voice of God. David found this treasure when He said, *"My souls sits in silence before the Lord."* (Ps. 62:5) This *"inner calm in the intercom"* for God to give you clear direction for your days.

So I challenge you; Get away with the Lord and wait patiently for Him. Hurry is the dagger that puts prayer to death. Don't rush through the most important part of your day. Give God your best. Give Him 100% of your attention. If you need an answer, He will illuminate His good, pleasing and perfect will for your life. He wants you to know *"the truth"* more than you do! So, don't be discouraged. God speaks to those who take time to listen.

In fact, this is the key to spiritual success; *Knowing and obeying the voice of the Lord.* My prayer is that God would open your ears of spiritual understanding to be led by His still small voice. Somebody say, "*Speak Lord, I'm listening.*"

<u>Step to Start Strong</u>:

Be Still and Wait for the Word of the Lord

OCTOBER 17.

God-Chasers

"He made David their king. God testified concerning him: 'I have found David son of Jesse, a man after my own heart; he will do everything I want him to do."

Acts 13:22

God found David the Son of Jesse in the field tending to his fathers sheep. Young David was a servant and God saw Him in his obedience way before he found great success. Don't miss this: *Your servants heart will take you way farther than your talent could ever sustain you.* David was a man after God's own heart because He was willing to do everything God wanted Him to do. He was totally dependent upon the Lord as He walked through the valley of the shadow of death but He was also repentant for His sins when they seemed to be overtaking Him. He wasn't perfect but He learned to follow after the perfect one. His problems never changed His posture of prayer and praise. This is why He wrote most of the Psalms. He had deep, deep desire to *"to see God face to face."* Indeed, He was a God Chaser, a man after God's own heart.

Tommy Tenney put it this way, "*worship and spiritual hunger make you so attractive to God that your circumstances cease to matter anymore. He will move Heaven and earth to find a worshiper. When you begin to worship with all your being and desire, your heart turns Him toward you. You capture His attention and you attract His affection.*"

If your problems are too big; Maybe your worship is too small? Don't let spiritual complacency strangle your calling. Jeremiah wrote these words during his journey in life, *"If you seek God you will find God if you seek God with all of your heart."* God is not hiding so you can't find Him, He is hiding so you can! Go hard after God today and you will develop His heart for tomorrow. Be a Good God-Chaser! It's the highest calling!

Step to Start Strong:

Serve your Way to the Top

OCTOBER 18.

LET IT GROW

"For if you possess these qualities in increasing measure, they will keep you from being ineffective and unproductive in your knowledge of our Lord Jesus Christ."

2 Peter 1:8

Spiritual gifts are given but the Fruit of the Spirit is grown. The word "gift" in the greek is "charisma." When we say a certain person is charismatic, what we are really saying is, they are extremely gifted. God has given each man at least one spiritual gift *"for the edification of the Church."* These gifts are given by the Holy Spirit and there are many mentioned in scripture. However, just because somebody has a spiritual gift and walks in great power doesn't mean they are spiritually mature and strong in character. (Read 1st Corinthians 12 & 13)

On the contrary, you can't fake the fruit. *"Every tree will be identified by its fruit."* The Fruit of the Holy Spirit is the scale to weigh our personal walk with Christ. Fruit grows and becomes ripe when placed in the right atmosphere. Our fruit will be ever-increasing, effective and productive, if we are firmly planted in a genuine relationship with Christ Jesus.

The nine fruit of the spirit are love, joy, peace, patience, kindness, goodness, faithfulness, gentleness and self-control. (Gal. 5:22) Try to memorize these this week.

"The greatest gift is ***Love****. The* ***Joy*** *of the Lord is your strength. You have the* ***Peace*** *of God that surpasses all understanding. So let* ***Kindness*** *guide your way and make your paths straight; For every* ***Good*** *and perfect gift comes from God. Even when you are faithless, He is* ***Faithful*** *so let faith arise inside of your soul and let your* ***Gentleness*** *be evident to all while being* ***Self-Controlled."***

"Against such there is no law. And those who are alive in Christ have crucified the flesh with its passions and desires. So, If we live in the Spirit, let us also walk in the Spirit." (Galatians 5:23-25)

Let's walk, water and watch it grow. Glory to God! Hallelujah!

Step to Start Strong:

Memorize the Fruit of the Spirit

OCTOBER 19.

God's Goal

"For you are receiving the goal of your faith, the salvation of your souls."

1st Peter 1:9

What is God's ultimate goal? The salvation of souls! *For God is not slack concerning His promise, but He is patient, not wanting anyone to perish but for ALL to come to a place of repentance.* Indeed, He will leave the ninety-nine to go after the one lost sheep. He will dig and dig in the depths of the sea to redeem lost coins and give them a destiny. Yes, God knows your name but more importantly, He knows your pain. He relentlessly pursues because of his passion and He eagerly awaits no matter whats happening. He seeks the distant and damned souls of man. 'This is God's Goal; a well devised plan. So don't lose sight of why you're still here. God wants to use you in a mighty way this year. You may ask what would Jesus do? For most of mankind they have not a clue. For Jesus came to seek and save and this my friend is the only way. Exalting Jesus is the key, by doing so, He'll set you free.

So, what's the only thing left to do? Biblically, it's the exceedingly great joy of sharing the Good News! And never, ever, ever forget; Nothing can stop God's goal for you but you. This is the goal of your faith and by fighting for it; many souls will be saved. Whoa! This is God's goal!

If you believe it, do anything to achieve it!

<u>Step to Start Strong</u>:

Set a Soul-Saving Goal

OCTOBER 20.

FAITH WORKS

"Faith without works is dead."

James 2:26

Ministers love to meet and eat! It can be a blessing or a curse depending upon a persons self-control. For me, I had to find a way out; I do this by working out. My weekly routine is to go to the gym at least three to four times a week. Personally, it's a great release; physically, emotionally and even spiritually. When I work out, clarity comes to my mind and creativity fills my soul. It's amazing to me, when I run, stretch and begin to lift weights, I know longer eat food for fun but I use it for fuel. My diet is much healthier when I'm working out. When I'm not doing anything, I eat everything.

This reminds me of a sign I saw a few weeks ago, it said, "*I missed my work out today. This makes 7 years in a row!* Does this hit home?

Furthermore, working out is a lot like exercising your faith. If you know anything about working out, you know your muscles hit personal plateaus of growth. When you first start working out, your muscles get sore, they tighten up and begin to grow. However, overtime, your body gets accustomed to the reoccurring routine. The weight that broke down the muscle fibers before, doesn't do what they use to do. It takes more and more weight and more and more repetitions to create the same results.

In the same way, if you're not careful, you'll get used to living in a certain level of faith and the good that you do today will cripple the greatness that God has planned for you. This is called; growing from faith to faith. Faith enables God's word to come alive and work through you because James said, *"faith without works is dead!"* You can't work for faith but faith can work for you! In fact, the only way for your faith to work and grow is by exercising it everyday.

With this in mind, if you don't work out for weeks, your physical body will deteriorate. It works the same way spiritually. Faith keeps you fit. Faith stretches you into your God-given destiny. Faith challenges you to keep believing for a desired outcome. On the contrary, it's so easy to get stuck in a rut and never grow to your maximum potential in the Kingdom. The great strive of yesterday that shocked your religious system into something new can become an act of complacency that stunts your growth today. Maybe this is why Jesus never performed a miracle the same way twice? Just a thought? My challenge to you today: Exercise your FAITH. Pray and push through spiritual plateaus and don't let fear keep you from fulfilling your calling. Let faith be your servant.

Step to Start Strong:

Exercise your Faith

OCTOBER 21.

ANGELS AMONG US

"Are not all angels ministering spirits sent to serve those who will inherit salvation?"

Hebrews 1:14

Are angels just for kids? My mom made it a habit growing up to share an angel story with her Sunday School class and they loved it! What was she doing? She was creating a hunger for the supernatural in the heart of her young hearers. But the truth is, angels are not just for kids! Angels are for adults too. Have you ever encountered an angel? Has supernatural intervention ever flashed before your eyes? The Bible shares numerous stories about angels and to me it's very intriguing. In Hebrews 1:14, the word salvation means, "*deliverance, protection or preservation.*" So think about this; God has created mighty spiritual beings who are specifically designed and assigned to protect and preserve the children of God from the evil one. This sheds a whole new light on the scripture that says, "If God be for us; who can be against us?" Just imagine what your angelic bodyguard looks like at night? Psalm 103:20 gives us some more insight; "*Bless the Lord, you angels of His, Who excel in strength, who do His word, Heeding the voice of His commands."* So what you do in times of struggle, temptation and doubt determines what happens in the spirit realm. If you speak the word of God; angels are dispatched. In fact, they watch over God's word to accomplish it. Angels heed the word of God. I believe one of the greatest tragedies of prayerlessness is the unemployment of angels. We have to give our angels something to do.

Notice that angels are sent *"to serve those who will inherit salvation."* This means, all of Heaven stands at attention, watching and waiting to fulfill God's word for your life. So, don't be afraid. Rest in the best protection. ADT doesn't compare to G.O.D. If we could see in the spirit for a split second; our prayer life would change forever. We would know that there really are *"angels among us."* Give your angels something to do; speak, shout and declare the word of the Lord over your life.

Step to Start Strong:

Employ Angels

Psalm 91:9-16 *"Because you have made the Lord, who is my refuge, Even the Most High, your dwelling place. No evil shall befall you, Nor shall any plague come near your dwelling; For He shall give His angels charge over you, To keep you in all your ways. In their hands they shall bear you up, Lest you dash your foot against a stone. You shall tread upon the lion and the cobra, The young lion and the serpent you shall trample underfoot. "Because he has set his love upon Me, therefore I will deliver him; I will set him on high, because he has known My name. He shall call upon Me, and I will answer him; I will be with him in trouble; I will deliver him and honor him. With long life I will satisfy him, And show him My salvation."*

OCTOBER 22.

HOLY, HOLY, HOLY

"He who has My commandments and keeps them, it is he who loves Me. And he who loves Me will be loved by My Father, and I will love him and manifest Myself to him."

John 14:21

The word *Holy* means a cut above; dedicated and consecrated to be used for God's divine purposes. This only happens when you make a decision to please God in every activity of our life. In this dimension of obedience, Jesus promises to manifest Himself unto you.

When you study past movements of revival, you'll find the groups of people who experienced supernatural outpourings of the Holy Spirit became discontent with temporal possessions and popularity. Daily encounters with Christ became first priority. Everything that displeased God was quickly forsaken as their eyes and heart were undivided toward their King. Over time, the world started to call these individuals *"holiness people or holy-rollers."*

This name derived because the people were so different from everybody else. They didn't follow current trends and try to fit in. They changed their culture and turned their cities and communities upside down (Acts 17:6). Now, it would be easy to focus on the outward consecration of these people but what truly brought the mighty manifestations of the Holy Spirit was the condition of their postured heart. Their inner purity, holiness and submissiveness to prayer moved the Hand of God.

Very few people understand holiness today and even fewer people understand the manifestation of the spirit that comes from it. However, if you implement God's instruction into your daily life, your life will begin to change. You won't have to stand on a street corner waving your Bible; people will quickly notice the difference in your daily walk. The glow of God will come upon your countenance and people will take notice. All this will come from soaking in His presence and heeding His commands which ultimately creates holiness in your heart and consecration in your walk.

1st Peter 1:15-16 says, "*He who called you is holy, so you also be holy in all your conduct, because it is written, "Be holy, for I am holy.*" Holiness is a habit. It doesn't happen by accident. Make a decision to obey the still small voice of the Holy Spirit today. It will change your perspective, produce in you a newfound love for God and ultimately, it will manifest the presence of Jesus to people all around you.

Step to Start Strong:

Be Holy

OCTOBER 23.

THE MOST HOLY PLACE

"Now the first covenant had regulations for worship and also an earthly sanctuary. A tabernacle was set up. In its first room were the lamp-stand and the table with its consecrated bread; this was called the Holy Place. Behind the second curtain was a room called the Most Holy Place, which had the golden altar of incense and the gold-covered ark of the covenant. This ark contained the gold jar of manna, Aaron's staff that had budded, and the stone tablets of the covenant. Above the ark were the cherubim of the Glory, overshadowing the mercy seat."

Hebrews 9:1-5

When Jesus cried out with a loud voice, and yielded up His spirit, the veil of the temple was torn in two from top to bottom. A powerful picture of the new covenant being established. Josephus, a first century historian reported, *"that the veil was 4 inches thick, renewed every year, and that horses tied to each others side could not pull it apart. This veil barred all but the High Priest from the presence of God, but when it was torn in two because of the death of Jesus of Nazareth (see Mark 15:38), and access to God was made available to ALL who come through him."*

The Blood of Christ pardons us from sin and invites us to pass from the Outer Court of the temple into the Holy of Holies. Andrew Murray describes this thought in His exposition on the book of Hebrews, that there are still those who have not entered into this granted area:

> *"Many believers never experience this life of the inner sanctuary-the more complete and abiding nearness to God. They have, in the outer court, seen the altar and received the pardon of sin. They have entered upon the service of God and seek to do His will, but the joy of His presence as their abiding portion they know not. Very often, they do not know that there is a better life, an entering within the veil, a real dwelling in the secret of God's presence. They need the Holy Spirit to work in them the conviction that to them the way into the Holiest hath not yet been made manifest. Oh let us, if we have not yet entered in, give ourselves to pray for the discovery that there is an inner chamber; and that there is still the veil of the flesh-the life of the carnal Christian-that prevents the access. Only the Spirit that came from the throne when Jesus had rent the veil will bring us in."*

Holy Spirit help us to make the most of our all-access pass to your throne of grace today. May we live, breathe and find ourselves in the Most Holy Place of your presence. Take us into all the inner chambers of your heart by the Blood of the Lamb. We want to know you more. This is our prayer.

Step to Start Strong:

Tear Down the Veil in your own Heart

OCTOBER 24.

What you See is What you Get

"When the Lord was about to take Elijah up to heaven in a whirlwind, Elijah and Elisha were on their way from Gilgal. Elijah said to Elisha, "Stay here; the Lord has sent me to Bethel." But Elisha said, "As surely as the Lord lives and as you live, I will not leave you." So they went down to Bethel."

2 Kings 2:1-2

Elisha has to be one of the most persistent people in all of the Bible. His predecessor, Elijah, the miracle man, basically told him to get lost three times. He said, you stay here, I'm going to another place but the young man knew that there was something that his mentor had that He needed. So he persistently proclaimed, "*As surely as the Lord lives, and you live, I will not leave you.*" So they stayed close together.

This principle is not only powerful but it is foundational. Elisha represents the younger generation and Elijah represents the old. The young prophet understood the importance of watching the way the more mature man of God lived his life. The wisdom and faith that comes from God cannot be replaced with fervor alone. Yes, at times, we need passion and enthusiasm to rekindle our spiritual flame but passion without godly wisdom will soon turn to chaff. What we need is for God to grant us a holy kiss between the young and old generations. In fact, hose who do not learn from history are doomed to repeat it. The apostle Paul put it this way, "*Remember your leaders, who spoke the word of God to you. Consider the outcome of their way of life and imitate their faith.*" I'll never forget my first ministry position as I had the honor of serving up under my Spiritual Father. The impact of his ministry was profound and remarkable. It not only changed my life but it birthed in me a call for evangelism. When I watched him minister under the anointing; I could clearly see what I could be if I aligned myself under the umbrella of the same authority. For two years, I followed his ministry closely until I felt released from his leadership. It was time to go learn from another man's example and glean more life lessons. However, the key was watching and listening with great intent. For what you see is what you get. Elijah told Elisha, *"if you see me when I am taken from you, it will be yours—otherwise, it will not." (2 Kings 2:10)* The key was the willingness and submission of the younger generation to learn from the old. Elisha stayed so close to Elijah that He received what He was looking for; a double-portion of the anointing. This young man's heart of humility opened the door to what everybody was searching for. I wonder who you are watching in this season of your life and what impact they are having in your heart? Better yet, who is your mentor and who are you mentoring? At this point, we need to make sure we are sowing seeds for the next generation to see. For ultimately, the greatest testimony is the outcome of your life. It will speak louder than words. May we ever be watching, listening and learning.

Step to Start Strong:

Be a Mentor and Mentee

OCTOBER 25.

Losing Jesus

"Every year Jesus' parents went to Jerusalem for the Festival of the Passover. When he was twelve years old, they went up to the festival, according to the custom. After the festival was over, while his parents were returning home, the boy Jesus stayed behind in Jerusalem, but they were unaware of it. Thinking he was in their company, they traveled on for a day. Then they began looking for him among their relatives and friends. When they did not find him, they went back to Jerusalem to look for him. After three days they found him in the temple courts, sitting among the teachers, listening to them and asking them questions."

Luke 2:41-46

Joseph and Mary with a whole company of other Jews traveled a great distance to Jerusalem to celebrate Passover. We know now that the songs and sacraments of this 8 day festival were all signs and symbols that pointed to the death, burial and resurrection of our

Lord and Savior Jesus Christ. Indeed, He was the pure and spotless lamb that was slain for the sins of the world. Symbolically, this yearly celebration was all about Jesus.

However, when the family and friends of Mary and Joseph began their 5 day journey back to Nazareth, they forgot the one in whom the festival was for. They finally realized they had lost Jesus; the Son of God and this passage proves a powerful point.

If we are not careful, we can go to our modern day temples to worship and leave the reality of the risen Christ in the building. We can go through all the right religious rituals; we can shout, we can sing and we can read the scriptures that are all about Jesus. But what happens we when leave? Is Jesus someone we converse with on Sunday or do we involve Him in every activity throughout the week?

In this story, Mary & Joseph left Jesus is the temple. Religion caused them to lose sight of pleasing the most important person. Around the world, many people keep Jesus in the corner of their heart when He desires fill every area of their life. So, whatever you do; don't lose Jesus. Don't allow the distractions of this world deter you from your God-given destiny. Don't lose your focus. Fix your eyes on Jesus, the author and the finisher of your faith. Do you know where Jesus is right now? Scripture says, He's sitting at the right hand of the Father interceding for the saints. This is Jesus' job description today. Praying for all people. May we never lose sight of where He is, who He is and what we're supposed to be doing.

Step to Start Strong:

Keep your eyes and affection on the Risen Christ

OCTOBER 26.

OUR RESPONSIBILITY TO REST

"My soul finds rest in God alone; my salvation comes from Him. He alone is my rock and my salvation; He is my fortress, Therefore, I will never be shaken."

Psalm 62

Recently, the Lord reminded me of a word He whispered into my heart one Fall. We were in Jacksonville, Florida for the weekend working at the Fire Conference for Christ for All Nations. It was the first night of the event and the atmosphere was electrifying. Thousands of people came in from the four corners of the country to be touched by God and empowered for personal evangelism. After everyone was settled, I slipped down to the second row to sit in the reserved section to enjoy the show. After a great a line-up of songs and speakers, the key note speaker was about to conclude the night but before he did, He surprisingly walked right up to me in front of everybody. Obviously, my first reaction was to look to the left as if He were staring at the guy sitting next to me. However, when my head whipped back around,

I was wrong; He proceeded to call me out in front of the crowd. What happened next was simple; All he said was these two sentences, "*You're working tonight right?*" With a smile, I stood to my feet and nodded my head. He then proceeded with a smirk, "*Not anymore.*" When he laid His hands on me, the power of God shot through my body and the rest was history.

Now why did I share this story? Because these two sentences have profound implications for all of us. Of course, in the moment I didn't grasp the revelation of what was said to me and maybe you didn't either but on the flight home the Lord brought these words back to my remembrance. *"You've been working haven't you. Not anymore!"* Was the Lord calling me to quit my job? Now don't misinterpret what I'm saying. The message that God was trying to convey is this; *Our responsibility is to remain in the rest of the Lord.* In the Old Testament, the place of rest for God's people was the Promised Land. In the New testament, the place of rest is in the person of Jesus Christ. For all of God's promises are YES in Christ Jesus. However, sometimes we can find ourselves working for grace, working for the approval of God and people and even working for the overall good of society but not working with God. The truth is, we are called to be co-laborers with Christ. Don't miss this: *When we labor without the Lord, we carry the responsibility of the effort and the outcome.* With this in mind, We are not called to be beasts of burden. A sheep wasn't created to carry heavy loads. They were created to follow; meaning our responsibility is to remain in the rest of the Lord because He is our Good Shepherd. When this word was spoken over me, the Lord convicted my heart of trying to do His job. The first order of theology is, *"There is a God and I am not him."* Let God be God. Trust in His goodness and grace. Rest in your relationship with Jesus. Don't worry about tomorrow. If we proclaim His promises today, tomorrow will take care of itself. When we work, we work! And we feel the repercussions from it! However, when we believe God and pray, God works! And we work with Him and not without Him. This is the better way. I have to ask; Have you been "working?" If so, not anymore; "From now on, your responsibility is to rest in your relationship with the Lord."

Step to Start Strong:

Rest, Rest, Rest

OCTOBER 27.

A New Beginning

"Then the word of the LORD came to Jonah a second time."

Jonah 3:1

Whenever I first read this verse years ago; I marked these 3 words in the margin of my Bible; *a new beginning*. Aren't you so glad the word of the Lord keeps coming to you despite your disobedience and reluctancy. For God's mercies are anew every morning; meaning if we missed it yesterday, He's willing to give us another chance today. Some call it amazing but I call it grace!

In this story, God was so determined to use this selfish, timid prophet that he wouldn't give up on him even though he had given up on himself. After falling into a deep, dark pit of self-pity, Jonah found himself as low as He could go; In the belly of a great fish, at the bottom of the ocean floor. Can anybody top this testimony? Indeed, God has a way of getting our attention.

Tony Evans said it best when He said, *"Sometimes God will let you hit rock bottom just so you will know that He is the rock at the bottom."* For me, rock bottom became the solid foundation for which I built my life and if Jonah could speak up today, he would probably say, *"Amen."*

For in distress Jonah cried out to God and said, *"salvation comes from the Lord!"* and instantly, the fish spewed this man out on the seashore. After gaining his composure, the word of the Lord came to Jonah a second time. Now don't miss this; The word was the test to see if what He said in distress came from his head or his heart. *See, the original call for Jonah's life never changed.* God was determined to use Jonah for His glory but more importantly, he wanted to see the lost souls in Nineveh saved.

Have you been given God lip service? Are you being disobedient to the call of God placed upon your life? You can run from God but remember, He can run faster than you can! A matter of fact, He can fly faster than you can fall. He knows your shortcomings and He knows all your fears. So, call out to God this morning and ask Him what He wants you to do. You never know; He may relent and leave behind a blessing and ultimately, give you a new beginning for the second or third time.

Step to Start Strong:

Ask God to give you another Chance

OCTOBER 28.

A TITLE OF HONOR

"For the sake of Jacob my servant, of Israel my chosen, I summon you by name and bestow on you a title of honor."

Isaiah 53:4

Honor is the key to success. Mike Murdock says, "*Your future is determined by who you choose to honor, and if you fail in your life, it will be because of a person you have chosen to dishonor.*" Honor means to highly esteem and respect the office of another or literally, *"to weigh heavily."* When you sow seeds of honor, it will open up a boulevard of blessing to your life, family and ministry? Think about it; What do you do when someone highly esteems you publicly? Typically, in due time, you would return the favor and so on.

For example, the Bible mentions a man that cried out to the God of Israel for prosperity, influence and protection and God gave it to him. But what most people miss is in the first verse accredited to his life which gives us a key to his great success: *"For*

Jabez was <u>more honorable than all of His brothers</u>." Jabez bore the Title of Honor and in return God honored him and granted him great success.

I though about Jospeh; Joseph was judged by His brothers and sent away into slavery but the common thread that held his life together was honor. He gave honor to the jailor and in return he received great favor and blessing. Later, when He approached Pharaoh, He shaved his beard even though it was customary for an Israelite to have a beard. This showed his public respect to the Egyptian authority because everyone else was clean shaven. These small steps of esteem taken by Joseph compounded to giant strides of prosperity and promotion.

With this in mind, we have to give honor where honor is due and within the Kingdom of God, *every individual is extremely valuable and should be respected.* Honor is respecting who a person is instead of who they're not. The world is so used to coming into the church and being confronted with who they are not that they don't want to come back. The church is not a club, its a community of believers who operate as the body of Jesus Christ even though they are different. We should celebrate people because they are children of God. (period) Anything less is dishonor and disrespect and this attitude induces darkness.

So, who do you need to give honor to today? Your spouse? Your kids? Your employer? Your employees? How about your Pastor or even the stranger on the street? Honor will grant you access which will ultimately bring you great success. Never forget: *Honor is the highest seed you can sow. True Story.*

<u>Step to Start Strong:</u>

Sow the Seed of Honor

OCTOBER 29.

STANDING IN THE GAP

"I looked for someone among them who would build up the wall and stand before me in the gap on behalf of the land so I would not have to destroy it, but I found no one. So I will pour out my wrath on them and consume them with my fiery anger, bringing down on their own heads all they have done, declares the Sovereign Lord."

Ezekiel 22:30-31

The first time I read this passage, it all made sense to me. After God miraculously delivered me from a life of drugs and alcoholism, I had to wonder why me? How did I survive when so many die by overdose and suicide. This could've been me so easyily but by God's grace I'm still standing and for this I am forever grateful. I know it is by grace that I am saved but why was this grace given to me over and over again? I think Ezekiel's conversation with God will bring some clarity to this conversation. For God is slow to anger, full of compassion and rich in love not desiring for anyone to perish but for all to come to a place of repentance. It took me 10 years but I finally bowed my knee, waved the white flag and God's grace set me free. Yes, God's love for us in unconditional but if we reject it; His judgment has to come.

This is how it happened: Ezekiel wrote, *"God looked for a man to stand in the gap because He wanted to grant this city grace but He found no-one. So He had to pour out His wrath upon the people for what they had done."* Do you sense God's heart here? He was patiently waiting and searching for someone to rise up and pray for the people in Jerusalem because He wanted to relent His judgment. Death and destruction was the last thing He wanted to see but without the partnership of a praying man evil prevailed. Do you see where I'm going with this? God is searching for praying men and women to stand in the gap on behalf of this generation. People are staggering toward the slaughter and their only hope is for our prayers to hold them back. This reminds me of Moses interceding for Israel when God said, *"He would destroy them - had not Moses, his chosen one, stood in the breach before him to keep his wrath from coming."* (Ps. 106:23) Abraham also pleads for Sodom and Gomorrah. Jeremiah weeps for Jerusalem. Now, we find Ezekiel wrestling with the same idea pertaining to the will of the Lord. The bottom line is this: Sin creates a gap in the wall of protection around God's people but prayer fills it with the power of God's grace. No prayer; No protection. It's as simple as this. What gap do you need to fill? Who's life is heavy on your heart this morning? Be intentional. Start praying for people who need salvation? Do you know someone struggling with addiction? Shoot arrows prayers up to the throne of God's grace today. What if you're the only one standing between their life and eternal damnation? God says, all He needs is one. For me, it was my family. When I read these verses, it all made sense to me. The only reason why I made it was by prayer and the only reason why I'm here today is by grace.

<u>Step to Start Strong</u>:

Stand in the Gap and Pray

OCTOBER 30.

God's Best

"For the Lord God is a sun and shield; the Lord bestows favor and honor. No good thing does he withhold from those who walk uprightly."

Psalm 84:11

Do you desire God's best? If so, you have a part to play. The scripture says,*"No good thing does God withhold from His children."* I believe this sentence represents God's best! Doesn't this sound great? Are you ready to reap this 100 fold reward? If so, don't miss the next two words; *"If you want God's best you have to walk uprightly."*

What does this mean? Walking in an upright spirit calls for a consistent commitment to Christ and His word. God's best doesn't come when you make a vow before the Lord one week and forget about your faith the next. Reaping the best requires daily diligence and an undivided heart regarding your devotion to God.

Are you walking in an upright manner? The word upright refers to a persons character. No one is perfect but you can be pleasing to the perfect one by being obedient to His precepts. When God asks you to do something; Are you quick to obey or slow to listen?

If you want God's best, you have to give Him your best. He doesn't desire to withhold any good thing from you. He wants you to have the best of the best. So, don't you settle for anything less. "*For the Lord is a sun and shield; the Lord bestows favor and honor. No good thing does he withhold from those who walk uprightly.*"

May God bless you with His best both now and forevermore in Jesus name I pray. May we keep believing for the best!

Step to Start Strong:

Don't settle for God's Second Best

OCTOBER 31.

After Easter Intentions

"And when he had apprehended Peter, he put him in prison, and delivered him to four quadrants of soldiers to keep him; intending after Easter to bring him forth to the people."

Acts 12:4

Hear me; God has big, big plans for your life. They are exceedingly and abundantly more than you could ever ask or think. His plan is to prosper you and not to harm you; plans to give you a hope and a bright, bright future. This is so true. However, Satan has a plan for you too. His plan is to steal your joy, kill your ambition and destroy your dreams. He's the author of confusion, the backbone of bitterness and the Father of all Lies. This is his plan; to stop the masterplan that God has written for your life.

At least this is what happened to Simon Peter. It was the week of the Passover Celebration for the first century church. King Herod, a type of Satan in scripture, just beheaded James for sharing his faith. Who was next on the hit list? You said it,

Simon Peter. His goal was to completely eradicate the fiery faith of these so-called Christ followers. Peter's life was now in grave danger. He was placed in the inner prison of a dark dungeon and the scripture says that Herod had planned to bring him out after Easter for public trial. This was his *after easter intentions;* To keep stealing, killing and destroying the life of every disciple. His thinking was this; Let the church celebrate Passover and when life gets back to normal, I will continue my killing spree. See, Satan has a plan but God's plan is greater. We read how Simon Peter was miraculously delivered from the devil for one reason; because the church was earnestly praying for him. (Acts 12:5) This was a divine disruption.

So, don't be distracted by the devil's devices. We know what His intentions are after easter but what are your after Easter intentions? Are you planning to go back to life as normal or do you have a desire for change. Do you have a drive for more of God or are you ok with where you are spiritually? I say, let's continue the celebration! Let's change from glory to glory and faith to faith. We've come way too far to go back now. I pray God's plan would come to pass in your life in Jesus name. Place your faith in Him today. There's so much more in store for you if you don't give up!

Step to Start Strong:

Believe for a Divine Disruption

NOVEMBER 1.

HANG TEN

"If you faint in the day of adversity, Your strength is small."

Proverbs 24:10

Surfers use a term called *Hang Ten.* In order to do this, the surfer has to position the surfboard where the tail end of the board is covered by the wave. This process produces great pressure on the backside of the board which allows the surfer to walk freely to the front without flipping over. To keep from wiping out, the surfer will go as far as he can go and *"Hang all Ten of His Toes over the Edge."* This is hanging ten or what I like to call hanging tough.

The Bible gives us great insight about the waves of pressure that come in this life. Pressure can bog you down or it can cause you to rise to the top. It all depends on how you deal with it. For in this world, you will have trouble but take courage because Jesus has overcome the world. (John 6:33) The Bible is your surfboard. It will keep you afloat during times of adversity and stress. So hang tough to the truth of God's word. Don't give up. Don't allow the pressures of the world to push you away from God. Let pressure push you to prayer. People who worry can actually be the greatest prayer warriors if they will just learn to channel their thoughts in the right direction. Are you a worrier or a warrior? It's your choice. Every time you feel the waves of the world crashing all around you, just hang ten. Walk to the fore-front of God's word and ride the wave all the way to the shore; right into the loving arms of Jesus. This is where we want to be anyway.

Step to Start Strong:

Hang Ten

NOVEMBER 2.

GRAND CENTRAL STATION

"For though we live in the world, we do not wage war as the world does. The weapons we fight with are not the weapons of the world. On the contrary, they have divine power to demolish strongholds. We demolish arguments and every pretension that sets itself up against the knowledge of God, and we take captive every thought to make it obedient to Christ."

2nd Corinthians 10:3-5

The battlefield for every believer begins in the mind. Unfortunately, weapons of mass destruction cannot shut the mouth of the Satan. If so, he would no longer be a threat to the church. Being a spiritual being, he is unharmed by our physical retribution. So, there must be another way to overcome his schemes and strategies. How can we win the war over our enemy?

The scripture says, *"we disarm the devil when we take every thought "captive" and bring it under the obedience of Christ."* We win the war in our personal spiritual walk when we watch over our thought life.

Our mind is like Grand Central Station. All day long, we have hundreds and for some thousands of thoughts traveling through our mind at a rapid pace. What train we decide to board mentally will ultimately determine our final destination and state of well-being.

Overall, our goal is to be transformed by the renewing of our mind. When a train pulls up trying to lead you down the wrong track, turn your back and let it fly on bye. Don't lose you train of thought today. Keep your mind focused on Christ and the plans He has for your life. Stop looking in the rearview mirror of past failures and defeats. Fix your eyes on the hope that you are alive in Jesus Christ. All-aboard!

Step to Start Strong:

Train your thoughts to Think like Christ

NOVEMBER 3.

THE PROMISES OF GOD

"For no matter how many promises God has made, they are "Yes" in Christ. And through Him the "Amen" is spoken by us to the glory of God."

2nd Corinthians 1:20

Has anybody ever told you they would do something and they didn't do it? Sure they have and you've done the exact same thing to somebody else but not God. God is not like a man who says one thing and does another; In essence, He cannot lie. For no matter how many promises He has made in His word, they are "Yes" in Christ Jesus. This means if you place all of your trust in Jesus Christ the promises of God will start to come to pass in your life. Since God is a promise keeper, this makes us promise reapers.

Charles Spurgeon puts it this way; *Get a promise every day and take it with you wherever you go. Mark it, learn it, and inwardly digest it. Don't do as some men do-who, out of Christian duty, read a chapter every morning, and they read one as long as your arm without understanding it at all. Instead, take out some choice text and pray for the Lord to remind you of it during the day.* Do as Luther says: *"When I get hold of a promise, I look upon it as I would a fruit tree. I think, there hangs the fruit above my head, and if I would get it, I must shake the tree to and fro. In the same way, I take a promise and meditate on it. I shake it to and fro and sometimes the mellow fruit falls into my hand. At other times, the fruit is less ready to fall, but I never give up until I get it. I shake and shake all day long. I turn the text over and over again and at last, the fruit drops down and my soul is comforted with it."*

May we approach the promises of God with the same attitude because they will not fail if we faint not.

Let God's promises shine on your problems today.

Step to Start Strong:

Find a Promise for every Problem

NOVEMBER 4.

FRUIT-TESTING

"But the fruit of the Spirit is love, joy, peace,
forbearance, kindness, goodness, faithfulness,
gentleness and self-control. Against such things
there is no law."

Galatians 5:22-23

Abraham Lincoln said, *"It's not the years of your life that count, it's the life in your years."* What a profound statement! What kind of life do you want to live? Some people live a long life but live it for themselves. Others live a short life but their legacy lives on forever. So it was with our Lord & Savior Jesus Christ. Scholars say, He lived 33 years but we still stand in awe of His life and study His teaching today. Why? Jesus lived His life in view of eternity because He knew eternity is what matters most.

It amazes me the amount of people who care nothing about the next life. This is the million dollar question: *Where will you spend eternity?* I don't know? Well, if I were you I would try to figure it out! Google is great for finding answers, Siri is fast and genius for most information but the two of these cannot help you when it comes to eternity. Only Christ can.

Let the Life of Christ be your compass. Let the Holy Spirit be your tour guide. Let the Fruit of the Spirit be found in your life. By living this way, you will leave a lasting legacy and your years will be full of the life. *For the Fruit of the Sprit is Love, Joy, Peace, Patience, Kindness, Goodness, Gentleness, Faithfulness & Self-Control.*

How do you know if you are bearing spiritual fruit? Place your name in front of each fruit: John is Love. John is Joyful. John is Peaceful? And so on…

Give it a try? Test yourself to see if your fruit is ripe. If not, make some changes and ask God to help to become like Christlike.

Step to Start Strong:

Test your Spiritual Fruit

NOVEMBER 5.

RISE OF CHRISTIANITY

"Of the increase of His government and peace; There will be no end."

Isaiah 9:7

The first century church was birthed on the Day of Pentecost when the Holy Spirit was poured out upon 120 believers in the upper room. This transference of power from Heaven to earth compelled the church to reach out and love those in their community and beyond. Christianity quickly spread across Judea and eventually made its way to the Roman Empire. Acts 2:41 says that, *"God added to their number daily those who were being saved."* Everyday someone decided to make Jesus Lord of their life and the cycle has never stopped. Christianity is still on the rise. The 120 has multiplied to over 2.5 billion people with Christianity representing over a third of the world's population. There are more Christians alive today than any other time in History. God is fulfilling His promise as He keeps pouring out His spirit upon all flesh. (Joel 2)

The best part? You get to be a part of a Great End Time Revival! Jesus is coming back soon and He wants to empower you to bring in a harvest of souls. Yes, you; Everyday is an opportunity to advance the Kingdom of God. Leonard Ravenhill said, *"the opportunity of a lifetime must be seized during the lifetime of the opportunity."* Yes, we are living in perilous times but revival never breaks out during the best of times. Revival breaks out when people of God are pressed to pray. So lift your eyes unto hills today, help is on the way. Jesus chose you to re-present Him to your generation. You don't have to do it alone. He wants to be your ever-present help in time of need. Let your Christ arise among you this year! Christianity is still the fasting growing religion in the world and it always will be if we do what we are called to do.

Step to Start Strong:

Let Christ Rise Among You

NOVEMBER 6.

THE SPIRIT OF PRAYER

"Watch and pray so that you will not fall into temptation. The spirit is willing, but the flesh is weak."

Matthew 26:41

In the words of Jonathan Edwards, *"Prayer is as natural as an expression of faith as breathing is to life; and to say a man lives a life of faith, and yet lives a prayerless life, is every bit as inconsistent and incredible as to say that a man lives without breathing."*

Charles Finney was equally expressive about this topic 100 years later. This was his analysis: *"The lack of prayer is evidence of a backslidden heart. When the love of Christ remains fresh in the soul, the indwelling Spirit of Christ will reveal Himself as the Spirit of grace and supplication. He will instill strong desires in the soul for the salvation of sinners and the sanctification of saints. He will often make intercessions in them, with great longings, strong crying and tears, with groaning that cannot be uttered in words, for those things that are according to the will of God. If the spirit of prayer departs, it is a sure indication of a backslidden heart, for while the first love of a Christian continues he is sure to be drawn by the Holy Spirit to wrestle much in prayer."*

Do these words describe your current situation? Are you back-slidden in your heart? Is prayer an unknown language in your life? If so, seek forgiveness today; Ask God to restore you to your first love. Open your mouth and begin to pray. God is the only one who can satisfy your souls desire. If your spirit is willing but your flesh is weak, slip down on your knees this morning and begin cry out to God in worship. Don't hurry. Just wait. By doing so, times of refreshing will come from the Lord. It's His promise. We need God to release *"The Spirit of Prayer"* upon His people in this hour. May it be rebirthed in the modern day church.

Step to Start Strong:

Receive the Spirit of Prayer

NOVEMBER 7.

MOVED WITH COMPASSION

"Now a leper came to Him and begged Him on his knees saying, "If You are willing, You can make me clean." Then Jesus, moved with compassion, stretched out His hand and touched him, and said to him, "I am willing; be cleansed." As soon as He had spoken, immediately the leprosy left him, and he was cleansed."

Mark 1:40-42

True compassion demands action. When we study the life and ministry of Jesus Christ, we see a distinct model of love and empathy toward humanity. You never see the word compassion coupled in scripture without a corresponding action. Jesus was filled with compassion because of His connection to His Heavenly Father. For example, His love overflowed into the life of a leper and He healed Him instantaneously. Compassion was the motivating force that moved the hand of God across the earth. Compassion hit the heart of Christ when He saw the 5,000 sitting on a hillside without anything to eat. What did He do? He multiplied a little boys bag lunch and sent everyone away satisfied. Later, He looked across the city of Jerusalem with tears flooding His face because His people were like sheep without a shepherd. Indeed, true compassion was at the core of the ministry of Jesus Christ.

The Greek word for compassion is *"splagchnizomai."* (It's way easier to write than it is to say:) But it literally means *"to yearn in the bowels; to feel deep sympathy and at best to be moved to action."* Compassion is way different from concern. The Biblical word for compassion means *"to be moved in the deepest part of your being."* In fact, *"to say that you care and do nothing is to really say that you do not care at all."* Christlike compassion demands a step of action.

Do you want to know what the will of God is for your life? Find a need and fill it. This is how Jesus lived His life. His love for humanity permeated His heart in such a way that He could not turn a cold cheek. The leper asked, *"Lord, are you willing to help me?"* And Jesus said, *"I am,"* and His answer has never changed. He is the Great I AM.

However, this question remains relevant, *"Are you willing?"* Will you allow the Lord to use you? Yes, there's an overwhelming need in the world that can cause a callousness of heart but I always say, *"you can't help everyone but you can help someone."* Be moved with the compassion of Jesus Christ today. The world is waiting for someone to care.

Step to Start Strong:

Be Moved with Compassion

NOVEMBER 8.

POWER RELATIONSHIPS

"Two is better than one."

Ecclesiastes 4:9

People are like elevators. They will take you up or they will take you down. The Apostle Paul put it this way, *"Bad company corrupts good character." (1st Cor. 15:33)* The people you allow into your life hold the power to prosper you or to keep you from fulfilling your purpose. Jesus understood this principle; There were hundreds of people in the outer court of His life. Everyone was pushing and pulling to be a part of His ministry. However, *"He knew the heart of man." (John 2:24))* He only took 12 individuals into the inner chambers of His life. This is Discipleship 101. People come and people go. You can't be best friends with everybody. Embrace who the Lord has led into your life and let humility allow you to learn from one another.

For example, at the beginning of every year, I pray this prayer; *"Lord, strengthen my current relationships and help me to birth new ones."* Why would I pray such a prayer? Because I have learned a principle; *"When the Lord wants to use me or bless me, He brings somebody into my life."* Since the beginning of time, God has used people to bless people. This is why the enemy is working overtime to destroy your family, friends and ministry; because he knows if he can bring division within your relationships he can remove the bridge of blessing from your life. The same is equally true; *"when Satan wants to distract you or deter you from your destiny, He will bring someone into your life."* This is why we should be good gatekeepers of who we allow into the inner circle of our lives. Someone said, show me your 5 best friends and I will show you the next 5 years of your life. Who are you 5 best friends? Who do you follow? Who has the greatest influence in your life? What relationships need to be mended? Which ones need to be suspended? It's worthy to think through today.

Pray this prayer with me: *"Lord, strengthen my current relationships by your grace and help me to birth new ones for your glory, In Jesus Name. I need to be in right relationship with you and your people."*

Step to Start Strong:

Be in Right Relationships

NOVEMBER 9.

STRUGGLING WITH SIN

"Direct my footsteps according to your word; let no sin rule over me."

Psalm 119:133

Sin is crouching at the doorstep of your soul and it desires to overtake you. What took years to build can be destroyed with one hasty decision. It happens all the time. One politician falls into a ponzy scheme. Another pastor embezzles money. A husband commits adultery. Some student succumbs to peer pressure and starts living an alternate lifestyle. The sin cycle never stops and no one is spared from its effect. So where do we find hope and who do we turn to for help? I think this short discourse from the Apostle Paul's struggle with sin will shine some light on the subject: Let's Read Romans 7:13-25 in the Message Version

> *"Sin simply did what sin is so famous for doing: using the good as a cover up to tempt me to do what would finally destroy me. By hiding within God's good commandment, sin did far more mischief than it could ever*

> *have done on its own. I can anticipate the response that is coming: "I know that all God's commands are spiritual, but I'm not. Isn't this also your experience?" Yes,. I'm full of myself—after all, I've spent a long time in sin's prison. What I don't understand about myself is I decide one way, but then I act another, doing things I absolutely despise. So if I can't be trusted to figure out what is best for myself and then do it, it becomes obvious that God's command is necessary. But I need something more! For if I know the law but still can't keep it, and if the power of sin within me keeps sabotaging my best intentions, I obviously need help! I realize that I don't have what it takes. I can will it, but I can't do it. I decide to do good, but I don't really do it; I decide not to do bad, but then I do it anyway. My decisions, such as they are, don't result in actions. Something has gone wrong deep within me and gets the better of me every time. It happens so regularly that it's predictable. The moment I decide to do good, sin is there to trip me up. I truly delight in God's commands, but it's pretty obvious that not all of me joins in that delight. Parts of me covertly rebel, and just when I least expect it, they take charge. I've tried everything and nothing helps. I'm at the end of my rope. Is there no one who can do anything for me? Isn't that the real question? Thank God! The answer is that Jesus Christ can and will. He acted to set things right in this life of contradictions where I want to serve God with all my heart and mind, but am pulled by the influence of sin to do something totally different."*

Where do you find hope? Where do you find Help? Where do you find deliverance from sin? You can only find it in one place; In the grace that comes with a personal relationship with Jesus Christ.

<u>Step to Start Strong</u>:

Stop Struggling with Sin and Surrender

NOVEMBER 10.

Mere Motivation

"The way of the righteous is like the light of dawn. It grows brighter and brighter until it is full daylight."

Proverbs 4:18

Notice the pathway of the righteous grows brighter and brighter, not darker and dimmer. Yes, at times, we have to walk through the valley of the shadow of death but it's just a shadow. You can choose to stop in the middle of your mess and build your own theology around it or you can make up your mind to keep marching through the valley and end up in pleasant places. No more excuses. Excuses are the crutches for the uncommitted. There's always a reason to quit. Defy the odds today. Rise above your circumstances, release your potential that dwells on the inside of you and remember, God's promises don't have expiration dates. You can do anything you put your mind to.

Ray Crock was 54 years old when He left His sales job in Chicago to start a cheeseburger chain called McDonalds. Who recognizes the Golden Arches? Everybody does! Colonel Sanders was 65 when he started KFC, the finger licking good fried chicken. Better yet, Moses was 80, Abraham & Sarah were 100 and so many others in the Bible kept the faith and finished the race despite sudden delays and dire circumstances. The Scripture says, *"God's mercies are new everyday."* What are you going to do? Magnify your problems or magnify your God? It's all about perspective. You're living in the best years of your life. If the Lord is the light of your salvation; whom shall you fear? Its time to arise and shine for the glory of God. Can you feel faith after this short exhortation? This is Mere Motivation! The victory is already yours! Take it today by faith.

Step to Start Strong:

Stay Motivated

NOVEMBER 11.

Cry out to Jesus

"Then Moses cried out to the LORD, "What am I going to do with these people!"

Exodus 17:4

Whenever you walk through the wilderness of life, whatever is in your heart will eventually come out. The Bible says, the children of Israel complained during times of trial but Moses, the man of God, cried out to the Lord. There's such a big difference! Do you have a complaining spirit or does your spirit cry out to God? Your answer will determine your destiny. When was the last time you complained? If you don't remember ask your spouse or your best friend. Ok; When was the last time you really cried out to God and I don't mean during a tragic event. When was the last time you cried out to God just because you were desperate for His divine touch? Moses *"cried out to God"* on a regular basis because He knew the one who called Him was the one who could keep Him. Abraham, Isaac and Jacob all tapped into the same vein. *"When the righteous cry out, the Lord hears them and He delivers them from all of their troubles"* (Psalm 34:17). Complaining will cripple your call but crying out to God will cover you with fresh faith to finish the race!

Luke 6:45 says, *"A good man brings good things out of the good stored up in his heart, and an evil man brings evil things out of the evil stored up in his heart. For out of the abundance of the heart so a man speaks."*

Don't complain. When you do, what you're really saying is; *"God, what you've given me is not good enough."* I'm discontent and dissatisfied. May this condition be for from the church! What we need is a fresh baptism of gratefulness that results in a heart felt cry of praise to God.

Step to Start Strong:

Cry out to God

NOVEMBER 12.

What's in your House?

"A certain woman of the wives of the sons of the prophets cried out to Elisha, saying, "Your servant my husband is dead, and you know that your servant feared the Lord. And the creditor is coming to take my two sons to be his slaves." So Elisha said to her, "What shall I do for you? Tell me, what do you have in the house?" And she said, "Your maidservant has nothing in the house but a jar of oil."

2nd Kings 4:1-2

In Biblical times, if you didn't pay your bills, a creditor could come and enslave your children so they would have to work to pay off the debts of the parents. This is what was happening in this story. A widow lady had lost her husband and the creditors were coming to her house to capture her two sons to work and pay off the shortcomings of the previous generation. Symbolically, what we see here is the spirit of the world trying to come into our houses, our churches and our schools to lure our kids away from their hope and future. The spirit of the world boldly declares everyday, *"I'm going to enslave your children!"* Culture is trying chain them and bind them to all kinds of addictions so they will be confused mentally, physically & sexually. It's happening all around us! The enemy is tearing the family apart. Why is this so? Because He knows we will never experience revival in God's House until we start having revival in our own houses. If the devil can divide and destroy the parent-child relationship, the overall health of the church doesn't have a chance. In scripture, God gives us clarity on how to keep the next generation in a place of freedom. The Prophet Elisha poses this question to the widow, "What's in your house? Whatever is in your house will be the deterring factor of freedom for you, your kids and your grandkids. What you allow in your house will help you or hinder you. You can't control what happens in the world but all of us can control what comes into our houses. *The widow woman represents someone who is in covenantal relationship with God but at the same time they have lost their first-love.* Remember, she had lost her husband. The one she loved. However, the prophet highlighted the only thing she had left. *Elisha said, "What's in your house? And the woman said, "all I have is a jar of oil."* Oil in the Bible represents the Holy Spirit. Whenever you read oil, wind, water, wine, fire, cloud or dove, you know the Lord is referencing the Holy Spirit. So, I would like to submit to you today that the only thing that can preserve a generation and ultimately, set a person free is the power of the Holy Spirit. In essence, this is His presence. David said, *"take anything from me O'God, but don't take your presence."* Moses said, *"what else will distinguish us of from the rest of the people in the world? None other than your presence God!"* The presence of God was already in the House and His presence of God set this lady and her family free. End of Story! So this leaves us with a question: What's in your house? All the widow had was an empty vessel and a little bit of oil. If this is all you have left; this is all you need to gain the victory! Yes, emptiness and holiness! This two ingredients are prerequisites for God's power rest upon you and your family.

Step to Start Strong:

Guard your House

NOVEMBER 13.

JEHOVA SHAMMAH

"The name of the city from that day shall be; The Lord is there."

Ezekiel 48:35

One of the covenantal names of the Lord is Jehovah Shammah meaning, *"The Lord is There."* According to scripture, there are three types of presence: the omni-presence, the inner presence and the manifest presence. Omni means ALL so a good working definition of the omni-presence is this: *"All of God, everywhere, All the time."* David said in Psalms 139:7, *"Where can I go from your spirit? Where can I flee from your presence? If I go to the Heavens, you are there! If I make my bed in the depths of Hell. You are there?"* What He meant was this; Our God is everywhere!

However, there's another facet of His presence. In John 14, Jesus said, *"I am with you but when I leave, He will be in you"* speaking of the Holy Spirit. God is everywhere but to be more intimate, He sent His precious Holy Spirit to reside in every born-again believer. This is what the church calls the *Inner presence.*

Lastly, I want you to notice the *Manifest Presence.* The word *manifest* means, *"to make known."* Moses made this statement to the Lord in Exodus 33:14, *"If your presence doesn't go with us, do not send us up from here. What else will distinguish us from all of the other people on the face of the earth?"* What was He talking about? If God is always with you; how could He not go with you wherever you go? What Moses was really referring to was the manifest presence of God. How will the world know that He is the one true and living God? When He manifests Himself among us! Moses' statement alluded to the fact that He refused to go through life without allowing the Lord to manifest Himself in His midst. Most people don't understand this part of the trinity. They know God is everywhere and they know His Spirit lives inside of every saint but they neglect the fact that God wants to reveal His glory in the earth. Do you desire *"to make God known?"* If so, Jehovah Shammah will show up and show off in your life. Don't be ashamed of the Gospel. Share it. The Gospel is the power of God unto salvation. I hope this helps your understanding of the presence for God. My prayer is that He would manifest Himself among you today in a very special way.

Step to Start Strong:

Practice the Presence of God

NOVEMBER 14.

The After Glow

"When Moses came down from Mount Sinai with the two tablets of the Testimony in his hands, he was not aware that his face was radiant because he had spoken with the Lord."

Exodus 34:29

Before he had quite turned 16 years old, William Jay began preaching. He is said to have delivered no less than 1,000 sermons by the time he reached 21 years of age. Perhaps the very thing that drew the people to listen was the afterglow of God's glory emanating from him after spending time in God's presence. Here is an excerpt of one of his famous sermons. It will do you well to read his revelation slowly and meditate upon it:

"Resemblance to God results from our intimacy with Him. "Evil communications corrupt good manners." But while a companion of fools shall be destroyed, he that walks with wise men shall be wise. We soon assume the manners and absorb the spirit of those with

whom we are most familiar, especially if the individual is distinguished as someone we esteem and dearly love. Upon this principle, the more we have to do with God, the more we shall grow into His likeness and "be followers of Him as dear children." When Moses descended from communion with God, his face shone; and although he was not aware of the luster himself, the people could not look directly at him because of the glory of his countenance, and he was compelled to hide his face under a veil. The Christian, too, may be unaware of such radiating brilliance; but it will appear unto all men-who will take note that he has been with Jesus."

How many around you every day are suffering in darkness? Remember, light dispels darkness. Jesus is the Light of the world. The more time you spend in His presence, the more His light illuminates in you which will ultimately shine onto those still walking in darkness. You are a city set on a hill. Let your light shine ever so brightly that the world may see your good works and glorify your Father in Heaven.

Step to Start Strong:

Let your Light Shine Bright

NOVEMBER 15.

Leading Yourself

"Follow my example, as I follow the example of Christ."

1st Corinthians 11:1

Every person is a leader. The question remains: Are you leading others in the right direction or the wrong direction. Statistics say, even the most introverted individuals influence over 20,000 people in their lifetime. I would describe this as leadership. John Maxwell defines leadership in one word; *"influence."* Do you desire to influence others in the right way? Do you want to be a good leader? If so, you must learn this; In order to be a good leader, you must lead yourself well. The toughest person to lead is you. It's easy to tell everybody else what to do. Its even easier to point out the flaws in your family and fellow church members. However, it's hard to examine yourself and make changes accordingly. So, here's a few keys to lead yourself well:

1) In order to be a good leader; you must be a good follower. Only those who follow well, can lead well? The Apostle Paul said, *"Follow my example because I follow Christ."* Are you submissive to the leading of the Holy Spirit? Do you feel His impression on your heart and quickly abandon your plans? Secondly, Do you easily submit to authority? Do you follow the guidelines that have instituted around your life for a reason? Living a life of submissiveness will keep you safe spiritually and ultimately lead you in the right direction.

2) Secondly, in order to be a good leader, you have to have accountability. Influential people know a secret? They can't trust themselves. This is why it is important for you to keep people around you that will be brutally honest with you. Harry Truman once told a story about a friend who approached him after he won the presidency. He said this, *"Now from here forward, everybody is going to tell you how great a man you are but remember, we know it's not true."* The only one who is great is God. He deserves the glory and honor for all of our accolades and accomplishments. Accountability will keep your character in check.

3) Lastly, never ask anyone to do something that you are not willing to do yourself. Jesus Christ modeled this principle perfectly. Scholars call it *"Servant Leadership."* Your actions speak louder than words. Lead by example and your impact will reach eternity. Ask yourself this question: Would you follow you? If you're not willing to follow yourself, why would you expect anyone else to do so? Follow Christ! Keep Accountability! And Be the Best at Servanthood!

Step to Start Strong:

Lead Yourself Well

NOVEMBER 16.

HOUSEHOLD SALVATION

"and your children I will save."

Isaiah 49:25

During one my devotions on international soil, I came across this simple but powerful promise in scripture. Isaiah prophesied long ago that God would *"contend with those who contend with us and our children He would save."* Now, I don't know who I'm talking to today but don't miss this; God said, *"your children He will save!"* Do you believe the word of the Lord? If so, stop worrying and start worshipping! I hear the Lord saying, *What they are doing is not who they are!* God has heard your prayer and the day of their salvation is closer than you think. *"If you trained your child up in the way that he or she should go; even when they are old he or she will not depart from it."* (Proverbs 22:6) This is good news! Stand on this promise today and refuse to be moved! God says, *He will save your children.*

As for me, I wrote my childrens name beside this verse in my Bible and put down the date. God's word never comes back void. He will save our kids from their sins. From now on, may we not waiver concerning what we see. The truth is; *"Today is the day of salvation for you and your whole household."*

Acts 16:31 says, *"Believe on the Lord Jesus Christ, and you will be saved, you and your household."*

<u>Step to Start Strong</u>:

Believe for Household Salvation

NOVEMBER 17.

The Secret Place

"He that dwelleth in the secret place of the most High shall abide under the shadow of the Almighty."

Psalm 91:1

Last Tuesday morning at 4:29am, I walked out of my house and headed to the State of Telegana in Central India. By the time we caught three planes and two taxi's, we arrived at our hotel Wednesday night at 10:30pm. A total travel time of over 42 hours with not mush sleep. After I took a shower and got settled in, there was only one thing left to do; *Go to the Secret Place.* I got down on my knees, opened my Bible and began to read some of my favorite scriptures to stir myself up in the spirit. As I remembered the goodness of God, His manifest presence began to fill the room. If you read my daily devotional thoughts, you'll remember a few weeks ago, I wrote a short teaching on the three types of presence; the omni-presence, the inner-presence and the manifest-presence of God. The word manifest means *"to make known."* I have learned after you have traveled to an unfamiliar place, in a distant land, it is vitally important to have the affirmation of your Heavenly Father. As I prayed, His presence got stronger and stronger as He wrapped His loving arms around my tired and weary body. I could literally feel the tangible presence of God as I wept and worshipped Him for His glory and majesty. This is all a son or daughter ever needs to know; that they are loved, forgiven and accepted. This truth will endue you with great power to climb the highest mountain and cross the widest sea. In this moment, my soul found rest in the God of my salvation and I knew I was ready to stand and minister on His behalf.

Don't miss this: *"This is where our strength comes from; when nobody else is around in the stillness and solitude of the Secret Place."* If we will take time to seek His face privately, He will manifest Himself on our behalf publicly. Knowing that He is with me is all I need to know. If He doesn't go with me; I don't even wanna go to the grocery store much less the other side of the world.

The Psalmist said this way, "*He that dwelleth in the secret place of the most High shall abide under the shadow of the Almighty*." Where is your favorite place to pray and worship? Go there today.

Scripture calls it, *"The Secret Place."*

Step to Start Strong:

Find a Secret Place

NOVEMBER 18.

Running Out of Time

"Make the most of every opportunity for the days are evil."

Ephesians 5:16

One day, I went for a run during my lunch break as I do quite often to get away from work. It was a beautiful sunny afternoon with a slight breeze to my back as I coasted around our community. When I turned the corner, to my surprise, a pack of dogs pounced off my neighbors front porch and started running at me as if I were a pork-chop. You know the feeling. What else do you do? Your heart pounds, you pray and you run as fast as you can! Don't tell anyone but this is exactly what I did. Thankfully, four of the dogs stopped at the ditch but the last little guy darted out into the road. It was too late. An old man driving a truck and trailer timed it all wrong as he ran over the families best friend; right in front of me. Grievingly, the whole family was sitting on the porch and watched it all unfold. The little girl hysterically sprinted across the yard screaming with her mother right behind her. It was an unpleasant picture. The elderly gentleman kindly pulled over to the shoulder of the street. By that time, the mother was cradling the little puppy in her arms as we walked over together to give our condolences. With only a few breaths left, I had to ask; *"Anyway I can I pray?"* In one minute, I shared the Gospel in my prayer and asked the Lord to comfort this broken-hearted family. When I said, *"Amen,"* they wrapped the puppy in a sheet and walked away. I said, *"I'm so sorry ma'am,"* and the mom said, *"Thank you for stopping. It wasn't your fault."* I am telling you all this so I can tell what happened next; When the man and I walked back to his truck, I could see his nerves were shot and I knew in my spirit he wasn't saved. So, what did I do? I said, *"Sir can I ask you a question?'If you were that dog today and you died; do you know for sure if you would go to Heaven?* He gave me the All-American answer; *"Well, I've tried my best to be good all my life so I think so?"* With his heart being heavy, God prepared a freeway for me to share the story of salvation; So I did. As I talked about the love of God, the old man's eyes began to water. With quivering lips, He said, *"Sir, thanks for stopping. I want to make it right with God today."* I said, *"Good answer."* Let's pray. All I can say is, *"we're running out of time."* Theologically, I'm not sure if all dogs go to Heaven but I know its not a guarantee for all men. Yes, we're all created by God but we're not all children of God. Yes, everyone is born of flesh but not everyone is born of the spirit. 1st John 5:13 says, *"I have written this to you who believe in the name of the Son of God, so that you may know you have eternal life."* It is important that you KNOW that you, your family and your friends are saved. It's the most important question you could ever ask yourself or anyone else. This is why the

Apostle Paul said, *"make the most of every opportunity for the days are evil."* Church; we're running out of time.

Step to Start Strong:

Make the Most of Every Opportunity

NOVEMBER 19.

PRAY FOR YOUR PASTOR

"And I will give you shepherds after my own heart, who will feed you with knowledge and understanding."

Jeremiah 3:15

Over the past fifteen years of being in christian leadership, I've the had the opportunity to serve under some mighty men and women of God who have influenced my life greatly. However, when you walk close with people, its inevitable; you see their flaws and guess what? They see yours too! So here's a quick reminder, Pastors are people and all people need prayer. I'll never forget this incident because it taught me a valuable lesson. There was a certain guy that I grew close to who wasn't walking in the purity and character that I was accustomed to for a minister. After some thought, I knew it wasn't my position to bring correction but as time passed, I noticed my heart starting to callous and my relationship with him started to spoil. In my mind, this was the reward for his unrighteousness as other relationships started to suffer as well. After all, the scripture says, *"your sin will find you out."* So, I just waited for this to be fulfilled.

However, one year ended and another year began so we celebrated. As always, we began our 21 Day Fast as a first fruit offering unto the Lord. It's the best way to consecrate yourself and clearly hear the voice of the Lord. So, after a few days of not eating, I pulled out of my driveway headed to work with a complaining spirit. Now, I know this has never happen to you but this is what I was complaining about; *church people.* What was I complaining about? The minister who was living a live of sin and as quick as one, two, three; the Holy Spirit checked me in my spirit; *"When was the last time you prayed for him?" Ummm...*

To be honest, I could not remember the last time I prayed for him. What did I have to do? Sure, I repented right then and there and said, "I'm so sorry Lord." From now on, I'll pray for Him. Do you wanna know what happened? He didn't change but I did. Prayer changed my perspective before it changed my situation. Ultimately, prayer gives you the grace to love the unlovable, the faith to do what you really don't want to do and it even releases hope when you don't see any progress in people.

From that day forward, I have made it a holy habit to pray for my spiritual authority. I do my best to pray for my spouse, my parents, my family, my employers and especially my pastor and pastor friends.

Seriously, when was the last time you *"really"* prayed for your Pastor? Take a few minutes to pray for him every Sunday morning as he prepares to minister to you and your family. Pray a blessing over the one who blesses you every week. Take time right now to pray for your Pastor.

Step to Start Strong:

Pray for your Spiritual Authority

NOVEMBER 20.

Leaning on My Beloved

"Who is that coming up from the wilderness, leaning on her beloved? Under the apple tree I awakened you."

Song of Solomon 8:5

Song of Solomon is read on the Sabbath during the Passover Feast. This marks the beginning of the grain harvest and commemorates the Exodus from Egypt for the Israelites. Scripturally, the Song of Songs is unique in its celebration of intimate love. It gives the voices of two lovers, praising each other, yearning for each other and proffering invitations to enjoy. Jewish tradition reads the poem as an allegory of the relationship between God and Israel. However, Christian tradition, reads the poem as an allegory of Christ and His Bride. Despite the viewpoint, the issue remains the same; *God is explicitly in love with His children.* In fact, you are His Beloved and the Beloved is mine.

This is what Song of Songs 8:5 implies; *"Who is this coming up out of the wilderness?"* The wilderness represents a time of testing and trial but notice who is by your side? The Beloved. He's never left you nor forsaken you. No matter what's going on in your life this morning. Jesus Christ is our constant.

Are you leaning this morning? Do you feel lost in a world of pain and displeasure? If so, my message to you this today is this; *"you're not alone."* God is with you. Don't lean on your own understanding; Lean on the Lord. He loves you with an everlasting love. You will come out the wilderness because thou art with you.

Step to Start Strong:

Lean on the Lord

NOVEMBER 21.

GRACE, GRACE

"For who has despised the day of small things? You will bring it forth with grace, grace!"

Zechariah 4:6-10

This is a miracle formula that God wants to get deep into your spirit today. When you study the history of Zechariah, you'll discover the city of Jerusalem was in ruins during his day; the nation was unstable, families were in frantic, the city walls were broken down and the temple was utterly destroyed. Despite popular belief, the man of God said, *"Let's rebuild the House of God."* He didn't say, let me take care of my four and no more, He said, "As for me and my house, we're gonna build back the House of God. Now here's a Biblical principle, *"when you seek ye first the Kingdom of God and His righteousness, everything else will be added unto you."* (Matthew 6:33) So, He laid the foundation for the House of God. When He did so the enabling grace of God came upon His life to do what He could not do without it. When your life is laced with grace, you can make what is hard for others seem easy and effortless with God. However, as soon as He started the work a mountain popped up spiritually. Mountains represent anything that stands in the way of you fulfilling your God given destiny. So what does He do? He speaks to the mountain because He understands his authority as a child of God. Jesus teaches us this in Mark 11:22 to speak to our mountains! Zerubbabel obeys but in the midst of intense spiritual warfare the temple renovation ceases for 16 years. I can only imagine the doubt and depression in the mind of this man. Remember, God was the one who told him to start the work in the first place but just like many of us life happened. The job site looked like an abandoned western town with tumbleweeds blowing around. No fruit from your labor and no hope for the future. *However, what happens next changes everything.* The prophet shows up on the scene and says to,*"Go get the capstone."* Now the capstone is the final piece of the project. Now picture this; after 16 years of no progress, the prophet says to go get the final piece of the project but what does He have to lose? He picks up the capstone and the prophet says, *"to shout Grace, Grace to it!"* Another translation says, *"God bless it! God bless it!"* However, when Zerubbabel begins to shout grace and blessings to the temple of God something shifts and the Bible says, *"the people were awakened to work and the temple was rebuilt in a very short amount of time."* Here's the miracle formula: *When we give grace, God gives us grace.* When we bless others, God blesses us. Its inevitable. Grace and blessing bounce back off of whatever we are trying to build in our life and it enables us to finish the race. See, the capstone represents Jesus Christ. HE was the cornerstone that the builders rejected. What the prophet was implying is this: *"You've lost your focus. The reason why nothing is happening in the house of God is because Jesus is not being glorified."* So, Go grab a hold of God and give Him your undivided attention. Worship and adore Him. When you do so, a shift will take place in your spirit and you will reap what you sow. Do you believe it? If it happened for Zerubbabel it can happen for you. Fix your eyes on Jesus, He is the author and finisher of your faith. Give an extra amount of grace to everybody that crosses your path and get ready for the blessing. *Do not despise the day of small beginning; for the Lord rejoices when a work is begun.* He will complete the work that He started in you.

Step to Start Strong:

Shout Grace!

NOVEMBER 22.

THE CHOICE IS YOURS

"O foolish Galatians! This only I want to learn from you: Did you receive the Spirit by the works of the law, or by the hearing of faith? Are you so foolish? Having begun in the Spirit, are you now being made perfect by the flesh."

Galatians 3:1-3

Paul the apostle was having a difficult time with the Church in Galatia. They had received the truth, they were living for God, but for some reason they began to fall away. He was dealing with both the carnal man and the spiritual man. Notice how Andrew Murray differentiates between the two...

> *"I cannot with too much earnestness urge every Christian reader to learn well the two stages of the Christian. There are the carnal, and there are the spiritual; there are those who remain babes, and those who are full-grown men. There are those who come up out of Egypt, but then remain in the wilderness of a worldly life. The call to*

> *holiness, the call to cease from the life of wandering and murmuring, and enter into the rest of God, the call to the life of victory over every enemy and to the service of God in the land of promise, is not obeyed. They say it is too high and too hard. There are those who follow the Lord fully and enter the life of rest and victory. Let each of us find out where we stand, and taking earnest heed to God's warnings, with our whole heart press on to go all the length in following Jesus, in seeking to stand perfect and complete in all the will of God."*

Members of the church in Galatia had made a serious mistake. They had allowed the world's philosophy to weave its way into the fabric of their lives. Don't make the same mistake. Are you carnal or spiritual? The choice is yours.

Step to Start Strong:

Be a Person of Purity

NOVEMBER 23.

HEDGE OF PROTECTION

"Have You not put a hedge [of protection] around him and his house and all that he has, on every side? You have blessed the work of his hands [and conferred prosperity and happiness upon him], and his possessions have increased in the land."

Job 1:10

The Book of Job is the oldest book in the Bible. Scholars say, Job was the wealthiest man alive during his day. He was a very powerful man with great influence. His wealth was tied up in livestock with thousands of bulls, sheep and goats. Everyone knew who he was because of His prosperity but we also know he was a man who valued his relationship with the Lord. How do we know this? Because we read how Job offered up sacrifices to God morning and night. There was always blood on the family altar. He worshipped God with his whole heart and cared about his kids. In light of this truth, God had placed a hedge of protection around Job and everything under his authority. This hedge referred to angelic protection. Psalm 34:7 says, *"The angels of the Lord encamp around those who fear him, and he delivers them."* *Hebrews 1:14 says, "aren't angels ministering spirits sent to serve those who will inherit salvation?"* I believe this hedge was placed around this man's life because of the blood sacrifice that was applied to his heart and home on a daily basis. In the New Testament, the altar of God is the heart of man. When we apply the blood of Jesus to the doorpost of our spirit, angels are dispatched to protect and serve us. How do we apply the blood of Christ? By daily confession. This is why the greatest hindrance to the blessing and protection of God is unforgiveness. When we arbor unconfessed sin in our heart we open the door to the devil and destroy the supernatural hedge that has been placed around our lives. Notice the first thing Satan desired to destroy was Job's livestock. Satan hated the daily sacrifice. Why is this so? The Exodus story gives us some clarity into this subject: On the night of the Passover, God instructed the children of Israel to apply the blood of a pure and spotless lamb above the entryway to their home. This was the sign that stopped the death angel from harming anyone in their home. All over Egypt, you could hear the cries of helpless people who didn't take the time to apply the blood to their home and the repercussions fell upon their kids. However, for the children of God, the blood of the pure and spotless lamb stopped the destruction at the door! The presence of evil could not come into the home that had been consecrated and set apart by the blood. This is a powerful truth. Jesus Christ was the lamb that was slain for the sins of the world. Consecrate your home today. Confess your sins. Worship in the morning and at night. Apply the blood the Jesus, the perfect sacrifice. Confess the truth. Angels are all around you. Build a hedge around you and your family.

Step to Start Strong:

Plead the Blood of Jesus by Daily Confession

NOVEMBER 24.

HACKSAW RIDGE

"Therefore, He is able to save completely those who come to God through him, because he always lives to intercede for them."

<u>Hebrews 7:25</u>

One day, I was on a twelve hour flight back from Jerusalem and I was watching the real life story of Hacksaw Ridge. This was the day American forces stormed the nation of Japan during World War II. The plot was written after a man by the name of Desmond Doss. After nearly killing his brother while they were young and seeing His mother severely beaten by His father, He vowed to never use any weapons during His life. However, when war broke out in our nation, He couldn't stand to sit around and see all the other guys going to fight for our freedom. So what did He do? He enlisted himself to be a medic so he wouldn't have to bear arms in times of war. Of course, you could imagine the persecution and public scrutiny from other soldiers for such a decision. They beat him, laughed at him and even tried to throw him in prison. All the while, he stood his ground and never opened his mouth. When the day came for his platoon to go and fight in Okinawa, they approached the Hill of Hacksaw Ridge. Many American soldiers lost their life in this place. However, in the midst of mass destruction, there was a courageous soldier by the name of Desmond Doss, who chose not to kill, but to help his fellow man. History tells us, in the line of fire and in grave danger, he rescued seventy-five men and saved their lives. The part of the movie that moved my heart the most was what he prayed after each rescue. With bullets, bombs and blood all around him, He would bow his head and whisper these words, *"Heavenly Father, please help me to save just one more." Just one more!* And then he would fearlessly run back into enemy territory to save one more soul. Why did I tell you this? Because I believe with every ounce of my being that there is a God in Heaven who loves you and He sent His son into the world to do for you what you could not do for yourself. They laughed at Him, they mocked him and ultimately they threw him in prison for false accusations. However, he never opened his mouth. They impaled him on a tree for a public spectacle to see. When He breathed His last breath; He didn't say, *"I am finished!"* He said, *"It is finished!"* Meaning the price for our sins had been paid in full. Now, Jesus is sitting at the right hand of the Father saying, *"Help me save just one more." Just one more soul!* One more family member! One more backslidden teen ager! One more father and one more mother! One more co-worker and one more friend! May this be our prayer today as we step into the enemies territory; *"God, use me to save one more soul."* Make me fearless, make me courageous, Make me like Desmond Doss! A hero in the faith! In fact, Desmond

Doss became the first conscientious objector to be awarded the Medal of Honor for service above and beyond the call of duty during the Battle of Okinawa. May we do the same spiritually for our fellow man, Amen.

Step to Start Strong:

Lead One More Soul to Christ

NOVEMBER 25.

REWARD FOR FAITHFULNESS

"The things which you have heard from me in the presence of many witnesses, entrust these to faithful men who will be able to teach others also."

2nd Timothy 2:2

After the ascension of Christ in Acts Chapter 1, the disciples returned to Jerusalem to make preparations for the Festival of Pentecost. As they were praying in the upper room, the Apostle Peter stood up and quoted Psalm 69:25 concerning the betrayal of Judas, He said, *"May another take His place of leadership." Therefore it was necessary to choose one of the men who have been with us the whole time the Lord Jesus was living among us, beginning from John's baptism to the time when Jesus was taken up from us. For one of these must become a witness with us of his resurrection. So they nominated two men: Joseph (also known as Justus) and Matthias. Then they prayed, "Lord, you know everyone's heart. Show us which of these two you have chosen to take over this apostolic ministry, which Judas left to go where he belongs." Then they cast lots, and the lot fell to Matthias; so he was added to the eleven apostles.*

Notice the only qualification that it took to fill the spot of the 12th Apostle: the scripture says, *"choose one of the men who has been with us the whole time."* This is the definition of faithfulness; fidelity, reliable and staying true to the standard! Matthias was faithful a man. He followed Jesus everyday while He was alive. The Bible doesn't record Matthias performing any miracles, preaching any powerful sermons or doing anything that we would call spectacular. However, he was grafted into greatness for this one quality; faithfulness.

This principle proves a powerful point; showing up is more than half the battle. Presenting yourself to be used by God is what God is looking for. *Availability is more important in the Kingdom of God than man's ability.* What we need in this hour is men and women who will simply show up. If Matthias did anything right it was this; He was there. He was faithful. He showed up to serve, pray and freely give of himself. By doing so, Matthias earned a spot amongst the Holy Scripture and better yet; Revelation 21:14 says that, *"the wall around the Heavenly City called New Jerusalem bears the name of the 12 Apostles."* Matthias' faithfulness on earth made a permanent mark in eternity! How did this happen? By just showing up to pray! By following Jesus everyday! By being faithful my friend!

Indeed, Faithfulness releases the fruit of great reward.

<u>Step to Start Strong</u>:

Be Faithful in all Things

NOVEMBER 26.

BY FAITH

"By faith we understand."

Hebrews 11:3

Say this with me; *"Goodbye Fear. Good morning Faith."* The scripture says, *"By Faith, we understand."* It's not the other way around meaning we will never fully understand the walk of faith. Faith is not intellectual in nature. *"Faith is the assurance of things hoped for (divinely guaranteed), and the evidence of things not yet seen —faith comprehends as fact what cannot be experienced by the physical senses]. (Hebrews 11:1)* Just because you can't see something in the natural doesn't mean its not a reality in the spiritual world. This is how Jesus called Simon Peter the Rock before the Day of Pentecost even though he was unstable and carnal in his thinking. Real faith encourages the true calling of God's children while the spirit of fear cripples the call.

So, what lens are looking through today? Faith sees what most people cannot perceive.

This is why Christ is calling us *"to continually renew our mind by the washing of the word."* (Eph. 5:26) A renewed mind sees from a different perspective. A renewed mind will walk by faith and ultimately understand the times and seasons in the spirit. If the church is going to grow into greater dimensions of God's glory, we have to change the way we think. The old carnal way of thinking cannot contain the new wine of God's word. It will burst and cause the church the crumple in confusion and disarray.

So, how do we finish the race? By receiving a new measure of faith. The word repent literally means *"to change the way you think."* In order to receive anything from God, you have to repent saying my way didn't work, I'm ready to do your will O'God. The fear of walking by faith will never bear fruit. Therefore, don't let fear dictate the way you think. When you start walking by faith, you will soon understand why.

Furthermore, nothing is more liberating and life-changing than living totally and dependently upon God. Give it a try!

Here's a Point to Ponder: "How would your thinking change if nothing were impossible?"

Step to Start Strong:

Make the Supernatural the Natural

NOVEMBER 27.

WAKE-UP CALL

"For this reason He says, "Awake, o' sleeper, And arise from the dead, And Christ will shine upon you and give you light."

Ephesians 5:14

History isn't clear about the origin of a wake-up call but I can only imagine what it was like before cell phone service. You were suddenly startled out of your sleep by a scream from the bottom of the steps or even worse; the foot of the bed. Now to me, nothing is more disturbing than someone shouting when I am in a deep sleep. Also, if its up to me, I'm not using alarm clocks unless I have to. Most of the time, something on the inside of me tells me its time to roll out of bed and start my day. An internal alarm clock if you will.

And For this reason He says, "Awake, o' sleeper and rise from the dead." For what reason? The scripture beforehand says, "that God is going to make everything visible that is invisible" meaning whatever you are doing that no-one knows about will be brought to the light one day;

both good and bad. We will be held accountable for every idle word and every little deed done on secret. *(Matthew 12:36)* With this is mind, Jesus Christ is sending a wake-up call to the church.

There's a lot of people in the church today who have been lured to sleep by the wine of this world. It's evident that they are not watching the signs of the times. There is a lethargy, a passiveness—even a laziness—in some Christians. There is an apparent disconnect between their so-called spiritual lives and their real lives. Greg Laurie says, *"Instead of walking in the Spirit, some believers are sleepwalking."* It's time we wake up. We need revival of the Bible. The Apostle Paul says it this way, *"Be on your guard, don't fall asleep like the others. Stay alert and always be sober minded."* (1 Thessalonians 5:6).

Revelation 3:1-3 reiterates this point in closing; *"These are the words of Him who has the seven Spirits of God and the seven stars: 'I know your deeds; you have a name (reputation) that you are alive, but [in reality] you are dead. <u>Wake up</u>, and strengthen and reaffirm what remains [of your faithful commitment to Me], which is about to die; for I have not found [any of] your deeds completed in the sight of My God or meeting His requirements. So remember and take to heart the lessons you have received and heard. Keep and obey them, and repent [change your sinful way of thinking, and demonstrate your repentance with new behavior that proves a conscious decision to turn away from sin]. So then, if you do not wake up, I will come like a thief, and you will not know at what hour I will come to you."*

<u>Step to Start Strong</u>:

Wake up!

NOVEMBER 28.

RAPTURE READY

"Be dressed and ready for active service, and keep your lamps continuously burning."

Luke 12:35-40

Surely this morning, I say to you that Jesus Christ is coming back soon! Today could be the day! You don't know? Even in the early church; 2,000 years ago, the disciples greeted one another with the word, *"maranatha"* meaning *"The Lord is coming back soon." If it was soon in the first century, the world's time clock has to be coming to a close. There are many prophetic voices in the earth that believe we are in the last seconds of the last days. (Amos 3:2) So, what does this mean for me and you? Here are 3 thoughts:*

1) We need to GET READY: Jesus uses four word pictures in Luke 12:35-40 to emphasize the same point: To be ready for His return. He says *"to be dressed in readiness"* or *"to let your loins be girded."* In that day, everyone wore long robes which were a hindrance if you needed to move quickly or freely. If a person planned to run or work, he would tuck his robe into a sash around his waist so that it would not interfere with his movements. The verb here indicates *"a state of perpetual readiness for action."* The second figure, *"keep your lamps burning,"* comes from a day when there was no electricity. There were no streetlights outside and certainly no night-lights to help you find your way to the bathroom. If you were expecting a midnight visitor, you would keep an oil lamp burning so that when he or she knocked on the door, you could see to let him in. Again, the idea is, *"to be ready for the Master's coming."* The third picture is of servants who are awaiting their master's return from a wedding feast. Such feasts could last for days, often for a week. The servants would need to be ready when they heard their master arrive so that they could open the door and serve him. Scholars debate whether Luke is using a Roman or Jewish reckoning of the watches of the night, but the point is the same: *"the master could come in the middle of the night when you least expect him, so you must be ready."* The fourth picture is of a thief breaking into a house in the middle of the night. If the homeowner had known when the thief was coming, he would not have allowed his house to be broken into. He would have been ready and waiting. Then Jesus states the application of all four figures: *"You, too, be ready; for the Son of Man is coming at an hour that you do not expect"* (12:40). **2) Secondly; Work while it is Day:** John 9:4-5 says, "We must work the works of Him who sent Me while it is day because night is coming when no one can work. As long as I am in the world, I am the Light of the world [giving guidance through My word and works]." My point: Now is not the time to be passive when it comes to proclaiming the Gospel. The scripture says, "to let your light shine BRIGHT before men so that they will see your good works and glorify your Father in Heaven. No-one who has a lamp hides it under a shade so why should you? It's time for the church "to rise and shine for the Glory of God has come among us."(Is. 60) Preach! **3) Lastly, Be Watchful and Pray:** Luke 21:36 says, "But keep alert at all times [be attentive and ready], praying that you may have the strength and ability [to be found worthy and] to escape all these things that are going to take place, and to stand in the presence of the Son of Man [at His coming]." Maranatha my friend! Indeed, Jesus is coming back soon! Don't forget; Get Ready and work while it is day and always be watchful and pray!

Step to Start Strong:

Be Rapture Ready!

NOVEMBER 29.

JUST JESUS

"A woman in that town who lived a sinful life learned that Jesus was eating at the Pharisee's house, so she came there with an alabaster jar of perfume. As she stood behind him at his feet weeping, she began to wet his feet with her tears. Then she wiped them with her hair, kissed them and poured perfume on them."

Luke 7:37-38

Notice the sinful lady "lived" a sinful life. When she came in contact with Jesus, He set her free from her past. Every ounce of guilt and shame was washed away when she fell at the feet of the one who is worthy of praise. While the world is searching for self-help antidotes to heal people from depression and addiction; this is all we need; Just Jesus! This has been one my quotes lately; *"All I need is Jesus. Just Jesus."*

Notice she was surrounded by sinners and Pharisees who thought they were justified by their faithfulness to the law. Both individuals could see the Savior but only one recognized their need to be saved from their sins. It amazes me how some people can be so close to Jesus but yet so far away. It breaks my heart to know that we have the answer that the world is searching for but yet we can so easily keep it to ourselves. The church can be so selfish and self-centered.

So what are we really? We can liken ourselves to an usher. An usher escorts people to their designated seat. Ultimately, God wants to raise us up so we can sit with him in heavenly realms with Christ Jesus. (Eph. 2:16) This is where this lady lay.

Lastly, she wiped the feet of Jesus with expensive oil. The Bible says, *"the fragrance filled the room."*This symbolizes the presence of the Holy Spirit. The Holy Spirit is attracted to acts of self-sacrifice. As in the Old Testament, *"the fire will fall on the altar of your heart when you humble yourself before the King."* However, notice who left with the aroma of Christ on their life; The one who saw their need and fell at His feet. The lady left with the fragrance of Christ; Just like Jesus. May we fall at the feet of Jesus by faith today and worship for a few minutes. All you need is Jesus; Just Jesus.

Step to Start Strong:

Be Christ-Centered

NOVEMBER 30.

GONE WITH THE WIND

"When the day of Pentecost came, they were all together in one place. Suddenly a sound like the blowing of a violent wind came from heaven and filled the whole house where they were sitting."

Acts 2:1-2

With over 9,000 promises spoken in scripture only one is mentioned as *"the promise of the Father."* (Luke 24:49 / Acts 1:4) The Promise of the Father alludes to the outpouring of the Holy Spirit in Acts Chapter 2; what we call, *The Birthday of the Church.* Our tour group stood in the place where this promise was fulfilled in the Old City of Jerusalem. As we prayed and sang a few songs, I could only imagine what it was like on the Day of Pentecost. The hairs on the back of my neck began to stand up and as I sensed the Holy Spirit was still hovering in the Upper Room of that house. With this in mind, it has been said,*"that the sin of the Old Testament was the rejection of the Father, the sin of the New*

Testament was the rejection of the Son but the sin of the present age has been the rejection of the Holy Spirit." The teaching of Jesus was quite contrary. He said in John 14:12 *"that whoever believed in Him would do the same works that He did and even greater works than these, because He was going to the Father."* The truth is most experience the pardon of passover but sadly, few experience the power of pentecost. If we are going to do the same works that Jesus did, we certainly need the same power that He received. The wind of the Holy Spirit is still blowing today. In fact, *The Wind of the Holy Spirit carried 4 things away of that day:*

1) The Wind of the Holy Spirit carried away The Cowardice of Witnessing: Acts 1:8 says, *"But you will receive power when the Holy Spirit comes on you; and you will be my witnesses in Jerusalem, and in all Judea and Samaria, and to the ends of the earth."*

2) The Wind of the Holy Spirit carried away The Coldness of Worship: The upper room was literally shaken by the fervency of prayer that day. It was so passionate that passerby's thought everyone was drunk even though it was only 9 o'clock in the morning (Acts 2:13). It was the wind that rekindled the fire in everyone's heart to worship.

3) The Wind of the Holy Spirit carried away The Contention in people's Walk: When the wind of the Holy Spirit began to blow, it created perfect unity. People helped one another who ended up in need (Acts 2:44). The truth is you can't fish and fight at the same time. If there is contention or disagreement in your house, it proves people are gazing at people rather than people praising God. You cannot serve the Lord is discord.

4) Lastly, The Wind of the Holy Spirit carried away The Complacency in God's Work: The 120 disciples quickly multiplied because they lived a crucified life. They crossed over from being saved to living surrendered. There was no room for causal christian living. Everyone sought after the Kingdom and everything was added unto thee. Indeed, this was the Promise of the Father fulfilled. May the Wind of the Holy Spirit blow away our cowardice to witness, our coldness in worship, our contention in our daily walk and our complacency in God's work. Pray this with me: Have your way in me Holy Spirit, in Jesus name, Amen.

Step to Start Strong:

Go with the Wind

DECEMBER 1.

STUMBLING BLOCKS

"Jesus turned and said to Peter, "Get behind me, Satan! You are a stumbling block to me; you do not have in mind the concerns of God, but merely the concerns of men."

Matthew 16:23

Are you a stepping stone or a stumbling block? Romans 14:13 says, *"Therefore let us stop passing judgment on one another. Instead, make up your mind not to put any stumbling block or obstacle in the way of a brother or sister."* It's not all about you. *The scripture is clear; We should not do anything that would cause another brother or sister to sin even if we think it's ok (1st Cor. 8:13).*

As Christians, we live in glass houses. Everyone is peering into our personal lives to see if our relationship with God is genuine and worth seeking after. Jesus said, *"whoever causes one of these little ones to stumble and sin [by leading them away from My teaching], it would be better for him to have a heavy millstone hung around his neck and to be drowned in the depth of the sea." (Matthew 18:6)* This is strong terminology but surely something to think about. Are you helping people fulfill their purpose or are you pulling them down by your so-called freedom?

It's easy to be a stumbling block to those closest to you. The reason why? Because you are too close to the situation.Take a step back today and re-examine the way you treat your closest peers.

It's all about perspective.

Simon Peter allowed He's emotion to get in the way of what God wanted to do for eternity. The outcome? An open rebuke. Don't be influenced by Satan by what you say.

Be a Stepping Stone and not a Stumbling Block.

Step to Start Strong:

Take a Step Back

DECEMBER 2.

THE GRACE OF GIVING

"He who is gracious to a poor man lends to the Lord, and He will repay him for his good deed." (NASB)

Proverbs 19:17

I have had the privilege of working all over the world. My travels have taken me to some of the most poverty-stricken areas on the planet. My heart breaks as I see the stark contrast between those who have much and those who have nothing. In America, it is common for a family to spend $50 for a meal in a restaurant, while in other nations, that is more than a month's wages. Why is it so easy for us to give a restaurant $50 for an hour of gratification, and so difficult to give an offering of $50 for mission? It seems I am not alone in my views on money. As a matter of fact, the Bible speaks clearly of how we should handle our finances. Robert Murray McCheyne spoke to the idol of money in much the same way as I do today:

> *"If you have felt the love of God, you must dash down the idol of money. You must not love money. You must be more open-hearted*

and more open-handed to the poor. May God be praised for what He has been done: but you must do far more. You must give to missions, to send the knowledge of Jesus to the world. How can you grasp your money in your hand so greedily, while there are hundreds of millions perishing on the other side of the planet? You that give tens must give your hundreds. You that are poor must do what you can. Let us resolve to not only give the tenth of all we have to God but give offerings as well."

The truth is God owns it all.

We're just stewards of a very small portion of God's great wealth.

Who are we to argue when He wants to give a little away?

(Excerpt Taken from Evangelist Steve Hill.)

<u>Step to Start Strong</u>:

Give to World Missions

DECEMBER 3.

REAPING THE HARVEST

"So shall My word be that goes forth out of My mouth: it shall not return to Me void [without producing any effect], but it shall accomplish that which I please and purpose, and it shall prosper in the thing for which I sent it."

Psalm 118:8

Recently, I was approached by a young man in the altar after I preached a Sunday morning service and this is what He said; "You don't know me but a few years ago you preached my Baccalaureate Service when I graduated from High School. To this day, I don't recollect anything you said but this: You turned around at the very beginning of your message and said, *"most of you won't remember anything I say tonight. To be honest, most of you have your eyes set on your next step in life but others have your eyes set on party and getting plastered this summer."* When you said this I thought, *"He's right. I can't wait to get out of here so I can go get high and drink some beer with my friends."* Sadly, the young man went on to say that this is all

He'd done for the past three years. He shared a heart wrenching story about how drugs and alcohol had destroyed his families life and he didn't want to become the same statistic.

However, what He said next is why we do what we do. He said, *"I don't normally come to church but I felt like I was supposed to be here this morning and now I know why. I want to give my life to Jesus."* And the rest is History. We prayed. He repented and I sensed the sweet presence of the Holy Spirit filling His heart with love and grace.

My point: The Bible says, *"when Jesus is lifted up in the earth, He will draw all men unto Himself."* (John 12:32) Jesus is the one who brought this broken young man to church that morning. He always leaves the fold to find the one lost sheep. He found you and He found me, Now He wants to use us for His glory. The Apostle Paul said, *"I planted the seed, Apollos watered it, but God has been making it grow. So neither the one who plants nor the one who waters is anything, but only God, who makes things grow."* (1st For. 3:6-7) Take time to plant some seed today. The thing the young man remembered about me wasn't even scripture but He remembered the compassion behind what was said and He came back to me when times were tough. The result? The salvation of his soul! So keep watering the seedlings that are being rooted and grounded in His love. God is faithful. I believe with my whole heart that this growth will change the course of many generations. Sometimes you plant, sometimes you water and at others times you *"Reap the Harvest."* Church; It's Harvest-Time!

Step to Start Strong:

Lift up the Name of Jesus!

DECEMBER 4.

The Atmosphere for Increase

"Jesus took the loaves, gave thanks, and distributed to those who were seated as much as they wanted. He did the same with the fish. When they had all had enough to eat, he said to his disciples, "Gather the pieces that are left over. Let nothing be wasted." So they gathered them and filled twelve baskets with the pieces of the five barley loaves left over by those who had eaten."

John 6:11-13

Jesus feeding the 5,000 is one of my all-time favorite story's! This encounter is one of the only few stories that is mentioned in all four Gospels. This proves the importance of the principles that lie therein.

John 6:11 says, *"Jesus took the loaves, gave thanks, and distributed to those who were seated as much as they wanted."* If there is one characteristic that we need to engulf as the children of God; it's thankfulness. Your level of thankfulness is a mirror of your hearts humility. This is why Jesus had the people sit down on the hillside. You can't receive anything from God unless you humble yourself. Pride says, I can personally provide for me and my family but humility says, *"I am poor and needy."* Spiritually poor of course. This means *"God, I am totally dependent upon you."* This is what makes your bread multiply; a posture of hunger and humility within an atmosphere of thanksgiving. This releases the anointing to build the Kingdom of God.

When you sow seeds of thankfulness, you give God the opportunity to give you more. Otherwise, why would God give you more to complain about? When the heart of humility and the attitude of thankfulness kiss, you create an atmosphere for increase. Just ask the 5,000 who walked away full that day. They reaped the benefit of God's blessing because they were willing to humble themselves and be thankful even though they started with nothing. However, the little became large because the Lord blessed it.

Guard the atmosphere of your life. Fill it with spiritual hunger, humility and thankfulness. If so, increase will come according to your need.

Step to Start Strong:

Develop an Atmosphere for Increase

DECEMBER 5.

THE 4 CALLS OF GOD

"So the last shall be first, and the first shall be last: for many are called, but few are chosen."

<u>Matthew 20:16</u>

There are "4 Calls" that come from God during your lifetime. Whatever you do; don't drop these calls:

1) The Outward Call. This is the voice of the Shepherd, saying, *"Come home."* It happens when the Word of God is preached and the Holy Spirit convicts the lost soul. The Bible says, *"For many be called, but few are chosen"* (Matthew 20:16). The truth of this scripture is that few choose to be chosen.

2) The Inward Call. This is the deeper call. The first call gets your attention; the second call your adoration. The outward call brings men to a profession of Christ, the inward call to a possession of Christ. The outward call tells you who He is; the inward call, He tells you who you are.

3) The Forward Call. Once a person has answered the outward call and obeyed the inward call, he is ready to put his hand to the plow. It is one thing to tell the Lord that we will go wherever He wants us to go, while it is quite another to actually do it. Jesus said, *"Go into all the world and preach the gospel."* This is the Forward Call. It's not an option but a heavenly mandate.

4) The Upward Call. This is the final call. Jesus is coming back for a spotless Bride. It is this call that the first three are in preparation for. As Paul wrote to Timothy, *"Henceforth there is laid up for me a crown of righteousness, which the Lord, the righteous judge, shall give me at that day: and not to me only, but unto all them also that love his appearing"* (2 Timothy 4:8). *Don't miss the upward call.*

Go ahead; *"Call unto Him and He will answer you, and tell you great and mighty things, which you do not know."* (Jeremiah 33:3)

<u>Step to Start Strong</u>:

Call unto the Lord

DECEMBER 6.

My Favorite Verse

"For I know the plans I have for you," declares the Lord, "plans to prosper you and not to harm you, plans to give you hope and a future."

Jeremiah 29:11

What's your all-time favorite verse? This was the question I was presented with. Hard question huh? This coming Sunday I am the guest speaker for a new sermon series on what topic? You guessed it; *"My Favorite Verse."* How could we ever boil the whole Bible down to choose just one scripture.

However, my all-time favorite verse really depends upon what I need in the *"now-moments"* of my everyday life. If I feel pressured and need peace, I will pray; *"God, give me the peace that surpasses all understanding."* (Phil. 4) If I'm boarding a plane, I always pray; *"Father, command your angels to guard and protect me in all of my ways!"* (Psalm 91) If someone I know is sick, I will pray; *"By your stripes they have been healed! Hallelujah!"* (Is. 53) These verses just bubble out of my remembrance when I need them the most. These are my favorite verses; The ones I need the most in the moment.

Secondly, an old wise man once said, *"we serve an adverse God."* When we gain revelation of who God is through the scripture, He *"adds a verse and seals it in our heart"* and we end up knowing Him better because of it. For example, when He saved me, I understood the scriptures pertaining to salvation and Satan could no longer steal the reality of my eternal destination. When He delivered me, I fully understood freedom because I was truly free and so on. The Bible is full of living power and sharp enough to cut the lies of Satan right off of your life. May He add scriptural understanding and insight to you as you seek Him through His Word.

What's your favorite verse?

What verses have been bound around your heart?

What do you need God to do for you today?

Find a verse and stand on its promise until you see it come to pass.

<u>Step to Start Strong</u>:

Memorize your Favorite Verses

DECEMBER 7.

What's in your Hand?

"So God said, 'What's that in your hand?'"

Exodus 4:2

There's a story of an old wise man who lived in a village: "This man was considered wise because there was never a riddle that he could not solve. In the village, there was also a little boy who watched the old man in all his wise ways but one day he decided he was going to trick the old man once and for all. At least one time, he would prove that this old man didn't know it all.

So this is what he decided to do…

He would go and catch a butterfly and put it in his hand. He would later find the old man and ask him is the butterfly in my hand dead or alive? If he said, *"alive,"* he would crush him and say, *"You're wrong. I win."* If he said, *"dead,"* he would open his hand and let him go free.

Either way, the old man would finally be wrong!

So, when the timing was right, the little boy approached the old man with a butterfly in his hand…

He said, *"Old man! Is the butterfly in my hand, dead or alive?"*

The old man stood their for a moment, stroked his beard, gazed intently into the eyes of the little boy and noticed what the little boy was trying to do. So, he thought for a few more moments and this is what he said, *"Young man, the answer is in your hands. The answer is in your hands."*

This is also true for you and your life. It's all up to you.

God has given you everything that you need to live a life of godliness in Christ Jesus

This is your moment: The answer is in your hands!

Salvation, healing, hope and deliverance has been extended into the earth by the strong of the Holy Spirit. The provision has already been provided. Its up to you and I to call upon the name of Jesus because He is among us.

Nobody can do it for you but you can do all things through Christ who gives you the strength that you need!

Step to Start Strong:

Believe in the Strong Hand of the Holy Spirit

DECEMBER 8.

THE FIRST STATE

"But you walked away from your first love—why? What's going on with you, anyway? Do you have any idea how far you've fallen? "Turn back! Recover your dear early love. No time to waste, for I'm well on my way to removing your light from the lamp-stand."

Revelation 2:5

The author of the following passage is unknown but the divine inspiration is apparent:

"Our knees then, must bow to Him who walks in the midst of the golden candlesticks. Back we must go until the glorious Lord stands among us in all the majesty of His holiness. The Church, which is His by gift of the Father and by His own purchase, comes under His complete control. For too long our remiss ways have shut the gates against the heavenly breathing of this Holy Spirit. Back we must go until the Lord Jesus is gloriously unveiled so

> that the fragrance of His Holy Presence becomes again the saving power of the Gospel. It is only our full return to the first state of the church which will once again make our worship spiritual and our prayers and devotions fervent and zealous. Those mighty acts wrought by the apostles are possible again but only when those who love Him walk with Him in white. Therefore, He says, *"Do the first works"*-that is, do as the first Christians did."

Whoever penned these words knew the secret of revival. There must be a passionate love for the Savior before a mighty move of God will ever take place. This love must be daily demonstrated in our prayers and actions. We must return to the first state, that is, when we first fell in love with Jesus Christ. This should be our constant condition: radically and passionately in love with the Lord.

Step to Start Strong:

Return to your First Love

DECEMBER 9.

MATTHEW

"As Jesus was walking along, he saw a man named Matthew sitting at his tax collector's booth. "Follow me and be my disciple," Jesus said to him. So Matthew got up and followed him. Later, Matthew invited Jesus and his disciples to his home as dinner guests, along with many tax collectors and other disreputable sinners."

Matthew 9:9-10

The name Matthew means *"Gift of God."* Matthew was one of the men who was chosen by Christ to be one of the original apostles. (Luke 6:12) He worked as a publican otherwise known as a tax collector in the city of Capernaum by the Sea of Galilee. Little is known about his upbringing but we do know that the Holy Spirit touched his heart in such a way that he forsook everything and followed Jesus.

However, before his radical encounter with the Messiah, Matthew was called Levi but after his conversion God changed his name to Matthew. I wonder why? Jews often marked major life changes by changing their names and the names always proved to be prophetic in a sense. Simon was changed to Peter, Saul was later called Paul and Jacob was named Israel. The point? When you meet the risen Christ, He gives you a brand new life and a gripping new mission. *The old is gone; Behold, the new has come!* Jesus Christ changes everything. In fact, if you say you met Christ and nothing has changed, I have to wonder if you really met Christ at all?

For Matthew, He was so mesmerized with *"the Son of Man"* that 25% of his Gospel is filled with the words of Jesus; verbatim. If anything, Matthew was not ashamed of the Gospel of Jesus Christ and neither should we. He opened His house to sinners, wrote *"love letters"* to lost Jews and overall was a great gift from God. His life indicates miraculous transformation. No matter how many people have written you off, when God writes your name in the Lamb's Book of Life, He empowers to impact your community. He not only gives you new life but He gives you a new mission. Matthew crossed over from a tax collector to a soul-harvester.

Be like Matthew. Be bold. Reach out to sinners. Don't look back. Allow God to change the landscape of your life. Fill your mouth with the words of Christ. Forsake everything and follow the one who will never forsake you.

Step to Start Strong:

Be like Matthew

DECEMBER 10.

JOHN MARK

"After this the Lord appointed seventy-two others and sent them out two by two ahead of him to every town and place where he was about to go."

Luke 10:1

As you can see, John Mark was not listed as one of the original twelve apostles but many theologians believe that He was one of the *"seventy-two"* recorded in Luke 10. Most likely his conversion took place under the ministry of Simon Peter because Peter calls him son in 1st Peter 5:13. In the early church, believers used to gather in homes for worship and we read how they used Mark's mothers house in Acts 12:12. It was during one of these worship services that the Holy Spirit spoke to Mark to set sail with Paul and Barnabas on a missionary journey. However, somewhere along the way Mark and Paul parted ways due to a disagreement. The scripture doesn't leave us wondering if they ever made amends though. Prior to the Apostle Paul's death in Rome, what does he do? He calls on John Mark to come and be with him (2 Timothy 4:11). After the reconciled relationship in Rome, history tells us Mark planted a church in Alexandria, Egypt. His Gospel was written around 64 AD.

So, what can we gather from the life of John Mark?

1) **John Mark had ears to hear.** The fear of the Lord will always precede the ability to hear God's voice.

2) **John Mark feared the Lord.** He probably adopted this principle from following his Pastor Simon Peter through his public fall.

3) **John Mark cleared his calendar for the agenda of Christ.** We see Mark's flexibility when it came to his faith. He was an early follower of Christ despite public opinion. He was willing to open his home for worship during times of uncertainty and persecution. When the Holy Spirit spoke, he packed his bags and set sail to preach the gospel, making personal amends and planting a church. Charles Spurgeon said, *"Millions have never heard of Jesus. We ought not to ask, Can I prove that I ought to go?' But can I prove that I ought not to go?"* Indeed, John Mark had a passion to go and preach the Gospel of Jesus Christ.

John Mark feared the Lord, He heard the Lord and He served the Lord wholeheartedly.

Step to Start Strong:

Be like John Mark

DECEMBER 11.

From Bad to Worse

"When the enemy comes in like a flood, the Spirit of the Lord shall lift up a standard against him."

Isaiah 59:19

What do you do when bad becomes worse? What do you do when one beer becomes a six pack which can lead to a keg? How about one fight with your spouse leading to the verge of divorce? There's so many scenarios in life that can go from bad to worse but this is the truth; *Our enemy seems to overplay his hand when trying to destroy people's lives.* He should've stopped pushing you around when things got bad but here's what happens when things go from bad to worse: People get back up and go after God. This plot is all though the Bible. I thought about the prodigal son. The scripture says, *"He wasted his life."* He spent all of his time getting wasted but something changed when he found himself in the pig pen. In this moment, the scripture says, *"He came to his senses and arose to go back to his Father's House."* People go back to church when things go from bad to worse. I thought about Daniel when he and his family were exiled to the wicked city of Babylon. This was a bad situation for this young man but what happened next was even worse. The King ordered he and his friends to eat food sacrificed to idols to defy the principles in which they were raised. So what did he do? He arose and went into his prayer closet to fast and pray. People fast and pray when things go from bad to worse. People start reading their Bible again. They cry out to God with a sincere heart when things go from bad to worse! So why am I reiterating this phrase today? If you are in a situation that seems to be overbearing or impossible; I've got good news for you! You are closer to your miracle than ever before! All through scripture, Satan pushes God's people into their divine purpose. It's true! *"What the devil meant for evil, God is turning around for your good and for the saving of many lives."* (Gen. 50:20) Don't miss this: *The level of the attack is directly proportional to the level of blessing that is coming your way. This is what the attack is all about. If things are going from bad to worse for you; just worship your way back to the Father's feet.* And remember; *"When the enemy comes in like a flood, the Lord raises up a standard against thee." So stand strong mighty warrior! I've got better news! Read the same verse with the comma in a different place. "When the enemy comes, LIKE A FLOOD the Lord will raise up a standard against thee!" I like it better the second time around. Receive this word by faith today. If God be for you; who can be against you? Your life is about to go from bad to better. Just believe and whatever you do; don't back down or turn around. Turn your pain into praise and watch God show up on the scene!*

Step to Start Strong:

Believe for Better

DECEMBER 12.

7 Keys to Christian Living

"Rejoice always, pray without ceasing, in everything give thanks; for this is the will of God in Christ Jesus for you. Do not quench the Spirit. Do not despise prophecies. Test all things; hold fast what is good and abstain from every form of evil."

1st Thessalonians 5:16-22

In this passage of scripture the Apostle Paul gives us *"7 Keys to Successful Christian Living."* These are seven daily duties that when applied in practical ways will assist you in your spiritual growth and maturity.

#1 Rejoice! at ALL Times.
#2 NEVER Cease to Pray.
#3 Always BE Thankful.
#4 Refrain from QUENCHING the Holy Spirit meaning not to allow the fire and zeal burning within you to be extinguished.

#5 Don't consider USELESS the prophetic utterances occurring within the church.

#6 PROVE all things meaning to put spiritual manifestations or teachings to the test to make sure they line up with scripture.

#7 Abstain from EVIL...If you must question whether or not something is right or wrong to do; then side with not doing it.

These are seven guidelines are keys to grant you great success within your walk with Christ Jesus. They will also keep you pure and holy as you anticipate His return in these last days.

<u>Step to Start Strong</u>:

Use your Keys of Authority

DECEMBER 13.

PRAYER OF A MINOR PROPHET

"Watch and pray, lest you enter into temptation. The spirit indeed is willing, but the flesh is weak."

Matthew 26:41

This is the prayer A. W. Tozer wrote after the day of his ordination service on August 8, 1920. May these words encourage you and convict you to never forget why we are here in this world. *"O Lord, I have heard Thy voice and was afraid. Thou has called me to an awesome task in a grave and perilous hour. Thou art about to shake all nations and the earth and also heaven, that the things that cannot be shaken may remain. O Lord, my Lord, Thou has stooped to honor me to be Thy servant. No man taketh this honor upon himself save he that is called of God as was Aaron. Thou has ordained me; Thy messenger to them that are stubborn of heart and hard of hearing. They have rejected Thee, the Master, and it is not to be expected that they will receive me as thy the servant.* My God, I shall not waste time deploring my weakness nor my unfittedness for the work. The responsibility is not mine, but yours. Thou has said, "I knew thee - I ordained thee - I sanctified thee," and

Thou hast also said, "Thou shalt go to all that I shall send thee, and whatsoever I command thee thou shalt speak." Who am I to argue with you or to call into question Thy sovereign choice? The decision is not mine but yours. So be it, Lord. Thy will, not mine, be done. Well do I know, The God of the prophets and the apostles, that as long as I honor Thee Thou will honor me. Help me therefore to take this solemn vow to honor Thee in all my future life and labors, whether by gain or by loss, by life or by death, and then to keep that vow unbroken while I live.

It is time, O God, for Thee to work, for the enemy has entered into Thy pastures and the sheep are torn and scattered. And false shepherds abound who deny the danger and laugh at the perils which surround Thy flock. The sheep are deceived by these hirelings and follow them with touching loyalty while the wolf closes in to kill and destroy. I beseech Thee, give me sharp eyes to detect the presence of the enemy; give me understanding to see and courage to report what I see faithfully. Make my voice so like Thine own that even the sick sheep will recognize it and follow Thee. Lord Jesus, I come to Thee for spiritual preparation. Lay Thy hand upon me. Anoint me with the oil of the New Testament prophet. Forbid that I should be come a religious scribe and thus lose my prophetic calling. Save me from the curse that lies dark across the modern clergy, the curse of compromise, of imitation, of professionalism. Save me from the error of judging a church by its size, its popularity or the amount of its yearly offering. Help me to remember that I am a prophet - not a promoter, not a religious manager, but a prophet. Let me never become a slave to crowds. Heal my soul of carnal ambitions and deliver me from the itch for publicity. Save me from bondage to things. Let me not waste my days puttering around the house. Lay Thy terror upon me, O God, and drive me to the place of prayer where I may wrestle with principalities and powers and the rulers of the darkness of this world. Deliver me from overeating and late sleeping. Teach me self-discipline that I may be a good soldier of Jesus Christ.

I accept hard work and small rewards in this life. I ask for no easy place. I shall try to be blind to the little ways that could make life easier. If others seek the smoother path I shall try to take the hard way without judging them too harshly. I shall expect opposition and try to take it quietly when it comes. Or if, as sometimes it falleth out to Thy servants, I should have grateful gifts pressed upon me by Thy kindly people, stand by me then and save me from the blight that often follows. Teach me to use whatever I receive in such manner that will not injure my soul nor diminish my spiritual power. And if in Thy permissive providence honor should come to me from Thy church, let me not forget in that hour that I am unworthy of the least of Thy mercies, and that if men knew me as intimately as I know myself they would withhold their honors or bestow them upon others more worthy to receive them. And now, O Lord of heaven and earth, I consecrate my remaining days to Thee; let them be many or few, as Thou wilt. Let me stand before the great or minister to the poor and lowly; that choice is not mine, and I would not influence it if I could. I am Thy servant to do Thy will, and that will is sweeter to me than position or riches or fame and I choose it above all things on earth or in heaven. Though I am chosen of Thee and honored by a high and holy calling, let me never forget that I am but a man of dust and ashes, a man with all the natural faults and passions that plague the race of men. I pray Thee, therefore, my Lord and Redeemer, save me from myself and from all the injuries I may do myself while trying to be a blessing to others. Fill me with Thy power by the Holy Spirit, and I will go in Thy strength and tell of Thy righteousness, even Thine only. I will spread abroad the message of redeeming love while my normal powers endure.Then, dear Lord, when I am old and weary and too tired to go on, have a place ready for me above, and make me to be numbered with Thy saints in glory everlasting.

Step to Start Strong:

Major in the Minors

DECEMBER 14.

God's Medicine

"My son, pay attention to what I say; turn your ear to my words. Do not let them out of your sight, keep them within your heart; for they are life to those who find them and health to one's whole body. Above all else, guard your heart, for everything you do flows from it."

Proverbs 4:20-23

Have you taken your medication today? The one prescribed by your Heavenly Father? If not, according to Proverbs 4:22, the Lord says, *"that His word is health to your bones."* The Hebrew word health can also be translated into medicine meaning God's word is like medicine to your body. I love this verse! However, just like any other medicine, it will never do you any good unless you take it! You have to ingest it, break it down and apply it to the proper place in order to receive the full measure of its power. So it is so with God's word; It is like medicine. Just like any prescription, you have to follow the doctor's orders. So, this is the instruction that Proverbs Chapter 4 implies:

Step One: *Attend to My Words...*
These aren't just anybody's words, THE BIBLE comes from the mouth of the God Almighty. His Word is to your spirit what food is to your flesh. Your body cannot be physically healthy without physical food and neither can your faith be strong and healthy without the Word of God.

Step Two: *Incline thine ear to My Sayings...*
Romans 10:17 says, *"Faith comes by hearing and hearing by the Word of God."* Notice the phrase *"by the word"* meaning The Word should be our filter in all manner of conversation. If what we hear and what we say doesn't line up with what God says, we should steer clear from it. God's Word is the standard. Secondly, notice the word *"incline."* This word means *"to lean in the same direction."* When we incline our ears to the Word of God, we lean not on our own understanding but we lean toward what God is saying. Make sense?

Step Three: *"Let them not depart from thine eyes."*
The ears and eyes work together as a team. If you watch something long enough you'll end up doing it too! It's true. Your life follows what you look at. When you gaze upon the goodness of God's Word long enough, The Word will transform you from the inside out and you will begin to see yourself as God sees you. As Rick Warren says, *"stop listening for a voice and start looking for a verse."*

Step Four: *Keep them in the Middle of your Heart...*

Proverbs 4:23 says, *"keep thy heart with all diligence; for out of it flows the issues of life."* Issues can be translated forces. Another translations says, *"Guard your heart; for it determines the course of your life."* It can't be any clearer than this. Attend to God's Word, Incline your ear to Him, Let not the truth depart from your eyes and be sure to guard your heart for all these things will determine the course of your life. This medicine is a miracle formula and more important than any other part of our day. Be sure to take the Gos-pill every time you get a chance. It will save your soul, heal your body and set you completely free from yourself and your enemy.

Step to Start Strong:

Take your Medicine!

DECEMBER 15.

The Ark

One night, a group of us were fellowshipping at the house for dinner and afterwards we decided to have a spontaneous worship service. My buddy broke out his ole' guitar and we all gathered in the living room to sing and give praises unto God. It's amazing how quick God will show up if you will just turn your attention to Him. As we closed our eyes and lifted our hands toward Heaven a sweet presence of the Holy Spirit filled the room. What did God say to me in this moment? He said, *"Build an Ark for me in your heart."* See, the Bible is full of types and shadows. I always say, you should approach the Bible as a literal composition of content but secondly, there are symbolic aspects of each passage as well. One of my all-time favorites is the story of Noah and the Ark. Yes, there was a man by the name of Noah who was called by God to build a big boat and yes, it did rain for 40 days and 40 nights. In this moment, every living creature on the face of the earth died except Noah and His household with all the animals. However, there is a deeper meaning to the manuscript. The Ark is a type and shadow of our salvation. All of the elements of the ARK point to our Savior Jesus Christ. Check this out:

1) Just as the Ark was provided for God's people so was Jesus Christ provided for you and me. God sent Jesus to the earth to be our provision and propitiation for our sins

2) After the Ark was built it was sealed with *"pitch."* The root word in Hebrew for the word pitch is translated *"atonement."* The tar like substance symbolizes the blood of Jesus Christ that covers a believers life. Noah and His whole family was ultimately protected because the wind and waves of the world could not penetrate the pitch that covered their vessel. It's the same way when the blood of Jesus is applied to our heart and soul.

3) The Ark only had one door. God said, *"make an ark and put only one door to provide entryway."* It's the same way with salvation. There's only one way to Heaven. Jesus said, *"I am the way, the truth and the life and no one gets to the Father except through me."*

4) Once God shut the door; no one could enter and no one could get out. God gives us a doorway of opportunity to repent and receive Him as Savior. Once the door is closed; you've missed the boat and after death there are no second chances. Sad but true.

5) The Ark was a place of total security. Once you were inside; you were safe and secure. This speaks of Heaven in the presence of the Lord with all the saints. Are you eternal secure? Are you sure?

Matthew 24:37-39 says, *"As it was in the days of Noah, so it will be at the coming of the Son of Man. For in the days before the flood, people were eating and drinking, marrying and giving in marriage, up to the day Noah entered the ark; and they knew nothing about what would happen until the* *flood came and took them all away. That is how it will be at the coming of the Son of Man."*

6) & Lastly, the Story of Noah represents the Rapture. Once the church is secured in the Ark of Salvation, the rains of judgment will come down from Heaven and the saints of God will be raised to safety in the presence of the Lord. This is the Good News my friend! When the rain comes down, the church will go up! If you want to read the whole story of Noah check out Genesis 5 through 9. There's more symbolism to be sought after so happy hunting! I hope this wets your spiritual appetite to look for Jesus in every story of the Bible. Make an ARK in your heart for God.

Step to Start Strong:

Build an Ark in your Heart

DECEMBER 16.

Upside Down

"These men who have turned the world upside down have come here too."

Acts 17:6

Jesus came to serve the unserved. In fact, He said, *"He was sent by His Father to minister to the poor, the captives, the blind and the oppressed (Luke 4:18-20)."* Jesus didn't come for the healthy or for those who didn't think they needed His help. He came for the sick and the spiritually distraught individuals. So how did He do it and what did He do first? Jesus' mission was compelled by His compassion for mankind. Out of this compassion, Jesus met people right where they were and He simply met their needs. So often, we feel like if we could just get a person to church they could be healed but Jesus' ministry shows us a better way. Jesus saw entire communities of people in need but then met the personal needs of each individual, never expecting a payback (Luke 14:13-14). This illustration proves a powerful point: If we minister to meet people's need on site, they will experience the love and faith that comes from God and Lord willing, one day they will end up in church doing exactly what we're called to do; Serving the unserved.

So I challenge you: *"Be light and not lightening."* Lightening brings a big flash with a lot of loud thunder, and then it's gone. It certainly gets lots of attention but then it disappears. But light, like a street light for example, doesn't even get noticed most of the time, but it quietly blesses a city everyday. With this in mind, God calls us *"children of light."* By being light, you will guide the world to the Savior's side and ultimately, *"turn the world upside down."* Just like the early disciples; Keep helping the hopeless, loving the unlovable and keep serving the unserved! You're making a huge difference.

Step to Start Strong:

Be Light and Not Lightening

DECEMBER 17.

Do You Love Him?

"He who has My commandments and keeps them, it is he who loves Me. And he who loves Me will be loved by My Father, and I will love him and manifest Myself to him."

John 14:21

According to the New Testament *"the law of God is written on the hearts and man, giving us no excuse not to know who He is and what He wants us to do (Romans 2:15)."* This reminds me of the response of the early disciples when they encountered Christ for the first time. The scripture says, *"they left everything to follow Him."*What would possess a man to make such a drastic decision? I'll tell you what it was; It was deep, deep conviction within each man's heart that he was made for such a time as this. The Word of God made flesh was literally right before their eyes and the Holy Spirit persuaded their soul to make the most important decision anyone could ever make; *The surrender of one's whole life to Jesus Christ.* This is your part; surrender. This is His part; the miracle of salvation. But there's one more thing; According to John 14:21, *"if you surrender your soul to God and submit to*

His ways, He will manifest Himself to you." The Amplified Version puts it this way, *"He will reveal Himself to you and make Himself real."* Has God ever revealed Himself to you? Has He ever made Himself real to you and your family? If not, get ready. I tell people all the time; Give God 30 days. Commit yourself to serve Him for a few weeks and see if He won't show Himself mighty on your behalf. As the young kids say, *"Won't God do it"* To be honest, I'll never forget the deep doubts I had in my heart when I first came to Christ. My tendency was to worry about everything. I worried about my past and I fretted over my future. It took some time to renew my carnal mind and come into agreement with the word of God. However, over time, God manifested Himself to me and proved Himself in presence, power and provision. These divine occurrences drew me into a deeper relationship with God. Did He have to do it? No! Did He want to? According to John 14:21, yes! The foundation of every relationship is built on trust. The deeper the level of trust, the greater revelation of love. *"How can you say you love me and you don't do what I say, says the Lord?"* You show your love for God by keeping His commandments. Your disobedience is a sure factor of your distrust. The reality is; you can trust the Lord. He has never broken one of my promises and He has never told a lie. Why would He start today? God is not like a man. If He says He will show up and show off. Why not allow Him to? Pray this prayer: "God, manifest yourself in our churches and communities. We ask you for divine interruptions and divine appointments all day and all week. May our daily obedience be the key that unlocks the door of unexpected opportunities and miracles. We trust you, we believe in your promises and we love you. Give us your heart, in Jesus name.

Step to Start Strong:

Trust and Obey.

DECEMBER 18.

EXPLAINING THE ECLIPSE

"The sun shall be turned into darkness, And the moon into blood, Before the coming of the great and awesome day of the Lord."

Joel 2:31

While not suggesting that I have all the answers for what happened but I still want to give a prophetic overview of the solar eclipse with Biblical reference. In history, God has used the sky as His billboard to speak clearly to His people. Psalm 24:1 says, *"The earth is the Lord's and the fullness thereof so on any given day God can use nature to paint a prophetic picture of the signs and times we are living in."* With this in mind, let me say this first. According to Jewish tradition, an eclipse of the moon always signified the nation of Israel. On the contrary, an eclipse of the sun always signified the nations of the earth. Why? As the nation of Israel is smaller than the nations of the earth so is the moon smaller than the sun. Secondly, a solar eclipse, represents judgment. With this being said, I am not a doom and gloom preacher but we have to pay attention to the signs of the times. Am I saying judgment is coming to America? Obviously, if we don't repent; yes. Am I saying it is coming today? Not necessarily so. There is a set order within creations time table where certain things happen on certain days, months and even years. With this said, God can definitely speak under these circumstances. However, there are also cataclysmic events that happen outside of natures systematic order. God can and will speak through the too. Next, it's important for us to understand that one of the tools that scholars use to follow the signs of the times is through the Hebrew calendar. When a solar eclipse covers one specific nation and no other nation on earth, you have witnessed a very rare occurrence. In fact, the last time this happened on American soil alone was on June 13, 1257,; far before America had become a nation. However, this did happen in Australia in 2012 but it won't happen in America again until January 25th, 2316 if the Lord so tarries. So here's my point: enjoy natural phenomenons, pray for America and lastly, be sure to spend some time in repentance. John the Baptist came with these words, *"Repent for the Kingdom of Heaven is near."* (Matthew 3:2) The last red letter words written in your Bible read this way, *"Behold, I am coming quickly!" (Rev.22)* Therefore, The Great American Eclipse on August 21st, 2017; is on the first day of the month of Elul in the Hebrew calendar. This month represents the month of repentance. *"Is God calling America to repentance?"* Let me put it this way; *"Is this God's way of calling the church, those who understand the signs of the times, to repentance?"* You bet. The scripture says, *"If my people, who are called by my name, will humble themselves and pray and turn from their wicked ways. Then will I hear from Heaven, forgive their sins and heal their land."* (2 Chronicles 7:14) It starts with us church. More importantly, let it start today. I challenge you: Spend some time in repentance today. Spend some time praying for our nation and it's leaders. Spend some time praying for Israel and the nations of the earth. In a solar eclipse, the moon passes between the sun and the earth. If the moon represents Israel, our nation is literally being covered by it's blessing. This is the hour where we as Americans should rise up and pray for the nation who gave us our three greatest blessings: The Messiah, The Bible and the world's greatest institution; the Church. This is why we honor our heritage. I hope this sheds some light on a few hours of darkness during an eclipse.

Step to Start Strong:

Spend some time in Repentance

DECEMBER 19.

RED LETTERS

"It is the Spirit who gives life; the flesh profits nothing. The words that I speak to you are spirit, and they are life."

John 6:63

Have you ever took the time to read *"The Red Letters?"* Do you know what I'm talking about? Within the New Testament, the letters written in red are the words that actually came out of Jesus' mouth; *verbatim.* It's quite the feat but well worth the wisdom. Recently, the thought crossed my mind to do just this so here are a few insights from my time of meditation.

#1 The Red Letters give us Diving Inspiration from the Heralds of the Past: The first thing I noticed when I was reading through the Red Letters was this; Jesus quoted the Old Testament Prophets quite often. One of His favorite weapons to war against the enemy were these three words; *"It is written!"* Isaiah understood this principle when He said, *"God's word will not* *come back to me void but it will accomplish the purposes for which it was sent (Is. 55:11)."* Even though Jesus was the Word, He spoke the word. If the Word is good enough for Jesus, I have to say, *"it's good enough for me."* In fact, the Word of God is really all we need. If we have the Word of God stored up in our heart and we speak it out of our mouth, we will walk in victory. As Reinhart Bonnke says, *"God's word is our mouth is just as powerful as God's word in His mouth." What does this mean? Speak the word! Live the Word! And be the Word! For you are a living epistle known and read by all men.*

#2 The Red Letters give us Divine Instruction for Holiness: The second principle I discovered while reading through the Red Letters was this; Jesus Christ is the greatest Rabbi and teacher of the Word. His insight is impeccable pertaining to living a life in, with and for the Spirit. The infamous message that we call *"The Sermon on the Mount"* makes up a good percentage of His instruction within the Four Gospels. As James, Jesus' half brother said, *"Be not hearers of the word only but be ye doers of the word!* He goes on to say, *"Do what the word says!" (James 1:22.)* What if we actually did what the word said to do verbatim? How would our lives look today? What difference would this make in our churches and communities?

#3 <u>Lastly, The Red Letters give us Divine Inquiry from Heaven</u>: When I read through the Gospels, I noticed Jesus asking a lot of questions. It almost reminded me of a child's reoccurring method to ask who, what, when, where and why? All the time! His questions were very simplistic and childlike. *"Why are you so afraid? Why do you worry about clothes? Why do you doubt? Who are you? Who touched me?"* And so on! The reality is; when God asks you a question, He's never seeking out information. He's

God remember! In fact, He's omniscient! He knows everything! The reason why God takes divine inquiries with people is this; When God asks a question, He's typically pointing to the problem. Let me put it this way; The question creates an awareness on the inside of you for something that needs to change. Has God ever asked you a question? Studies show Jesus asked 135 questions within the Gospel accounts. Divine inquiries lead to divine visitations if you answer correctly and obey. The Red Letters give divine inspiration from the past, divine instruction for our future and divine inquiries to help us walk in His good, pleasing & perfect will.

Step to Start Strong:

Read the Red Letters

DECEMBER 20.

A WORD OF ENCOURAGEMENT

"Be strong and of good courage, do not fear nor be afraid of them; for the Lord your God, He is the One who goes with you. He will not leave you nor forsake you." Then Moses called Joshua and said to him in the sight of all Israel, "Be strong and of good courage, for you must go with this people to the land which the Lord has sworn to their fathers to give them, and you shall cause them to inherit it."

Deuteronomy 31:6-7

From start to finish, the Heavenly Father would stir Joshua's faith with these few words in this midst of his ministry; *"Be strong and courageous, for I am with you and I will never leave you nor forsake you."* Notice the promise is always coupled with His presence. With this in mind, we live in a day where people need this kind of encouragement. Everyday the world is in our face bombarding our faith and many people are fed up and feel like giving up. Is this you this morning? If so, I want to give you a word of encouragement. You have come way too far to go back now! Just like the children of Israel in this situation; they had endured for over 40 years through the wilderness and now they had finally made it to the bank of the Jordan River. From where they were standing, they could see the promises of God even though they hadn't fully possessed them yet. According to scripture, they had one more step to take! Now this could represent you and your situation today. You're so close! You've come so far! Whatever you do; don't back down now! Here's the good news; God is with you and He will never leave you nor forsake you! Did you hear what I just said? Almighty God is right by your side and He's not going anywhere. All you have to do, is do what He says.

Does this encourage you? I sure hope so! The word encouragement simply means *"to give courage to someone."* In this day and age, people need to be surrounded by encouraging people. Do you know why? Because so many things in life can discourage us and pull us down. Discouragement simply means *"to take away the courage."* Has your courage been taken away? Does your pastor, spouse or co-worker need some encouragement? If so, write a note, send an email or simply give them a hug and say, *"you mean so much to me. Thank you for all you do."* Wow! Words of this caliber will encourage a man to endure another day. Go ahead! Give it a try! Encourage someone today and don't forget to encourage yourself in the Lord. This is a command I give you; *"Encourage one another."*

Step to Start Strong:

Encourage Everyone

DECEMBER 21.

It's Not About Me

"That is why the Scripture says: "God opposes the proud but shows favor to the humble."

James 4:6

When my need to be right is greater than my desire to display God's love, I will inevitably treat people with judgment, disrespect and condemnation. It happens all the time. People win the battle but sadly, they lose the war. The reality is; we don't have to be right all-the-time. Consider the church; In history, it seems all we're known for is what we're against and not what we love. Yes, the scripture is against same sex marriage, divorce and the abuse of alcohol but what about the other side of scripture? Like Love your neighbor as yourself and bare one another's burdens? If we will be known for what we love and who we love, I truly believe the rest will take care of itself. Am I saying there's not a time to address such issues? Certainly not! However, what I am saying is, they shouldn't be our focus. The Law never set anyone free. In fact, the Law brought forth death but on the contrary, the grace given by Jesus Christ set the captive free.

I wonder if we lived our lives in such a way that we didn't seek to be right but we sought to be sympathetic, benevolent and caring. How would this change the landscape of the church? Think about it. Our wise and persuasive preaching has never changed anybody. It takes the regenerating work of the Holy Spirit. Therefore, don't let the Law deter you from Heavens greatest reality; The Love of God.

Let's pray: *"Lord Jesus, Help me to see through the lens of your love today as I live your life out loud in front of my peers. Thank you that love conquers all, including my fears and the sin that keeps me from experiencing your love in a greater way in Jesus Name, Amen."*

Step to Start Strong:

Love the Sinner. Hate the Sin

DECEMBER 22.

MAGNIFY THE LORD

"I will praise the name of God with a song, And will magnify Him with thanksgiving."

Psalm 69:30

One of my teacher friends told me recently, *"the only way that He could get a bigger paycheck from the state was to look at it with a magnifying glass."* Funny for some people but maybe not so funny to you.

With this in mind, a magnifying glass doesn't change the size of what you're looking at all but it does change your perspective. In fact, it pulls the object of your affection into closer proximity so you can see it all the better. This is what the Psalmists was speaking of in this passage. He was calling the people of God to magnify the Lord. The Hebrew word for magnify is *"gadal"* which means *"to grow up" and "to make great."* In a sense, God is calling His people to grow up in their level of faith so that they can make Him great in their hearts. According to Psalm 69:30, we do this by giving God praise and giving God thanks.

Have you been magnifying your problems or magnifying God?
Have you been feeding your faith or feeding your fears?

It's all about perspective.

It's time to pull the truth of God's word into the forefront of your mind and focus on what He says about your future. Its time to make God great again in your heart by giving Him a sacrifice of praise today. Its time to magnify the Lord and let Him be the object of your affection.

Step to Start Strong:

Magnify the Majesty of God

DECEMBER 23.

How to Get to the Other Side

"Leaving the crowd behind, they took him along, just as he was, in the boat. There were also other boats with him. A furious squall came up, and the waves broke over the boat, so that it was nearly swamped. Jesus was in the stern, sleeping on a cushion. The disciples woke him and said to him, "Teacher, don't you care if we drown?" He got up, rebuked the wind and said to the waves, "Quiet! Be still!" Then the wind died down and it was completely calm. He said to his disciples, "Why are you so afraid? Do you still have no faith?" They were terrified and asked each other, "Who is this? Even the wind and the waves obey him!"

Mark 4:36-41

Envision the reality of this situation; The KJV says, *"a furious squall came upon the sea when Jesus and His disciples were trying to get to the other side."* The only other reference to this greek word for squall was during the moment of Jesus' death. When He breathed his last breath, the scripture is clear that the whole world could feel its effect. With this in mind, it is safe to say that the storm that these men were experiencing could resemble a tropical storm or even a hurricane. Historically, it was torrentous and terrifying.

Nevertheless, I want you to notice what Jesus was doing during the storm. While everyone else was screaming for their lives, Jesus was in a deep, deep sleep possibly snoring on the stern. Can you believe this? How could He sleep while the others shivered in fear? This is how.

In this story, Jesus sets the standard how we should face life-threatening storms effectively and successfully; By entering into His Rest. This principle illustrates how the Kingdom of God functions and how faith works. It happens within a heart or place of peace. This place can also be referred to as *"abiding in Christ."* Abiding means to live your everyday life connected to the mind, heart and Spirit of Christ. When you dwell in this place, you will embody the presence of peace. Notice how Jesus was resting in the midst of the storm but when He was awakened frantically, instead of growing anxious, He released the presence of peace that dwelled on the inside of Him. Don't miss this; Peace is the atmosphere of Heaven and you can experience this supernatural peace today. Jesus is the Prince of Peace and He can calm any storm you are facing. Don't let the squall scare you. Greater is He who lives in you than He that lives in the world. Take a spiritual nap. Proper rest will release the presence of peace that will compel you to arrive safely on the other side. This is the way to arrive safely in any storm.

Step to Start Strong:

Enter into the Rest of God

DECEMBER 24.

Have Faith in God

"Have faith in God," Jesus answered.

Mark 11:22

Romans 4:16 says, *"this is why it depends on faith, in order that the promise may rest on grace and be guaranteed to all his descendants—not only to the adherents of the law but also to those who share the faith of Abraham, for he is the father of us all."* Notice how the promise rests on grace and it is guaranteed to ALL of Abraham's descendants (which includes you). So how do you obtain grace to receive ALL of God's promises? The scripture is clear; by Faith. This is why it depends on faith.

No faith. No grace. No promises. *"Without faith it is impossible to please God."* (Hebrews 11:6) Why is this so? See, faith activates the amazing grace that is always available for God's sons and daughters. Grace gives us what we do not deserve but in order to receive it we must believe that He is the rewarder of those who diligently seek Him. Therefore, faith is the divine connector for those things hoped for. (Hebrews 11:1)

"What are you hoping God will do for you?"

Do you need a financial miracle? Have Faith in God!
Are you having physical complications? Have Faith in God!
Do you need household salvation? Have Faith in God!
Is your marriage falling apart? Have Faith in God!

Do you have a great need?
Let me remind you: You have a Great God!

Place your faith in the finished work of Christ today.

It will work for you just like it has worked for others if you have Faith in God's Word but remember, faith without works is dead. Faith always requires a corresponding action. Put your faith to work today and do whatever God tells you to do.

And Jesus answered them saying, *"Have faith in God."*

Step to Start Strong:

Have the God kind of Faith

DECEMBER 25.

The Parable of the Life-Saving Station

"And the Lord added to their number daily those who were being saved."

Acts 2:47

On a dangerous sea coast where shipwrecks often occur, there was once a crude, little life-saving station. The building was just a hut, and there as only one boat, but the few devoted members kept a constant watch over the sea, and with no thought for themselves, went out day and night tirelessly searching for the lost. Many lives were saved by this wonderful little life-saving station. So it became famous. Some of those who were saved and various others in the surrounding area, wanted to become associated with the station and give of their time and their money and their effort for the support of its work. New boats were bought, and new life-saving crews were trained, and the little life-saving station grew. Some of the members of the life-saving station were unhappy that the building was no crude and poorly equipped. They felt a more comfortable place should be provided as the first refuge of those saved from the sea. So they replaced the emergency cots and beds and put better furniture in the enlarged building. Now the life-saving station became a popular gathering place for its members, and they decorated it beautifully, and furnished it exquisitely because they used it as sort of a club.

Fewer members were now interested in going to sea on life-saving missions, so they hired lifeboat crews to do this work. The life-saving motif still prevailed in the club's decorations, and there was a liturgical lifeboat in the room where the club held its initiations. About this time, a large ship was wrecked off the coast, and the hired crews brought in loads of cold, wet, half-drowned people. They were dirty and sick, and some of them had black skin and some had yellow skin. The beautiful new club was considerably messed up. So the property committee immediately had a shower house built outside the club where the victims of shipwrecks could be cleaned up before coming inside. At the next meeting, there was a split in the club membership. Most of the members wanted to stop the club's life-saving activities as being unpleasant, and a hindrance to the normal social life of the club. Some members insisted upon life-saving as their primary purpose, and pointed out they were still called a life-saving station. But they were finally voted down and told if they wanted to save the lives of various kinds of people who were shipwrecked in those waters, they could begin their own life-saving station down the coast a little ways, which they did. As the years went by, the new station experienced the same changes that had occurred in the old one. It evolved into a club, and yet another life-saving station was founded. History continued to repeat itself, and if you visit that coast today, you will find a number of exclusive clubs along the shore. Shipwrecks are frequent in those waters, but most of the people drown. (E*xcerpt taken from the 1941* Presbyterian Journal)

Step to Start Strong:

Be a Life-Saver.

DECEMBER 26.

HELLO, MY NAME IS

"A good name is more desirable than great riches; to be esteemed is better than silver or gold."

Proverbs 22:1

Growing up most people have a favorite color, a favorite cartoon and even a favorite birthday cake. At least, I did and most of these things have never changed. I'm still a Carolina Blue Fan who loves me some Scooby-Doo and chocolate cake! On the same note, there's something else that stuck with me and this is my favorite number. My father wore the #22 on his back when he played sports in high school and this was pasted down to the next generation too. As long as I can remember, I wore the #22 on my back because I wanted to be like my father. Now, I not only want to be like my father but I want to be like my Heavenly Father! Therefore, when I came across the reference of this verse it made it easy for me to remember and also adhere to.

Proverbs 22:1 says, *"a good name is better than great riches."* Yes, your name is more priceless than silver and gold! In fact, your name has great value! Sadly, you can't sell it on craigslist but within the Kingdom of God it holds great weight and significance. When you were born you inherited a surname or family name if you will but you also received a first name or given name. Now obviously, you are called by your name but according to scripture, your name also describes your character. *Your character is the sum of the choices you have made.* When someone says your name, an image automatically pops up in their mind of who you are. Your name and character effects people emotionally and even spiritually per se. Your name reminds people of what you've done and what you're doing with your life.

Pastor Mike Murdock said it this way, *"all of us will be remembered by the problems that we cause and the problems that we cause."* Can I ask you a question: What will you be remembered by? What's the legacy that you are leaving to your family? Remember, your name is more important than money. What you do now will affect future generations. So here's my provoking thought: May we live our life with the end in mind. Jesus lived 33 years but His words and character changed the world forever and ultimately made it a better place. Pick a few words to live by today and do your best to portray them to your family and friends.

How about faithful, grateful and fun just to get started!
Overall, May God help us to become more like Jesus.

Step to Start Strong:

Be Remembered by the Problems you Solve.

DECEMBER 27.

THE POWER OF ONE

"Can one person chase away 1000 men? Can two men cause 10,000 men to run away? It will happen only if the Lord gives them to their enemy."

Deuteronomy 32:30

The scripture says, *"one can put a thousand to flight and two can put 10,000 to flight if the Lord is fighting for them and with them."* So yes! There is an exponential power when God's people come together to pray or work together in any way but what I want you to see is that we shouldn't ever neglect The Power of One. I have found out in life that there is hidden physical, mental and spiritual power in the secret places of every person. If you rise up in the midst of your circumstances and do what God has called you do, the possibilities are infinite and unimaginable. *(1st Cor. 2:9)*

Helen Keller made this statement, *"I am only one, but still I am one. I cannot do everything, but still I can do something; and because I cannot do everything, I will not refuse to do something that I can do."*

When you read the scripture, you will quickly see that God can use the willingness of ONE person to make an eternal impact:

> ONE man was used to save the world from extinction.... (Genesis 6)
> ONE woman was instrumental in saving a whole nation...(Esther 4)
> ONE little boy gave his bag lunch to feed 5,000 people... (John 6)
> ONE man met the Lord and took the Gospel to the Gentiles all over Asia...(Acts 9)
> ONE Savior redeemed the world by laying down His life so that we could live forever...(Matthew 27)

What do all these men and women have in common?
They all said, YES! To God and YES! To His leading...

So, what is God leading you to do?
Your life can impact the world in a profound way...
As one preacher said, *"We are an Army of ONE for an Audience of ONE!"*
So, *"Stop waiting on people to give you permission to do what God has already appointed you do...*

You can and you will make a difference in the world!
In fact, you are a World-changer!
Keep changing the world ONE Soul at a time…

Step to Start Strong:

Tap into God's Power

DECEMBER 28.

The Instructed Tongue

"The Sovereign Lord has given me an instructed tongue, to know the word that sustains the weary. He wakens me morning by morning, He wakens my ear to listen like one being instructed. The Sovereign Lord has opened my ears; I have not been rebellious, I have not turned away."

Isaiah 50:4-5

Praying the Word of God is the most powerful words you can pray. What you're doing is returning what God said in a personalized way. You're literally placing your will in the middle of who He is and what He already wants to do through you in prayer and in deed.

Numbers 23:19 says it this way, *"God is not a man, that he should lie, God is not a human being, that he should change his mind. Does he speak and then not act? Does he promise and not fulfill?"*

Many people build their house on human reasoning and church tradition but the scripture says for us to be like *"wise men who build their house on the rock."* What is the rock? The inerrant and infallible Word of God. Who is the Rock of Ages? Jesus Christ, the Word of God made flesh. Therefore, what we need to do in this hour is to run back to the Word of God and bury ourselves in the chest of its treasure. Read the word! Pray the Word! Be the Word! Nothing more! Nothing less! For James admonishes us *"to be not only hearers of the word but doers of the word also!* "Let's pray the Word and watch the word accomplish the reason for which it was sent. (Is. 55:11)

Start praying God word when we read it...

Isaiah 50 has always been one of my favorite passages to return back to God:

Pray this with me: *"The Sovereign Lord has given me an instructed tongue, to know the word that sustains the weary. He wakens me morning by morning, He wakens my ear to listen like one being instructed. The Sovereign Lord has opened my ears; I have not been rebellious, I have not turned away." Therefore use me today O' God. I thank you for giving me "the instructed tongue" to lift people up and not to tear people down. Open my ears today God. I want to hear your voice crystal clear. If you tell me to do it, I will be obedient. In every moment of the day, use my words to bring peace and healing to those around me, in Jesus Name. Amen!*

Step to Start Strong:

Pray the Word

DECEMBER 29.

Seeking the Lost

"For the Son of Man has come to seek and to save that which was lost."

Luke 19:10

Every organization has a mission statement. We at Chance Walters Ministries strive to preach the Gospel in all nations as we spread a message of prevention among the next generation. These themes come out of Matthew 28:19-20 and Proverbs 24:11. The First says: *"Therefore, Go and make disciples of all the nations, baptizing them in the name of the Father and of the Son and of the Holy Spirit, teaching them to observe all things that I have commanded you for I am with you always, even to the end of the age."* The Second says: *"Rescue those being led away to death; (this speaks of salvation) and hold back those staggering toward slaughter (this speaks of prevention).* Indeed, God has specifically commissioned us to these two callings.

But what about God? Why did He send His Son Jesus Christ into the world? Luke 19:10 sums it up, *"For the Son of Man has come to seek and save that which was lost"* and we can see this clearly from the beginning. In Genesis 3, after the fall of man, we find Adam and Eve hiding from their Heavenly Father and who initiates the conversation? God does. Adam and Eve feel a sense of shame and even guilt for eating the forbidden fruit but who takes the first step to start a dialogue? God does.

Check this out: *"When the man and his wife heard the sound of the Lord walking in the garden in the cool of the day, they hid from the Lord among the trees in the garden. <u>But the Lord God called to the man,</u> "Where are you?"* (Genesis 3:8-9) In fact, He's still calling out to sinners and saints alike! He's still pursuing people all cross the globe! And He'll never stop seeking and saving the lost at any cost! This is the heart of Heaven from the Book of Genesis to the Book of Revelation. He called Adam and Eve, He called the Apostle Paul and He chose you. Indeed, Jesus is still seeking, saving and calling whosever will open their ears to hear His voice. What a mission! What a statement! What a Savior!

<u>Step to Start Strong</u>:

Write Down a Personalized Mission Statement

DECEMBER 30.

The Law of Worship

"When the people of the land come before the Lord at the appointed festivals, whoever enters by the North gate to worship is to go out the South gate; and whoever enters by the South gate is to go out the North gate. No one is to return through the gate by which they entered, but each is to go out the opposite gate. ***10*** *The prince is to be among them, going in when they go in and going out when they go out."*

Ezekiel 46:9-10

There is only one Law concerning worship. You are forbidden to come in one way and leave the same. According to the appointed festivals in the Old Testament, when the children of God came to worship him, if they came in one door they were commanded to go out the opposite door when they left the place of worship. If you came in north gate, you had to go out the South gate and so on.

Here the point: You cannot come into the presence of the Lord and remain the same. If you come in struggling, you'll leave with strength, if you come in stressed, you'll leave blessed, if you come in bound by addiction, you'll leave set free! Whatever way you come, you cannot leave the same if you come before Him with a worshipful heart, ready to receive. It's the Law of Worship! May we never change our posture of prayer and praise! He is worthy of our worship this week church. Give Him the Glory that is due to His name. If you do; You will be forever changed for you can't leave the same way. It's the Law of Worship!

Step to Start Strong:

Abide by Spiritual Laws

DECEMBER 31.

If you will, He will

"If ye walk in my statutes, and keep my commandments, and do them; then I will give you rain in due season, and the land shall yield her increase, and the trees of the field shall yield their fruit."

Leviticus 23:4-5

Out of the ALL the promises in the Bible, and there are many, most of them are conditional promises. A condition is a provision upon which the carrying out of an agreement depends. Here's an example: A condition of employment might be that you must type 50 words per minute, have a high-school diploma and must not have a criminal record. If you qualify in meeting these three requirements, there is a chance you could be employed by the company in which you applied.

Furthermore, if you exercise and eat right, you will feel better, look better and hopefully live longer. If you don't drink alcohol, you won't be arrested for drunk driving. If you bathe regularly and brush your teeth, you won't cause people to avoid you in the check-out line. These are all results of certain conditions being met.

With this in mind, the Bible is full of conditions. In other words, if you will, God will!

Jeremiah 29:13 says, *"If you seek me, you will find me, if you seek me with your whole heart."* Of course, the key words are "IF."

Second Chronicles 7:14 goes on to say, *"If my people, who are called by my name, shall humble themselves, and pray, and seek my face, and turn from their wicked ways; then will I hear from heaven, and will forgive their sin, and will heal their land." Again, it's easy to see that the Bible is an "iffy Book."*

Psalm 37:4 says, "Delight yourself in the Lord and He will give you the desires of your heart." Lastly, the condition of such delight will release and deliver the desire.

So don't forget: "When you read, study and meditate upon the precepts in scripture, circle the word "if." This is God's way of saying, *"If you will, I will"* and He always upholds His end of the deal. In fact, as one preacher said, *"Our God is a promise-keeper! This makes us promise-reapers!"*

Step to Start Strong:

Circle the Word "IF" in your Bible

Made in the USA
Columbia, SC
13 June 2022